The Trinitarian Christology of St Thomas Aquinas

DOMINIC LEGGE, O.P.

OXFORD
UNIVERSITY PRESS

OXFORD
UNIVERSITY PRESS

Great Clarendon Street, Oxford, OX2 6DP,
United Kingdom

Oxford University Press is a department of the University of Oxford.
It furthers the University's objective of excellence in research, scholarship,
and education by publishing worldwide. Oxford is a registered trade mark of
Oxford University Press in the UK and in certain other countries

Nihil Obstat	*Imprimatur*
Rev. Thomas Joseph White, O.P.	Most Rev. Barry C. Knestout
Censor Deputatus	Auxiliary Bishop of Washington
	Archdiocese of Washington
	March 16, 2016

The *Nihil Obstat* and *Imprimatur* are official declarations that a book or pamphlet
is free of doctrinal or moral error. There is no implication that those who have
granted the *Nihil Obstat* and the *Imprimatur* agree with the content, opinions,
or statements expressed therein.

Published in the United States of America by Oxford University Press
198 Madison Avenue, New York, NY 10016, United States of America

British Library Cataloguing in Publication Data
Data available

Library of Congress Cataloging in Publication Data
Data available

ISBN 978-0-19-879419-6 (Hbk.)
ISBN 978-0-19-882909-6 (Pbk.)

Foreword

Dominic Legge's book needs no recommendation beyond itself: all its readers will be able to confirm the high value of this research, the conclusions of which are solidly based on a rigorous reading of the texts of Thomas Aquinas. This work demonstrates the essentially Trinitarian structure of the Christology of St Thomas. It is the first monograph that treats this in a comprehensive way, and it constitutes henceforth the reference work on the subject.

"Aquinas's Christology is intrinsically Trinitarian." The key to this affirmation resides in the recognition that the Trinitarian missions, discussed in the first two chapters, are the point of departure for St Thomas's Christology. The incarnation, life, and work of Christ are presented in those chapters as the "visible mission" of the Son. Combined with this, Legge shows convincingly that the Son's visible mission is inseparable from the visible mission of the Holy Spirit, and that these visible missions are ordered to the "invisible missions," that is, to the gift, at once interior and ecclesial, of salvation. To be even more precise, the key to this book's argument is that "a mission includes the eternal procession, with the addition of a temporal effect."[1] The mission of a divine person "is not essentially different from the eternal procession, but only adds a reference to a temporal effect."[2] This approach to reading Christology in light of Aquinas's theology of the divine missions brings numerous consequences in its wake; I would like to note four that, in my view, merit special attention.

First, in CHAPTER 4, the doctrine of the missions allows one to appreciate what, in the incarnation, pertains properly and distinctly to the person of the Son: the incarnation is a union in the "personal being" (*esse personale*) of the Son. This accounts for the personal identity of Christ as the incarnate Son. To consider Christ "in himself," in his personal being, is always to consider him in his relations to the Father and to the Holy Spirit. Based on this, because each divine person *acts* in a proper and distinct mode that corresponds to

---

[1] *STh* I, q. 43, a. 2 ad 3.   [2] I *Sent.* d. 16, q. 1, a. 1.

his mode of existing, Legge is able to uncover not only Christ's "filial mode of being," but also his "filial mode of acting." This mode of acting is also itself relational: Christ acts *from* the Father and leads *to* the Father. From one end to the other, and even unto the salvific effects of Christ's work, Thomas Aquinas offers a filial Christology.

Simultaneously, the Christology of Thomas Aquinas is a genuine Spirit Christology. The central text here is *STh* III, q. 7, a. 13, studied in CHAPTER 5. In becoming incarnate, the Son (with the Father) sends "the whole Spirit" to the humanity that he assumes in the unity of his person. The fullness of grace and knowledge in Christ (an effect of the invisible mission of the Holy Spirit) flows from the hypostatic union (the visible mission of the Son). This permits one to see why, according to St Thomas, the fullness of Christ's human knowledge, studied in CHAPTER 6, is sometimes attributed to the Son himself (by reason of the hypostatic union) and sometimes is more precisely attributed to the Holy Spirit (by reason of the mission of the Holy Spirit made to Christ at the instant of his conception): the Son sends his own Spirit to the humanity that he assumes. In this way, Thomas Aquinas shows that Christ *as man* is at the same time, under different but intrinsically linked aspects, the *beneficiary* and the *giver* of the Holy Spirit (CHAPTERS 7 and 8). The aspect of giving, which is explained by the instrumental efficiency of Christ's humanity, finds its foundation in Trinitarian doctrine. In his visible mission (see CHAPTER 3), the Son is sent as "the Author of salvation" (*sanctificationis Auctor*), that is, as the principle of and giver of the Holy Spirit, while the Holy Spirit is sent as "the Gift of sanctification" (*sanctificationis Donum*), the one who accomplishes our sanctification interiorly. Christ unites believers to the Father by pouring out upon them the Spirit with which his own humanity is filled. This presence of the Holy Spirit at the heart of Christology is a fruit of Thomas Aquinas's understanding of the deep significance of Trinitarian communion.

Second, a Christology centered on the divine missions presents the great advantage of reuniting the actions of Christ with his teaching. St Thomas presents the visible missions of the Holy Spirit (at Christ's baptism, at his transfiguration, at Pentecost) as the overflow of Christ's fullness of grace "by way of teaching" and "by way of operation." The teaching of Christ is an integral part of Christology. This approach joins Christology and Ecclesiology under the sign of the Holy Spirit, in the relation that Christ has with his Father. It avoids isolating the incarnation, the passion, and the resurrection, instead considering the whole of Christ's life as a work of *revelation* and of *salvation*. And in the perspective of the divine missions, the intrinsic link between revelation and salvation that one finds at the heart of Christology is illuminated. This is because, on Aquinas's account, the visible missions manifest the eternal processions of the persons (revelation of the Trinity) and they also manifest the invisible missions (the interior gift of salvation that is accomplished through the sending of the Son and the Spirit into the souls of the just).

Third, St Thomas's Trinitarian Christology accounts for the relation that believers have with each divine person. If one considers the effects of the divine missions under their "intentional" aspect—that is, in their dynamism toward the objects to which they lead us (the divine persons as known and loved)—one sees that the gifts of elevating grace (wisdom and charity) flowing from Christ's saving work refer us to the three persons inasmuch as these persons are distinct from each other and are apprehended in their proper singularity: the first as Father, the second as only-begotten Son, and the third as the Holy Spirit who comes forth from the Father and the Son. Christ and the Holy Spirit lead us to the Father by giving us a participation in the very relations that they have with the Father. St Thomas's Christology, intrinsically Trinitarian as it is, is thus much more personalist than is generally thought.

Finally, Aquinas's Trinitarian Christology invites us to restore the gifts of the Holy Spirit, so often neglected today, to their rightful importance. On this score, CHAPTER 7 offers an original contribution of the first importance. The hypostatic union *constitutes* the humanity of Christ as an instrument of the divinity, but it remains for the Holy Spirit to *perfect* that humanity to make it a suitable and worthy instrument of the divinity. The gifts of the Holy Spirit do not only imply a habitual "instinct" to follow the Spirit's promptings, but also the actual motion of the Holy Spirit in the soul. In Christology, then, along with St Thomas's account of the connection between the hypostatic union and Christ's fullness of grace (*STh* III, q. 7, a. 13), one can meditate upon a parallel truth found in Aquinas's commentary on Hebrews 9:14 about how the Holy Spirit moves Christ: "The cause why Christ shed his blood . . . was the Holy Spirit, by whose motion and instinct—namely, by charity for God and for neighbor—he did this."

Dominic Legge's book brings freshness and new life to our understanding of the Christology of Thomas Aquinas, because it successfully restores to its primacy the Trinitarian approach that guides the theology of the Dominican master. This permits the reader to avoid the snares of false oppositions (e.g. incarnation vs. paschal mystery, theocentrism vs. Christocentrism, Christomonism vs. pneumatology, ontology vs. salvific action, and so on), and to better grasp, as Legge writes in his conclusion, that "the Trinitarian shape of our salvation is derived from the Trinitarian shape of the mystery of the incarnation."

Gilles Emery, O.P.

Ordinary Professor of Dogmatic Theology
University of Fribourg (Switzerland)
Palm Sunday, 2016

Acknowledgments

I owe a great debt of gratitude to Fr. Gilles Emery, O.P., Professor of Theology at the University of Fribourg. His encouragement of my research stretches back to 2007 when, as a student at the Pontifical Faculty of the Immaculate Conception in Washington, D.C., my interest in this subject had just been kindled. His scholarship has given impetus to the present project, and his aid and advice have been invaluable. I cannot thank him enough.

Thanks are due to many others. My brethren in the Dominican Province of St Joseph have made this work possible in more ways than I can name, beginning with their acceptance of me as one of their own, in virtue of which I have had the opportunity to study St Thomas as a Dominican since my entry into the Order of Preachers. Likewise, the brethren of the Albertinum, the international Dominican priory in Fribourg where this book was written, have been a constant support. My time there was rich and deeply formative.

Two Dominican contemplative nuns—Sister Maria of the Angels, O.P. (of the Monastery of Our Lady of Grace in North Guilford, Connecticut), and Sister Mary Dominic of the Holy Spirit, O.P. (of the Monastery of Our Lady of the Rosary in Buffalo, New York)— read the entire manuscript and gave me invaluable help in editing and correcting it, both as to its form and its substance. In addition, their prayers, the prayers of the other nuns in North Guilford and Buffalo, and many others (I must mention especially Sr. Maria Dominic of the Incarnate Word, O.P. of Queen of Peace Monastery; the Dominican nuns of Linden, Virginia; of Paray-le-Monial, France; and of Summit, New Jersey; Sisters Maris Stella, O.C.D, and Mary Benedicta, O.C.D, of the Carmelite Monastery of Flemington, New Jersey; and the Carmelite nuns of Denmark, Wisconsin) have been an inestimable aid over the years of my research. Finally, I would like to thank my parents, whose love and support has been a firm foundation from the first moment of this project until the last.

Contents

PART III CHRIST AND THE HOLY SPIRIT

Abbreviations and Editions of Works of St Thomas Aquinas

Catena in Matthaeum	*Catena Aurea in Quatuor Evangelia*, vol. 1, edited by A. Guarienti, Turin and Rome: Marietti, 1953.
Compendium theologiae	*Compendium theologiae seu Brevis compilatio theologiae ad fratrem Raynaldum*, in *Sancti Thomae de Aquino Opera omnia*, iussu Leonis XIII P.M. edita ("Leonine edition"), vol. 42, 1979.
Contra errores Graecorum	*Contra errores Graecorum ad Urbanum papam*, Leonine edition, vol. 40, 1969.
Contra doctrinam retrahentium	*Contra doctrinam retrahentium a religione*, Leonine edition, vol. 41, 1970.
De Caritate	*Quaestio Disputata de Caritate*, in *Quaestiones Disputatae*, vol. 2, edited by P. Bazzi, M. Calcaterra, T. S. Centi, E. Odetto, and P. M. Pession, Turin and Rome: Marietti, 1949.
De Pot.	*Quaestiones Disputatae de Potentia*, in *Quaestiones Disputatae*, vol. 2, edited by P. Bazzi, M. Calcaterra, T. S. Centi, E. Odetto, and P. M. Pession, Turin and Rome: Marietti 1949.
De articulis fidei	*De articulis fidei et Ecclesiae sacramentis ad archiepiscopum Panormitanum*, Leonine edition, vol. 42, 1979.
De rationibus fidei	*De rationibus fidei ad Cantorem Antiochenum*, Leonine edition, vol. 40, 1969.
De unione Verbi incarnati	*Quaestio disputata 'De unione Verbi incarnati'*, edited by Walter Senner, Barbara Bartocci, and Klaus Obenauer, Stuttgart—Bad Cannstatt: Frommann-Holzboog, 2011.
De Verit.	*Quaestiones Disputatae de Veritate*, Leonine edition, vol. 22/1–3, 1970–6.
Ecce ego mitto	*Ecce ego mitto*, Leonine edition, vol. 44/1, 2014.
Ecce rex tuus	*Ecce rex tuus*, Leonine edition, vol. 44/1, 2014.

Emitte spiritum tuum	*Emitte spiritum tuum*, Leonine edition, vol. 44/1, 2014.
Expositio super Isaiam	*Expositio super Isaiam ad litteram*, Leonine edition, vol. 28, 1974.
Homo quidam fecit cenam	*Homo quidam fecit cenam*, Leonine edition, vol. 44/1, 2014.
Germinet terra	*Germinet terra*, Leonine edition, vol. 44/1, 2014.
In decem preceptis	*Collationes in decem preceptis*, in Jean-Pierre Torrell, "Les 'Collationes in decem praeceptis' de saint Thomas d'Aquin. Édition critique avec introduction et notes," in Jean-Pierre Torrell, *Recherches thomasiennes. Études revues et augmentées*, 65–117, Paris: Librairie Philosophique J. Vrin, 2000.
In Epist. ad Col.	*Super Epistolam ad Colossenses Lectura*, in *Super Epistolas S. Pauli Lectura*, vol. 2, edited by R. Cai, Turin and Rome: Marietti, 1953.
In Epist. ad Ephes.	*Super Epistolam ad Ephesios Lectura*, in *Super Epistolas S. Pauli Lectura*, vol. 2, edited by R. Cai, Turin and Rome: Marietti, 1953.
In Epist. ad Gal.	*Super Epistolam ad Galatas Lectura* in *Super Epistolas S. Pauli Lectura*, vol. 1, edited by R. Cai, Turin and Rome: Marietti, 1953.
In Epist. ad Hebr.	*Super Epistolam ad Hebraeos Lectura*, in *Super Epistolas S. Pauli Lectura*, vol. 2, edited by R. Cai, Turin and Rome: Marietti, 1953.
In Epist. ad Phil.	*Super Epistolam ad Philippenses Lectura*, in *Super Epistolas S. Pauli Lectura*, vol. 2, edited by R. Cai, Turin and Rome: Marietti, 1953.
In Epist. ad Philemon.	*Super Epistolam ad Philemonem Lectura*, in *Super Epistolas S. Pauli Lectura*, vol. 2, edited by R. Cai, Turin and Rome: Marietti, 1953.
In Epist. ad Rom.	*Super Epistolam ad Romanos Lectura* in *Super Epistolas S. Pauli Lectura*, vol. 1, edited by R. Cai, Turin and Rome: Marietti, 1953.
In Epist. ad Tit.	*Super Epistolam ad Titum Lectura*, in *Super Epistolas S. Pauli Lectura*, vol. 2, edited by R. Cai, Turin and Rome: Marietti, 1953.

In I Epist. ad Cor.	*Super Primam Epistolam ad Corinthios Lectura* in *Super Epistolas S. Pauli Lectura*, vol. 1, edited by R. Cai, Turin and Rome: Marietti, 1953.
In II Epist. ad Cor.	*Super Secundam Epistolam ad Corinthios Lectura* in *Super Epistolas S. Pauli Lectura*, vol. 1, edited by R. Cai, Turin and Rome: Marietti, 1953.
In I Epist. ad Thess.	*Super Primam Epistolam ad Thessalonicenses Lectura*, in *Super Epistolas S. Pauli Lectura*, vol. 2, edited by R. Cai, Turin and Rome: Marietti, 1953.
In II Epist. ad Thess.	*Super Secundam Epistolam ad Thessalonicenses Lectura*, in *Super Epistolas S. Pauli Lectura*, vol. 2, edited by R. Cai, Turin and Rome: Marietti, 1953.
In I Epist. ad Tim.	*Super Primam Epistolam ad Timotheum Lectura*, in *Super Epistolas S. Pauli Lectura*, vol. 2, edited by R. Cai, Turin and Rome: Marietti, 1953.
In II Epist. ad Tim.	*Super Secundam Epistolam ad Timotheum Lectura*, in *Super Epistolas S. Pauli Lectura*, vol. 2, edited by R. Cai, Turin and Rome: Marietti, 1953.
In Ioan.	*Super Evangelium S. Ioannis Lectura*, edited by R. Cai, Turin and Rome: Marietti, 1952.
In Matt.	*Super Evangelium S. Matthaei Lectura*, edited by R. Cai, Turin and Rome: Marietti, 1951.
In Psalm.	*In Psalmos Davidis Expositio*, in *Opera omnia*, vol. 14, Parma: Typis Petri Fiaccadori, 1863.
In Symbolum Apost.	*In Symbolum Apostolorum scilicet 'credo in Deum' Expositio*, Leonine text as published in *The Sermon-Conferences of St Thomas Aquinas on the Apostles' Creed*, trans. Nicholas Ayo, Notre Dame: University of Notre Dame Press, 1988. See also *Opuscula Theologica* vol. 2, ed. R. M. Spiazzi, Turin: Marietti, 1954.
Officium de festo Corporis Christi	*Officium de festo Corporis Christi* in P. M. Gy, *La Liturgie dans l'histoire*, Paris: Éditions Saint-Paul, 1990.

Puer Iesus	*Puer Iesus*, Leonine edition, vol. 44/1, 2014.
Quodlibet	*Quaestiones de Quolibet*, Leonine edition, vol. 25/1–2, 1996.
Rigans montes	*Breve Principium Fratris Thomae de Aquino "Rigans montes de superioribus,"* in *Opuscula Theologica*, vol. 1, edited by R. A. Verardo, Turin and Rome: Marietti 1954, 435–43.
ScG	*Summa contra Gentiles*, Leonine edition, vols. 13–15, Rome, 1918–30.
Sent.	*Scriptum super libros Sententiarum*. Prologue edited by Adriano Oliva in *Les débuts de l'enseignement de Thomas d'Aquin et sa conception de la* Sacra Doctrina: *avec l'édition du prologue de son Commentaire des* Sentences (Paris: Librairie Philosophique J. Vrin, 2006). Books I and II, edited by Pierre Mandonnet, Paris: Lethielleux, 1929. Books III and IV (up to dist. 22), edited by Maria Fabianus Moos, Paris: Lethielleux, 1933–47. Book IV (dist. 23–50), *Opera omnia*, vol. 7/2, Parma: Typis Petri Fiaccadori, 1858.
STh	*Summa Theologiae*, Leonine edition, vols. 4–12, 1888–1906.
Super Boet. De Trinitate	*Super Boetium de Trinitate*, Leonine edition, vol. 50, 1992.

All quotations of Aquinas in English are my translations from the Latin of the printed editions, except where noted.

Other Abbreviations

CCL   *Corpus Christanorum. Series Latina.*

PG   *Patrologiae cursus completus, Series Graeca,* edited by J. P. Migne.

PL   *Patrologiae cursus completus, Series Latina,* edited by J. P. Migne.

Introduction

Many of the witnesses in the canonization process for St Thomas Aquinas testify that he was a man of deep faith, much given to contemplation and to regular and fervent prayer, even with tears, and especially before teaching or writing. To some, however, St Thomas's writings seem analytical, dry, and bereft of the zest of the Gospel. Yet to the attentive reader, his texts offer important clues pointing to the fervor for the divine mysteries that fueled his labors.

The opening lines of Aquinas's *Compendium of Theology* are a good example.[1] St Thomas composed that short work, a condensation of the essentials of the Christian faith, for his longtime secretary and *socius*, Brother Reginald of Piperno, and he begins it with a rather striking commendation:

> I hand on to you, my dearest son Reginald, the condensed doctrine of the Christian religion, so that you might keep it always before your eyes.... The first thing necessary is faith, through which you may know the truth.... The whole knowledge of faith revolves around... two points, namely, the divinity of the Trinity and the humanity of Christ. Nor is this to be wondered at, since the humanity of Christ is the way to come to the divinity. As a wayfarer, [you] must know the way by which [you] can come to the end.[2]

Among all the doctrines that the Dominican Master might underline, he exhorts Reginald keep the divinity of the Trinity and the humanity of Christ always before his eyes. This is more than advice for success

---

[1] Many other examples could be cited; perhaps the most prominent is *ScG* I, cc. 2 and 8. See also *Rigans montes* (no. 1214); *Contra doctrinam retrahentium* cc. 1 and 16. St Thomas's sermons are also an excellent source.

[2] *Compendium theologiae* I, cc.1–2.

as a university theologian; St Thomas speaks of it as key to the Christian life, a recipe for beatitude. Does this not sound like St Thomas here reveals something at the heart not only of his doctrine, but even of his own life as a Christian? We come to the Trinity, our final end, through the humanity of Christ, who is our way to God, and therefore, above all else, it is Christ whom we must seek to know—and him crucified.[3] In fact, in bringing us salvation, Thomas continues, Christ sums up and condenses in himself, in the "abbreviated word" (*Verbum abbreuiatum*) of his own humanity, the mystery of the Triune God:

> The Word of the eternal Father, comprehending the universe by his immensity, . . . willed to be made brief by assuming our brevity, not by laying down his majesty. And that there would be no excuse for grasping the doctrine of the heavenly Word, . . . he compressed the doctrine of human salvation, for the sake of the busy, in a brief summary.[4]

St Thomas's commendation to Reginald, though unusually personal in its form, typifies his thought. Christ makes present in time, and for the sake of our salvation, the mystery of the Word's eternal procession from the Father. The Word comes in the flesh to save us, sending us the Holy Spirit, revealing the Trinity, and opening the way of our return to the Trinity. Consequently, Aquinas's account of the mystery of the incarnation leads us into the heart of the Trinitarian mystery. Indeed, there is no way to the Trinity but through Christ.[5] For St Thomas, Christology is intrinsically Trinitarian.

This is a controversial claim. Contemporary critics intone the refrain that the Dominican Master's Trinitarian doctrine is so trapped in abstractions and so "very remote . . . from the biblical data concerning the actual events of salvation history,"[6] that it ceases to

---

[3] *De rationibus fidei* c. 1.

[4] *Compendium theologiae* I, c. 1.

[5] This is why Aquinas sets Christ at the head of his explication of the articles of faith: "the whole Christian faith'—Thomas intends to include our knowledge of the Trinity—"revolves around the divinity and the humanity of Christ." *De articulis fidei* I. See also *In I Epist. ad Thess.* c. 1, lect. 1 (no. 5); *Compendium theologiae* I, c. 201.

[6] Anne Hunt, *The Trinity and the Paschal Mystery: A Development in Recent Catholic Theology* (Collegeville, MN: Liturgical Press, 1997), 4. See also Eugene Webb, *In Search of the Triune God: The Christian Paths of East and West* (Columbia, MO: University of Missouri Press, 2014), 224; Catherine Mowry LaCugna, *God for Us: The Trinity and Christian Life* (New York: HarperCollins, 1991), 143–80.

present the Trinity as a saving mystery. A generation ago, Karl Rahner accused Aquinas of divorcing Christology from the Trinity, above all because, according to Aquinas's teaching on the incarnation, any divine person could become incarnate. According to Rahner, if Aquinas's view were accepted, "[t]here would no longer be any connection between 'mission' and the intra-trinitarian life. Our sonship in grace would in fact have nothing to do with the Son's sonship, since it might equally well be brought about without any modification by another incarnate person. That which God is for us would tell us absolutely nothing about that which he is in himself, as triune."[7] Hans Urs von Balthasar leveled a similar accusation.[8] Many prominent theologians, both Catholic and Protestant, have since joined in.[9] Similarly, Aquinas's Christology is mistrusted for its alleged "one-sidedness," overemphasizing the hypostatic union and forgetting about the Holy Spirit's presence in Christ's life and ministry.[10] As we shall see, this is all based on a serious misunderstanding of Aquinas's thought. Clearing this away can only enrich contemporary theological debates, since it is precisely this sort of misunderstanding that has led some theologians quite far afield from the main lines of the Western theological tradition in their search for a Christology that is genuinely Trinitarian. We shall endeavor to show that such a Trinitarian Christology is already present in St Thomas, and that it offers a tested and sure theological account of the interconnection of the most fundamental Christian mysteries.

[7] Karl Rahner, *The Trinity*, trans. Joseph Donceel (New York: Herder & Herder, 1970), 30.
[8] Hans Urs von Balthasar, *The Theology of Karl Barth: Exposition and Interpretation*, trans. Edward T. Oakes (San Francisco: Ignatius Press, 1992), 260, 263–5. Balthasar even claims that, for Aquinas, the Trinity and Christology "have...little structuring impact in his theology," and that "the temporal nature of salvation history... recede[s] into the background." *Ibid.*, 263–4.
[9] Walter Kasper, *Jesus the Christ*, trans. V. Green, pbk ed. (London: Burns and Oates, 1977), 184; 249–50. See also Thomas G. Weinandy, "Trinitarian Christology: The Eternal Son," in *The Oxford Handbook of the Trinity*, ed. Gilles Emery and Matthew Levering (Oxford: Oxford University Press, 2011), 392–4; Robert Jenson, *Systematic Theology*, vol. 1, *The Triune God* (Oxford: Oxford University Press, 1999), 112–14; Jürgen Moltmann, *Der gekreuzigte Gott: Das Kreuz Christi als Grund und Kritik christlicher Theologie* (Munich: Chr. Kaiser Verlag, 1972), 226–8.
[10] Kasper, *Jesus the Christ*, 250–1; Philip J. Rosato, "Spirit Christology: Ambiguity and Promise," *Theological Studies* 38 (1977): 437. See also Bruce D. Marshall, "*Ex Occidente Lux*? Aquinas and Eastern Orthodox Theology," *Modern Theology* 20 (2004): 25, 40, articulating the criticisms of twentieth-century Orthodox theologians.

More important than any defense of Aquinas, however, is the positive reason for undertaking this study: the better we grasp how Aquinas's Christology is intrinsically Trinitarian, the better we will understand the unity of his thought and the intelligible order he discerns in the whole dispensation of salvation, as it emerges from the Trinity and leads us back to the Trinity. One could even say that, to the extent that we remain ignorant of this overarching perspective, the deepest significance of the mystery of the incarnation will be unknown to us. Indeed, as St Thomas's words to his *socius* Reginald suggest, our study of Christ can thus be far more than a merely academic exercise, since it is the very way by which we return to the Triune God.

In what follows, therefore, we will examine how Aquinas conceives of the mystery of the incarnation—in its origin and *ratio* (i.e., "reason," "meaning," or "explanation"), its shape, its structure, and its role in the dispensation of salvation—as intrinsically Trinitarian. The crux of our investigation will be the Trinitarian shape of the incarnation itself, which Aquinas conceives as the visible mission of the Son, sent by the Father, implicating the invisible mission of the Holy Spirit to his assumed human nature.

In doing this, we will not review the whole of Aquinas's Christology, nor even highlight every aspect of it that implicates the doctrine of the Trinity, which would produce a study both overlong and scattered. Neither do we propose a forced march through a long sequence of Aquinas's texts. Rather, we are after what makes Aquinas's theology of the incarnation essentially or intrinsically Trinitarian, its *ratio* and its ordering principles—its Trinitarian heart, bones, and lifeblood, so to speak. Consequently, we will treat only what helps us grasp this Trinitarian *ratio*, and especially what pertains to the structure of the mystery of the incarnation in itself.

Our study does not correspond to a given range of questions in the *Summa Theologiae*, though we will often find ourselves in the part especially devoted to the incarnation in the *Tertia pars*. In fact, this book's interest and originality stems partly from this fact. The Trinitarian dimension of Aquinas's thought is everywhere present in his Christology, but if we were to read only the *Tertia pars*, our perception of it would be dulled, since Aquinas assumed that his Christology would be read in continuity with his treatment of the Trinitarian processions, of the divine missions, of grace, and so forth. (Indeed, Thomas's own method in the *Summa Theologiae* is calculated to promote concision and avoid repetition.) Consequently, we will explore a wider terrain, venturing beyond the trusty but well-worn paths of the *Tertia pars* and into lesser-known regions of Aquinas's *oeuvre*—especially his biblical commentaries and his commentary on Peter Lombard's *Sentences*. We do so not for the sake of mere variety, but to bring to light the fundamentally Trinitarian shape of the incarnation in Aquinas's thought.

We have tried, as much as possible, to let St Thomas speak for himself. To achieve this, we have often brought together texts from a variety of different works. This cannot be done without discernment, however: we have paid close attention to the original context of each. Likewise, we have carefully studied the historical development of Aquinas's own thought. Though some of the key principles that guide St Thomas's theological reflection remain constant throughout his career, he changes his position on other points as he develops deeper insights into the Trinitarian and Christological mysteries that he treats. We have noted these changes when relevant to our discussion.

This book has three main parts. PART I examines how the eternal processions in God are "extended" into time in the divine missions, which link God in himself (*theologia*) with the economy or dispensation of salvation.[11] Though it may not at first seem to be part of Christology, this key prologue will enable us to understand what Aquinas means when he says that the incarnation is the visible mission of the Son, and hence to grasp an important reason why Christology is intrinsically Trinitarian: the incarnation's origin and cause is found in the eternal processions of the Son from the Father and of the Holy Spirit from the Father and the Son; Christ thus becomes the path of our return to the Trinity.

PART II analyzes the incarnation as the visible mission of the second person of the Trinity. We begin with Christ's identity as the eternal Son, which implies his relation, as both God and man, to the Father from whom he proceeds. We will probe why, for Aquinas, it was the person of the Son who became incarnate, and what this reveals to us about the Triune God and about the relation of creatures to distinct

---

[11] Aquinas rarely uses the term "economy," preferring to speak instead of the divine "dispensation" or *dispensatio*, by which God realizes in time his eternal plan, in particular through the Word's incarnation; we will follow St Thomas's usage. See Gilles Emery, "*Theologia* and *Dispensatio*: The Centrality of the Divine Missions in St Thomas's Trinitarian Theology," *The Thomist* 74 (2010): 517–18.

persons of the Trinity. We will also see how, in Aquinas's thought, the hypostatic union terminates in the personal being of the Son, which is "from the Father," and therefore accounts, at the deepest metaphysical level, for why Christ is oriented entirely to the Father and reveals the Father in all that he is and does.

PART III investigates the relation between Christ and the Holy Spirit, a relation much more important for Aquinas's approach to the incarnation than is usually recognized. The key here is that Christ receives, as man, an invisible mission of the Holy Spirit in the fullness of habitual grace. This presence of the Holy Spirit in Christ's humanity follows from the hypostatic union because the divine persons are never separated: when the Word joins a human nature to himself, he breathes forth the Holy Spirit in full to that human nature. This has important consequences for Christology. The Holy Spirit becomes an indispensable principle of the elevation of Christ's human nature, so that it receives every perfection it needs to be the perfect conjoined instrument of the eternal Word. We will pay special attention to the Holy Spirit's role in Christ's supernatural human knowledge, including both his beatific vision, by which Christ as man sees the divine essence and knows the divine will perfectly, and his infused supernatural knowledge. Likewise, we will show how the Holy Spirit both disposes Christ's humanity to act as an instrument of his divinity, and actually moves it to action. We will also consider how, having received the Holy Spirit in full as man, Christ becomes, as man, the source of the Holy Spirit for the world. In other words, for Aquinas, the order of the eternal processions of the persons is manifested through Christ's humanity and his saving actions: as the Word (with the Father) breathes forth the Holy Spirit from all eternity, so the Word made flesh (who is from the Father) breathes forth the Holy Spirit in time.

* * *

The Trinitarian shape of St Thomas's teaching on the Word's incarnation for our sake is a rich subject for theological study. It brings us into contact with some of the most important themes of Aquinas's overarching theological vision, which begins from the Triune God and sees all of creation as returning to the Trinity through the temporal missions of the Son and the Holy Spirit. Although at times they are rather technical and demanding, St Thomas did not write his theological works only as an academic exercise, but also to draw his readers into the search for the highest truths—and into the delightful contemplation of the divine mystery—that animated his own life. It is our hope that, in this study of the Trinitarian shape of Aquinas's theology of the incarnation, we too may share in some measure in the precious fruit of the Dominican master's contemplation.

Part I

The Trinity and the Dispensation
of Salvation

1

The Divine Missions

From the Trinity, to the Trinity

It is at the heart of the Gospel that the Father sends the Son into the world. "The Father has sent me," Jesus says (John 5:36). "I proceeded and came forth from God; I came not of my own accord, but he sent me (John 8:42)." And the Son tells the apostles: "Behold, I send the promise of my Father upon you (Lk 24:49)." "When the Counselor comes, whom I shall send to you from the Father, even the Spirit of truth, who proceeds from the Father, he will bear witness to me (John 15:26)." In these passages, Scripture alerts us to two interconnected truths: both the Son and the Holy Spirit *proceed* from another in God, and are *sent* into the world.

These truths (which St Thomas designates by the shorthand "eternal processions" and "missions") stand at the center of Aquinas's account of the whole of theology. Thus, in the opening prologue to his first systematic work, he places the Trinitarian processions at the origin of all things:

> The temporal procession of creatures [is derived] from the eternal procession of the persons. . . . For, as always, that which is first is the cause of what comes afterwards, according to the Philosopher. Thus, the first procession is the cause and *ratio* of every subsequent procession.[1]

The eternal processions of the divine persons *in* God—that is, the eternal generation of the Son (the Word) by the Father, and the Holy Spirit's procession from the Father and Son—are the cause and *ratio* of every other procession that comes forth *from* God.

---

[1] I *Sent.* prol.

If we are to grasp how Christology is Trinitarian for St Thomas, this must be our starting point. The eternal processions (the ultimate bases for the distinction of the persons within the Trinity)[2] are the *ratio*,[3] origin,[4] and exemplar[5] of the coming forth of the vast diversity of creatures.[6] This principle has an extraordinary importance for all of Aquinas's thought. It makes his theology deeply Trinitarian: the pattern of the Trinitarian processions is at the very foundation of the world, characterizes creation itself, and marks all of the Triune God's actions in it.[7]

A. THE ETERNAL PROCESSIONS AND THE *REDITUS* OF CREATURES TO GOD

Aquinas builds his theology of the divine missions on the fundamental principle that the eternal processions ground *both* the *exitus* of creatures from God *and* their *reditus* to God. Consider, for example, this text from his Commentary on Peter Lombard's *Sentences*:

> In the coming forth [*exitus*] of creatures from the first principle there is a certain circulation [*circulatio*] or circling-back [*regiratio*], such that everything returns to that from which it proceeded as a principle, as if returning to its end. And hence it is necessary that, through the same thing by which something comes forth [*exitus*] from a principle, it also returns [*reditus*] unto its end. Therefore, as . . . the procession of the persons is the *ratio* of the production of creatures from the first principle, so also the same procession is the *ratio* of returning unto the end, because just as we were created through the Son and the Holy Spirit, likewise we also are joined [through them] to our ultimate end; as is evident from the words of Augustine . . . where he says: "the principle to which we return," namely, the Father, "and the form we follow," namely, the Son, "and the grace by which we are reconciled." And Hilary says in the *De Trinitate* . . . : "Through the Son, we refer all things to one principle of all things without principle."[8]

---

[2] *STh* I, q. 27, prol.   [3] *STh* I, q. 45, a. 6.
[4] I *Sent.* d. 32, q. 1, a. 3.   [5] I *Sent.* d. 29, q. 1, a. 2, qla 2.
[6] Gilles Emery, *La Trinité créatrice: Trinité et création dans les commentaires aux Sentences de Thomas d'Aquin et de ses précurseurs Albert le Grand et Bonaventure* (Paris: Librairie Philosophique J. Vrin, 1995), 487–8.
[7] *Ibid.*, 248–528 (especially 514–28).   [8] I *Sent.* d. 14, q. 2, a. 2.

In this key text, St Thomas begins with the Neoplatonic conception of *exitus* and *reditus*, part of the common Dionysian heritage that he received from his master, Albert the Great (and that he shares with St Bonaventure):[9] *exitus* and *reditus* describes the circular motion by which goodness is diffused from God and returns to God. From this, Aquinas formulates a distinctively Trinitarian insight: *exitus* and *reditus* accounts for how the Trinitarian processions themselves ground both creation *and the Trinitarian dispensation of grace*. This is an original contribution of St Thomas, and he uses it to offer a fundamental theological explanation of the scriptural and Patristic teaching that we return to the Father through the missions of the Son and the Holy Spirit. As Thomas puts it, "just as we were created through the Son and the Holy Spirit, likewise we also are joined [through them] to our ultimate end."

The scope of St Thomas's principle is vast: it extends to the whole range of the divine missions, both visible and invisible. The eternal processions of the Son and Holy Spirit are the path of our return to the Father, as those persons are "sent" to us in time. Indeed, for Aquinas, this is the very reason for the missions: "to bring the rational creature unto God"[10] according to the pattern of the eternal processions.

This is why it is so important for us to begin here: the visible mission of the Son in the incarnation—accompanied by the missions of the Holy Spirit to Christ and, at Pentecost, to the Church—are the means, "the way," by which all of creation is brought back to the Triune God as its final end.[11] As Thomas puts it:

> The whole totality of the divine work is in a manner brought to completion through [the incarnation], since man, who was the last to

---

[9] Emery, *La Trinité créatrice*, 390–402. For more on Aquinas's reception of Dionysian thought, see, e.g., Bernhard Blankenhorn, *The Mystery of Union with God: Dionysian Mysticism in Albert the Great and Thomas Aquinas* (Washington, D.C.: Catholic University of America Press, 2015); Andrew Hofer, "Dionysian Elements in Thomas Aquinas's Christology: A Case of the Authority and Ambiguity of Pseudo-Dionysius," *The Thomist* 72 (2008): 409–42.

[10] I *Sent.* d. 15, q. 2, a. 1 ad 3.

[11] See, e.g., III *Sent.*, prol.; III *Sent.* d. 1, div. text.; IV *Sent.* d. 50, expos. text. Cf. *In Ioan.* c. 14, lect. 2 (no. 1873); *STh* I, q. 2, prol.; I *Sent.* d. 15, q. 5, a. 1, qla 1 ad 3; I *Sent.* d. 15, q. 5, a. 1, qla 4. See also Emile Bailleux, "Le cycle des missions trinitaires, d'après saint Thomas," *Revue Thomiste* 63 (1963): 165–86.

be created, returns by a certain circular movement to his first principle, united to the very principle of all things through the work of the incarnation.[12]

As we shall see, individual men and women are drawn into this return to the Father as they receive the invisible missions of the Son and Spirit in sanctifying grace. The ultimate consummation of these divine missions is the perfect completion of man's return, namely, the glory of heaven, in which human beings are united directly to the Father, Son, and Holy Spirit in the beatifying vision of God.[13]

When we recover this theological context for St Thomas's Christology—something that is a unique hallmark of his theology—then we begin to see how Christology for Aquinas is Trinitarian not only here or there, but in its deepest roots, in its most far-flung branches, and in its varied fruits. To understand this more clearly, however, we should discuss in more detail Aquinas's teaching on the divine missions in general, that we may better grasp how the Trinitarian processions are at the heart of the dispensation of grace.

B. THE DIVINE MISSIONS IN GENERAL

For St Thomas, a mission always involves two relations: "one is the relation [*habitudo*] of the one sent to him from whom he is sent; the other is the relation of the one sent to the terminus to which he is sent."[14] Thus, on one side, there is "a certain procession of the one sent from the sender," and on the other, a new relation to a terminus.[15] When speaking of the mission of a divine person, however, Thomas removes everything that hints of change in God, since a divine person "neither begins to be where he was not before, nor does he cease to be where he was."[16] This brings Aquinas to the following formulation:

> A mission can belong to a divine person, therefore, insofar as it implies, on one side, a procession of origin from the sender, . . . and on the other side, a new mode of existing in another.[17]

---

[12] *Compendium theologiae* I, c. 201.
[13] I *Sent.* d. 15, q. 4, a. 2 ad 5; IV *Sent.* d. 50, expos. text. See also III *Sent.* d. 1, div. text.
[14] *STh* I, q. 43, a. 1. See also I *Sent.* d. 15, q. 1, a. 1.   [15] *STh* I, q. 43, a. 1.
[16] *STh* I, q. 43, a. 1 ad 2.   [17] *STh* I, q. 43, a. 1.

This "new mode of existing in another" refers to "some effect in a creature . . . according to which a divine person is sent."[18] There are, therefore, two key elements that constitute a divine mission: (1) the person's eternal procession, and (2) the divine person's relation to the creature in whom this person is made present in a new way, according to some created effect.[19]

An Eternal Procession of Origin

Let us begin with the first of these two elements, the "procession of origin." The term "procession," drawn directly from Scripture,[20] here designates an immanent action in God that "does not tend into something exterior but remains in the agent himself."[21] "There are only two such actions in the intellectual and divine nature [of God], namely, to understand and to will."[22]

Aquinas understands the first of these, a procession by way of intellect, as analogous to the act by which an intellect conceives a word as the "fruit" of its understanding. Such a word is distinct from, and yet remains in, the mind that conceives it. In God, the Father "understands himself" by a single eternal act and so generates an eternal Word—as a conception proceeding from his act of understanding—that "expresses the Father."[23] To the second person also belongs the proper names "Image" (expressing his "likeness" to the Father) and "Son" (underscoring his consubstantiality with the Father).

The procession according to will is "the procession of love, by which the beloved is in the lover, like the reality spoken or understood through the conception of a word is in the one understanding."[24] This procession is ordered to the procession of the Word, since "nothing can be loved by the will unless it is conceived in the intellect."[25] The Holy Spirit is thus Love in person, the mutual love and nexus of the Father and the Son;[26] "Love" is a proper name for him.[27] From this,

---

[18] *De Pot.* q. 10, a. 4 ad 14.   [19] See Emery, "*Theologia* and *Dispensatio*," 521.
[20] *STh* I, q. 27, a. 1. Aquinas is fond of citing John 8:42 and 15:26. See Gilles Emery, *The Trinitarian Theology of Saint Thomas Aquinas*, trans. Francesca Aran Murphy, pbk ed. (Oxford: Oxford University Press, 2010), 52 n. 4.
[21] *STh* I, q. 27, a. 3.   [22] *STh* I, q. 27, a. 5.
[23] *STh* I, q. 34, a. 3.   [24] *STh* I, q. 27, a. 3.   [25] *Ibid.*
[26] *STh* I, q. 37, a. 1 and 3.   [27] *STh* I, q. 37, a. 1.

another proper name for the Spirit unfolds: he is "Gift," because love is the "first Gift" from which every other gift proceeds.[28]

We will examine the significance of the Word's procession in further detail in CHAPTER 3. For now, let us pause on an important but often overlooked point in St Thomas's theology: the significance of the Holy Spirit's procession for the dispensation of salvation. The names of "Love" and "Gift" point us to how the Spirit's procession founds the economy of grace—including the divine plan to save us in Christ—and is extended into time in the Spirit's missions.[29] In other words, the Holy Spirit's procession (along with the Son's) is a *ratio* and cause of both creation and salvation, of both *exitus* and *reditus*:

> Because the eternal processions of the persons are the cause and *ratio* of the entirety of the production of creatures, hence it is necessary that, as the generation of the Son is the *ratio* of the entirety of the production of creatures insofar as the Father is said to have made all things in the Son, so also the love of the Father towards the Son ... is the *ratio* in which God bestows every effect of love on the creature; and therefore the Holy Spirit, who is the Love by which the Father loves the Son, is also the Love by which He loves the creature by imparting its perfection to it.[30]

Every good bestowed on a creature (including existence itself) has its origin in the Holy Spirit, because a true gift—one which has absolutely no strings attached—flows from the giver's love.[31] This love is ultimately grounded in the divine procession of Love, and thus in the Holy Spirit.

This means that the economy of grace itself, with the incarnation at its center, has its origin in the Holy Spirit's procession as Love, just as much as in the eternal generation of the Word. Indeed, Aquinas affords such a central place to the Spirit that he even claims that "all gifts are given to us through him."[32] For this reason, the Spirit is rightly called the divine person "nearest to us" (an expression Aquinas credits to Augustine and Hilary).[33]

---

[28] *STh* I, q. 38, a. 2.
[29] These proper names do not mean that the Spirit is defined by a reference to creatures. Though the gift is only given to creatures in time, it is the eternal aptitude for being given (as Love from the Father and the Son) that grounds the name 'Gift' as a personal name. *STh* I, q. 38, a. 1 ad 4. See Emery, *Trinitarian Theology*, 251 n. 134.
[30] I *Sent.* d. 14, q. 1, a. 1.   [31] *STh* I, q. 38, a. 2.
[32] III *Sent.* d. 2, q. 2, a. 2, qla 2 ad 3.   [33] *Ibid.*, obj. 3 and ad 3.

This is an important point for our study of St Thomas's Christology. For Aquinas, it is inconceivable for there to be a visible mission of the Word in the incarnation apart from the Holy Spirit, just as it is inconceivable that there be a Father and Son without the Spirit who is the mutual Love who proceeds from them. The visible mission of the Son is necessarily accompanied by the invisible mission of the Holy Spirit to Christ's humanity, which is manifested by the Holy Spirit's visible missions to Christ at his baptism and transfiguration. Moreover, Christ's coming as man culminates in his sending of the Holy Spirit—visibly to the Apostles (on the evening of the resurrection and at Pentecost), and invisibly to all the faithful—through which the gift of salvation is given. In short, the eternal processions of *both* the Son and Holy Spirit are the origin, *ratio*, cause, and exemplar of our return to the Triune God in the dispensation of grace, in which the divine missions of the Son and Holy Spirit always work together.

A Divine Mission's Created Effect

The second element of a divine mission is the created effect in which a divine mission is made. It is this second element that distinguishes the divine missions from the eternal processions:[34] "A mission includes the eternal procession, and adds something, namely, a temporal effect."[35]

While essential, this created effect always remains secondary to the divine person's eternal procession: it accounts for how the eternal procession—or, better, the divine Person as proceeding—is received in a creature, and for the new way in which the Person is made present. But the eternal procession, and thus the proper presence of the divine person who is sent, is primary. This is always presupposed by Aquinas, even though he sometimes begins with the created effect.[36] A divine mission is the sending *of a divine person* as really present in time according to a created effect.

---

[34] I *Sent.* d. 15, q. 1, a. 2.   [35] *STh* I, q. 43, a. 2 ad 3.

[36] In fact, Aquinas offers two complementary explanations: one "ascending," which begins with sanctifying grace and the infused gifts of wisdom and charity that dispose a soul to receive the divine persons, and one "descending," which begins with the divine persons who come to us and emphasizes their personal presence as the cause of those gifts. Aquinas gives priority to the latter. See Gilles Emery, "L'inhabitation de Dieu Trinité dans les justes," *Nova et Vetera* 88 (2013): 165–77; Guillermo A. Juárez, *Dios Trinidad en todas las creaturas y en los santos: Estudio histórico-sistemático de la doctrina del* Commentario a las Sentencias *de Santo Tomás de Aquino sobre la omnipresencia y la inhabitación* (Córdoba, Argentina: Ediciones del Copista, 2008), 357–448.

A mission's created effect must also be "new." A divine mission is made according to something "specially made for that purpose,"[37] something that grounds a "new mode" of the divine person's presence. The divine person is sent "in" or "according to" this created effect. Thomas also puts it this way: the "effect in the creature" is that "by reason of which the divine person is said to be sent."[38]

> For since the divine persons are everywhere by essence, presence, and power, a person is said to be sent according to this, that he begins to be in [*esse in*] a creature in a new mode through some new effect.[39]

Thomas's words point us to a second aspect: through this new effect, a divine person begins to "be in" a creature. This expression, "*esse in*," is significant; it is the same one Aquinas uses when he speaks about the *perichoresis* or mutual co-inherence of the divine persons.[40] A divine mission is ultimately rooted in *being*: a divine person truly "exists in another in a new mode."[41] Of course, the divine person himself does not change: "that a divine person is in another by a new mode, or is possessed in time by someone, is not on account of a change of the divine person, but because of a change of the creature."[42]

Consequently, not just any created effect will serve: it must somehow imply "a relation [of the person sent] to the terminus to which he is sent, so that he begins in some way to be there."[43] This is the third aspect we want to underline: in a mission, a creature "is related to [a divine person] according to a new mode."[44] More specifically, the person sent "is in a creature according to a new relation."[45] What does Aquinas mean? How can a creature be related to a single divine person, such that the divine person is "in" the creature? This is an important question, and the stakes involved are substantial.[46]

[37] *STh* I, q. 43, a. 7 ad 2. Cf. I *Sent.* d. 15, q. 3, a. 1, where St Thomas examines in detail the senses of being and becoming involved in a divine mission.
[38] *Contra errores Graecorum* I, c. 14.   [39] *Ibid.*
[40] Emery, *Trinitarian Theology*, 367. See also Juárez, *Dios Trinidad*, 415–22.
[41] *STh* I, q. 43, a. 3; see also a. 1. Cf. I *Sent.* d. 14, q. 2, a. 2 ad 2, which underlines that the new relation of a creature to the divine person must involve the divine person's presence in the creature. Note, however, that the visible missions of the Holy Spirit involve a sign pointing to the Spirit's presence in someone—the Holy Spirit is not "in" the sign. See pp. 48–51.
[42] *STh* I, q. 43, a. 2 ad 2.   [43] *Ibid.*, a. 1.
[44] I *Sent.* d. 15, q. 1, a. 1.   [45] *Ibid.*, q. 3, a. 1 ad 3.
[46] For example, Étienne Vetö's study of the Trinity in Aquinas's Christology stumbles at precisely this point, with serious consequences. Having missed St Thomas's teaching that the created effect of a mission has a distinct relation to the divine person sent, he

How Can a Creature Be Related to
a Single Divine Person?

To answer, we must recall that Aquinas understands the relations between God and creatures as so-called "mixed relations." St Thomas explains what he means by drawing an analogy to how our senses are related to the objects they sense.[47] We can illustrate this with an example: when I look at the Washington Monument, my sense of sight is related to it. On the side of my sense impressions, the relation is what Aquinas calls "real," because my sight of the Monument is really ordered to—and dependent on—the Monument itself. When I see the Monument, something new is really *in* my sense of sight, and it really depends on the Monument itself.[48] (We could even say that a true "likeness" of the Monument is "in" me because of this relation.) But on the side of the Monument, it is not "ordered to" or dependent on my sense of sight, nor does it change. Nonetheless, it *is* genuinely related to my sense of sight, insofar as my sight of the Monument depends on the Monument itself. The relation from the Monument to me is not a fiction or an unreality, yet it is not "really in" the Monument itself, and so we use a different label to describe it; it is a "relation of reason," insofar as the Washington Monument is the "terminus" of my sight.[49] Considering both sides at the same time, then, we say that the relation between my sense of sight and the Washington monument is "mixed." On my side, it is "real"—that is, really grounded "in" my sense of sight—while on the other side it is not "in" the Monument and so is a relation "of reason."

A divine mission involves something analogous to this. When Aquinas says that a divine person "is in a creature according to a new relation," he means that, on the side of the creature, the new created effect *is really related* to the divine person who is sent—it is "referred" or "ordered" to the divine person as its terminus, like my sense of sight has

wrongly assumes that, considered on the side of its created effect, a mission could be attributed to a single divine person only by appropriation—and therefore that Aquinas must make a special exception for the incarnation in order to affirm that Christ's humanity belongs to the Son alone. As a result, Vetö concludes that Aquinas's Christology has irresolvable internal tensions, and that it systematically obscures the distinctive presence and action of the divine persons in the economy of salvation. Étienne Vetö, *Du Christ à la Trinité: Penser les mystères du Christ après Thomas d'Aquin et Balthasar* (Paris: Les Éditions du Cerf, 2012), 68–70, 196–205, 213–16.

[47] *STh* I, q. 13, a. 7.   [48] Cf. *De Pot.* q. 7, a. 9.
[49] *STh* I, q. 13, a. 7. See also *De Pot.* q. 7, a. 9; I *Sent.* d. 30, q. 1, a. 3.

the Washington Monument as its terminus. This relation "really exists in" the creature.[50] By contrast, there is not something new "in" the divine person; instead, there is a relation of reason[51] to the created effect insofar as the divine person is that effect's terminus.[52]

Aquinas takes this approach—and adds a new element—when he explains how a creature can have a distinct relation to one divine person and vice versa, consistent with Trinitarian faith. He writes: "A relation of God to a creature can be designated in two ways: either insofar as a creature is referred unto God as to a principle, or . . . as to a terminus."[53] Let us momentarily pass over the new element ("as to a principle"), because it is with respect to the second part ("as to a terminus") that St Thomas discerns a relation to a single divine person. Aquinas continues:

> If the relation of a creature to the creator is considered as to a terminus, this relation of the creature can be . . . something personal. This occurs . . . according to exemplar causality, as [for example] . . . in the infusion of charity there is a termination to a likeness of the personal procession of the Holy Spirit. Or there is a termination according to being, and this mode belongs uniquely to the incarnation, through which a human nature is assumed into the being and unity of the divine person, but not to the unity of the divine nature.[54]

We will enter into the details of these two different "terminations" ("according to exemplar causality" and "according to being") later. For now, we simply want to underscore that, in both cases, Aquinas

---

[50] I *Sent*. d. 30, q. 1, a. 2 ad 4.

[51] St Thomas distinguishes two kinds of relations of reason: (1) logical relations, where the order is *posited* by our intellect, and (2) relations that arise when we understand one thing as ordered to another. The latter relations are not posited or "invented" by our intellect, but rather follow upon our understanding by a kind of necessity. "Relations of the divine persons to creatures belong to the second kind . . . which 'are attributed by the intellect not to that which is in the intellect, but to that which has objective reality.'" Emery, "*Theologia* and *Dispensatio*," 525, quoting *De Pot.*, q. 7, a. 11.

[52] See e.g., I *Sent*. d. 14, q. 2, a. 1, qla 1 and ad 1 (discussing this point with respect to the Holy Spirit's mission).

[53] I *Sent*. d. 30, q. 1, a. 2. Note how Aquinas begins by speaking about God's relation to a creature, and immediately transposes this into the creature's relation to God. He does this because of his doctrine of mixed relations: God is related to creatures not because something new is in God, but because creatures are "really" ordered to him. Although we can rightly speak about God's relation to creatures, this relation is really "in" creatures, properly speaking.

[54] I *Sent*. d. 30, q. 1, a. 2.

has in mind a created effect that has a real relation to a single divine person because it "terminates" *to what is proper to that person.* This "termination" is something real in the creature; it is not only a manner of speaking. A divine mission's created effect really makes present a divine person's eternal procession "in" the creature, like the Washington Monument is, as it were, made present "in" my sense of sight when my seeing "terminates" in the Monument.

We can now return to the element we skipped over: every creature is also related to God "as to a principle." As the creator of all things, God is the principle of the entire universe and everything in it.[55] More specifically, creatures' relation to God "as a principle" is a relation to the divine essence, by which "the three persons are one principle" of all things and "produce creatures by one action."[56]

> Since the Father, the Son, and the Holy Spirit have the same power, just as [they have] the same essence, it is necessary that everything that God works in us as from an efficient cause would be at once from the Father, the Son, and the Holy Spirit.[57]

A divine mission's created effect, therefore, is always efficiently caused by all three divine persons acting together. This point is obviously fundamental: a created effect only exists as efficiently caused by the whole Trinity. (We have omitted it up to now in order to bring out more clearly the personal dimension of a divine mission's created effect.)

Aquinas's Synthesis: Distinguishing Principle and Terminus

We are now in a position to appreciate how Aquinas integrates both of these truths into a single synthesis of capital importance for our study. All three divine persons are a single efficient *principle* of a divine mission's created effect, while a single divine person can be, on the side of God, its *terminus.*[58]

---

[55] See I *Sent.* d. 30, q. 1, a. 1.
[56] *ScG* IV, c. 25. See also I *Sent.* d. 30, q. 1, aa. 1–2; *STh* I, q. 45, a. 6.
[57] *ScG* IV, c. 21.
[58] In fact, a divine mission has two *termini* or end points that are in relation to each other: on the side of God, it is the divine person who is sent; on the side of creatures, it is the created effect according to which the person is present in a new mode. Here, Aquinas is speaking about the terminus on the side of God.

The terms "sent," "incarnate," and such like, imply two relations, namely, that of a terminus and that of a principle. Regarding the one, the relation of a principle belongs to the whole Trinity, whence we say that the whole Trinity "sends" or "makes incarnate." But the other [the relation of a terminus] belongs to some distinct person, so that such names [e.g., "is sent," "is made incarnate"] are not said of the whole Trinity.[59]

All three divine persons together efficiently cause a divine mission's created effect, so on the side of the created effect, there is a real relation to all three divine persons as a single principle. (For example, all three divine persons efficiently cause Christ's human nature to be united to the Son in person.) But a divine mission's created effect has a second relation, also "really in" the creature, by which it "terminates to" the one divine person who is sent—and *not* to the others.

These two relations are intrinsically connected in a divine mission, says St Thomas:

This relation [*relatio*] by which a creature is drawn into God as into a terminus [i.e., the relation arising from a divine mission's created effect] also includes as an intrinsic consequence a relation [*relationem*] to God as a principle. Thus, in all cases where God is said to have a relation [*habitudinem*] to a creature because the creature is drawn into God as into a terminus, one must consider that, under the aspect of the relation [*habitudinem*] to the terminus, such things can belong to one of the divine persons alone. But the *ratio* of principle, which is included here, necessarily belongs to the whole Trinity. Therefore, under one respect, these things can make us think of a person; while, under the other, they make us think of the [divine] essence; as is clear when it is said that "incarnate" belongs only to the Son, because the incarnation terminates in the person of the Son alone, although the whole Trinity accomplishes this.[60]

This synthesis mirrors a basic insight of Aquinas's Trinitarian theology: when we speak of a divine person, we must also think of the divine essence in the background. The same is true here. When, in a divine mission, we highlight a creature's relation to a single divine person, we must remember that, in the background, there is also a relation to the divine essence (which is really identical with that person), as the efficient cause of the new created effect.

[59] I *Sent.* d. 30, q. 1, a. 2 ad 3.
[60] I *Sent.* d. 30, q. 1, a. 2. On this, see Emery, *La Trinité créatrice*, 314–16.

We can summarize Aquinas's teaching concerning the created effect of a divine mission thus: a mission's created effect is (1) something "new" in the creature, (2) through which the divine person sent "begins to *be in* a creature,"[61] in person, in a new mode, (3) "according to a new relation"[62] between the person sent and the creature, which is "really in" the creature and by which the creature uniquely "is referred to" that one divine person "as a terminus,"[63] and (4) this is efficiently caused by all three divine persons as by a single principle of the created effect. Precisely how this happens will become clearer as we examine in more detail the visible and invisible missions of the Son and Holy Spirit. It is to that examination that we now turn.

---

[61] *Contra errores Graecorum* I, c. 14. Emphasis added.
[62] I *Sent.* d. 15, q. 3, a. 1 ad 3.   [63] I *Sent.* d. 30, q. 1, a. 2.

2

Divine Missions

Invisible and Visible

When we read the New Testament, we cannot miss the visible missions: the Father sends the Son into the world as man; the Holy Spirit descends on Jesus in the form of a dove, and on the Apostles in tongues of flame. But invisible missions are clearly mentioned, too: "God has sent the Spirit of his Son into our hearts, crying, 'Abba! Father! (Gal. 4:6).'"

In St Thomas's longest extended examination of the divine missions (*STh* I, q. 43), he reverses this order. After clarifying the idea of missions in general (in aa. 1–2), he treats first the invisible missions (aa. 3–6), and then concludes with the visible missions (aa. 7–8). There is a good reason for this: the invisible missions of the Son and the Holy Spirit are, in a sense, simpler to explain. In every invisible mission, the created effect is an unseen *habitus* in the soul. In contrast, the visible missions, while easier to envision, are more complex to explain. For this reason, we will follow St Thomas's order: invisible missions first, then visible missions.[1]

---

[1] Gilles Emery has treated the divine missions repeatedly; this chapter builds on his work. See Emery, "L'inhabitation de Dieu Trinité dans les justes," 155–84; "*Theologia* and *Dispensatio*," 519–27; *Trinitarian Theology*, 372–95; "Missions invisibles et missions visibles: le Christ et son Esprit," *Revue Thomiste* 106 (2006): 51–99. We have also relied on Martin Sabathé, *La Trinité rédemptrice dans le Commentaire de l'évangile de saint Jean par Thomas d'Aquin* (Paris: Librairie Philosophique J. Vrin, 2011), 301–422; Bruno Drilhon, *Dieu missionnaire: Les missions visibles des personnes divines selon saint Thomas d'Aquin* (Paris: Éditions Téqui, 2009); Camille de Belloy, *La visite de Dieu: Essai sur les missions des personnes divines selon saint Thomas d'Aquin* (Geneva: Éditions Ad Solem, 2006); and Marshall, "*Ex Occidente Lux?*," 25–30.

A. THE INVISIBLE MISSIONS

The term "invisible mission" refers to the sending of a divine person to a human being (or an angel) "through invisible grace," and it "signifies a new mode of that person's indwelling, and his origin from another."[2] Both the Son and the Holy Spirit are sent invisibly "since it befits both the Son and the Holy Spirit to indwell through grace and to be from another;" although the Father also dwells in human beings "through grace," he is never "sent" because he is not "from another."[3] An invisible mission thus has the two elements that characterize every divine mission: an eternal procession of a divine person from another, and a created effect by which that procession is made present in a new way in a creature.[4]

These missions are called "invisible" because "the indwelling by grace"[5] is a spiritual reality in the soul that cannot be seen directly.[6] Aquinas underlines that this new presence can only be according to sanctifying or habitual grace[7]—and, more specifically, that it is according to the gifts of wisdom and charity that a creature receives in sanctifying grace. These are created effects given to the creature, but—this point is capital—*in* these created effects, the divine persons are sent in person and really begin to dwell in the creature: the Son in wisdom, and the Holy Spirit in charity.

Aquinas's teaching on this point is rather subtle and has often been either misunderstood or only partially grasped.[8] Our ambition is not to examine its every aspect, but to survey its principal elements, in order to clarify how Aquinas understands the Son and the Holy Spirit to be sent invisibly and in person, and thus to prepare the ground for later chapters.

---

[2] *STh* I, q. 43, a. 5.   [3] *Ibid.*

[4] Emery, "Missions invisibles et missions visibles," 52–3.

[5] *STh* I, q. 43, a. 5 ad 3.   [6] *STh* I–II, q. 112, a. 5.

[7] *STh* I, q. 43, a. 3. Though St Thomas's terminology varies—sometimes he says an invisible mission is "*secundum gratiam gratum facientem*," and at other times "*secundum gratiam habitualem*"—he is speaking about the same reality. Compare *STh* I, q. 43, a. 3 with *STh* III, q. 7, a. 13; q. 7, a. 1 sc.

[8] Consider, for example, David Coffey, "A Proper Mission of the Holy Spirit," *Theological Studies* 47 (1986): 227–50. Although he does not single out Aquinas, Coffey suggests that the Western theological tradition does not adequately account for a mission of the Holy Spirit in person in grace. For a discussion of a number of other contemporary theologians who misunderstand Aquinas on this point, see Marshall, "*Ex Occidente Lux?*," 23–50.

Created Gifts, Uncreated Presence

Let us begin with the point we have been stressing: the divine persons themselves are sent to, dwell in, and are possessed by human beings, in person, in the gifts of wisdom and charity received through sanctifying or habitual grace. These missions are absolutely primary for Aquinas: created grace is ordered to uncreated grace, the proper presence of the divine persons themselves.[9] He emphasizes, for example, that when grace is given, "not only the gifts of the Spirit, but the Holy Spirit himself proceeds temporally or is given."[10]

In order to expose to view the interlaced web of causality and presence involved here, however, it is easiest if we follow the same order as used by Aquinas in the *Summa Theologiae*. We will begin by examining the created effect of sanctifying or habitual grace and the further gifts it entails. From there, we can then ascend to the presence of the uncreated divine persons.

Habitual Grace and Its Gifts

Aquinas describes habitual grace as a quality, "a habitual gift infused by God into the soul," distinguishing it from the "gratuitous effect" whereby God moves the soul,[11] which Aquinas elsewhere refers to as the "*auxilium* [i.e., help] of grace,"[12] and which later authors often

---

[9] It is not uncommon to find theologians speaking as if Aquinas negated this proposition. For example, that Karl Rahner went to great lengths to show how one could, consistent with "scholastic theology," accord priority to the personal presence of the divine persons in the soul over the created effects of sanctifying grace, demonstrates this misunderstanding rather well. (Rahner's solution differs from Aquinas's position in important respects.) Karl Rahner, "Some Implications of the Scholastic Concept of Uncreated Grace," in *Theological Investigations*, vol. 1, trans. Cornelius Ernst (Baltimore: Helicon Press, 1961), 319–46. This misunderstanding persists. See, e.g., Roger Haight, "Sin and Grace," in *Systematic Theology: Roman Catholic Perspectives*, 2nd ed., eds Francis Schüssler Fiorenza and John P. Galvin (Minneapolis: Fortress Press, 2011), 404–5.

[10] I *Sent.* d. 14, q. 2, a. 1, qla 1.

[11] *STh* I–II, q. 110, a. 2. See also *In Ioan.* c. 1, lect. 6 (no. 154), where Aquinas distinguishes habitual grace from what he there terms "moving" grace.

[12] *STh* I, q. 62, a. 2. According to Joseph Wawrykow, Aquinas sometimes also uses "*auxilium*" in a broader sense that can include habitual grace, although its principal sense refers to a divine motion of the soul. Joseph Wawrykow, *God's Grace and*

call "actual grace."[13] (Aquinas is quite clear that the first sense of the term "grace" is the love of God that causes man to receive such a habitual gift,[14] but for the moment, let us leave this to one side.) Unlike a divine *auxilium* or motion of the soul by God, habitual grace is a quality of soul, and thus "acts in the soul not as an efficient cause, but as a formal cause."[15] It is the created formal cause by which a human being is elevated and given to participate in a new and higher nature, the divine nature itself. Aquinas calls this a "certain regeneration or re-creation," through which man "participates [in] the divine nature, through the nature of the soul, according to a certain likeness."[16] Habitual or sanctifying grace is, in effect, the beginning of the divinization that reaches its apex in glory, insofar as habitual grace is "in" the essence of the soul itself, elevating that essence to participate in the divine nature.[17] Consequently, the Thomist tradition (though not St Thomas himself) spoke of habitual grace as an "entitative *habitus*," in order to underline that it elevates the soul by producing in it a certain "spiritual being" not itself immediately ordered to operation.[18]

It follows from this participation in the divine nature by habitual grace that the human being receives further gifts: gifts of operative *habitus* that perfect his powers and dispose them to attain the new and higher end of his new and higher participated nature, according to a higher mode.[19] This derivation from the participation in the divine nature (habitual grace) follows the same pattern by which, on the purely natural level, a human being's distinct powers, including

---

Human Action: 'Merit' in the Theology of Thomas Aquinas (Notre Dame: University of Notre Dame Press, 1995), 171 n. 52.

[13] Some later commentators include actual graces within the larger category of sanctifying grace. See Réginald Garrigou-Lagrange, *De Gratia* (Turin: R. Berruti & Co., 1947), 122. In Aquinas's texts, however, when he speaks of sanctifying grace (*gratia gratum faciens*) without further specification, the context usually suggests that he is speaking about habitual grace. We will therefore use "habitual grace" and "sanctifying grace" as largely interchangeable terms.

[14] See, e.g., *STh* I–II, q. 110, a. 1.   [15] *STh* I–II, q. 110, a. 2 ad 1.

[16] *Ibid.*, a. 4; see also a. 3.   [17] *STh* I–II, q. 110, a. 4.

[18] Jean-Pierre Torrell, *Encyclopédie Jésus le Christ chez saint Thomas d'Aquin* (Paris: Les Éditions du Cerf, 2008), 1002–3. Provided that one avoids reifying grace, this can be an acceptable way to speak.

[19] *STh* I–II, q. 110, a. 4; cf. *De Verit.*, q. 27, a. 3. See also Emery, "Missions invisibles et missions visibles," 54.

his intellect and will, flow from his soul's essence, rooted in his human nature.[20] When a human being is elevated to participate in the higher divine nature, a parallel outflowing occurs on a supernatural level: supernaturally infused habitual gifts flow from the habitual grace that elevates his nature, and thus his powers receive new, supernatural perfections. These gifts are included *virtualiter* in habitual grace but are really distinct from it; habitual grace (which is "in" the soul's essence) is their principle and root, and they flow from it.

The most obvious examples of such gifts are the infused theological virtues of faith and charity. (For the sake of simplicity, let us set aside the infused moral virtues as well as the gifts of the Holy Spirit, though they also could be included here.)[21] These virtues are not the same as habitual grace, Aquinas explains, because habitual grace regards the *essence* of the soul while the infused virtues regard its *powers*: "rather, [habitual grace] is a certain disposition (*habitudo*) presupposed to the infused virtues as their principle and root."[22] As he clarifies elsewhere, "as the powers of the soul are derived from its essence, so also the virtues are certain derivations from grace."[23] This is what Aquinas is getting at by calling habitual grace the "principle and root" of the infused virtues: as a participation in the divine nature, habitual grace brings with it habitual gifts that perfect the human being's powers of knowing and loving so that he attains to God himself in faith and charity. The infusion of these theological virtues is simultaneous with habitual grace; when a wayfarer receives the gift of sanctifying grace, he also receives, simultaneously, the distinct gifts of the infused

---

[20] Aquinas established the pattern of relations between the soul's essence, its powers, operative *habitus*, acts, and the end of human nature in his largely philosophical analysis of human nature, the soul, and human virtue in the *Prima pars*. In brief, a human being has a variety of distinct powers (including the powers of intellect and will), each rooted in the single essence of the soul, from which these powers flow as from their principle. In the natural realm, therefore, the soul's distinct powers of intellect and will are said to flow from the single essence of the soul's human nature, in which they are rooted. Cf. *STh* I, q. 77, aa. 1–7. The soul's natural virtues are *habitus* perfecting these powers in reference to their acts. *STh* I–II, q. 55, a. 2.

[21] For a more detailed account of the virtues of faith and charity infused in habitual grace, and the relation between them, see, e.g., Michael S. Sherwin, *By Knowledge & By Love: Charity and Knowledge in the Moral Theology of St Thomas Aquinas* (Washington, D.C.: Catholic University of America Press, 2005), 127–31, 147–203.

[22] *STh* I–II, q. 110, a. 3 ad 3.   [23] *STh* III, q. 7, a. 2.

virtues of faith and love that flow from it. In other words, habitual grace elevates human nature (entitative *habitus*), while the infused virtues (as well as the gifts of the Holy Spirit) perfect its powers (operative *habitus*).[24]

The Presence of the Divine Persons in a New Mode

We have now laid the foundation for understanding the crowning gift given to human beings: the presence of the divine persons themselves. When Aquinas discusses this in Question 43 of the *Summa Theologiae*'s *Prima pars*,[25] he starts building his case in article 3, showing that it is only according to sanctifying grace that the divine persons are in a human being according to a new and special mode: "as the known is in the knower and the beloved is in the lover," so that God is not only in the rational creature as a cause, but also as the object of his knowing and loving. The only created effect by which this can happen is sanctifying grace: "no other effect can be the reason that a divine person would be in the rational creature in a new way."[26] Sanctifying grace is the root and principle in the essence of the soul according to which a human being can begin to know and love God in this way. But Aquinas immediately adds that this does not lead to an undifferentiated divine presence, but rather the presence of the Son and Holy Spirit themselves as sent and temporally proceeding: "Thus, the divine persons are sent and proceed temporally only according to sanctifying grace."[27]

This *Summa* article is sometimes mistakenly read as if Thomas were saying that God indwells the soul only insofar as one actually knows and loves God.[28] Elsewhere, however, Thomas explicitly clarifies that God dwells in the soul even when one is not actually knowing

---

[24] Emery, "L'inhabitation de Dieu Trinité dans les justes," 176–7.

[25] The following discussion of articles 3 and 5 of Question 43 is largely a summary of the work already done on this subject by Gilles Emery and Camille de Belloy. See Emery, *Trinitarian Theology*, 372–87; "Missions invisibles et missions visibles," 52–6; Belloy, *La visite de Dieu*, 98–147. See also D. Juvenal Merriell, *To the Image of the Trinity: A Study in the Development of Aquinas' Teaching* (Toronto: Pontifical Institute of Mediaeval Studies, 1990), 226–35.

[26] *STh* I, q. 43, a. 3.   [27] *Ibid.*

[28] See, e.g., Francis L. B. Cunningham, *The Indwelling of the Trinity: A Historico-Doctrinal Study of the Theory of St Thomas Aquinas* (Dubuque, Iowa: Priory Press, 1955), 299, 325–7.

and loving him.[29] This article does not deny that point; rather, as one recent author has shown, Aquinas deepens his teaching about the divine indwelling in this article to parallel the development of his insights into how the Trinitarian processions themselves are by way of knowledge and of love, uncovering the likeness between the processions in God, and their similitude impressed on the rational soul.[30]

Having established in article 3 that sanctifying grace is the necessary condition for the presence of the divine persons in the invisible missions, Aquinas shows in article 5 precisely *how* those persons are present in the soul according to their distinct personal properties. He begins by observing that, if one considers only sanctifying grace in itself, one discerns only the presence of the whole Trinity:

> [T]hrough sanctifying grace the whole Trinity indwells the mind. But that a divine person be sent to someone through an invisible grace signifies that person's new mode of indwelling, as well as his origin from another.[31]

Habitual grace, as a created effect of all three persons, does not yet disclose the distinct processions of the persons; it is how those processions are made present *within* habitual grace that Aquinas wants to highlight. In order to do this, he passes from habitual grace itself to the gifts perfective of a human being's intellect and will that are formal effects of habitual grace. It is according to those gifts that the soul is "assimilated" to—conformed to, made like, made the bearer and possessor of—the Son and Holy Spirit according to their eternal processions:

> [T]he soul is conformed to God through grace. So in order for a divine person to be sent to someone through grace, it is necessary that an assimilation, through some gift of grace, be made to the divine person who is sent. And because the Holy Spirit is Love, the soul is assimilated to the Holy Spirit through the gift of charity; hence, the mission of the Holy Spirit is observed according to the gift of charity. But the Son is the Word, not of whatever kind, but a Word breathing forth Love.... Therefore, the Son is sent ... according to an intellectual illumination

---

[29] See, e.g., *In I Epist. ad Cor.* c. 3, lect. 3 (no. 173).

[30] Belloy, *La visite de Dieu*, 103–4. As Emery explains, the acts of knowing and loving God are present *virtualiter* in the habitual dispositions to know and love God, and hence God is rightly said to dwell in the soul by means of those habitual dispositions even when they are not in act. Emery, *Trinitarian Theology*, 383.

[31] *STh* I, q. 43. a. 5.

by which [the soul] breaks forth into the affection of love.... [which is] properly called wisdom.[32]

A full accounting of an invisible mission requires Aquinas to identify not only habitual grace in general, but the distinct gift within habitual grace by which the human being is "assimilated to the divine person who is sent"—which is to say, by which a likeness to the divine person's mode of procession is impressed on the soul. In the gift of charity, which flows from habitual grace and perfects the human power of loving, the soul is "assimilated" to the Holy Spirit himself, receiving a likeness to the Spirit who is Love in person—and it is thus that the Spirit is "in" the soul.[33] Likewise, the gift of wisdom[34] also flows from habitual grace and perfects the human power of knowing, thereby assimilating the soul to the person of the Word.

Note the connection between wisdom and love: the Word breathes forth Love. Here we see the expanse, both broad and deep, of St Thomas's doctrine of the processions of Word and Love. Just as the perfect Word of the Father breathes forth the Holy Spirit (the Father and his Word spirate the Holy Spirit) so also the sending of the Word to the soul breaks forth into the love in which there is a mission of the Holy Spirit. By the very nature of the divine persons and the necessary order of their processions, the divine missions are inseparable and simultaneous. This intrinsic and necessary order between the processions is reproduced in the created likeness of those processions generated in the soul; the invisible missions in grace include the eternal processions and assimilate the recipient of sanctifying grace to them.[35]

---

[32] *STh* I, q. 43, a. 5 ad 2.

[33] That charity is not simply the Holy Spirit in the soul, but is a created *habitus* supernaturally infused by God that assimilates the soul to the Holy Spirit, is a distinctive note of Aquinas's theology that distinguishes him from his medieval contemporaries. Indeed, St Thomas posits this view in express disagreement with Peter Lombard. *STh* II–II, q. 23, a. 2.

[34] It is noteworthy that Aquinas uses the word "wisdom" and not "faith," so that our assimilation to the Son is not limited to faith as possessed by wayfarers but refers more generally to a gift that perfects man's intellectual power, and which therefore also is possessed by the blessed. See Emery, "Missions invisibles et missions visibles," 54; *Trinitarian Theology*, 375–9. See, e.g., I *Sent.* d. 15, q. 2, a. 1 ad 6. Neither the saints in glory nor Christ in his humanity have faith, but both nonetheless receive a gracious gift that perfects their intellects and assimilates them in their human natures to the Son in his procession as Word.

[35] We should add that the eternal exemplar of the relation between knowing and loving is found in the eternal processions themselves. In other words, while our understanding of the order of the divine processions is based on our grasp of the

In his *Sentences* Commentary, Aquinas argues in slightly different terms, explaining that, for the wayfarer, it is not enough to say that a divine person is sent by sanctifying grace, but that it is more specifically in the gifts of wisdom and love, given through that grace, that there is a "sealing" in the soul to conform it to the divine persons in their distinction. As Aquinas puts it, since in the mission of the Holy Spirit:

> the Holy Spirit himself must really be given, it is not enough for the creature to have a new relation to God of whatever sort; there must be some way by which the soul is drawn [*referatur*] unto the Holy Spirit himself as possessed, because what is given to someone is possessed by him. But a divine person cannot be possessed by us except either as enjoyed perfectly through the gift of glory, or as enjoyed imperfectly through the gift of sanctifying grace, or rather through that through which we are joined to the person we enjoy, insofar as the divine person himself by impressing his seal on our souls grants us certain gifts by which we formally enjoy the person, namely, by love and wisdom.[36]

Thomas's analogy here is vivid: as a seal, when pressed into hot wax (efficient causality), "seals" or "impresses" its image there (exemplar causality), so a divine person, "by impressing his seal on our souls," grants us the gift by which he is present, and by which the soul receives a new relation drawing it unto the divine person himself.[37] The passive verb *referri*—"to be borne" or "to be drawn"[38]—is significant; it and terms like it recur often in Thomas's *Sentences* Commentary. It has a much stronger sense than "to be referred" in contemporary English; it means not only a reference or relation to another, but also a real vector into the divine person himself. It is therefore analogous to the way Aquinas speaks of a relation that "terminates" in a divine person. Both expressions are attempts to articulate the mystery of the invisible missions, where a creature acquires a new relation that extends all the way into the divine person himself.

---

created realities of knowing and loving in a rational nature, the eternal exemplar of this is in God. For Aquinas, this is no projection from the creature onto God, but a true analogy, discernible in the creature, to a divine reality. The divine reality is first, and the created realities are certain likenesses of it.

[36] I *Sent.* d. 14, q. 2, a. 2 ad 2.

[37] For a careful examination of this analogy, see Belloy, *La visite de Dieu*, 41–5.

[38] *Referri* is the passive infinitive of *refero*, a compound whose root is *fero, ferre*, "to bring" or "to bear."

This "drawing unto" and "terminating in" the divine persons does not produce only a static quality in the soul.[39] Rather, the gifts of wisdom and charity elevate and, so to speak, energize man's powers so that he can know and love God in act.[40] They are, in dynamic actuality, how a creature is assimilated to the Son and the Holy Spirit, and consequently they are the vectors by which man returns unto the Father according to the pattern of the eternal processions of the Son and Holy Spirit.[41] "Through his gifts we are joined to the Holy Spirit himself, as by those gifts he is assimilating us to himself."[42] "The Spirit of God, namely, the love of God, descends to man from above and makes him ascend."[43] Aquinas offers his most detailed explanation of this in an important text from his *Sentences* Commentary that is well worth quoting at length: the rational creature's *reditus*, like its *exitus*, has those eternal processions as its origin, *ratio*, and exemplar. Just as a certain likeness to God is reproduced in creatures in their *exitus* from him, Aquinas explains:

> so also in the return of the rational creature unto God, a procession of a divine person is understood, insofar as the proper relation of a divine person is represented in the soul through a certain received likeness, which has its exemplar in and originates from that property of the eternal relation itself; as the proper mode by which the Holy Spirit points back [*refertur*] to the Father is love, and the proper mode by which the Son points back [*referendi*] to the Father is that he is the Father's Word itself manifesting him. Thus, as the Holy Spirit proceeds invisibly into the mind through the gift of love, thus also the Son does so through the gift

---

[39] Robert Faricy presents Thomas's theology of the divine indwelling as terminating in the divine persons themselves, but then concludes that this is a "static" understanding of that presence that lacks the "dynamism" that is necessary to understanding a vibrant and living Christian life. Robert L. Faricy, "The Trinitarian Indwelling," *The Thomist* 35 (1971): 369–404.

[40] The natural human powers of knowing and loving are supernaturally elevated by wisdom and charity so that, by means of those operative *habitus*, man can know and love God, who is infinitely above every creature. This does not mean that man is always actually knowing and loving God with all of his powers. He may think about other things, fall asleep, or be incapacitated, but in virtue of these *habitus*, he remains always ordered to knowing and loving God in act, and every intentional act of such knowledge and love has these *habitus* as its font. Aquinas would further hold that in each free act of exercising these virtues, man is moved and aided by a divine *auxilium*. See, e.g., *STh* I, q. 83, a. 1 ad 2–4; I–II, q. 109, a. 1.

[41] See Belloy, *La visite de Dieu*, 65–6; Emery, "L'inhabitation de Dieu Trinité dans les justes," 171.

[42] I *Sent.* d. 14, q. 2, a. 1, qla 1.   [43] *In Ioan.* c. 1, lect. 14 (no. 269).

of wisdom, in which is the manifestation of the Father himself, who is the ultimate person to whom we return.[44]

The gifts of wisdom and love reproduce a likeness in the soul of the very processions of the Word and Holy Spirit themselves. The exemplar and origin of those gifts are, therefore, the processions of the Son and the Spirit. And in those very likenesses, we are brought back unto the Father, since the processions of the Son and Spirit are always relative to the Father, eternally "pointing back to" and terminating in their principle, as, analogously, the created gifts point us back to the Son and the Spirit and terminate in them.

Because of this likeness to the processions of the Son and Spirit impressed on us in the respective gifts of wisdom and love, Aquinas continues, we are assimilated to those persons, and thus the persons themselves are really sent to us and are present in us:

> And because a likeness to the properties of the persons is caused in us according to the reception of these two gifts [of love and wisdom], the divine persons are therefore said to be in us to the extent that we are assimilated to them, insofar as a thing is in its likeness. . . . And for this reason, both processions are called missions.[45]

Finally, the divine persons are in us according to a dynamic movement by which they bring us back to our ultimate end, the Father himself:

> Further, as charity and wisdom originate from the properties of the persons, so also their effects follow only by the power of the divine persons who join us to our end (because in any form impressed by some agent there is the power of the impressing agent). Whence, in the reception of such gifts, the divine persons are possessed in a new mode, as if leading us [*quasi ductrices*] unto our end or joining us to it.[46]

Aquinas could hardly be more clear that the real motor behind this movement back to God is the procession of the divine persons themselves. Put otherwise, Aquinas's emphasis is on the procession and activity of the divine persons: it is the Son and Holy Spirit who reproduce in the human being a likeness of their processions, and by that likeness, they dwell in him and lead him back to the Father. Thomas speaks of the gifts of wisdom and love as created forms "impressed on" or "sealed in" us; he would not have us confuse

[44] I *Sent.* d. 15, q. 4, a. 1.   [45] *Ibid.*   [46] *Ibid.*

the likeness in us—a created effect—with the eternal persons themselves.[47] But it is the persons, according to their distinct processions, who are the exemplars and the origin of these created gifts, who impress them upon us and energize them (in the created gifts of wisdom and love lies the power (*virtus*) of the Son and Holy Spirit themselves), and who are the termini of the new relations in us in virtue of these gifts. The persons are therefore really present and active in us, impressing their likenesses on us, referring us back to, pointing us to, putting us in contact with, and drawing us into the Trinity according to their own distinct mode of proceeding.

We might now return with profit to the analogy we proposed about the Washington Monument. That example is helpful for illustrating a mixed relation, but it does not capture the element of "being drawn into" that Aquinas underlines in the invisible missions. We would need to imagine that, in seeing the Washington Monument, one would somehow also be drawn into the Monument. In fact, this is insufficient and even misleading; the gifts of charity and wisdom do not draw us into a place or a material thing, but into the infinite and perfect spirit who is the Triune God. They do so by making us more and more like the divine persons themselves, who are active in us without changing in themselves. To illustrate this, Aquinas, speaking of the Holy Spirit's mission, turns to a different analogy:

> How is [the Holy Spirit] sent? He draws us to himself, and to that extent is said to be sent, as the sun is said to be sent to someone when he participates in the sun's brightness. So it is with the Holy Spirit.[48]

When the sun shines on Socrates, Socrates becomes "bright" with the sun's brightness. If we imagine this brightness were somehow "in" Socrates—as if his new radiance were not just the sun's light reflecting off his body, but that it somehow entered into him and emanated thence, all the while being from the sun—we get a better idea of what Aquinas has in mind. The sun does not change when it shines on Socrates; the change is entirely on Socrates' side as he is "assimilated" to the sun's brightness. And if we try to transcend the limits of this

---

[47] See, e.g., I *Sent.* d. 14, q. 2, a. 1, qla 1. For example, charity in our souls is not the Holy Spirit himself. *STh* II–II, q. 23, a. 2. Rather, the Holy Spirit is really present as the origin and exemplar of charity, impressing that created form, a likeness to his procession, on our souls.

[48] *Emitte spiritum tuum.*

material example and think of "being drawn into" in terms of a spiritual participation—that is, if we do not think of Socrates moving into the sun as into an object in a place, but rather as becoming "closer" to or more like the exemplar of all brightness—then the more Socrates shares in the sun's brightness, the more he is "drawn into" the sun itself. In this way, a divine person is the "terminus" of a mission's created effect. The gifts of charity and wisdom not only make us *like* the divine persons, but in doing so they draw us *into* them as the terminus of a new relation that is *in* the creature.

Let us add a final word about distinguishing between these invisible missions: they are distinct, first of all, because of the distinction between the eternal processions of the persons. Secondly, "they are distinguished in the effects of grace," when living faith perfects a wayfarer's intellect (by which the believer's soul is assimilated to the Son's personal procession), while charity perfects his will (whereby there is an assimilation to the Holy Spirit's procession).[49] These two effects, though inseparable just as the divine persons are inseparable, are nonetheless distinct.

Four Types of Causality in Habitual Grace

We are now in a position to build on what we have discussed in CHAPTER 1 about the principle and terminus of a divine mission's created effect. In the created effect of habitual grace, with its accompanying gifts of wisdom and charity by reason of which the invisible missions are made, we can discern four interlaced types of causality.

Efficient Causality

First, with respect to efficient causality, Aquinas steadfastly maintains that habitual grace, as a created effect in the soul, has as its efficient cause all three persons of the Trinity acting inseparably.[50] In other words, the whole Trinity, acting in virtue of the one divine essence, is a single principle of habitual grace. Similarly, because the gifts of wisdom and charity flowing from habitual grace are also created effects, they too have the entire Trinity as their efficient cause. When

---

[49] See, e.g., *STh* I, q. 43, a. 5 ad 3.   [50] See *ibid.*, a. 4 ad 2; III, q. 3, a. 4 ad 3.

Aquinas speaks of one divine person as an efficient cause of sanctifying grace, or of a gift given in that grace, therefore, he does so by appropriation. Thus, he often suggests, by appropriation, that the Holy Spirit is the efficient cause of charity, and the Son of wisdom or faith.[51]

Appropriations are useful, though often misunderstood and underappreciated. It is often assumed that appropriation is only a manner of speaking; for example, in the context of grace, some think it is a way to pay lip service to the Holy Spirit's role while emptying it of any real content.[52] In fact, for Aquinas, the opposite is true. Appropriating grace to the Holy Spirit is a way of manifesting, even in an action common to all three persons, the kinship or likeness of this action to the Spirit's procession. Dominique-Marie Cabaret's detailed study of the Trinitarian appropriations in Aquinas shows that this kinship is really in God—it is not only a matter of our language or understanding. While appropriated attributes are not themselves based on a real distinction and plurality in God, and so cannot by themselves reveal the plurality and distinction of the persons, once we have come to know that plurality and distinction—that is, once we have come to know the persons in themselves—what is appropriated can disclose (though imperfectly) the real plurality and distinction of the persons in the unity of the one God. Appropriations help us to know better, although in limited fashion, the mystery of the divine persons in what is proper to them, by way of what is easier for us to grasp, namely, the attributes and actions common to all three persons.[53] In this context, then, Aquinas's doctrine of appropriations helps us see how the gifts of wisdom and charity, precisely as created *effects*, point us back to the personal properties of the Son and Holy Spirit, and to the way that, even as all three divine persons act inseparably together in the order of efficient causality, each of them acts according to a proper mode.[54]

---

[51] See, e.g., *STh* I, q. 43, a. 5 ad 1; ScG IV, c. 21. Likewise, the gifts of the Holy Spirit are efficiently caused by all three persons and appropriated to the Holy Spirit.

[52] See, e.g., Coffey, "A Proper Mission of the Holy Spirit," 228.

[53] Dominique-Marie Cabaret, *L'étonnante manifestation des personnes divines: Les appropriations trinitaires chez saint Thomas d'Aquin* (Les Plans-sur-Bex, Switzerland: Éditions Parole et Silence, 2015). See also Emery, *Trinitarian Theology*, 322–31.

[54] "Thomas lays little stress on appropriation within the question on the missions, but it has to come into its own when he explains how the *effects* are related to the divine persons.... [Appropriation] touches on the connection between the created gifts of wisdom and love and the personal properties of the Son and the Holy Spirit. Any created effect as such has the whole Trinity as its efficient cause. The mission itself is certainly not an appropriation, but proper to a given divine person.... By bringing

Exemplar Causality

Unfortunately, many readers of St Thomas stop at efficient causality. They think that, because habitual grace is a created effect efficiently caused by all three persons, all references to a single divine person as a cause of this gift must be by appropriation—that is, they conclude that there is no proper, personal causality of, or presence in, grace. This is a serious misunderstanding, because it overlooks a second type of causality: the exemplar causality of the divine persons and their eternal processions. Though often marginalized or forgotten, exemplar causality has a central place in Aquinas's thought.[55] In every exercise of efficient causality, the eternal processions are already exercising their influence as the origin, the *ratio*, and the exemplar of what comes forth from God.[56] Thus, in every gift of grace, Thomas identifies the special exemplary influence of the Holy Spirit: "every gift, insofar as it is a gift, is attributed to the Holy Spirit, because as Love he is the First Gift."[57] As Thomas puts it, charity is "properly representative of the Holy Spirit."[58] Although it "is from the whole Trinity efficiently, . . . according to exemplarity, it flows from Love, who is the Holy Spirit."[59]

---

about an assimilation to a divine person, the created gift opens the way to a real recognition of which divine person has been sent." Emery, *Trinitarian Theology*, 389.

[55] See, e.g., Gregory Doolan, *Aquinas on the Divine Ideas as Exemplar Causes* (Washington, D.C.: Catholic University of America Press, 2008), 156–90. Consider, in contrast, David L. Greenstock, "Exemplar Causality and the Supernatural Order," *The Thomist* 16 (1953): 1–31. Greenstock cites Aquinas's texts that speak about the exemplar causality of the personal processions, but concludes that they must not mean what they say.

[56] See Belloy, *La visite de Dieu*, 115–16. An intelligent agent only exercises efficient causality according to some exemplar idea that determines that activity. "This is a metaphysical law of action." Emery, *Trinitarian Theology*, 197.

[57] *STh* I, q. 43, a. 5 ad 1. See also *ScG* IV, c. 21, where Aquinas is particularly clear in delineating the distinction between the common efficient causality of all three persons in grace and the proper mode of the Holy Spirit's exemplar causality. This exemplarity does not suggest that the Spirit is the formal or quasi-formal cause of grace (*pace* Rahner and Mühlen). See Gilles Emery, "The Personal Mode of Trinitarian Action in Saint Thomas Aquinas," *The Thomist* 69 (2005): 47 n. 46. Cf. Rahner, "Some Implications," 319–46; Heribert Mühlen, *Der Heilige Geist als Person* (Münster: Aschendorff, 1963). Indeed, Aquinas insists that an uncreated divine person cannot be the finite form of a creature. See, e.g., III *Sent.* d. 13, q. 1, a. 1. Rather, habitual grace is the created form inherent in the creature by which the creature participates in the divine nature.

[58] *ScG* IV, c. 21.   [59] I *Sent.* d. 17, q. 1, a. 1.

More importantly, in the gifts of wisdom and charity, it is by exemplar causality that the soul is assimilated to a likeness of the divine persons: according to their eternal processions by way of knowledge and love, the Son and Holy Spirit are the models to which we are conformed by those gifts. This is to be related to a divine person "as to a terminus," as we discussed in CHAPTER 1: "This occurs . . . according to exemplar causality, as [for example] . . . in the infusion of charity there is a termination to a likeness of the personal procession of the Holy Spirit."[60] Here we have no fanciful medieval *marginalia*, but rather a deep and powerful principle pervading Aquinas's theology.

Final Causality

The third category, final causality, is closely associated with the second. God causes habitual grace in us in order that the divine persons would be present in us and would be enjoyed by us. This end is achieved insofar as we are assimilated to the processions of the Son and Holy Spirit, the eternal exemplars of the gifts of wisdom and charity. "Whence, in the reception of such gifts the divine persons are possessed in a new way, as if leading or conjoining [their recipient] to the end."[61] In short, the gifts of charity and wisdom act as vectors that lead us or bear us back to the whole Trinity.[62] This vector into the Trinity is imperfect in sanctifying grace and perfect in glory, but the goal and terminus of this movement is always the same: our divinization as we are conformed to the divine persons themselves. Thomas recognizes this as the same movement into God that St Paul describes in Romans: "You have received the Spirit of adoption of sons, whereby we cry: Abba, Father (Rom 8:15)." It is through this filial adoption (which comes from our reception of the Holy Spirit in charity) that we already possess, albeit imperfectly, our final end, our eternal inheritance from God, which is nothing less than God himself.[63]

---

[60] I *Sent.* d. 30, q. 1, a. 2.   [61] I *Sent.* d. 15, q. 4, a. 1.
[62] I *Sent.* d. 15, q. 2, a. 1, ad 4.
[63] See, e.g., *ScG* IV, c. 21. Regarding filial adoption and the divine indwelling, see Guillermo A. Juárez, *Dios Trinidad en todas las creaturas y en los santos: Estudio histórico-sistemático de la doctrina del* Commentario a las Sentencias *de Santo Tomás de Aquino sobre la omnipresencia y la inhabitación* (Córdoba, Argentina: Ediciones del Copista, 2008); Luc-Thomas Somme, *Fils adoptifs de Dieu par Jésus Christ: La filiation divine par adoption dans la théologie de saint Thomas d'Aquin* (Paris:

Habitual Grace as a Disposing Cause

There remains a fourth type of causality in grace about which we have as yet said little: the disposing causality of habitual grace. We are made fit to receive the divine persons by habitual or sanctifying grace. From our perspective, this created effect seems to come first—we receive faith and charity in sanctifying grace, and according to these gifts, the Son and Holy Spirit are invisibly sent to us.

Before we examine the details of this disposing causality, a clarification is in order. As we have seen, St Thomas mainly speaks about habitual or sanctifying grace in connection with the Holy Spirit, since he views the procession of the Holy Spirit as Love and Gift as the origin and exemplar of the whole dispensation of salvation and of every gracious gift given to creatures. "[A]ll gifts are given to us through him."[64] Because of the Spirit's special exemplar likeness to grace, St Thomas speaks most often about grace as caused by the Holy Spirit, and of grace as the created effect by which the Holy Spirit dwells in us. This exemplarity of the Holy Spirit with respect to God's gifts in general should not be confused, however, with the unique mode by which the Holy Spirit is personally present in an invisible mission. In the gift of charity, there is something new *in us* that makes us really like the Holy Spirit. When we receive the gift of charity, we begin to love God above all things by a supernatural, spiritual act of a rational nature, and so we are "assimilated to" and begin to resemble the Holy Spirit in a new and unique way, one that surpasses the way the Holy Spirit is an exemplar of other created gifts. Additionally, since charity is a gift always and only given in sanctifying grace, and everyone who receives it also receives habitual or sanctifying grace, and vice versa, sometimes St Thomas does not even mention charity. Instead, he simply says that the Holy Spirit causes habitual grace, and is especially made present "in" or "through" that grace. Aquinas does not mean by this that the Holy Spirit indwells the soul in person in some way other than by charity, nor that the Holy Spirit is an exclusive efficient cause of sanctifying grace (all three persons are

Librairie Philosophique J. Vrin, 1997). See also A. N. Williams, *The Ground of Union: Deification in Aquinas and Palamas* (Oxford: Oxford University Press, 1999), 55–64; Emile Bailleux, "A l'image du Fils premier-né," *Revue Thomiste* 76 (1976): 181–207.

[64] III *Sent.* d. 2, q. 2, a. 2, qla 2 ad 3.

its efficient cause), nor again that the Holy Spirit is sent without the Son (who is also sent in habitual grace, according to the gift of wisdom that is also always given with it).

With this clarification in mind, let us return to the formal disposing causality of habitual grace. In the *Summa Theologiae*, St Thomas starts his analysis of the indwelling of the divine persons by speaking first about grace as a created effect that disposes the creature to receive the Holy Spirit in person. This is but a first step in Aquinas's depiction of a reciprocal relation between charity as a created effect and the mission of the Holy Spirit made "in" that gift of grace. (The same analysis could be applied to the mission and personal presence of the Son in the gift of wisdom, which is always given with charity in habitual grace, though Aquinas speaks more often of the Holy Spirit in this context.) On the side of the creature, sanctifying grace disposes the creature to receive the divine persons. On the side of God, the gifts of grace (wisdom and charity) are not only *ordered to* the indwelling of the divine persons, but are given *in the sending of* the Son and Holy Spirit, in person, to the creature. Thomas states this quite clearly in the *Summa Theologiae* (he speaks only of the invisible mission of the Holy Spirit, but the context includes the Son's invisible mission as well):

> Sanctifying grace disposes the soul to possess the divine person, and this is signified when we say that the Holy Spirit is given according to the gift of grace. But nonetheless, this very gift of grace is from the Holy Spirit, and this is signified when we read that "the love of God is infused into our hearts through the Holy Spirit (Rom. 5:5)."[65]

Thomas, then, affords only a relative priority to habitual grace. The true priority in a divine mission is not on the side of the creature or created effect, but on the side of the divine person who is sent.[66] Speaking again about the Holy Spirit, Aquinas writes:

> A natural ordering between two things can be looked at in two ways. (1) On the side of the one who receives ... the disposition takes priority over that to which it disposes: in this sense, the receipt of the gifts of the Holy Spirit has priority over that of the Holy Spirit himself, since it is by receiving these gifts that we are conformed to the Holy Spirit. (2) But on

---

[65] *STh* I, q. 43, a. 3 ad 2.
[66] Emery, "*Theologia* and *Dispensatio*," 522–4.

the side of the agent and end, priority belongs to what falls closer to the agent and end: in this sense, the receipt of the Holy Spirit has priority over that of his gifts . . . and this kind of priority is absolute.[67]

Consequently, the very word "grace" can itself designate either the personal presence of the Holy Spirit (and, by implication, the presence of the Father and Son as well), or the created effect in the creature wrought by that presence:

There is a certain freely given gift that is uncreated, namely, the Holy Spirit. But that this gift begins to be possessed at one moment when before it was not, is not the result of some change in the Holy Spirit, but of a change in the one to whom he is given. Thus, it is necessary from the fact itself that the Holy Spirit is given to someone, that the creature acquires something that he did not have before, according to which he is said to have obtained the Holy Spirit. Therefore, the term 'grace,' in whatever sense it is used, signifies that something freely given is created in the soul, although it also can signify something uncreated—either the divine favor itself or the uncreated gift that is the Holy Spirit.[68]

This is extremely important for our study: the Spirit's personal presence and the created effect in the soul cannot be separated. For Aquinas, even the term "grace" is itself capable of signifying both sides of this single reality. Sanctifying grace cannot be divorced from the personal presence of the Holy Spirit; it is a created gift, a temporal effect that is "caused by the Holy Spirit," and that "disposes us to receive the Holy Spirit himself."[69] To put it most simply, the charity that always is given in habitual or sanctifying grace is the created dimension of an invisible mission of the Holy Spirit in person. (The same can be said for the Son's invisible mission by the gift of wisdom informed by love.) As Thomas puts it: "Where there is charity, there is the Holy Spirit. . . . With charity, it is necessary that the Holy Spirit is present."[70]

[67] I *Sent.* d. 14, q. 2, a. 1, qla 2. The translation is from Emery, "*Theologia* and *Dispensatio*," 523.

[68] II *Sent.* d. 26, q. 1, a. 1.

[69] Emery, "*Theologia* and *Dispensatio*," 523. Other contemporary authors have also noted this point in passing; see, e.g., Nicholas M. Healy, *Thomas Aquinas: Theologian of the Christian Life* (Burlington, Vt.: Ashgate, 2003), 111.

[70] *In decem preceptis*, prol.

Integrating the Modes of Personal
Presence and Causality

St Thomas carefully distinguishes different modes of causality and presence in the created effect of an invisible mission, but he nonetheless emphasizes that they are aspects of a single reality that is a unified whole. This is evident in a number of texts.

The first, an important text from the *Summa Contra Gentiles* on the Holy Spirit, offers an excellent example. St Thomas begins with efficient and exemplar causality:

> Those things that are in us from God are traced back to God as to their efficient cause and their exemplar cause: to their efficient cause, since something is done in us by the divine operative power; to their exemplar cause, since what is in us from God imitates God in some way.[71]

These two types of causality in grace are not mutually exclusive but rather complementary: what God does in us by his operative power necessarily also creates a likeness to God in us. There is a single divine action in giving us grace, but there are two distinct aspects to God's causality discernible within it. As to efficient causality, Thomas continues, "everything that God works in us" is at once "from the Father, the Son, and the Holy Spirit" since they have "the very same power" and "the very same essence."[72] But Aquinas immediately adds that, viewed in terms of exemplar causality, the gifts of grace in us produce a likeness to the Son and Holy Spirit according to their distinct properties.

> Nonetheless, the word of wisdom sent to us by God, by which we know God, is properly representative (*proprie repraesentativum*) of the Son. And likewise, the love by which we love God is properly representative (*proprium repraesentativum*) of the Holy Spirit. And thus the charity that is in us, although an effect of the Father, Son, and Holy Spirit, nonetheless is said to be in us in a particular way through the Holy Spirit.[73]

In other words, God's efficient causality, common to all three persons, is shaped by the pattern of the Trinitarian processions (or the personal properties of the Son and of the Holy Spirit), and thus it impresses

---

[71] *ScG* IV, c. 21.   [72] *Ibid.*   [73] *Ibid.*

on the creature an effect that bears the distinctive marks of the divine persons.

As we have seen, in his *Sentences* Commentary, Aquinas used the analogy of a seal to explain this: when pressed into hot wax (efficient causality), a seal impresses its image in it (exemplar causality).[74] Here, in the *Summa Contra Gentiles*, St Thomas draws an analogy to action and the actor, and to motion and the moved, to reach the same conclusion:

> Because divine effects not only begin to be but also are held in being by divine action (just as . . . nothing can act unless it is present, so it is necessary that the one acting and his action exist together at the same time, just as the one moving and the motion must exist together), it is necessary that, wherever there is an effect of God, there would be God himself causing it. Thus, since the charity by which we love God is in us through the Holy Spirit, it is necessary that the Holy Spirit himself would also be in us, as long as charity is in us. Therefore the Apostle says, "do you not know that you are the temple of God, and that the Holy Spirit dwells in you (1 Cor. 3:16)?"[75]

It is not as if God impresses his image on us in the gift of charity and then withdraws, as the earlier analogy of the seal might suggest.[76] By drawing an analogy to the relation between an action and the agent who does it, and to motion and the one who is moved, Aquinas underlines both the dynamism of an invisible mission's created effect, and the inseparable presence of the divine person who causes it. Charity is in us only so long the Holy Spirit is really there, insofar as he actively impresses and conserves (by the efficient causality common to all three persons) the pattern of his personal property in us.

Finally, the presence of the Holy Spirit in charity brings with it the presence of the Father and the Son, so that we are joined to the Triune God as to our perfect and ultimate end:

> Since, therefore, through the Holy Spirit we are made lovers of God, and every beloved is in the lover as such, it is necessary that through the Holy Spirit the Father and the Son also dwell in us. Therefore the Lord says, "we will come to him," namely to the one who loves God, "and we will make our dwelling with him (John 14:23)." And we read, "we

---

[74] See I *Sent.* d. 14, q. 2, a. 2 ad 2.   [75] *ScG* IV, c. 21.
[76] See I *Sent.* d. 37, q. 1, a. 1 ad 3.

know that he remains in us from the Spirit that he has given us (1 John 3:24)."[77]

Put otherwise, through the invisible missions, we are brought into God himself: "Therefore it is necessary that, through the Holy Spirit, not only is God in us, but we also are in God."[78] Thomas continues at length, explaining that this makes us friends of God, lifting us up into God by our operations of knowing and loving, and granting us a pledge of the perfect beatitude that we now experience in part. This is our adoption as sons and daughters of God, and our reception of an eternal inheritance.[79]

In his *Disputed Question on Charity*, Aquinas uses two additional analogies to illustrate the impossibility of separating charity from the Holy Spirit's presence in the soul:

> [C]harity is infused "into our hearts by the Holy Spirit who is given to us," as Romans 5:5 says. But God does not cause charity in the soul as if he were a cause only of its coming-to-be and not of its conservation—as if God were like a builder who is only the cause of a house coming to be, so that when the builder goes away, the house remains. Rather, God is the cause of charity and grace in the soul both in its coming-to-be and in its conservation, as the sun is the cause of light in the atmosphere.... As Augustine says ... "man is illuminated by God being present to him so that, when God is absent, he continues in darkness."[80]

When the Holy Spirit infuses charity into our hearts, he is more like the sun than a builder of a house. Further, *both* the divine efficient causality *and* the personal presence of the Holy Spirit are continuous. These examples free us from a static idea of charity; he would have us conceive of it less as a "thing" in the soul, and more as a power elevated and energized—supernaturally supercharged, as it were—by the actualizing presence of God in the soul ("illuminated by God being present to him").

St Thomas integrates all of the foregoing into the overarching perspective of the *exitus* of creatures from God and their return to him in his Commentary on Romans 5:5 (a text likely written in the last years of his life), on charity and the Holy Spirit's presence.

---

[77] *ScG* IV, c. 21.   [78] *Ibid.*   [79] *Ibid.*
[80] *De Caritate*, a. 13.

"The love of God" can be taken in two ways: in one way, for the love by which God loves us: "I have loved you with an everlasting love (Jer. 31:3);" in another way, "the love of God" can be called the love by which we love God: "I am certain that neither death nor life will separate us from the love of God (Rom 8:39)." Both these "loves of God" are poured into our hearts by the Holy Spirit who has been given to us. For the Holy Spirit, who is the love of the Father and of the Son, to be given to us is for us to be drawn into a participation in the Love who is the Holy Spirit, by which participation we are made lovers of God. And that we love him is a sign that he loves us: "I love those who love me (Pr. 8:17)." "Not as if we" first "loved God, but that he first loves us," as 1 John 4:10 says. But the love by which he loves us, is said to be poured into our hearts, because it is clearly shown to be in our hearts through the gift of the Holy Spirit imprinted in us.[81]

Here, Aquinas's starting point is charity's eternal foundation: God's love for us. On this score, the Spirit as Love (or his procession by way of Love) is the *ratio* of God's love for creatures, and therefore a cause of every grace. Aquinas then adds the personal presence and causality of the Holy Spirit: both God's love for us, and the love by which we love God, are "poured into our hearts through the Holy Spirit who has been given to us." The Holy Spirit is the divine person "nearest us," through whom grace, the created gift of all three persons, is given[82]—Aquinas always identifies the gift of grace with the action and presence of the Holy Spirit. Taken in itself, efficient causality is appropriated. But this text underlines the Holy Spirit's exemplar-efficient causality as Love in person who "imprints" his gift of charity "in our hearts." This imprint, a created effect, is the "sign" of his presence. Finally, when he is sent to us, the Spirit grants us a dynamic participation in his very procession as Love, so that we become lovers of God. This is our assimilation to the Holy Spirit and our movement into the Triune God who is our final end.[83]

We cannot omit mentioning one final text (also from one of Aquinas's mature works), since it is both evocative and clear. Jesus in John's Gospel tells the Samaritan woman that he will give a "spring of living water welling up to eternal life" (John 4:14). This image, thinks St Thomas, is perfect for underlining the intrinsic

---

[81] *In Epist. ad Rom.* c. 5, lect. 1 (no. 392).
[82] III *Sent.* d. 2, q. 2, a. 2, qla 2 ad 3.
[83] See also *In Epist. ad Rom.* c. 8, lect. 1 (no. 603).

connection between the Holy Spirit and charity (and grace understood more generally):

> Living water...is connected to its source and flows from it. In this sense, the grace of the Holy Spirit is rightly called living water, because the grace itself of the Holy Spirit is given to men in such a way that the very fount of grace is given, namely, the Holy Spirit. Nay, rather grace is given through him: "The charity of God is diffused into our hearts through the Holy Spirit who is given to us (Rom. 5:5)." For the Holy Spirit himself is the unfailing fountainhead from whom all gifts of grace flow: "one and the same Spirit does all these things (1 Cor. 12:11)," etc.[84]

Aquinas dwells on this image because it permits him to show both that all graces come to us through the Spirit, and that the Spirit is in us, in person, in his sanctifying gifts. The living water of grace is living precisely because it is "connected to its source and flows from it."

> And thus if anyone would have some gift of the Holy Spirit, and not the Spirit himself, the water would not be connected to its source, and hence it is dead rather than living.[85]

The Holy Spirit gives himself to us when he gives us charity, through which we receive grace. Were one to disconnect grace from its vital source, the Holy Spirit personally present in the soul, it would cease to be life-giving; indeed, it would cease to be sanctifying grace at all: it would be "dead rather than living."

Conclusion

To summarize the foregoing: if we think of grace as the created effect by reason of which the invisible divine missions are made according to charity and wisdom—as St Thomas clearly does—then the four causes we have discussed above, and the modes of personal presence of the divine persons, are integrated into a single overarching synthesis. For St Thomas, habitual grace (a) comes from and through the Holy Spirit (the Holy Spirit's procession as Love and Gift is the origin, *ratio*, and exemplar of every grace given to creatures). It is given to human beings (b) through the joint efficient causality of all three persons, an efficient causality that is nonetheless shaped by the

---

[84] *In Ioan.* c. 4, lect. 2 (no. 577).
[85] *Ibid.* See also *In Ioan.* c. 7, lect. 5 (no. 1090).

exemplarity of the Trinitarian processions, and that is appropriated to the Holy Spirit. Viewed from the side of the creature, habitual grace (c) disposes man to receive the divine persons by elevating his human nature to share in the divine nature (entitative *habitus*), thereby also elevating his power of loving in the gift of charity and his power of knowing in the gift of sanctifying wisdom (both are operative *habitus*) that flow from that grace. But in fact the true priority is on the side of the divine missions, by which (d) the Son and Holy Spirit come to dwell in man in person: in the gift of charity, the Holy Spirit impresses in man's soul a likeness of his personal property as Love (a special mode of exemplar causality), thus assimilating this soul to himself; the Son does likewise in the gift of wisdom. The Son and Holy Spirit are therefore invisibly sent to the human being, in whom they are personally present in a new way. And this presence is not static: (e) in the order of final causality, these invisible missions lead man back into the Triune God according to the pattern of the eternal processions by way of knowledge and love, so that we "return" to the Father through the Son and in the Holy Spirit.

B. THE VISIBLE MISSIONS

When Aquinas speaks of the "visible missions," he is designating the incarnation of the Son, the visible manifestations of the Holy Spirit as resting on Christ (at Christ's baptism and at his transfiguration), and the visible outpouring of the Holy Spirit on the Blessed Virgin Mary and the Apostles after the resurrection (Christ breathes on them on the evening of the resurrection, and then tongues of fire descend on them at Pentecost).[86] Speaking about a visible mission of the Holy Spirit, Aquinas formulates its elements as follows:

> A visible mission is not essentially different from an invisible mission of the Holy Spirit; it adds only an element of manifestation through a visible sign. Three things come together in the definition of the Holy Spirit's visible mission, therefore: that the one sent is from another, that he is in another according to some special mode, and that one or the

---

[86] Recent studies of Aquinas's theology of the visible missions include Drilhon, *Dieu missionnaire*, 51–176, and Sabathé, *La Trinité rédemptrice*, 328–422.

other of these is shown through some visible sign, by reason of which the whole mission is called visible.[87]

The first two elements of this definition are, by now, familiar to us. It is the new third element, concerning the mission's "visibility," that is (rather unsurprisingly) the distinguishing mark of a visible mission.

"Visible" in Different Ways

A visible mission involves some sort of manifestation. Of what? By what? The definition we have just quoted is, on this point, quite broad. A visible mission involves "some visible sign" that "shows" the divine person either as "from another," or as "in another according to some special mode." That is, what is visible always points to some invisible reality, but precisely what sort of invisible reality may vary from case to case: it could be the mission's personal *principle* (procession from another), or the mission's *terminus* (a new mode of existing in another) that is "shown through some visible sign." To the extent that these are different, the relations between what is visible and what is signified will also be different. In other words, the "visibility" or "manifestation" involved here is an analogical notion, not a univocal one.[88] What is made visible, and how, will be different in different visible missions.

This is evident when we compare the visible missions of the Holy Spirit to the visible mission of the Son. Since we will examine the Son's visible mission in PART II of this book, and the visible mission of the Holy Spirit to Christ in PART III, we will not enter into all of the details of these differences here. Suffice it to say for now that what is "visible" in the Son's visible mission—Christ's humanity itself—is an absolutely unique case, quite unlike the visible sign in the Holy Spirit's visible missions. Aquinas explains it thus:

> The visible creature according to which a mission is called "visible" is different in the visible mission of the Son and the visible mission of the Holy Spirit, because in the mission of the Son, [that creature] is constituted not only as that *through which* or *in which* the mission is shown, but also as that *to which* the mission is made, since [the Son] assumed a visible human nature into the unity of [his] person. He is said to be sent

---

[87] I *Sent.* d. 16, q. 1, a. 1.
[88] Emery, "Missions invisibles et missions visibles," 64.

visibly in the flesh according to this assumption. Therefore, he exists in some new mode in that visible nature itself, namely, through a union not only in the soul, but even in the body. But in a visible mission of the Holy Spirit, the visible creature is not constituted as that *to which* the mission is made, but only as what shows the invisible mission made to someone else. Thus, it is not necessary that [the Holy Spirit] be *in* that visible creature in a new mode, except as in a sign; rather, [the Holy Spirit] is, in a new mode, *in* him to whom the mission is made.[89]

In Christ, a human nature is taken up, in an utterly singular way, into a personal union with the invisible divine person *who is thus made visible as man*. Because it is united to the Son in person according to being, that human nature is more than a visible sign: the man Jesus *is* the Word made flesh.[90] In other words, if we consider the person or supposit, there is no distinction between what is visible, on the one hand, and his "new mode of existing" in the world on the other: "the Son exists in some new mode *in* that visible nature itself."[91] We can add that, as we shall discuss in CHAPTER 4, Christ's humanity bears the Son's personal property ("from the Father") in virtue of the hypostatic union; Christ manifests this "being from the Father" in his humanity itself and in all of his actions. (Indeed, this is one of the main reasons why the Word became flesh: "to manifest the Father.")[92] In the Son's visible mission, Christ's human nature is both the created terminus of the mission, and what manifests the two elements of a divine mission (procession from another, and a new mode of existing). Further, the Word assumes a human nature so as to *act* as man, and thereby to effect our salvation: it is through what he does and undergoes in that humanity, above all in his passion, that he becomes the Author of sanctification who sends the Holy Spirit as the Gift of sanctification (more on this just below).

The visible missions of the Holy Spirit do not work like this. "As Augustine says . . . the Holy Spirit is said to have descended on Christ in bodily form like a dove, not that the substance itself of the Holy Spirit—which is invisible—was seen."[93] The Holy Spirit is not united to the visible creature that serves as a sign. Rather, that sign points to the Holy Spirit's invisible presence according to a new mode

---

[89] I *Sent.* d. 16, q. 1, a. 1 ad 1. Emphasis added.   [90] *STh* III, q. 16, a. 2.
[91] I *Sent.* d. 16, q. 1, a. 1 ad 1. Emphasis added. See *Contra errores Graecorum* I, c. 14; *STh* I, q. 43, a. 1.
[92] *In Ioan.* c. 1, lect. 1 (no. 31).   [93] *STh* III, q. 39, a. 6 ad 2.

that also remains unseen in itself (i.e., the Spirit's sanctifying gifts in the soul). Moreover, the Spirit is not "in" the sign; rather, the sign shows that the Spirit is "in" someone else. For example, the dove at Christ's baptism points to the Spirit's mission to, and presence in, Christ, and the tongues of fire point to the Spirit's mission to, and presence in, those gathered in the upper room.

The *Summa Theologiae*'s Synthesis

This brings us to St Thomas's treatment of the visible missions in *Summa Theologiae* I, q. 43, a. 7. Even though his focus is ostensibly the visible mission of the Holy Spirit, this text is quite rich. In it, Aquinas distinguishes the visible and invisible missions of the Son and Holy Spirit while showing how they are intrinsically ordered to each other, in a perspective as broad as the whole dispensation of salvation itself. St Thomas begins:

> God provides for all things according to the mode of each. But the mode connatural to man is that he is led through the visible to the invisible, . . . and hence it was necessary that the invisible things of God would be manifested to man through the visible.[94]

The unstated premise here is that God wills to save human beings by manifesting himself to them (this is the reason why "it was necessary that the invisible things of God would be manifested . . . "), so that they will be "reduced into" God as they know and love him. We are a special type of rational creature: rational animals who, unlike angels, naturally come to know the invisible through the visible. A visible manifestation especially befits our nature,[95] and God tailors his saving action accordingly.

> Therefore, as God has in a certain way demonstrated himself and the eternal processions of the persons to men through visible creatures, according to certain signs, so also it was fitting that the invisible

[94] *STh* I, q. 43, a. 7.
[95] This is consistent with what Aquinas will say in the *Tertia pars*—that a visible mission of the Son was especially necessary as a remedy for sin because of the blindness to supernatural realities that sin entails—because, before sin, our first parents had a knowledge of God both from visible creatures *and* from a grasp of intelligible realities. *STh* I, q. 94, a. 1. Even while possessing the latter, it was still fitting for them to rise to the invisible through the visible.

52   *The Trinitarian Christology of St Thomas Aquinas*

missions of the divine persons would also be manifested according to some visible creatures.[96]

Note how Aquinas coordinates the two sides of this comparison. The first refers to God's revelation of himself and of the eternal processions of the divine persons through visible creatures. He places the accent on the *manifestation* of the invisible through visible creatures, for the sake of man's return to God. Aquinas then draws a conclusion concerning our *sanctification* accomplished in the invisible missions: as the eternal processions were "demonstrated" through something visible, so also the invisible missions, the vectors of our return, are fittingly revealed by visible creatures.

Still, the visible sending of the Son works differently from that of the Holy Spirit: the Son is sent as the Author of our sanctification, while a visible sign is given that the Holy Spirit is sent as Sanctifier.[97]

> Yet the Son differently than the Holy Spirit. For it belongs to the Holy Spirit, insofar as he proceeds as Love, to be the Gift of sanctification, but to the Son, as a principle of the Holy Spirit, it belongs to be the Author of this sanctification. And hence the Son was visibly sent as the Author of sanctification, while the Holy Spirit [was visibly sent] as the sign of sanctification.[98]

St Thomas is speaking of how the visible missions manifest the invisible missions, but his reasoning has much broader implications. Above all, we see that, for St Thomas, the deepest explanations of the divine missions always involve a reference back to the eternal processions: the visible mission of the Son both *precedes* and *entails* the visible mission of the Holy Spirit, because the Son is a principle of the Holy Spirit's eternal procession.[99] The meaning of the title "Author of sanctification" is therefore that the Son is the eternal principle (with the Father) of the Holy Spirit, who is the "Gift of sanctification," and that the Son gives that gift of sanctification through his visible mission.[100]

---

[96] *STh* I, q. 43, a. 7.   [97] Emery, *Trinitarian Theology*, 410.
[98] *STh* I, q. 43, a. 7.
[99] Aquinas notes elsewhere that the Son's mission is "prior according to the order of nature" to the Holy Spirit's, but he notes that, as to their eternal processions, there is no such "priority." Both processions are eternal, with only an "order of nature" between them. *STh* III, q. 7, a. 13. See pp. 147–50. In the first moment of the Son's existence as man, he receives the Holy Spirit in full, but the visible mission of the Holy Spirit certainly comes after the visible mission of the Son.
[100] See CHAPTER 3, SECTION D.

As a corollary to this, Aquinas explains that the created effect of each visible mission is especially tailored to manifest that person in particular.

Although those visible creatures are made by the whole Trinity, none-theless they are created especially to demonstrate this or that person. For as the Father, Son, and Holy Spirit are signified by different names, so also they can be signified by different things, although there is no separation or diversity between [the persons].[101]

Just as the proper names of the divine persons are not arbitrary impositions, but truly point to and disclose the real distinction between the persons, so also a visible mission's created effect is always adapted to the divine person it manifests. Christ's humanity truly reveals his sonship—it is from the Father—as well as his *auctoritas* with respect to grace and to our reception of the Holy Spirit. Similarly, the Holy Spirit is sent visibly according to a variety of creatures as signs: a dove (at Christ's baptism), a radiant cloud (at his transfiguration), Christ's breath (the evening of the Resurrection), and tongues of fire (at Pentecost). St Thomas's exegesis of the meaning of these signs, which might strike contemporary readers as strained, should not be too quickly dismissed: if the Spirit's visible missions are to be taken as revelations of the Spirit himself, the sign of his presence surely has something to teach us about the Spirit himself. (For this, Aquinas uses Scripture to interpret Scripture. For example, Jesus says at Matt. 10:16 that a dove is "simple," which explains why the Holy Spirit appeared in the form of a dove, since the Spirit gives us a single-hearted regard for God.)[102]

In the dispensation of salvation, therefore, the Son is sent visibly such that, by his visible actions, his eternal *auctoritas* or "authorship" of the Holy Spirit[103] and of our salvation is revealed—indeed, it is even more than a simple revelation, because his actions also *cause* our salvation, especially insofar as Christ sends the Holy Spirit to us.[104] "The Son appeared not only as a manifester, but as a savior."[105] As Aquinas argues:

[I]t was necessary for the person of the Son be declared [to us] as the Author of sanctification, ... and hence it was right [*oportuit*] that the

---

[101] *STh* I, q. 43, a. 7 ad 3.   [102] *In Ioan.* c. 1, lect. 14 (no. 272).
[103] *ScG* IV, c. 24.   [104] *STh* I, q. 43, a. 7 ad 4.
[105] *In Ioan.* c. 1, lect. 14 (no. 270).

visible mission of the Son be made according to a rational nature, to which it belongs to act, and which is capable of sanctifying.[106]

This is a point of prime importance. Aquinas has in mind the causality of Christ's humanity, especially the instrumental causality of his human acts ("capable of sanctifying"). In the Son's visible mission, therefore, the visible creature of Christ's humanity does more than simply manifest his eternal procession. As man, Christ becomes a source of grace both through his teaching and through his actions (*"per instructionem et per operationem"*), by which he effects our regeneration through the Holy Spirit and leads us to a sanctifying knowledge of the Father.[107]

From this, we begin to see how St Thomas's Christology is Trinitarian to its core. By the very fact that the Son's visible mission is founded in his eternal procession from the Father, *it is also ordered to the sending of the Holy Spirit*, who proceeds from the Father and the Son. The Son's visible mission does not—indeed, cannot—stand alone (nor can Christology without Pneumatology), because the Father's sending of the Son is intrinsically ordered to and culminates in the gift of the Holy Spirit to the world.

The Visible Mission: The Pinnacle of the Dispensation of Salvation

Despite the important distinctions between the incarnation and the Holy Spirit's visible missions, there is a good reason why St Thomas places them under the single heading of "visible missions." "They constitute the summit of the historical revelation of the Triune God in the visible events that founded the Church and its mission."[108] The visible missions are therefore (1) a revelation of the divine persons, making known the invisible things of God, and (2) the historical events at the center of the economy of grace (since all grace comes to us through, and in virtue of, Christ's incarnation). These dimensions are interrelated: the visible missions *manifest* the mystery of the Triune God, and *save* us as they draw us into that mystery. This

---

[106] *STh* I, q. 43, a. 7 ad 4. See also *In Ioan.* c. 2, lect. 14 (no. 270).
[107] I *Sent.* d. 16, q. 1, a. 3.
[108] Emery, "Missions invisibles et missions visibles," 64.

double aspect of manifestation and salvation is a fundamental trait of the entire dispensation of salvation.

More specifically, the manifestations are for the sake of our salvation: the visible missions are ultimately ordered to the invisible missions. In one of his sermons, Aquinas puts this rather bluntly: the Son's visible mission as man:

> leads to another coming of Christ, which is into the mind. It would have been worth nothing to us if Christ had come in the flesh unless, along with this, he would come into the mind, namely, by sanctifying us.[109]

We see a good example of this in St Thomas's treatment of Christ's teaching. When Christ teaches and preaches to his disciples, he reveals "the Father's name" "by exteriorly instructing [them] through words." But this exterior instruction, a kind of exterior manifestation, culminates in an invisible mission to the disciples, which is salvific. Christ makes his teaching interiorly effective in his hearers "by giving them the Holy Spirit" so that the faithful will know the Father in the present life "by the knowledge of faith ('we see now through a mirror darkly')" and "through the sight of glory in heaven, where we will see 'face to face' (1 Cor. 13:12)."[110] But note that that interior knowledge remains genetically linked to the words Christ pronounced exteriorly. The visible missions not only have the invisible missions as their aim, but their very historical shape continues to mark and condition the invisible missions that flow from them. In fact, all of Christ's activity in his earthly life—the whole of his visible mission—is ordered to, and reaches its accomplishment in, the invisible missions of the Son and Holy Spirit, and the Father's indwelling presence that accompanies them.[111]

Likewise, in all that he does and suffers (above all in his passion), Christ establishes the pattern and exemplar—"the way of truth"—for our return to God:

> [O]ur Savior, the Lord Jesus Christ, "saving his people from their sins," as the angel announced, has demonstrated to us the way of truth in himself, through which we can come by rising to the beatitude of immortal life. . . .[112]

---

[109] *Ecce rex tuus.*   [110] *In Ioan.*c. 17, lect. 6 (no. 2269).
[111] *Ibid.* (no. 2270).   [112] *STh* III, prol.

Our salvation consists in being drawn, by grace, on this "way," entering into the mystery made visible in the Son's visible mission. Or, to put this another way, the visible missions, as the historical events that found the economy of grace, establish the pattern for our return to God. This is accomplished in us above all when the Holy Spirit is sent to us, since he conforms us to Christ and makes us like him. "God sent the Spirit of his Son in your hearts. And . . . it follows that he makes those to whom he is sent like the one whose Spirit he is."[113] "[W]e are assimilated to the true Son through this, that we have his Spirit."[114] The Holy Spirit thus conforms us to Christ, first in his sufferings, by which our sins are removed, and then in his resurrection and glorification, by which we attain to glory in conformity with him.[115]

Finally, St Thomas underlines that the visible missions of the Holy Spirit—first to Christ, and then to the Apostles—play a special role in the foundation of the Church, which is to say, of the New Covenant itself.[116] They manifest not only the presence of the divine persons according to a "personal" or "private" gift to individuals, but in a "public" grace, brought about by Christ's life in the flesh and especially by his passion,[117] given for the good of the whole world. "It is not necessary that an invisible mission always be manifested by some visible exterior sign, but, as 1 Cor. 12 says, 'the manifestation of the Spirit' is given to someone 'for the good,' namely, of the Church."[118] Thomas continues, "therefore a visible mission of the Holy Spirit especially should be made to Christ and to the Apostles and to others of the first saints, in whom the Church was in a certain way founded." Those who receive a visible mission of the Spirit—first, Christ as man (as a sign of the fullness of the Holy Spirit that he possessed from the first moment of his conception, a fontal fullness whereby Christ as man is the head of the Church and the source of all graces) and then his Apostles—are thus "those through whom many graces are diffused, insofar as through them the Church was planted."[119]

For Aquinas, the four visible missions of the Holy Spirit (at the baptism of Christ, at the transfiguration, in Christ's breath in the

---

[113] *In Ioan.* c. 15, lect. 5 (no. 2062).   [114] *In Ioan.* c. 3, lect. 1 (no. 442).
[115] *STh* I–II, q. 85, a. 5 ad 2.
[116] See Emery, "Missions invisibles et missions visibles," 64–6.
[117] See *STh* III, q. 46, a. 3; q. 48, a. 1, ad 3; *Compendium theologiae* I, c. 231; *Quodlibet* II, q. 1, a. 2.
[118] *STh* I, q. 43, a. 7 ad 6.   [119] *Ibid.*

upper room on the evening of Easter Sunday, and at Pentecost) therefore manifest the genealogy of the propagation of grace, given first to Christ's humanity, then handed on from him to the Apostles, and which comes down to us in the sacraments and teaching of the Church:

> It should be noted that the Holy Spirit was sent upon Christ first in the appearance of a dove at [his] baptism (John 3:5), and in the appearance of a cloud at the transfiguration (Matt. 17:5). The reason for this is that the grace of Christ, which is given through the Holy Spirit, was to be derived to us through the propagation of grace in the sacraments (and thus he descended at the baptism in the appearance of a dove, which is a fruitful animal), and through teaching (and thus he descended in a luminous cloud). Hence also Christ is there shown [to be] a teacher, so it says "Listen to him." But the Holy Spirit first descended on the Apostles in [Christ's] breath, to designate the propagation of grace in the sacraments, of which they were ministers. For this reason, he says: "Whose sins you will forgive, will be forgiven (John 20:23)," and "Go therefore and baptize them in the name of the Father, and of the Son, and of the Holy Spirit (Matt. 28:19)." Second, [the Holy Spirit descended on the Apostles] in tongues of fire, to signify the propagation of grace through teaching. Thus, Acts 2:4 says that when they were filled with the Holy Spirit, they immediately began to speak.[120]

Just as Christ as man received two visible missions of the Holy Spirit—one manifesting him as endowed with the Spirit in order to give grace through the sacraments, and the other showing him as graced by the Spirit for the sake of teaching—so also the Apostles receive from Christ two visible missions of the Spirit, which makes them qualified to be his ministers in this twofold path of the propagation of grace. "Through the giving of the Holy Spirit, they are made qualified for this office: 'who also makes us qualified as ministers of a new covenant, not in the letter but in the Spirit (2 Cor. 3:6).'"[121]

Thus, Benoît-Dominique de La Soujeole has pointed out that the visible mission of the Holy Spirit to the Apostles inaugurates the abundant outflow of graces through their ministry, which is a kind of extension of Christ's action in the visible activity of the Church he sends to all nations. This happens above all through her preaching and her celebration of the sacraments.[122] Always shaped by the historical

---

[120] *In Ioan.* c. 20, lect. 4 (no. 2539).   [121] *In Ioan.* c. 20, lect. 4 (no. 2538).
[122] Benoît-Dominique de La Soujeole, "De l'actualité des missions *visibles* du Fils et de l'Esprit," *Revue Thomiste* 113 (2013): 399–410. See also Áron Fejérdy, *L'Eglise de*

events of Christ's life and passion, since the grace that flows from the Son's visible mission always bears the imprint of his humanity— "baptism and the other sacraments have no efficacy except by virtue of the humanity and the passion of Christ"[123]—this apostolic activity makes Christ known and brings his salvation to its recipients, insofar as they receive the Holy Spirit who conforms them to Christ and makes them adopted sons and daughters of the Father. That is, the Spirit of Christ conforms us to Christ according to all that he did and suffered in the flesh, our perfect exemplar and the "way" by which we return to the Father. And this "way" continues to be demonstrated to us and is opened to us through the Church via her preaching and sacraments, which perpetuate the saving action of Christ on earth even after his humanity is no longer directly visible to our sight. In sum, the Son is sent visibly by the Father as the Author of salvation precisely in order that, through his incarnation (including his passion and exaltation), and through the vicarious visible activity of the Church, grace would be poured out in abundance for the salvation of the whole world.

* * *

If we think of the organizing structure of the *Summa Theologiae*, our study to this point has remained in the *Prima pars*—we have discussed (briefly) the divine processions and (in greater detail) their extension into the dispensation of the salvation in the divine missions—but we have not yet entered into the interior of the mystery of Christ in itself. As we now turn to that task, the work of these opening chapters will continue to bear fruit as we see more clearly, and in more detail, how Christology for Aquinas builds on his theology of the eternal processions and of the divine missions—in short, how it is thoroughly Trinitarian.

---

l'Esprit du Christ: La relation ordonnée du Christ et de l'Esprit au mystère ecclésial: une lecture de Vatican II (S.T.D. thesis, Université de Fribourg, 2012), 280–4; M. J. (Yves) Congar, *Chrétiens désunis: Principes d'un 'oecuménisme' catholique* (Paris: Les Édi-tions du Cerf, 1937), 67–8.

[123] *In Epist. ad Tit.* c. 3, lect. 1 (no. 93).

Part II

Jesus Christ, the Word of the Father
Sent in the Flesh

3

Why the *Son* Became Incarnate

What does it mean to say that the incarnation is the visible mission *of the Son*? Why was it the *Son* who became incarnate? These questions are extremely important, because in grasping what is distinctive about Christ precisely as the Word made man sent to bring us to the Father, we are led into the deepest mysteries of the Trinity. Indeed, revealing God's Triune identity is at the heart of the Son's visible mission in the incarnation: "The Son of God came . . . publishing the name of the Trinity," explains St Thomas.[1] The more we come to grips with Aquinas's insights into why the Father sent *the Word* to assume our flesh, the more we understand why he locates the Word at the center of the vast horizon of the whole of theology, from the mystery of the divine processions in the Triune Godhead itself, to the creation of the universe through the Word, and finally our return to the Father through the Word's mission in the incarnation. In doing so, we find a potent confirmation of what we have already noted: Aquinas's theology of Christ is not only suffused by his Trinitarian doctrine which is everywhere present, but his treatment of Christ is itself the central movement in the whole symphony of his account of God in himself (*theologia*) and how God, having created creatures out of his goodness, draws them back into himself (*dispensatio*). To quote again a text from CHAPTER 1:

> The whole totality of the divine work is in a manner brought to completion through [the incarnation], since man, who was the last to be created, returns by a certain circular movement to his first principle, united to the very principle of all things through the work of the incarnation.[2]

---

[1] I *Sent.*, prol.   [2] *Compendium theologiae* I, c. 201.

The divine work of restoring and recreating man in the incarnation is the consummation of all things as they proceed from the Trinity and return to the Trinity. This entire movement of coming-forth and returning follows the Trinitarian patterns of the divine processions: just as the processions of the divine persons served as the *ratio* of the procession of creation from God, so also the return of creation to God—accomplished above all through the incarnation—takes place according to the same *ratio* of the divine processions.[3]

St Thomas's teaching on this point, and his texts probing the reasons why it was the Word who became man, are often underappreciated and misunderstood.[4] This is especially true for the principal text on this point in the *Summa Theologiae, STh* III, q. 3, a. 8, which we will take as the starting point of our inquiry and to which we will return throughout this chapter. There, Aquinas argues that it was supremely fitting (*"convenientissimum"*) that the Word become incarnate. Frequently read only as if it were a footnote to Aquinas's view that, in theory, any of the divine persons could assume a human nature, it contains in miniature an often-overlooked theological richness. In fact, the themes it evokes are so important that they are implicated in virtually the whole of Aquinas's Christology, and even the whole of his account of the dispensation of salvation.[5]

Aquinas refers in this article to three proper names and one proper designation of the second person of the Trinity in order to manifest the deep intelligibility of this mystery. He is Word, Son, Image, and the giver of the sanctifying gift who is the Holy Spirit (or, to apply the concise title Aquinas uses to express this idea earlier in the *Summa*

---

[3] I *Sent.* d. 14, q. 2, a. 2. Cf. CHAPTER 1, SECTION A.

[4] Francesco Neri's book-length study of this issue in several medieval authors, *Cur verbum capax hominis: Le ragioni dell'incarnazione della seconda Persona della Trinità fra teologia scolastica e teologia contemporanea* (Rome: Editrice Pontificia Università Gregoriana, 1999), although helpful for giving an overview of St Thomas's approach to this question in its historical context, does not adequately acknowledge how Thomas's approach is grounded on what is proper to the second person as Word, Son, Image, and Author of sanctification. As a consequence, Neri offers a critique of St Thomas along the lines of de Régnon's paradigm. See, e.g., *ibid.*, 162. We aim to show that this misunderstands Aquinas's approach.

[5] Joseph Wawrykow, "Hypostatic Union," in *The Theology of Thomas Aquinas*, ed. Rik Van Nieuwenhove and Joseph Wawrykow (Notre Dame: University of Notre Dame Press, 2005), 239–41; Joseph Wawrykow, "Wisdom in the Christology of Aquinas," in *Christ among the Medieval Dominicans: Representations of Christ in the Texts and Images of the Order of Preachers*, ed. Kent Emery and Joseph Wawrykow (Notre Dame: University of Notre Dame Press, 1998), 175–96.

Theologiae, he is the *Auctor sanctificationis).* This four-fold approach is not novel in the *Summa Theologiae;* in a parallel article of his *Sentences* Commentary, Aquinas uses these four titles to structure his investigation.[6] We will structure our inquiry according to these four names.

A. THE INCARNATION OF THE SON *AS WORD*

Perhaps the most fundamental Trinitarian theme in St Thomas's Christology is that Christ is the *Word* made flesh. This is unsurprising, since "the doctrine of the Word is incontestably the heart of Thomas' Trinitarian theology."[7] We will begin with a brief summary of Thomas's doctrine of the Word in general. We will then explore the way that this Trinitarian doctrine suffuses Aquinas's whole conception of the central truth that the Word became flesh for our salvation.

Aquinas's Trinitarian Doctrine of the Word

Four elements of Aquinas's Trinitarian doctrine of the divine Word are important for our study: first, the central insight of Aquinas's doctrine of the Word itself; second, the relation to creatures implied in the name "Word"; third, the theme of the Word as begotten Wisdom; and finally, the Word as intrinsically manifesting the Father.[8]

To begin, Aquinas builds his mature doctrine of the divine Word on a philosophical insight, only fully articulated in his later writings,[9] that

---

[6] See III *Sent.* d. 1, q. 2, a. 2. These four titles also structure St Thomas's study of the Son in the *prima pars* of the *Summa Theologiae*: Word and Son (q. 34), Image (q. 35), and Author of sanctification (q. 43). Though St Thomas uses the title "*Auctor sanctificationis*" in neither III *Sent.* d. 1, q. 2, a. 2 nor in *STh* III, q. 3, a. 8 (the key text where Aquinas gives that name to the Son is *STh* I, q. 43, a. 7), the rationale behind that title—that the Son is a principle of the Holy Spirit whom he gives to us for our sanctification—is present in both.

[7] Emery, *Trinitarian Theology*, 179.

[8] This summary of Aquinas's doctrine of the Word is drawn from Emery's detailed study. See Emery, *Trinitarian Theology*, 176–218.

[9] For Thomas's mature account of "Word" as a proper name for the Son, see, e.g., *STh* I, q. 34, a. 1; *In Ioan.* c. 1, lect. 1 (nos. 23–33); *De Pot.* q. 8, a. 1 and q. 9, a. 5.

an interior "word" in us is the terminus of the act of understanding, a concept that "the intellect conceives by knowing,"[10] a 'conception of the intellect.'[11] As such, a word always *proceeds* from the intellect in its perfect act of understanding, and is really distinct from it. Given this insight, Aquinas teaches that the second person of the Trinity is not merely dubbed "the Word" by convention or tradition; rather, "Word" itself means "something proceeding from another, which belongs to the nature of personal names in God, inasmuch as the divine persons are distinguished by origin."[12] "Word" is thus, in the fullest sense, "a proper name for the person of the Son, for it signifies a certain emanation of the intellect."[13] It really discloses to us, by a certain analogy, how he proceeds from the Father. As the word of our understanding is conceived by our intellect, so the divine Word is the "eternal conception"[14] who proceeds from the Father by way of intellect.

In the *Summa Theologiae*, Aquinas passes immediately from this to the Word's relation to creation.

> "Word" implies a respect to creation, since, in knowing himself, God knows every creature. But the word conceived in the mind is represen-tative of everything that is actually understood. Thus, in us there are many words, according to the many things that we understand. But because God understands himself and all things in one act, his single Word is expressive not only of the Father, but also of creatures. And as the knowledge of God is simply cognitive of God, while the knowledge of creatures is both cognitive and causative [*factiva*], so also the Word of God is simply expressive of what is in God the Father, while of creatures it is both expressive and operative. For this reason, Psalm 32 says "He spoke and they were made [*facta sunt*]," because the Word includes the design [*ratio factiva*] of what God makes.[15]

In knowing himself, God knows all things. The divine Word expresses "all that is in God the Father," including the Father's know-ledge or ideas of all things. In fact, Thomas elsewhere explains that

---

The earliest appearance of Aquinas's mature theory is *ScG* I, c. 53 and *ScG* IV, c. 11. For an example of Thomas's early approach to this question, see I *Sent*. d. 27, q. 2, a. 1. See also Harm Goris, "Theology and Theory of the Word in Aquinas: Understanding Augustine by Innovating Aristotle," in *Aquinas the Augustinian*, ed. Michael Dau-phinais, Barry David, and Matthew Levering (Washington, D.C.: Catholic University of America Press, 2007), 62–78.

[10] *STh* I, q. 34, a. 1 ad 2.   [11] *Ibid.*, a. 1.   [12] *Ibid.*
[13] *STh* I, q. 34, a. 2.   [14] *STh* III, q. 3, a. 8.   [15] *STh* I, q. 34, a. 3.

creatures participate in diverse and finite ways in the exemplar likeness of the Word.[16] This divine knowledge of creatures in the Word is also creative. "The Father 'utters' all creatures through the Word in which he 'speaks' himself."[17] All that God creates, all that God does in the world, is contained in the one divine Word and brought into existence through him.

Aquinas's theological exegesis in his John Commentary complements his teaching on this point. When he treats John 1:3 ("through him all things were made"), Aquinas takes great care to explain that it is proper to the Word that the Father acts "through" him in the world, although the Father is never moved to act by the Word: the Word is neither an efficient cause nor a formal cause of the Father's action.[18] The Son never causes anything in the Father; rather, he receives everything from him. Instead, "through" designates the Word's causality with respect to creatures. It underlines that the Word receives his action from the Father,[19] so that the Father and the Son act together. "The Son exists in the eternal reception of his being from the Father, and the way he acts conforms to this, that is, he eternally receives his action from the Father."[20] There is one divine action of creating: *from* the Father who acts *through* his Word *in* the Holy Spirit.

Aquinas recognizes the deep scriptural resonances between the theme of divine wisdom and that of the divine Word, and he directly links the two in his theology.[21] "The Word is 'begotten Wisdom,' which is nothing other than the very conception of Wisdom itself," he says.[22] Now, generally speaking, divine wisdom is an attribute shared by all three divine persons; it is appropriated to the Son because of its affinity to the Son's procession by way of intellect. Even so, Aquinas

[16] "The Word of God . . . is the exemplar likeness of all creatures. . . . [C]reatures are instituted in their own species through participation in this likeness." *STh* III, q. 3, a. 8. Thomas also speaks more generally of God as the first exemplar cause (*STh* I, q. 44, a. 3), and of creatures' diverse and partial participation with respect to the divine essence (*STh* I, q. 15, a. 2), divine goodness (*STh* I, q. 47, a. 1), and being (*STh* I, q. 44, a. 1).

[17] Emery, *Trinitarian Theology*, 196.

[18] The Father has no principle but himself. Consequently, that the Father acts "through" his Word cannot refer to efficient causality, Aquinas says, because that would suggest that the Father is prompted or caused to create by the Son. Likewise, properly speaking, "through" cannot designate the Word as a formal cause of the Father's action—a cause remaining within the Godhead, as it were, as a principle of divine action. *In Ioan.* c. 1, lect. 2 (no. 76). See Emery, "Personal Mode," 49–50; *Trinitarian Theology*, 198–9 and 349–55.

[19] *In Ioan.* c. 1, lect. 2 (no. 76).   [20] Emery, *Trinitarian Theology*, 351.

[21] *Ibid.*, 192.   [22] *STh* I, q. 34, a. 1, ad. 2.

insists that the Word is *properly* the begotten Wisdom of the Father (or Wisdom as proceeding). "[T]he Son is the *fruit* of the knowledge sown by the Father, he is the term conceived by the Father, he is the Word of the Father's wisdom, and, under this rubric, he is properly engendered Wisdom. It is in this sense that the Father knows all things *in his Word, in his begotten Wisdom*."[23]

The Father creates and governs all things through his begotten Wisdom, 'Christ, the power of God and the wisdom of God (1 Cor. 1:24)." Here, we see clearly how Aquinas's thought springs from the rich and fertile soil of sacred Scripture, which he quotes often. "How great are your works, O Lord; you have made all things in wisdom (Ps. 103:24)." "She reaches from end to end mightily, and orders all things sweetly (Wis. 8:1)." Aquinas deploys this theme to great effect to explain that the Son is at the center of the entire movement of *exitus* and *reditus*. "Through the wisdom of God, the hidden things of God are manifested, the works of creatures are produced, and not only are they produced, but they are restored and perfected . . . insofar as each attains its proper end."[24] "What was established through wisdom, should be repaired through wisdom: 'Through wisdom those were saved who pleased you from the beginning (Wis. 9:19).'"[25]

Finally, the Word, precisely as the Word, manifests the Father. "The Word is the manifestation of the Father himself."[26] The heart of the term's meaning lies here, says St Thomas: "the name 'Word' is principally imposed to signify a relation to the speaker."[27] St Thomas asserts this with such confidence precisely because of his insight that a word is an intrinsically relational term, a conception "in which" (*in quo*) one understands, which proceeds as the fruit of the understanding. "For everything which is from another manifests that from which it is. Thus the Son manifests the Father because he is from the Father."[28]

This suffices as an initial summary; we will have much more to say on these themes later, as we examine the principal Christological texts in which they appear. It is to that task that we now turn.

---

[23] Emery, *Trinitarian Theology*, 193.
[24] I *Sent.* prol. (critical edition of A. Oliva).   [25] *Ibid.*
[26] *In Ioan.* c. 6, lect. 4 (no. 918).   [27] *STh* I, q. 34, a. 3 ad 4.
[28] *In Ioan.* c. 16, lect. 4 (no. 2107). See also Sabathé, *La Trinité rédemptrice*, 292.

Why the *Word* became Incarnate

Aquinas gives three reasons why it was the Word who became incarnate. The first has a cosmic scope: just as the universe was created through the Word, so should it be restored through him. This argument is not original to Aquinas—one finds it in the Fathers and in other scholastics[29]—but St Thomas gives it a new depth by means of his doctrine of the Word. Aquinas's second reason regards the Word as begotten Wisdom: by joining a human nature to himself in the incarnation, the divine Word offers us a participation in the Wisdom that is both our path of return to God and our ultimate perfection. The third reason springs from the heart of Thomas's Trinitarian doctrine: since it is proper to the Word to manifest in the world the Father who speaks him from all eternity, the Word becomes incarnate to bring us back to the Father, 'the ultimate person to whom we return.'[30]

Creation and Recreation through the Word

The first reason Aquinas gives in *STh* III, q. 3, a. 8 for why it was the second person of the Trinity who assumed a human nature (the most important of St Thomas's texts on this point) is that, as all things were created by the Word, so they should be recreated through the Word's incarnation. He begins with a general principle: "Things that are similar are fittingly united," and then shows that creatures are in a certain way "similar" to the divine Word:

> [T]he Word of God [has] . . . a certain kind of universal affinity to the whole creation, because the word of an artisan, that is, his concept, is an exemplar likeness of the things that the artisan makes. Thus, the Word of God, which is his eternal conception, is the exemplar likeness of the whole creation.[31]

This analogy, of an artisan or architect who forms a concept (a "word") in his mind of what he sets about to make, is often used by

---

[29] See Emery, *Trinitarian Theology*, 199; F. Ocáriz, L. F. Mateo Seco, and J. A. Riestra, *The Mystery of Jesus Christ* (Dublin: Four Courts Press, 1994), 84–5.

[30] I *Sent.* d. 15, q. 4, a. 1. See also *In Ioan.* c. 14, lect. 3 (no. 1883).

[31] *STh* III, q. 3, a. 8.

Aquinas to explain exemplar causality.[32] Its use here shows how effectively Thomas deploys in his Christology the insights generated by his mature doctrine of the Word. Before an artisan fabricates a chest or builds a house, he must already have "in mind" what he wants to produce. That idea will guide his action. Even when he has his idea, however, the artisan still must make an act of will to start working—that is, first he *conceives* the idea by way of knowledge, and then he *wills* actually to build it.[33] In this way, the exemplar or idea of the artisan guides his efficient causality, and is rightly named a cause of his finished product.[34] If well made, the chest or house will correspond to the mental concept with which he began his work.[35] In this sense, the exemplar in the artisan's mind is "the rule and measure of the thing produced;" we judge the final product to be "more or less perfect according to the degree of accuracy with which it represents the idea in the mind of the person who produced it."[36]

This is exactly what Aquinas means when he says that the divine Word has "in a certain way, a universal fit to all creatures;" the "affinity" or "match" (*convenientia*) is that between an exemplar and the thing made to its likeness.[37] In the *Summa Contra Gentiles*, Aquinas explains more fully, and in slightly different terms, this same idea:

> The Word has a certain aspect of affinity [*quandam affinitatis ratio-nem*] to all creatures, since the Word contains the ideas [*rationes*] of everything created by God, just as the human artisan comprehends the ideas of what he makes by the conception of his understanding. Thus, all creatures are nothing but a certain real expression and

---

[32] On exemplar causality in Aquinas, see Doolan, *Aquinas on the Divine Ideas*, 1–42. See also L. B. Geiger, "Les idées divines dans l'oeuvre de S. Thomas," in *St Thomas Aquinas 1274–1974: Commemorative Studies*, ed. Armand A. Maurer et al. (Toronto: Pontifical Institute of Mediaeval Studies, 1974), 175–209; Greenstock, "Exemplar Causality," 1–31.

[33] See, e.g., *ScG* IV, c. 13.

[34] Doolan argues that exemplar causality has a "unique causal status" as an extrinsic formal cause (that is, a formal cause that does not inhere in the thing) closely connected to efficient causality, because, on the one hand, an exemplar guides the efficient causality of an artisan, and on the other, the idea is a true exemplar insofar as efficient causality has made something like it. It is also closely connected to final causality, insofar as the concept in an artisan's mind arouses his will to make the thing. Doolan, *Aquinas on the Divine Ideas*, 34–41.

[35] See *In Epist. ad Hebr.* c. 11, lect. 2 (no. 564).

[36] Greenstock, "Exemplar Causality," 6.

[37] This use of *convenientia* is perhaps most clear at *In Epist. ad Hebr.* c. 11, lect. 2 (no. 564).

representation of the things comprehended in the conception of the divine Word. It is also for this reason that all things are said to be made through the Word. Therefore, the Word is fittingly united to a creature, namely, to a human nature.[38]

The divine Word is the perfect expression of God himself. In the Word is included not only all that God knows of himself, but also, within that knowledge of himself, the ideas of all creatures.[39] As a corollary, Thomas says that creatures are in a certain sense expressions and representations of what is in the Word. "As the art of the craftsman is manifested in what he makes, so also the whole world is nothing other than a certain representation of the divine wisdom conceived in the mind of the Father."[40] "It is also for this reason" that all things were made through the Word.[41]

This theme, the "affinity" or "fit' between the divine Word and creatures,[42] is inseparable in Aquinas's mature thought from his teaching on God's Triune action in the world. Thus, commenting on John 1:3, Aquinas says:

> If the...phrase, "through him all things were made," is rightly considered, it is quite clear that the evangelist spoke most properly. For whoever makes something, must preconceive it in his wisdom, which is the form and blueprint [*ratio*] of the thing made, just as the preconceived form in the mind of the artisan is the blueprint [*ratio*] of the chest he is going to make. Thus, God makes nothing except through the concept of his intellect, who is wisdom conceived from all eternity,

---

[38] *ScG* IV, c. 42.

[39] On the divine ideas as "in" the Word who is the "expression" of all that God knows and the exemplar of all creatures, see Vivian Boland, *Ideas in God according to Saint Thomas Aquinas: Sources and Synthesis* (Leiden: Brill, 1996), 235–61; see also *STh* I, q. 34, a. 3, quoted above. Cf. Doolan, *Aquinas on the Divine Ideas*, 120–2; Greenstock, "Exemplar Causality," 29–31. Greenstock holds that all divine exemplarity is appropriated to the divine persons and cannot be said of them properly. He neglects to take into account, however, the way St Thomas regards the Word as properly the expression of all that is in God (the divine essence and the divine intellect *as conceived*), and hence of the idea of every creature. In this sense, the divine exemplar ideas are properly "in" the Word.

[40] *In Ioan.* c. 1, lect. 5 (no. 136). Cf. *In Epist. ad Hebr.* c. 1, lect. 1 (no. 15), which holds that, while creation is an "expression" of the Word, the incarnation is the perfect "manifestation" and "speaking" of the Word.

[41] *ScG* IV, c. 42. See also *In Epist. ad Col.* c. 1, lect. 4 (no. 37).

[42] Of course, the Word is in no way dependent on creatures; he is the divine Word from all eternity, and would be the Word even if no creatures existed. See *STh* I, q. 34, a. 3 ad 2.

namely, the Word of God and Son of God; and hence it is impossible that he would make anything except through the Son. And so Augustine says in *De Trinitate* that the Word is the art full of the patterns of all living things. And thus it is clear that everything that the Father makes, he makes through him.[43]

Aquinas is categorical: it is *impossible* that God would make *anything* except through his Word, because the Father always acts in the world through the Word, the eternal conception of his wisdom. Note the dynamism implicit here: Aquinas is not speaking only about one moment at the beginning of time, but of the creative plan by which God governs and provides for all things, by which God does all that he does in the world. Its scope is as broad as the entire *dispensatio* itself. At every moment from the beginning of the world until its final consummation, the Father always acts through his Word, who is the exemplar likeness of all things.[44]

To return to the principal Christological text on this theme (*STh* III, q. 3, a. 8), we can now see that Thomas has precisely such a far-reaching idea in mind when he argues that it is most fitting that the Word be the divine person who becomes man. The Word has a unique "fit" to "the whole creation" as its exemplar-efficient cause. Aquinas means both that the Word expresses the exemplar idea of particular creatures—including man—and that the entire wisely arranged order of creation in a certain way "fits" and "corresponds to" the divine Word, who is begotten wisdom itself. He makes the latter quite clear in his Commentary on Hebrews:

Because the whole creation is perfectly arranged, as produced by an artisan in whom no error can fall, nor any defect, it most fully corresponds [*convenit*], in its own way, to the divine conception. Thus Boethius says in the *De Consolatione*, "The most beautiful himself bearing the beautiful world in his mind, forming it in [his] likeness and image." Hence [Hebrews 11:3] says "we understand by faith that

---

[43] *In Ioan.* c. 1, lect. 2 (no. 77). Thomas's quotation from Augustine reads: "Verbum est ars plena omnium rationum viventium." A modern critical edition of Augustine's *De Trinitate* differs slightly: "plena omnium rationum uiuentium incommutabilium." Augustine, *De Trinitate* VI.X.11 (CCL 50).

[44] Properly understood, the Word's causality is both exemplary and efficient, since the Word acts according to the divine power in all things. In fact, Aquinas is expressing a fundamental truth of God's triunity: every divine action *ad extra* is an action of the three divine persons acting together, each according to a mode of action proper to him. See Emery, "Personal Mode," 48–50.

the world," that is, the whole universe of creatures, "was framed," that is, fittingly corresponds [*respondentia*], "to the Word," that is to the concept of God, as artifacts to their art. "He poured her out," namely, his wisdom, "on all his works (Sir. 1:10)."[45]

The beautiful ordering of the whole cosmos is a certain creaturely reflection of divine wisdom itself. What is more, God reveals that the universe's beauty, harmony, and intelligibility correspond to the Word, who is both begotten wisdom and the divine exemplar of all things. We can detect echoes here of several key themes in Aquinas's theology: the whole creation as proceeding from and imbued with divine wisdom,[46] the divine processions themselves as the *ratio* and cause of creation,[47] as well as the doctrine of the *imago Dei*.[48]

Let us return again to the key Christological text from the *Summa Theologiae* that we are examining. There, Thomas extends the scope of his reasoning from creation to restoration:

And hence, just as creatures are established in their own species through a participation in this likeness [to the Word], though changeably [*mobiliter*], so also, through the Word's union (not participated but personal) to the creature, it was fitting that the creature be restored in its order to an eternal and immutable perfection; for, if the work of an artisan were to collapse, he would restore it through the conceived form of his art by which he first built it.[49]

Thomas's reasoning about the Word's incarnation nests it in the vast movement of *exitus* and *reditus*, with the Word's personal procession playing a key role: the second person of the Trinity is the exemplar of all creatures insofar as he proceeds by way of intellect as the divine Word. The whole of the created order is made through him, so that each species of creature is what it is through its participation in a likeness of the Word. Further, creation is sustained by the Word[50] and is brought to its final perfection through the Word's incarnation. It is precisely the Word's procession as the conception of the divine understanding that grounds the fittingness of the Word's incarnation: "if the work of an artisan were to collapse, he would restore it through

[45] *In Epist. ad Hebr.* c. 11, lect. 2 (no. 564).
[46] See, e.g., *STh* I, q. 44, a. 3; q. 47, a. 2; *In Epist. ad Rom.* c. 1, lect. 6 (no. 118).
[47] See, e.g., *STh* I, q. 45, a. 6.   [48] See, e.g., *STh* I, q. 93.
[49] *STh* III, q. 3, a. 8.   [50] *In Ioan.* c. 5, lect. 2 (no. 740).

the conceived form of his art by which he first built it." In other words, for Thomas, there is something distinct about the Word *precisely as Word* that undergirds the divine plan to send the Word in the flesh, and (as we will see later), Christ's identity as the Word in person is absolutely central to the work that the Father gives him to do, and to the way he carries it out.

Also notable is the breadth of Thomas's sense of "restoration." The incarnation is ordered not only to the satisfaction for sin (though surely that has an important part to play), but also to the restoration of the whole order of creation, through the supreme union—personal, not by participation—of the immutable and perfect Word with a weak and changeable human nature. This union orders human nature to God, its immutable perfection. To be sure, Thomas regards the fall of human nature by sin as prompting this extraordinary remedy,[51] but his accent here is not on the collapse or on the details of the repair work (i.e., satisfaction, redemption),[52] but on the restoration of creatures to the ultimate end for which they were made, the perfect and immutable perfection which is God himself. The incarnation involves nothing less than the recreation of the world through the Word. "The first creation of things was done by the power of God the Father through the Word; hence recreation should also be done through the Word by the power of God the Father, so that the recreation would correspond to creation, as 2 Cor. 5[:19] says: 'God was reconciling the world to himself in Christ.'"[53]

This same reasoning is clearly visible in a concise version of this argument that Thomas offers in his Commentary on Romans:

> For it is fitting that, as all these things were made through the Word of God (as John 1:3 says), so also through him, as through the art of the almighty God, all things would be restored: just like an artisan repairs a house by the same art by which he built it. As Col. 1:20 says: "Through him" it pleased God "to reconcile all things, whether in heaven or on earth."[54]

---

[51] See, e.g., *STh* III, q. 1, a. 3.

[52] Cf. *Epist. ad II Cor.* c. 5, lect. 5 (nos. 197–8), where Aquinas does place the accent on the incarnate Word reconciling the world to God by offering satisfaction for sin.

[53] *STh* III, q. 3, a. 8 ad 2.   [54] *In Epist. ad Rom.* c. 1, lect. 4 (no. 60).

The incarnate Word restores all things (*'omnia'*), whether in heaven or on earth, reconciling them to God, their perfection.[55] He does this by restoring man, who is a microcosm of the whole creation.[56]

This argument about the supreme fittingness of the incarnation of the Word in Thomas's later works (especially the *Summa Theologiae* but also his Commentary on Romans)[57] is particularly notable because of the way it exploits his mature doctrine of the Word. In his *Sentences* Commentary, by contrast, this doctrine is missing. In that early work, Thomas does hold that "[s]omething should be repaired by the same thing through which it was made; hence it is fitting that those things created through wisdom would be restored through wisdom."[58] But as he explains it there, divine wisdom is appropriated to the Son but is not a personal property of the Son.[59] Later in his career, armed with the insight that the Word is, properly speaking, the Father's begotten Wisdom, Aquinas is able to discern the "fit" or "affinity" of the incarnation's work of restoration to the Word's personal property, and thus to sound the depths of the intelligibility that Christ is the *Word* incarnate.

Of course, Thomas was by no means the first medieval to argue that creation should be restored by the divine person through whom

[55] See also *De rationibus fidei* c. 5, which adds an additional step to this argument, explaining that the incarnation restores man, the highest creature in the visible universe. Since all other visible creatures "are subservient to and seem to be ordered to the rational creature," Thomas's reasoning suggests that the restoration of man is in fact the restoration of the whole of creation. *Ibid.*

[56] See, e.g., *In Epist. ad Rom.* c. 8, lect. 4 (no. 673); I *Sent.* prol. Cf. III *Sent.* d. 2, q. 1, a. 1, where Thomas takes care to show that this argument does not commit him to the view that the incarnation was necessary for the perfection of the universe. That man is a microcosm of the whole creation is an important theme in Aquinas, and one that he places at the head of his treatment of Christ in the third book of his *Sentences* Commentary. III *Sent.*, prol. See Jean-Pierre Torrell, *Saint Thomas Aquinas*, vol. 2, *Spiritual Master*, trans. Robert Royal (Washington, D.C.: Catholic University of America Press, 2003), 253–4; M. F. Manzanedo, "El hombre come 'Microcosmos' según santo Tomás," *Angelicum* 56 (1979): 62–92; Édouard-Henri Wéber, *La personne humaine au XIIIe siècle: l'avènement chez les maîtres parisiens de l'acception moderne de l'homme* (Paris: Librairie Philosophique J. Vrin, 1991), 73. For this argument in a slightly different form, see *Compendium theologiae* I, c. 148.

[57] *STh* III, q. 3, a. 8; *In Epist. ad Rom.* c. 1, lect. 4 (no. 60); *De rationibus fidei* c. 5.

[58] I *Sent.* prol. (critical edition of A. Oliva). See also III *Sent.* d. 1, q. 2, a. 2.

[59] This is especially clear at III *Sent.* d. 1, q. 2, a. 2, where Thomas expressly asks whether it was most fitting for the Son to become incarnate. His response distinguishes between what is proper to the Son and what is appropriated. Under what is appropriated, Thomas presents the argument that what was created through wisdom should be restored through wisdom.

it was made. (For example, Gilles Emery documents this theme in Alexander of Hales, Peter of Poitiers, William of Auxerre, and Bonaventure.[60] Jean-Pierre Torrell adds Guerric of Saint Quentin to this list.)[61] But the arguments of these other theologians are quite summary and do not explore why or how this is the case, nor do they identify why or how the work of restoration corresponds to what is proper to the Son. Aquinas's mature explanation, built on his doctrine of the Word and the Word's proper exemplarity for the whole creation and using the example of the artisan who repairs what he has made, is thus a significant development in the history of theological reasoning about the fittingness of the incarnation. Moreover, it reveals that the deepest foundations of the mystery of Christ—why it was the Son who became incarnate—are in a sense the elaboration and rearticulation of the Trinitarian mystery and the proper mode of Trinitarian action in the world: creation is restored and thus returns to God according to the same way in which it came forth from him, with the Father always acting through his Word.

The Word, Saving Wisdom and the Manifestation of the Father

Aquinas offers a second reason for the Word's incarnation in *STh* III, q. 3, a. 8, based on the Word's personal property as "Begotten Wisdom" and thus as the source of all human wisdom.

> In another way, [the Word] has a special fittingness with human nature, from the fact that the Word is the concept of eternal wisdom, from which all human wisdom is derived. And hence man grows in wisdom, which is his proper perfection insofar as he is rational, by participating the Word of God: as the disciple is instructed by receiving the word of the master. Hence Sir. 1:5 also says: "The Word of God on high is the fount of wisdom." Thus, for the consummate perfection of man, it was fitting that the Word of God himself would be personally united to a human nature.[62]

Aquinas here unites in one concise argument two important themes in his theology. The first is that the Word is the source of all human

---

[60] Emery, *La Trinité créatrice*, 287–8.
[61] Torrell, *Encyclopédie Jésus le Christ*, 108.   [62] *STh* III, q. 3, a. 8.

wisdom. The second person of the Trinity is "the concept of eternal Wisdom," that is, he proceeds by way of intellect as the Father's Word. As Thomas recounts elsewhere, this itself—the fact that he is the divine Word or *Logos* and hence has "a certain kinship" with reason and thus with man's rational nature—is already a reason why the Word is "most fittingly united" to a human nature.[63] But, in this text, Thomas delves deeper into the nature of this kinship: "all human wisdom is derived" from the Word, as a participation in him who is begotten Wisdom. Interestingly, while Aquinas notes earlier in the *Summa Theologiae* that human wisdom is a participation in divine Wisdom considered as a divine attribute,[64] it is only here, speaking of the incarnation in the *Tertia pars*, that he underlines the dependence of human wisdom on the distinct person of the Word.[65]

This is a theme found in several of Aquinas's commentaries on Scripture,[66] but it has a prominence above all in his Commentary on John's Gospel, where Aquinas repeatedly insists that "whatever light and wisdom is in men comes to them by a participation in the Word" who has a "causality with respect to human wisdom,"[67] both natural and supernatural. As to the first, "[a]s soon as human beings use their own natural reason, their knowledge flows from the Word, because 'it is from this true Light that human participation in the natural light of knowledge derives.'"[68] True wisdom ultimately consists in knowing God himself,[69] a knowledge derived from God's own knowledge of himself; in divine revelation through the Word, a knowledge of

---

[63] *ScG* IV, c. 42. See also *De rationibus fidei* c. 5.

[64] *STh* I, q. 41, a. 3 ad 4; II–II, q. 23, a. 2 ad 1. Cf. *ScG* III, c. 162. Aquinas does say, in the *Prima pars*, that the rational creature knows God by participating the Word. *STh* I, q. 38, a. 1.

[65] Likewise, Thomas's *Sentences* Commentary gives a central place to the theme of divine Wisdom, the source and end of all creation; his prologue frames the entire dispensation of creation, of restoration, and of the final perfection of all things, in terms of the working of and manifestation of divine Wisdom. Yet as we have noted, at that stage in his career, Aquinas regarded divine Wisdom as appropriated to the Son rather than as anchored in his proper identity as begotten Wisdom. See, e.g., I *Sent.* prol.; III *Sent.* d. 1, q. 2, a. 2. For a careful study of this theme in the prologue of Aquinas's *Sentences* Commentary, see Emery, *La Trinité créatrice*, 252–301.

[66] See, e.g., *In Epist. ad I Cor.* c. 1, lect. 4 (no. 71); *In Epist. ad Col.* c. 3, lect. 3 (no. 166); c. 2, lect. 1 (nos. 80–2).

[67] *In Ioan.* c. 1, lect. 13 (no. 246).

[68] Emery, *Trinitarian Theology*, 201–2 (quoting *In Ioan* c. 1, lect. 9, no. 129).

[69] See, e.g., *STh* I, q. 1, a. 6; II–II, q. 9, a. 2; I *Sent.* prol.; III *Sent.* d. 35, q. 2, a. 3, qla 1.

God is given that surpasses what natural reason can reach. Thomas's language is bold and broad:

> The root and fount of the knowledge of God is the Word of God, namely Christ: "The Word of God on high is the fount of wisdom (Sir. 1:5)." But human wisdom consists in the knowledge of God. This knowledge is derived to men from the Word, because insofar as they participate the Word of God, they know God. Hence he says: The world has not known you in this way, "but I," the fount of wisdom, your Word, "have known you," by the eternal knowledge of comprehension.... From this knowledge of the Word, which is the fount and root, are derived, like streams and branches, all the knowledge of the faithful.[70]

Thomas goes on to explain (following Augustine) that we know God according to God's own self-knowledge because of the mission of the Word in the incarnation, which manifests the Father's name to men and bears witness to the truth.[71] In other words, we know God (and therefore become wise) insofar as we participate in the Word of God, who proceeds as begotten Wisdom; we are brought to the pinnacle of that participation in the divine revelation through the incarnate Word, who manifests the Father to us. Aquinas thus links the order of things in themselves (*ordo secundum naturam*)—that is, that human wisdom is metaphysically dependent on the Word from which it is "derived" and in which it participates—with the order by which we become wise (*ordo quoad nos*), namely, by receiving what the incarnate Word teaches and reveals to us.[72] So, when we say that the Father created and restored humankind (and, in humankind, the entire universe) through his Word, this statement implicates both salvation and revelation, which are intrinsically connected and are brought about by the Word incarnate.

At every step in this progression, Aquinas adverts to the personal procession of the Word. Indeed, this theme is but a corollary of Thomas's foundational theological insight that the processions of the divine persons are the cause, the *ratio*, the origin, and the exemplar of both the production of creatures and of their return to God—and consequently, that the Son's procession by way of intellect (that is, his *generation as Word*) has a proper mode of causality for the

[70] *In Ioan.* c. 17, lect. 6 (nos. 2267–8).   [71] *Ibid.*
[72] See *In Ioan.* c. 1, lect. 1 (no. 34).

return of the rational creature to God by wisdom.[73] The Word is Truth in person who *reveals* the Father, bringing us and joining us to him.

This brings us to a second theme, closely linked to the first: man's dynamic perfection as a rational creature is precisely his growth in wisdom, the ultimate terminus of which is the beatific vision. As Aquinas puts it: "man grows in wisdom, which is his proper perfection insofar as he is rational, by participating the Word of God."[74] In other words, there is not only a static "kinship" or "likeness" of the Word to human nature[75] but in "participating the Word" more and more perfectly—which is to say, growing more and more in the true wisdom which is the beatifying knowledge of God—man approaches his ultimate perfection, which is to be drawn into the very life of the Trinity. Aquinas offers an analogy: it is like the way "the disciple is instructed by receiving the word of the master."[76] The more deeply the disciple receives his master's word, the more the master's wisdom is *in* the disciple, and the more the disciple becomes like the master in his knowledge.[77] At work here is the same theological principle that we discussed in CHAPTER 2: when one receives the gift of wisdom (for those of us *in via*, Aquinas means especially the theological virtue of faith), he is assimilated to the person of the Word according to the Word's personal property, so that the Word dwells in him in person.[78] The gift of wisdom (like the gift of charity) is thus a vector by which we are drawn in dynamic actuality into the life of the Holy Trinity according to the pattern of the Word's procession.[79] Indeed, for us to "participate the Word" is nothing other than our divinization, "to be made a god," and æ to become god by participation."[80]

[73] See, e.g., I *Sent.* d. 15, q. 4, a. 1, and our discussion of this point at page 39.
[74] *STh* III, q. 3, a. 8, as quoted at p. 74.
[75] This is Thomas's argument at *ScG* IV, c. 42, where he notes that, on account of the *"affinitas"* between the Word and man's rational nature, both the Word and man are called *"imago Dei."*
[76] *STh* III, q. 3, a. 8. For a detailed study of this theme in Aquinas, see Paweł Klimczak, *Christus Magister: Le Christ Maître dans les commentaires évangéliques de saint Thomas d'Aquin* (Fribourg: Academic Press Fribourg, 2013).
[77] Cf. *ScG* IV, c. 12.
[78] *STh* I, q. 38, a. 1; q. 43, a. 5; I *Sent.* d. 14, q. 2, a. 2 ad 2; d. 15, q. 4, a. 1.
[79] I *Sent.* d. 15, q. 4, a. 1; see also Belloy, *La visite de Dieu*, 65–6.
[80] *In Ioan.* c. 10, lect. 6 (no. 1460). Thomas is commenting on Christ's own quotation of Psalm 81: "I have said, you are gods." See also *STh* I, q. 38, a. 1.

This is exactly what Aquinas says in *STh* III, q. 3, a. 8, when he explains why it is fitting that the Word would become incarnate in view of the nature of the sin of our first parents:

> to which a remedy is applied through the incarnation. For the first man sinned by desiring knowledge, as is clear from the words of the serpent promising man "knowledge of good and evil." Thus, it was fitting that through the Word of true wisdom, man, who by an inordinate appetite for knowledge withdrew from God, would be brought back unto God.[81]

The theme remains the same: as before, man reaches his final end through wisdom. Yet, here, Aquinas changes the perspective from which he views it; he does not simply appeal to the Word as the exemplar and source of all human wisdom in general.[82] Rather, he builds on this more general truth to make the more specific point that it is through the Word's incarnation that the remedy for sin is applied, so that man is "brought back unto God"—or, to translate literally, man is "reduced into God," *reduceretur in Deum*, the very phrase Aquinas uses in his *Sentences* Commentary to speak about our final return to the Father through wisdom.[83]

Thus, man's "consummate perfection," the ultimate and supernatural perfection of man as a rational creature, is reached through the Word. As the "fount and root" of "all the knowledge of the faithful,"[84] it is fitting that, after the fall, the Word himself would assume a human nature in order to instruct man in divine wisdom and thus lead him to this final end, which is nothing other than the perfect knowledge of the Holy Trinity in the beatifying vision of God. Built on some of the most important Trinitarian themes of Aquinas's theology, this conclusion reveals the unity in his thought: Thomas understands our salvation by the Word's incarnation as the unfolding of the Word's eternal procession in his visible mission in time, by which we receive a participation in the fount of Wisdom on high.

The Word Manifests the Father

Though it does not appear in *STh* III, q. 3, a. 8, Thomas frequently offers elsewhere a third reason why it was fitting that the Word be the

---

[81] *STh* III, q. 3, a. 8.
[82] Irrespective of sin—that is, even before the fall, and in the case of the holy angels—the Word is the exemplar and source of all created wisdom. Cf. *STh* I, q. 62, a. 1 ad 3.
[83] I *Sent.* d. 15, q. 4, a. 1; cf. *ScG* IV, c. 21.   [84] *In Ioan.* c. 17, lect. 6 (no. 2268).

divine person who becomes incarnate, derived from the second reason (that is, from what is proper to his identity as Word):

> [I]nsofar as he is the Word, he has a suitability [*congruentiam*] to the office of preaching and teaching, because a word manifests the speaker, and he himself manifested the Father: "Father, I have manifested your name to men (John 17:6)."[85]

While Aquinas's explanation here is brief, this is a point of no small importance. In fact, it has a long patristic heritage. Likewise, in the prologue to his *Sentences* Commentary, Aquinas gives it a prominent place at the center of his account of the whole *dispensatio* of salvation.

> The manifestation [of the hidden things of God] is found to be made especially through the Son, since he is the Word of the Father, as John 1 says. Thus, the manifestation of the speaking Father and of the whole Trinity befits him. Thus Matt. 11:27 says: "no one knows the Father except the Son and he to whom the Son wills to reveal him."[86]

In the logic of his *Sentences* prologue, the Word occupies a unique place in the *dispensatio* because he is the one through whom the Father is manifested to the world—and thus also the one through whom the whole Trinity is manifested (since to know one divine person in his personal property implies knowledge of the other two). In the Trinity's plan of creation and grace, this manifestation is the way that we are drawn back into the Trinity. In short, the Word's special role of manifestation is conceived there as the heart and the completion of the whole movement of the procession of creatures from God and their return to him.

This theme is also present in the *Summa Theologiae*,[87] but it is in his Commentary on John where Aquinas gives it a crowning prominence, not only treating the incarnation of the Word as the manifestation of the Father, but bringing to light its deep roots in Trinitarian doctrine. Aquinas uses the example of a man who speaks a word that reveals what is hidden in his heart:

> As the Apostle says, "no one knows the [secret] things of a man except his spirit which is in him"—in other words, except insofar as he wills to manifest himself. But someone manifests his secret through his word: and hence no one can come to a man's secrets except through that man's word. Because, therefore, no one knows "the things of God except

---

[85] III *Sent.* d. 1, q. 2, a. 2.   [86] I *Sent.* prol. (critical edition of A. Oliva).
[87] See, e.g., *STh* I, q. 34, a. 1 ad 3.

the Spirit of God," no one can come to know the Father except through his Word, which is his Son. "No one knows the Father except the Son (Matt. 11:27)."[88]

Aquinas thus clarifies his concise formula that "a word manifests its speaker." While it is true that, when one hears a word, one rightly infers that that word was spoken by someone (as an effect points back to its cause), Aquinas has in mind something more personally revelatory.[89] His analogy refers to not just any word, but an intimate and innermost word, the "secret" in the speaker's heart that manifests who the speaker truly is, the inner truth of his personality.

At work here, yet again, is Aquinas's mature doctrine of the Word as the perfect conception and thus as perfectly expressive of the Father. "His one Word is the expression of the Father."[90] This note of revelation belongs *properly* to the Word; indeed, it was to emphasize this aspect of disclosure, Thomas says, that St John chose to use the name "Word" in the prologue to his Gospel.[91] Consequently, Aquinas explains that the Word brings us to know, through his incarnation, not only that God is the creator of all things, and that he alone should be worshipped, but also that God is Triune.[92] Indeed, he brings us to know the Father, Son, and Holy Spirit *personally*, according to what is proper to each.[93]

Having recognized this, we can now grasp the significance behind Aquinas's repeated use of the dictum, "a word manifests its speaker." Manifesting the Father is, he says, "the proper work (*proprium opus*) of the Son of God, who is the Word, to whom it is proper (*proprium*) to manifest the speaker."[94] Thomas means this in the strict sense:

---

[88] *In Ioan.* c. 14, lect. 2 (no. 1874).
[89] This is clear even in his *Sentences* Commentary when Aquinas speaks about the name "Word" as a personal name. I *Sent.* d. 27, q. 2, a. 2, qla 2 ad 1. See also *STh* I, q. 34, a. 2 ad 5.
[90] *STh* I, q. 34, a. 3; *In Ioan.* c. 1, lect. 1 (no. 29). See also *De Verit.*, q. 4, a. 3, where Thomas explicitly connects the Word's manifestation to his proper procession by way of intellect. Cf. *De Pot.* q. 10, a. 4 ad 4.
[91] Emery, *Trinitarian Theology*, 201, quoting *In Ioan.* c. 1, lect. 1 (no. 31).
[92] *In Ioan.* c. 17, lect. 2 (no. 2195). God the Father was known before the incarnation, but not as the natural Father of the Son. *Ibid.*, c. 5, lect. 7 (no. 830). Further, according to *In Ioan.* c. 10, lect. 2 (no. 1382), Christ is the door through which we enter into "the secrets of God." Similarly, at *In Ioan.* c. 13, lect. 4 (no. 1807), Aquinas explains that the closer one is to Jesus, the more the secrets of divine wisdom are revealed to one.
[93] See, e.g., *In Ioan.* c. 8, lect. 8 (nos. 1282–4); *Compendium theologiae* II, c. 8.
[94] *In Ioan.* c. 17, lect. 2 (no. 2194).

manifesting the Father is *proper* to the Word as Word. This is because, as the conception of the Father proceeding by way of intellect, the Word is the perfect likeness of the Father, including and expressing all that is in the Father and all that the Father is. St Thomas states this boldly: the Word is "the manifestation of the Father himself."[95]

In terms of his Trinitarian doctrine, this claim involves three complementary elements. First, "Word" is an intrinsically relational term—as we have seen, the mature Aquinas teaches that it is the conception "in which" (*in quo*) one understands, which proceeds as the fruit of the complete act of understanding—and hence it includes a reference to its principle. This relational "pointing-back" includes, per se, a manifestation, "[f]or everything which is from another manifests that from which it is: for the Son manifests the Father because he is from the Father."[96] This property of his very personality marks everything that the Son does in his assumed humanity. "Whatever the Son has, he has from the Father, and hence it is necessary that, through the things he does, he manifest the Father."[97] Second, the Word manifests the Father *perfectly* because a perfect word is the perfect likeness (*similitudo*) of what is understood.[98] 'The Word in God is a likeness of him from whom he proceeds, . . . coeternal, . . . always in act, . . . equal to the Father, since it is perfect and expressive of the whole being of the Father."[99] Finally, properly speaking, every manifestation is founded upon an act of understanding (before a speaker speaks a word out loud, he conceives it in his heart), and is ordered to an act of understanding (that the hearer would conceive the same word in his understanding). The Word's procession by way of intellect thus makes it proper to him to manifest what is understood, namely, the Father himself.[100] Consequently, in his visible mission (as we will discuss in detail in CHAPTER 4), the incarnate Word, who is eternally spoken by the Father, reveals in his very person the "speaking Father" to us.

---

[95] *In Ioan.* c. 6, lect. 4 (no. 918).   [96] *In Ioan.* c. 16, lect. 4 (no. 2107).
[97] *In Ioan.* c. 17, lect. 1 (no. 2185).   [98] Sabathé, *La Trinité rédemptrice*, 292.
[99] *In Ioan.* c. 1, lect. 1 (no. 29).
[100] *STh* I, q. 34, a. 1 ad 1; *De Verit.*, q. 4, a. 3; I *Sent.* d. 27, q. 2, a. 2, qla 2. Cf. *In Ioan.* c. 1, lect. 1 (no. 29).

He spoke only the Father and the words of the Father because He was sent by the Father, and because He Himself is the Word of the Father. Thus, he also says that he speaks the Father.[101]

The Word's incarnation is thus the heart of the entire *dispensatio*, because it is through him, and through his manifestation of the Father, that we are brought back to the Father, "the ultimate person to whom we return."[102] The Word incarnate is, indissociably, the agent of revelation and salvation. "As the Christ, he is the Word of God, and the manifestation of the Father. In this way, the Son draws [us] unto the Father."[103]

B. THE INCARNATION OF THE SON *AS SON*

Why was it the *Son* who became incarnate? Let us return to the master text of the *Summa Theologiae* (*STh* III, q. 3, a. 8) for the answer. It is fitting that it be the Son who joins a human nature to himself, viewed "from the end of the union," that is, considering the goal or finality of the incarnation, "the fulfilling of predestination." The incarnation is ordered to the completion of God's eternal plan of salvation, a plan that "those who are preordained to a heavenly inheritance" would be "nothing other than sons, as Rom. 8 says: "sons and heirs.'"

> And hence it was fitting that, through him who is the natural Son, men would participate the likeness of this filiation by adoption, as the Apostle says in the same place: "Those he foreknew he also predestined to be conformed to the image of his Son."[104]

This succinct argument has a long pedigree, beginning with the Church Fathers and extending to the present.[105] In fact, St Thomas's teaching on our filial adoption is a significant theme in his theology, and has been the subject of numerous studies.[106] Rather than delving

---

[101] *In Ioan.* c. 3, lect. 6 (no. 540).   [102] I *Sent.* d. 15, q. 4, a. 1.
[103] *In Ioan.* c. 6, lect. 5 (no. 936).   [104] *STh* III, q. 3, a. 8.
[105] See, e.g., the citations of Hilary of Poitiers and Ambrose in Emery, *Trinitarian Theology*, 204 n. 111, as well as the list of citations to the works of Augustine offered by Ocáriz, Mateo Seco, and Riestra, *The Mystery of Jesus Christ*, 84–5.
[106] See, e.g., Emery, *Trinitarian Theology*, 204–9. For a catalog and study of all of Thomas's texts on the matter, see Somme, *Fils adoptifs*. See also Torrell, *Spiritual Master*,

into this subject for its own sake—a task that would take us rather far afield—it suffices for our purposes to clarify what Aquinas means when he says that, through the incarnation, we "participate the likeness" of the eternal Son's filiation. This will help us grasp the force of the argument, anchored in his Trinitarian doctrine on the Son's natural filiation, of why it was the Son who took flesh. This is yet another case in which Aquinas articulates against the backdrop of his Trinitarian doctrine how the eternal processions of the divine persons unfold in the *dispensatio* and draw us into the heart of the Trinity.

The term "Son," one of the three principal proper names by which the Son's personal property is designated,[107] brings to light his consubstantiality with the Father[108] and the fact that he is begotten.[109] Only the eternal Son is Son of God by nature, per se—this is divine sonship in the fullest and most proper sense.[110] A rational creature can participate in the Son's natural sonship "by adoption" in grace and glory.[111] This adoptive sonship can be imperfect or perfect, "insofar as we are conformed to [Jesus Christ] and serve [him] in spirit."[112] Wayfarers who receive sanctifying grace have an imperfect adoptive sonship, as do those who do works of justice as moved by grace, while the blessed in glory have a perfect conformity to the eternal Son's filiation and hence have a perfect adoptive sonship.[113] Finally, there are other analogous senses of sonship: rational creatures have a certain likeness to God as created in his image, by virtue of their capacity to know and love, while irrational creatures have a certain sonship (in a qualified sense) insofar as

---

140–5; Gregory Vall, "*Ad Bona Gratiae et Gloriae*: Filial Adoption in Romans 8," *The Thomist* 74 (2010): 593–626; A. N. Williams, "Deification in the *Summa theologiae*: A Structural Interpretation of the Prima Pars," *The Thomist* 61 (1997): 219–55; Bailleux, "A l'image du Fils premier-né," 181–207.

[107] The other two principal names underline other aspects of the "perfection" of the personal property of the second person: the name "Image" stresses his perfect likeness to the Father, and the name "Word" emphasizes his immaterial procession by way of intellect, as well as his manifestation of the Father. Emery, *Trinitarian Theology*, 177; see *In Ioan.* c. 1, lect. 1 (nos. 31 and 42); Matthew Levering, *Scripture and Metaphysics: Aquinas and the Renewal of Trinitarian Theology* (Oxford: Blackwell Publishing, 2004), 179–85.

[108] *In Ioan.* c. 1, lect. 1 (no. 42).   [109] *Ibid.* (no. 31).

[110] *STh* I, q. 33, a. 3; *STh* III, q. 23, a. 4.   [111] *STh* III, q. 23, a. 3.

[112] *In Epist. ad. Eph.* c. 1, lect. 1 (no. 9).

[113] *In Ioan.* c. 1, lect. 6 (nos. 150 and 156); *STh* III, q. 45, a. 4; *In Epist. ad Ephes.* c. 1, lect. 1 (no. 10).

everything in the created universe comes from God and points back to him as its cause.[114]

We can set aside these latter analogous senses, since our goal is to expose to view the significance that Aquinas discerns in our adopted filiation through the incarnation *of the Son*. Through the incarnation, we receive a participated likeness of precisely what dimensions of the Son's eternal sonship? Aquinas identifies four.

The first is familiar to us; it concerns a participation by knowledge:

> Certain ones are called sons of God insofar as they participate a likeness of the only-begotten and natural Son, according to Rom. 8: "Those he foreknew [. . .] to be conformed to the image of his Son," who indeed is begotten wisdom. And hence by receiving the gift of wisdom, man attains to the sonship of God.[115]

When we grow in wisdom, we are made like the Son who is begotten wisdom; this participation in a likeness of the Son is rightly considered a form of adopted sonship. We are accustomed to hearing Aquinas speak about this as an assimilation to the Son's procession by way of intellect, an aspect of the Son's personal property best highlighted by the name "Word;" Aquinas lays this down as the principal speculative foundation for our assimilation to the second person. Yet Thomas sometimes also refers this assimilation to the name "Son" and speaks of it as a participation in the Son's filiation. For example, commenting on John 1:18 ("No one has ever seen God; it is the Only Begotten Son, who is in the bosom of the Father, who has made him known"), Aquinas offers a meditation on how we are sons through knowing God, by a participated likeness of the sonship of the eternal Son.

> Inasmuch as someone is called a son of God, so he participates a likeness of the natural Son; and inasmuch as he knows [God], to that extent he has [a share] of his likeness, since knowledge is had by assimilation: "Now we are sons of God," and it continues, "when he appears, we will be like him, and we will see him as he is (1 John 3)."[116]

Somewhat surprisingly, in his Commentary on the first chapter of St John's Gospel, Thomas does not fold this analysis back into his doctrine of the Word; rather, hewing closely to the biblical text, he

---

[114] *STh* I, q. 33, a. 3; Emery, *Trinitarian Theology*, 204–6.
[115] *STh* II–II, q. 45, a. 6. See also ad 1.   [116] *In Ioan.* c. 1, lect. 11 (no. 216).

underlines instead how the Son knows the Father since he is "Only-begotten" and "consubstantial."

He is called "Only-begotten" because he is the natural Son, having the same nature and knowledge as the Father. "The Lord said to me: 'You are my son' (Ps. 2)."... Then, when he says "in the bosom of the Father," he adds... his consubstantiality with the Father.... In that bosom, that is, in the most hidden things of the paternal nature and essence, which exceeds every creature's power, is the Only-begotten Son, and so he is consubstantial with the Father. What the evangelist here signified by "bosom," David expressed by "womb," saying [in Ps. 109] "from the womb, before the daystar," that is, from my most intimate and hidden essence, incomprehensible to every created intellect, "I have begotten you," consubstantial with me, and of the same nature, virtue, power, and knowledge.[117]

As the Son knows the secrets of the paternal nature as Only-begotten and consubstantial, he shares those secrets with us. The name "Son" is the point of departure, indicating that he has the very same divine nature and thus the same divine knowledge as the Father. Our adopted sonship, a participation in his eternal sonship, is therefore also a participation in the Son's divine knowledge. Thus, while the doctrine of the Word remains primary in Aquinas's thought (as other texts on the Son's divine sonship clearly show),[118] Aquinas offers us here a concrete example of the complementarity of the different proper names for the second person, each of which helps us grasp, according to our partial and limited way of knowing, what is the single personal property of the Son. Our knowledge of God can be conceived of both as a participation in the Word, and also as a participation in a likeness of the Son's natural filiation.

The second dimension of the sonship of the Son in which we participate is his unity with the Father.

Adoptive filiation is a certain likeness to natural filiation. But the Son of God naturally proceeds from the Father as an intellectual Word, while existing as one with the Father himself.... A creature is assimilated to the eternal Word according to the unity that he has with the Father; this occurs through grace and charity. Thus, the Lord prays "that they may

---

[117] *In Ioan.* c. 1, lect. 11 (nos. 217–18).
[118] See, e.g., *In Ioan.* c. 14, lect. 6 (no. 1874) (quoted above, explaining that the Son shares the secrets of the Father as the Father's Word); Emery, *Trinitarian Theology*, 185–209.

be one in us, as we also are one (John 17)." Such an assimilation perfects the *ratio* of adoption, because an eternal inheritance is due to those so assimilated. Whence it is clear that to be adopted belongs to a rational creature alone, and not to all such, but only to those who have charity, which is poured into our hearts by the Holy Spirit, as Rom. 5 says. And thus the Holy Spirit is called the "Spirit of adoption of sons (Rom. 8)."[119]

Among the several elements in play in this text (e.g., our union with God by grace and charity, our assimilation to the Word who proceeds by way of intellect), the Son's unity with the Father has an important role: when we are made adopted sons through grace and charity, we participate in the divine filiation that is shaped by the Son's consubstantial unity with the Father. Aquinas thus gives full weight to Jesus's prayer that, as he is one with the Father, so we would be one in them. We receive a participation in this consubstantial divine unity from the Holy Spirit. Assimilated to the Son by the Spirit's gift of charity (a point we shall discuss at length in CHAPTER 8), we are likewise "assimilated to that divine nature through which the Father and Son are one,"[120] and are thus drawn into the unity of the consubstantial Trinity. We are here at the heart of the Trinitarian mystery of our filial adoption.[121]

Next, we participate as adopted sons in a third dimension of the Son's natural filiation, specifically, his being begotten. To be sure, the divine Son's eternal begetting is absolutely unique. "There is this difference between adopted sons of God and the natural Son of God: the natural Son of God is 'begotten, not made,' while an adopted son is made, as John 1 says, 'he gave them the power to be made sons of God.'"[122] Yet, even though we are *made* adopted sons of God, this is nonetheless a sort of begetting; we are begotten anew, that is, we are "born again" or "regenerated." Thomas uses this vocabulary because it is the way Scripture itself speaks of the transformation accomplished in us by grace. "An adopted son is sometimes said to be begotten because of a spiritual regeneration" by grace.[123] By this grace, "we are regenerated as sons of God, to a likeness of the true Son."[124]

[119] *STh* III, q. 23, a. 3.
[120] *In Ioan.* c. 17, lect. 5 (no. 2240). See Emery, *Trinitarian Theology*, 207.
[121] For an account of our "inclusion" in the Trinitarian communion with a particular reference to the Father, see Emmanuel Durand, *Le Père, Alpha et Oméga de la vie trinitaire* (Paris: Les Éditions du Cerf, 2008), 73–92.
[122] *STh* III, q. 23, a. 2.   [123] *Ibid.*
[124] *In Ioan.* c. 3, lect. 1 (no. 442).

It is for this reason—the fact that we are rightly called "born" as children of God by the grace that comes from Christ—that Christ is also called "first-born" ("those he foreknew and predestined, he conforms to the image of his Son, so that he would be the first-born of many brothers (Rom. 8:29)"):

> [T]he Son of God willed to communicate a conformity to his filiation to others, so that he would not only be the Son, but the first-born of [many] sons. And thus, he who through an eternal generation is the only-begotten, "the only begotten who is in the bosom of the Father (John 1:18)," "would be," according to the bestowal of grace, "the first-born of many brothers." ... Therefore Christ has us as brothers, both because he communicates a likeness of filiation to us, as is said here [by St. Paul], and because he assumes a likeness of our nature.[125]

The structure of St Thomas's reasoning here contains an echo of his doctrine of the divine missions. Just as the Son's mission includes the Son's eternal procession, adding to it a temporal effect by which that procession is disclosed, so the Son's personal property considered under the aspect of "Only-begotten" is included in and disclosed by Christ's title as "first-born,"[126] and by his resulting invisible mission in the grace in which we are made like the Only-begotten insofar as we are re-born as adopted sons.[127] (Thomas offers a similar argument to show why it was fitting for Christ to be born of the Virgin Mary.)[128]

This leads us to the fourth and final dimension of the Son's sonship in which we participate, namely, the Son's eternal inheritance. We have already seen a good example of St Thomas's straightforward reasoning on this point: insofar as we are assimilated to and thus

---

[125] *In Epist. ad Rom.* c. 8, lect. 6 (no. 706). This text is also remarkable when read in a slightly broader context. Aquinas is arguing that just as God willed to communicate the goodness he has by nature to creatures so that they would share in that goodness by participation, so also the Son willed to communicate his natural filiation to creatures by becoming incarnate and thus making possible their participation in it by adoptive sonship. *Ibid.* Aquinas thus gives a striking new twist to the Dionysian theme of the good as self-diffusive, applying it to the Son's personal property (the Son wills to diffuse his natural filiation by participation). In addition, see *STh* III, q. 1, a. 1, where St Thomas cites this Dionysian principle in accounting for the fittingness of the incarnation. See also Torrell, *Encyclopédie Jésus le Christ*, 92.

[126] He holds this title in virtue of his visible mission in the incarnation. When referred to the Son in his divinity, "first-born" is only metaphorical. *STh* I, q. 41, a. 3.

[127] See also *In Ioan.* c. 1, lect. 8 (no. 187), which makes essentially the same argument.

[128] e.g., III *Sent.* d. 1, q. 2, a. 2.

united to the Son, the Son's "eternal inheritance is due" to us.[129] He takes this directly from St Paul: 'if sons, then heirs, heirs of God and co-heirs with Christ (Rom. 8:17).' St Thomas comments: "Since [Christ] is the principal Son from whom we participate filiation, he is thus the principal heir to whom we are joined in the inheritance."[130] In short, our title to this eternal inheritance runs through our relation to the Son. This is why it was the Son who became incarnate, says Aquinas: "This especially pertains to the Son, who, since he is the true and natural Son of God, leads us into the glory of the Father's heritage."[131]

We should not fail to mention, however, that the Holy Spirit also plays a decisive role here, uniting us to the Son.

> Because [the Holy Spirit] is given to us, we are made sons of God. For through the Holy Spirit we are made one with Christ, "if anyone does not have the Spirit of [Christ], he does not belong to him (Rom. 8:9)," and by consequence we are made adopted sons of God, from which we have the promise of an eternal heritage, because "if sons, then heirs (Rom. 8:17)."[132]

As we will discuss in detail in CHAPTER 8, the Holy Spirit is given to us through Christ, uniting us to Christ and conforming us to him, so that through the Spirit we become adopted sons and daughters in Christ and thus obtain a share in his inheritance.

What exactly is this inheritance?

> [St. Paul] describes it with reference to God the Father, saying "heirs of God." Now, one is called someone's heir who obtains or attains his principal goods, and not someone who receives something small.... But the principal good by which God is rich, is himself.... Thus, sons of God attain to God himself as an inheritance. "The Lord is my inheritance (Ps. 15:5)."[133]

When we are joined to the Son and made like him, we receive by adoption what he has by nature from the Father: God's own "heritage of blessedness," "the enjoyment [*fruitione*] of God, through which

---

[129] *STh* III, q. 23, a. 3.   [130] *In Epist. ad Rom.* c. 8, lect. 3 (no. 649).
[131] I *Sent.* prol. (critical edition of A. Oliva).
[132] *In Epist. ad Ephes.* c. 1, lect. 5 (no. 42). The Marietti edition records St Thomas as misquoting Rom. 8:9, saying "spiritum Dei," whereas the Vulgate reads "spiritum Christi."
[133] *In Epist. ad Rom.* c. 8, lect. 3 (no. 647).

God himself is blessed and, through himself, rich, namely, insofar as he enjoys himself."[134]

Having reviewed these four dimensions, we can now return to the text with which we began (*STh* III, q. 3, a. 8) to grasp the full significance of Aquinas's argument that it was supremely fitting for the Son, *as Son,* to become incarnate, since the goal or end of the incarnation is our adoption as sons. While that adoption by sanctifying grace is efficiently caused by all three divine persons, we receive in sanctifying grace and by way of knowledge a participated likeness of the Son's proper filiation, just as the Son, as Son, *knows* the Father perfectly (the first dimension discussed above). Our filial adoption draws us into the Son's *unity* with the Father (the second dimension); "born again" or "regenerated" by grace, we are made like him who is eternally *begotten* (the third dimension). We thus participate in a likeness of his eternal and perfect reception of the riches or *inheritance* of the Father (the fourth dimension). Under each of these aspects, the salvation that comes to us through the incarnation generates a likeness in us of the eternal filiation of the Son. In other words, Aquinas brings to light the wisdom of the divine plan which, through the Son's visible mission in Christ, draws us into the Trinity—and ultimately, to the Father—as adopted sons and daughters through and in the Son.

C. THE INCARNATION OF THE SON *AS IMAGE*

That the Son is the "Image" of the Father is the basis for a third important argument for why it was he who became incarnate. This appears only briefly in *STh* III, q. 3, a. 8, where Thomas quotes St Paul in explaining our participation in a likeness of the Son's natural filiation: "Those he foreknew he also predestined to be conformed to the image of his Son (Rom. 8:29)."[135] While this is little more than a nod of the head, it evokes not only Thomas's discussion of "Image" as a proper name of the Son in the *Prima pars*, but also the way that name describes the "end" of the creation of man (also in the

---

[134] *STh* III, q. 23, a. 1. The Son *is* the divine nature as received from the Father, and so also "enjoys" God in a filial mode, but the divine nature and the divine fruition of the Son are numerically the same as the Father's.

[135] *STh* III, q. 3, a. 8; see also II–II, q. 45, a. 6.

Prima pars).[136] It then blossoms into a major theme of the *Secunda pars*: man is made to the image of God (more specifically, there is an "image of the Trinity" in man's soul, according to the Trinitarian doctrine of Word and Love). Deformed by sin, this image in man is restored in grace and perfected in glory.[137] In the *Tertia pars*, Aquinas then accounts for how the Son, who is the perfect Image, restores the image in man through the incarnation.[138] The same theme is on display in Aquinas's John Commentary, where St Thomas succinctly articulates a wide-angle overview of the entire *dispensatio* along these lines:

> Among the other inferior creatures, man is a special work of God, because, according to Gen. 1:26, God made him to his image and likeness. And this work was, in a sense, perfect in the beginning, because God made man upright, as Eccl. 7:30 says. But afterwards, through sin, he lost this perfection and fell away from uprightness. And hence, in order that this work of the Lord would be perfect, he needed to be repaired—which perfection is through Christ.[139]

The incarnation is the divine repair project by which the image that God created in man is restored and perfected; this is an important facet of Aquinas's account of the *dispensatio*. What remains to be seen, however, is the deeper intelligibility Aquinas detects in this in light of the Son's identity as Image—that is, why it was especially fitting for the Son, *as Image*, to become incarnate.

As a prelude to answering this question, let us review St Thomas's teaching on "Image" as a proper name for the Son. This is, first of all, a biblical name, as well as an important theme of the Church Fathers.[140] In the *Summa Theologiae*, Thomas discusses this name immediately following his analysis of the personal names of "Son" and "Word." Like those names, Aquinas holds that "Image" is a proper

---

[136] *STh* I, q. 93.
[137] See, e.g., *STh* I, q. 35; I, q.45, a. 7; I–II, prol.; I–II, q. 109, a. 4 ad 1. This subject has been well treated by many commentators. See, e.g., Torrell, *Spiritual Master*, 80–100, and the voluminous sources he cites, as well as Michael A. Dauphinais, "Loving the Lord your God: The *Imago Dei* in Saint Thomas Aquinas," *The Thomist* 63 (1999): 241–67, and Leo J. Elders, *Sur les traces de saint Thomas d'Aquin, théologien: Étude de ses commentaires bibliques, Thèmes théologiques*, trans. Véronique Pommeret (Paris: Presses universitaires de l'IPC, 2009), 417–42.
[138] See, e.g., *STh* III, q. 5, a. 4 ad 1; q. 32, a. 3.
[139] *In Ioan.* c. 4, lect. 4 (no. 643).
[140] See Col. 1:15; 2 Cor. 4:4; in general, see Emery, *Trinitarian Theology*, 209–10. For a detailed patristic study on the Son as Image, and human beings as made to the image, see A. G. Hamman, *L'homme image de Dieu* (Paris: Desclée, 1987).

name for the second person of the Trinity. Thomas's explanation bases this conclusion on his doctrine of the Word: Image refers properly to the Son "because the Son proceeds as Word, the *ratio* of which includes a likeness of species to that from which it proceeds."[141] The Holy Spirit, while connatural with the Father, proceeds by way of love and hence is not properly called an image of the Father.[142] Finally, even though creatures are also called "images of God," they are only images in a way analogous to the true and perfect image of the Father, who is the connatural divine Son.[143]

Why is it the Image who restores the fallen image of God in man? If we read Aquinas carefully, he articulates two dimensions or levels of fittingness to the second person's image-restoration work. The first is straightforward: as the perfect Image of the Father, the Son is especially fitted to assuming and thereby restoring human nature, which is made "to the image" of God.

> Insofar as he is the Image, he has a fittingness with him who was to be restored, namely, with man, who was made "to the image of God (Gen. 1:27)." Hence it was fitting that the Image would assume the image, [that] the Uncreated [would assume] the created.[144]

On this level, the fittingness is between the Son's personal property as Image and human nature itself, which in a certain way reflects or represents that personal property.[145]

As Gilles Emery has documented, this depends heavily on Aquinas's doctrine of the Word. It is, in essence, another way of formulating the "fit" between the Word and rational creatures.[146] The analogy of

---

[141] *STh* I, q. 35, a. 2.   [142] *Ibid.*   [143] *Ibid.*, ad 3.

[144] III *Sent.* d. 1, q. 2, a. 2. A few lines later, Aquinas reprises this theme with respect to titles appropriated to the Son: "*species*" and "*pulchritudo*." See also I *Sent.* d. 3, q. 3, a. 1 ad 5.

[145] Man is not made to the image of the Son *alone*; Aquinas thinks this would be impossible because the Son is the perfect image and likeness of the Father, according to an absolute equality, so that a likeness to the Son is necessarily a likeness to the Father as well. *STh* I, q. 93, a. 5 ad 4. Rather, Thomas says that man is made to the image of God "both with respect to the divine nature and with respect to the Trinity of persons." *STh* I, q. 93, a. 5. That is, as we explained in CHAPTER 2, there is in man a "likeness" or "representation" not only of the divine essence, but also of the personal processions of Son and Holy Spirit—but never of one divine person without the others. *Ibid.* and ad. 5; a. 6 ad 2. Consequently, man is an image of God insofar as he has a "likeness" to or "represents" the divine essence, and to the personal processions of the Word and of Love. *STh* I, q. 93, a. 6.

[146] Emery, *Trinitarian Theology*, 214–17.

the mental word thus remains primary for Aquinas. Just as his treatment of the name "Image" follows that of "Word" in the Trinitarian treatise,[147] so also Thomas's account of the fittingness of the incarnation of the person who is the Image follows his account of the fittingness of the Word's incarnation. In the *Summa Contra Gentiles*, for example, Thomas explicitly links "Word" and "Image" on this point. The *ratio* of "Word" has to do with the intellect, and hence possesses an affinity with human nature.

> [O]n account of that aforesaid affinity, divine Scripture also attributes the name "Image" to both the Word and to man; for the Apostle says about the Word that "he is the image of the invisible God (Col. 1)," and says the same thing about man, that "man is the image of God (1 Cor. 11)."[148]

Because man's rational nature has an affinity to the Word, there is a parallel analogy or similitude between the divine Word who is the perfect Image, and man who is a created image of God—and therefore, for reasons rooted in Trinitarian doctrine, Aquinas concludes that it was most fitting for the divine person who is Word and Image to become incarnate.

The second dimension has to do with the way Christ himself, as man, is the perfect image of God in a human nature, through whom the divine image in each of us is repaired and perfected. We are no longer talking here only about the "fit" between the divine person who is "Image" and human nature in general, but also about how, in joining a human nature to the divine Image in person, every potentiality to be an *imago Dei* in human nature was supremely realized in Christ.[149] As we are conformed to Christ's humanity (including all that Christ lived, did, and suffered in that humanity), the image of God in us, damaged and defaced by sin, is refashioned and repaired.[150]

---

[147] *Ibid.*, 211–14. See also José Ramón Villar, "Christo, imagen de Dios invisible (Col 1, 15a). Tradición exegética y comentario de santo Tomás de Aquino," *Scripta Theologica* 42 (2010): 665–90.

[148] *ScG* IV, c. 42. See also *ScG* IV, c. 11.

[149] See, e.g., *Compendium theologiae* I, c. 213; *STh* III, q. 5, a. 4 and ad 1.

[150] This very contention plays a pivotal role in one of the key passages of the Second Vatican Council's *Pastoral Constitution on the Church in the Modern World*: "The truth is that only in the mystery of the incarnate Word does the mystery of man take on light . . . He Who is 'the image of the invisible God' (Col. 1:15), is Himself the perfect man. To the sons of Adam He restores the divine likeness which had been disfigured from the first sin onward." *Gaudium et Spes* 22. See also

Aquinas integrates these two dimensions into a genuine Trinitarian Christology. Consider, for example, how he approaches a key Pauline text (Rom. 8:29, "that we would be conformed to the image of his Son") in his Commentary on Romans. Christ as God is the Image (i.e., the Image of the Father in person) who repairs the damaged image of God in us, and this repair is accomplished when we are conformed to Christ *as man*, the perfect human image of God.

> The phrase "to the image of his Son" can be understood in two ways. The first is as an appositive construction, so that the meaning would be: "conformed to the image of his Son, who is the image." "He is the image of the invisible God (Col. 1:15)." The other way it can be understood is as a transitive construction, so that the meaning would be: "He has predestined us to be conformed to his Son in this, that we bear his image." "As we have borne the image of the earthly man, thus let us bear the image of the heavenly man (1 Cor. 15:49)."[151]

Using St Paul to comment on St Paul, Aquinas highlights the double resonance of the term "image." It is, first, a proper name of the Son. We are conformed to the Image, who is the Son, the divine exemplar through whom we are created and recreated. But there is also an *imago Dei* in man, and it is perfect in the "heavenly man," Jesus Christ. Indeed, Christ bears the Father's perfect image even in his humanity, as "wax retains the entire figure of a seal" pressed into it. "In this, something of the mystery of the incarnation is understood, because God the Father impressed the Word, who is 'the splendor and figure of his substance, (Heb. 1:3),' in a human nature."[152] (We will have much more to say elsewhere about how this is accomplished: how Christ's humanity bears what is proper to the Word (Chapter 4), and how it is elevated and sanctified by the Holy Spirit in Christ's perfect fullness of grace (Chapters 5–8.) Our salvation consists in being conformed to this perfect heavenly but also human image who is God incarnate. Speaking about Christ as image, therefore, permits Aquinas to pivot effortlessly from a Trinitarian truth (the Son is the Image of the Father) to a Christological one (we are conformed to the Son, the perfect image, by being conformed to Christ's human nature).

David Schindler, "Christology and the Imago Dei: Interpreting *Gaudium et Spes*," Communio 23 (1996): 156–84.

[151] *In Epist. ad Rom.* c. 8, lect. 6 (no. 705).
[152] *In Ioan.* c. 6, lect. 3 (no. 898).

This easily translates into the spirituality, at the same time Christocentric and Trinitarian, that Aquinas himself preached. Progress in the Christian life consists in a growing conformity to Christ the God-man, the perfect image who restores the image of God in us. A sermon probably delivered in Paris by the Dominican master on the first Sunday of Advent in 1271 offers a good example:

> This image [of God] was created in man, but...it is blackened and obscured by sin. "You will bring their images back to nothing (Ps. 72:20)." For this reason, God sent his Son to reform this image deformed by sin. Let us be zealous, therefore, to be reformed, as the Apostle says: "Stripping off the old man, clothe yourselves in the new man who is created to be like God and who is renewed in the image of him who created him (Col. 3:9–10)." And how are we renewed? Certainly, when we imitate Christ. This image, which in us is deformed, is perfect in Christ. We should therefore bear the image of Christ. This is what the Apostle writes to the Corinthians: "as we have borne the image of the earthly man, let us bear the image of the heavenly man (1 Cor. 15:49)," and in the letter [to the Romans], "put on Christ," that is, imitate Christ. The perfection of the Christian life consists in this.[153]

Aquinas does not only mean that Christ, as the perfect human image of God, is a moral example that we ought to follow (though this is undoubtedly part of what he means—"every action of Christ is our instruction," he says elsewhere),[154] but also that this imitating of Christ is itself the fruit of the grace that Christ gives.[155] As Christ refashions the image of God in us, we imitate him, becoming more like the true Image. We "put on Christ" and are "conformed to Christ" as we are moved, healed, elevated, and transformed by the grace that comes from and is given by Christ,[156] through his sacred humanity (as an instrument of the divinity—more on this below and in CHAPTER 8). Our salvation—and sanctifying grace itself—is therefore Christ-shaped. "In this world,

---

[153] *Ecce rex tuus.*   [154] *In Ioan.* c. 11, lect. 6 (no. 1555).

[155] *In Ioan.* c. 15, lect. 1 (no. 1993). Torrell points out that Thomas speaks of Christ as both a moral example, and as an ontological exemplar through the gift of grace. Jean-Pierre Torrell, *Christ and Spirituality in St Thomas Aquinas*, trans. Bernhard Blankenhorn (Washington, D.C.: Catholic University of America Press, 2011), 119–21. We can see a good example of how St Thomas approaches this at *In Ioan.* c. 4, lect. 4 (no. 641), where he explains that Christ not only teaches us how to go to the Father, but, in his passion, opens the way for us and gives us the power to reach that exalted end.

[156] See, e.g., *In Epist. ad I Cor.* c. 15, lect. 7 (no. 998).

no one comes to the state of perfection unless he follows in the footsteps of Christ."[157]

Moreover, Christ is not only the agent of our restoration as the source and efficient cause of the grace that heals us; as the perfect Image, he is also the *exemplar cause* of our present life of grace and our eventual life of glory.[158] In the incarnation of the Father's perfect Image, the divine exemplar has also made himself into a human exemplar, the "unfailing exemplar of holiness,"[159]—that is, not only an example but also an exemplar cause of our regeneration.[160] St Thomas makes just this point in his Commentary on 1 Corinthians:

> Things lower in being imitate those things that are higher insofar as they can. Thus, even a natural agent, insofar as it is a higher being, assimilates to itself those it acts upon. But the primordial principle of the whole procession of things is the Son of God, as John 1:3 says: "through him all things were made." And hence he is the primordial exemplar, which all creatures imitate as the true and perfect image of the Father. Thus, Col. 1:15 says: "He is the image of the invisible God, the first-born of all creatures, because in him all things were created." ... But, formerly, this exemplar of God was very far removed from us, as Eccl. 2:12 says: "What is man that he can follow the king his maker?" Therefore, he willed to be made man, to offer to men a human exemplar.[161]

The first part of this text repeats a familiar central claim of St Thomas's doctrine on the Trinity and creation: the Son, as Word and Image, is the perfect representation of the Father, and thus the primordial exemplar and principle of the procession of all creatures. "Through him all things were made." As a cause of an infinitely higher order, the eternal Son assimilates us to himself (as Thomas says elsewhere, "our

---

[157] *In Matt.* c. 24 (no. 2003).

[158] St Thomas makes this clear in a great number of texts when he speaks about the exemplar causality of different aspects and events in Christ's life. For example, the resurrection of Christ's body is both an efficient cause (as instrument of the divinity) and an exemplar cause of our resurrection (since Christ's body is personally united to the Word, it is the most perfect resurrected body, and thus is the exemplar that we will imitate in our resurrection.) *STh* III, q. 56, a. 1 ad 3. See also III *Sent.* d. 10, q. 3, a. 1, qla 3 (Christ's predestination is the formal exemplar cause of ours, insofar as we are conformed to his image); III *Sent.* d. 20, a. 3 (Christ's satisfaction); III *Sent.* d. 21, q. 2, a. 2 ad 1 and ad 2 (Christ's resurrection); *STh* III, q. 24, a. 3 (Christ's predestination); *STh* III, q. 28, a. 1 (Christ's conception); *STh* III, q. 39, a. 8 (Christ's baptism); *STh* III, q. 46, aa. 3 and 4 (Christ's passion); *STh* III, q. 56, a. 1 ad 4 (Christ's death); *In Epist. ad Rom.* c. 6, lect. 1 (no. 472) (Christ's death).

[159] *In Epist. ad I Cor.* c. 11, lect. 1 (no. 583).

[160] *STh* III, q. 62, a. 5 ad 1.   [161] *In Epist. ad I Cor.* c. 11, lect. 1 (no. 583).

regeneration is to a likeness of the Son of God" who is the Image in person).[162] To this, St Thomas now adds an important Christological truth: when the perfect Image of the Father becomes incarnate, that primordial exemplar comes "closer" to us (Thomas's doctrine of the divine missions, which include and disclose the eternal processions, is at work in the background here), so that Christ's humanity becomes the path through which we are assimilated to the Son.[163] Further, the logic of the Dominican Master's argument is precisely that the divine Image is acting upon us as we are assimilated to him in his divinity *through* his humanity that comes toward us and brings us near to him.

In sum, the incarnate Image (1) *demonstrates* in all that he does and suffers what a perfect human life is, lived as the image of God; (2) he *becomes the way* for our return, inasmuch as we conform our lives to what he lived in the flesh; and (3) through what he does in the flesh, he also *accomplishes* our salvation and *acts* to conform us to himself (the latter, above all, by giving us the Holy Spirit). This is, then, an excellent example of how Thomas understands the incarnation as the visible mission of the Son. The eternal procession of the second person of the Trinity is made present to us in a new way, acting upon us as the Image who reforms our fallen humanity through his human nature. As we imitate Christ the human exemplar, we are configured to and become more like the Son, the perfect divine Image and exemplar. In this way, we pass by faith through Christ's humanity to his divinity, and thus to the source of the Image, the Father himself.[164] We will find no other path of return unto God than the divine processions themselves, as they "come close" to us (in the created effects that disclose them and make them present) in the divine missions—first among them, the visible mission of the Image in the incarnation.[165]

D. THE INCARNATION OF THE SON AS THE *AUTHOR OF SANCTIFICATION*

St Thomas adverts to one more dimension of the Son's personal property in the master text of the *Summa Theologiae* discussing the

---

[162] *In Ioan.* c. 3, lect. 1 (no. 435).   [163] Cf. *In Ioan.* c. 3, lect. 1 (no. 443).
[164] *In Ioan.* c. 12, lect. 8 (no. 1712); see also c. 14, lect. 2 (nos. 1868, 1870–2).
[165] *In Ioan.* c. 14, lect. 2 (nos. 1878–9).

fittingness of his incarnation (*STh* III, q. 3, a. 8): the Son is a principle and giver of the Holy Spirit. Thomas thus implicitly refers to a title he used for the Son in the *Prima pars*: he is the *Auctor sanctificationis*, "Author of sanctification," because he gives the Holy Spirit who is himself the Gift of sanctification in person.[166]

Thomas speaks of this in response to article 8's third objection, which argued that

> the incarnation is ordered to the remission of sins, according to Matt. 1:21: "You will call him Jesus, for he will save his people from their sins." But the remission of sins is attributed to the Holy Spirit, according to John 20:22–3: "Receive the Holy Spirit: whose sins you forgive will be forgiven." Therefore it was more fitting for the person of the Holy Spirit to become incarnate than the person of the Son.[167]

This objection combines two unimpeachably true statements drawn directly from Scripture: the incarnation aims at the forgiveness of sins, and the means to that end is the sending of the Holy Spirit. Aquinas certainly does not doubt these truths; they are at the center of his whole treatment of the *dispensatio*. He is famous for maintaining that "the work of the incarnation is principally ordered to the reparation of human nature through the abolition of sin."[168] Further, he is quite clear that the Holy Spirit "causes the life of grace: 'it is the Spirit who gives life (John 6:64),'" because "sin is remitted by the Holy Spirit.... And this is because he is the Spirit of life: 'Come, spirit, from the four winds, and blow upon these slain, and let them live again (Ez. 37:9).'"[169]

What the objection has not done, however, is grasp the intrinsic relation between these two truths. Aquinas's reply articulates precisely what the objector missed: these truths are ordered to each other because of the order and relation of the divine persons themselves in the heart of the Trinity, and consequently because of the order of the divine missions that extend the processions of the persons into time. Aquinas writes:

> It is proper to the Holy Spirit to be the Gift of the Father and the Son. But the remission of sins is made through the Holy Spirit as through the

[166] See *STh* I, q. 43, a. 7; cf. III *Sent.* d. 1, q. 2, a. 2.
[167] *STh* III, q. 3, a. 8 obj. 3.   [168] *STh* III, q. 1, a. 5.
[169] *In Epist. ad Rom.* c. 8, lect. 1 (no. 605).

gift of God. Hence, it was more fitting for man's justification that the Son would become incarnate, of whom the Holy Spirit is the Gift.[170]

Aquinas begins with a fundamental Trinitarian truth about the Holy Spirit: he is "Gift" in person. As is clear from the *Prima pars*, the Spirit is *properly* called the Gift of the Father and the Son because he proceeds from both Father and Son by way of love ("Love" is another proper name of the Spirit).[171] The name "Gift" is properly his, therefore, not because of his acts in creation or because of his relation to creatures, but simply "because of an eternal relation at the heart of the Trinity."[172] Nonetheless, this name does imply an aptitude to be given to human beings in the Spirit's invisible mission according to grace.[173] Consequently, when Aquinas begins his reply by speaking about the Holy Spirit's proper name as "Gift," he is making a Trinitarian reference that also points to the particular way that the Spirit is "sent" and "given" to man in an invisible mission. At the same time, Aquinas notes that it is proper to the Holy Spirit to be from the Father and the Son. This expresses the eternal order of the divine processions. This order is revealed and made present in salvation history when the Son is sent visibly as the one who gives the Holy Spirit.

The second sentence of St Thomas's reply turns to the effect of the Spirit's mission in us. "But the remission of sins is made through the Holy Spirit as through the gift of God." It is by the gift of the Holy Spirit in person—that is, by the Father and Son "sending" and "giving" the Spirit to us in an invisible mission—that sin is forgiven, on account of the intrinsic connection between the invisible mission of the Spirit, the gift of sanctifying grace (in which man receives faith formed by charity), and the forgiveness of sins. The Spirit's invisible mission to man's soul, and hence the Holy Spirit's personal presence in man, is absolutely primary here.[174] "For the Holy Spirit, who is the Love of the Father and the Son, to be given to us, is for us to be brought to a participation of the love who is the Holy Spirit, by which participation we are made lovers of God."[175] When the Holy Spirit is sent to us in this way, we are assimilated to the Holy Spirit's procession by way of love as we love God and neighbor. "Because the Holy Spirit is Love, when someone is made a lover of God and neighbor,

---

[170] *STh* III, q. 3, a. 8 ad 3.   [171] *STh* I, qq. 36–8; see especially q. 38, a. 2.

[172] Emery, *Trinitarian Theology*, 251.   [173] See, e.g., *STh* I, q. 38, a. 1.

[174] See I *Sent.* d. 14, q. 2, a. 1, qla 2, discussed in CHAPTER 2, SECTION A.

[175] *In Epist. ad Rom.* c. 5, lect. 1 (no. 392).

the Holy Spirit is given to him."[176] It is precisely in giving man this supernatural charity that the Holy Spirit forgives sins,[177] unites man to Christ, and makes him an adopted son of God.[178]

The final sentence of Aquinas's reply connects this truth about the Holy Spirit's invisible mission in grace to the visible mission of the Son in the incarnation. "Hence, it was more fitting for man's justification that the Son would become incarnate, of whom the Holy Spirit is the Gift." Here, Aquinas is briefly rearticulating in the *Tertia pars* his teaching on the necessary interconnection and order of the divine missions of the Son and the Holy Spirit from question 43 of the *Prima pars* (which we discussed in detail in CHAPTER 2, SECTION B). As Aquinas explained there,

> it belongs to the Holy Spirit, insofar as he proceeds as Love, to be the Gift of sanctification, but to the Son, as a principle of the Holy Spirit, it belongs to be the Author of this sanctification. And hence the Son was visibly sent as the Author of sanctification, while the Holy Spirit [was visibly sent, e.g., as a dove at Christ's baptism] as the sign of sanctification.[179]

This seemingly simple statement expresses a complex theological insight. First, as we have already observed, the Holy Spirit himself is the Gift of sanctification in person. "The Holy Spirit is not the Giver but rather is the Gift itself."[180] (It is foreign to Aquinas's thought to approach sanctification as some "thing" separate from the Spirit's presence. Rather, it is a way of speaking about the Spirit's invisible mission itself, which consists in the Spirit's personal procession with the addition of a created effect in man's soul, according to which the Spirit is said to be sent. "Human beings are sanctified through the donation of the Holy Spirit."[181]) Second, because the Son is a principle of the Holy Spirit, the Son is likewise *necessarily* a principle of the Spirit's mission, whether invisible (i.e., in grace) or visible (at Christ's baptism, his transfiguration, or at Pentecost). The Son is thus

---

[176] *In Epist. ad Ephes.* c. 1, lect. 5 (no. 41).
[177] See, e.g., *STh* III, q. 79, a. 5; *In Epist. ad Titum*, c. 3, lect. 1 (nos. 94–5). This gift of charity is inseparable from the gift of faith, which it "informs" and vivifies. Both are given in sanctifying grace. Thus, Aquinas explains that we are justified by faith insofar as that faith is formed by charity. *In Epist. ad Rom.* c. 3, lect. 3 (no. 302); c. 15, lect. 1 (no. 1162).
[178] *In Epist. ad Ephes.* c. 1, lect. 5 (no. 42).
[179] *STh* I, q. 43, a. 7.   [180] Emery, '*Theologia* and *Dispensatio*,' 530.
[181] *In Epist. ad Rom.* c. 1, lect. 3 (no. 58).

the "Author of sanctification," the source (with the Father) of the Gift by which human beings are saved and sanctified.

This title, *Auctor sanctificationis*, itself derived from Scripture,[182] is therefore something proper to the Son even before we consider how, by his actions and his sufferings, Jesus Christ merited our salvation or sent the Holy Spirit in time. That is, for Aquinas, this title refers principally to the order of the divine missions themselves as derived from the relations of the divine persons in the heart of the eternal Trinity. The Son's visible mission extends his eternal procession from the Father into time, making the Son present and revealing him as from the Father, and, in addition, revealing his *auctoritas* with respect to the Holy Spirit. Since the Son is an eternal principle (with the Father) of the Holy Spirit's procession, the Son's visible mission also reveals this dimension of the Son's divine identity and makes it present in the world in a new way. The Son is sent as the Holy Spirit's eternal principle in the flesh, or, as Thomas puts it here, as the Author of the Gift of sanctification.[183] By the very fact that the Son's visible mission is founded in his eternal procession from the Father, it is also ordered to the sending of the Holy Spirit, who proceeds from the Father and the Son.

This is why St Thomas uses the title "Author of sanctification" (and the idea behind it, that the Son is a principle of the Holy Spirit) to explain the fittingness that it be the Son who becomes incarnate, since

---

[182] Heb. 2:10 identifies Christ as the *"auctorem salutis,"* while Rom. 1:4 calls the Holy Spirit the *"Spiritus sanctificationis"* in whom Christ was predestined as Son of God. Cf. *In Epist. ad Rom.* c. 1, lect. 3 (no. 58).

[183] St Thomas also refers to Christ as the "Author of salvation," *auctor salutis*, a title drawn directly from Heb. 2:10. These two titles, *auctor sanctificationis* and *auctor salutis*, refer to the same reality—that the Son is a principle of the invisible mission of the Holy Spirit in grace—but Thomas seems to employ them somewhat differently in speaking about different aspects of that truth. In general (though not exclusively), Aquinas uses *auctor sanctificationis* to refer to the Son as the principle of the Holy Spirit's mission insofar as the Holy Spirit eternally proceeds from the Son. In other words, it looks at the missions vis-à-vis what is proper to the Son as a divine person. In contrast, Aquinas principally uses *auctor salutis* to speak more widely about how Christ, even as man—that is, in virtue of his full reception of the Spirit and in virtue of his merits, his actions, his passion, etc.—gives the Holy Spirit. "According to his human nature, Christ . . . is the author of human salvation [*auctor humane salutis*]." *Compendium theologiae* I, c. 213. Consequently, this latter term also includes all of the things that Christ did and suffered in his human nature that are the foundation and cause of the sending of the Holy Spirit. See, e.g., *STh* III, q. 59, a. 2 ad 2; *In Epist. ad Hebr.* c. 2, lect. 3 (no. 128); cf. *De Verit.*, q. 27, a. 4; *In Epist. ad Rom.* c. 1, lect. 3 (no. 58).

it expresses the fundamental and necessary order between the divine missions. Because human beings are rational creatures, it is connatural to them that they be led to grasp the invisible things of God (namely, the divine processions themselves) through what is visible (in this case, Christ's coming in the flesh and his giving of the Holy Spirit).[184] Thus, Aquinas reasons, in order that:

> the person of the Son be declared [to us] as the Author of sanctification, . . . it was right [*oportuit*] that the visible mission of the Son be made according to a rational nature, to which it belongs to act, and which is capable of sanctifying.[185]

Thomas thus does not propose an absolute necessity that the Son become incarnate, but a kind of conditional necessity.

In general, St Thomas's use of the terms "necessity" and "fittingness" (*convenientia*) is complex, nuanced, and often overlapping. Without entering into all the details here, necessity generally designates something that cannot be otherwise, while fittingness in a broad sense bespeaks the coherence of a wise order.[186] The latter term is therefore especially important for theological arguments like this one, where a strict syllogism concluding to a logically necessary truth may not be possible. The incarnation of the Son was not necessary in the strictest sense, yet Aquinas does think that there is a kind of necessity here:[187] it was necessary given that God wanted to reveal himself and to save the world by the Son as Author of sanctification (i.e., as a principle of the Holy Spirit), and given that God wanted to do so through man's active cooperation (i.e., Christ's human act working with his divine

---

[184] See Chapter 2, section B.   [185] *STh* I, q. 43, a. 7 ad 4.

[186] For a more detailed treatment of these questions, see Dominic Legge, "Fittingness and Necessity in the Manifestation of the Trinity According to St Thomas Aquinas" (Licentiate Thesis, Pontifical Faculty of the Immaculate Conception, Washington, D.C., 2008). See also Gilbert Narcisse, *Les raisons de Dieu: Argument de convenance et esthétique théologique selon saint Thomas d'Aquin et Hans Urs von Balthasar* (Fribourg: Éditions Universitaires, 1997); Corey L. Barnes, "Necessary, Fitting, or Possible: The Shape of Scholastic Christology," *Nova et Vetera*, English ed. 10 (2012): 657–88.

[187] In general, even though, on the most fundamental level, everything created is in some sense contingent, one can discern within that created order some things that are necessary within that order (e.g., that a thing be what it is), many things that have a combination of fittingness and necessity (including things that are conditionally necessary, e.g., in view of a certain end—"if you want to visit the tomb of St Peter, it is necessary to go to Rome"), as well as many things that are fitting in view of the *ordo* as a whole (e.g., that St Paul receive certain gratuitous graces).

act). In order to use a created reality to demonstrate that sanctification comes through the action of the Son who gives the Spirit to us, it was necessary that the Son join a visible creaturely nature to himself capable of positing free acts and sanctifying others—that is, that the Son become man. This conditional necessity is precisely what Aquinas expresses in different terms in the final sentence of *STh* III, q. 3, a. 8 ad 3: it was "most fitting" for the Son to become incarnate so that, in his human nature and by his *acta et passa*, he would accomplish the world's salvation by the forgiveness of sins, giving to the world the Gift of sanctification (i.e., the Holy Spirit in person).

* * *

Our examination of the first principal facet of St Thomas's Trinitarian Christology—why it was the Word who became flesh—has brought to light some of the most important themes of his theology as a whole, grouped under four different names or designations of the second person of the Trinity (*Word*, *Son*, *Image*, and *Auctor sanctificationis*). We now turn to another important aspect of St Thomas's Trinitarian Christology, one that also centers on Christ's identity as the divine Son made man: Aquinas's account of the hypostatic union, and, specifically, how that union terminates in the person of the Son precisely as *from the Father*.

4

The Hypostatic Union and the Trinity

St Thomas's theology of the union of Christ's two natures is a central building block of his Christology, a theological achievement of paramount importance. Many commentators rightly focus their attention on Question 2 of the *Tertia pars*, where Aquinas investigates "the mode of the incarnate Word's union . . . with respect to the union itself,"[1] namely, that the union is in the person or "hypostatis" of the Word (hence the term "hypostatic union"). They see Question 2 as providing the speculative key to Aquinas's affirmation, in continuity with the Church Fathers and the great Christological councils, that Christ is truly God and man, without any mixing or confusion of natures, and without endangering divine immutability and impassibility.[2] This is a vast and important subject in Christology to which the present work cannot do justice. Instead, we have a more modest (but more specific) purpose: to bring to light the Trinitarian dimensions of Thomas's theology of the hypostatic union. For this, we will focus on Question 3 of the *Tertia pars*,[3] where Thomas considers "the union on the part of the person assuming."

---

[1] *STh* III, q. 2, prol.

[2] See, e.g., Michael Gorman, "Christ as Composite according to Aquinas," *Traditio* 55 (2000): 143–57.

[3] Though space does not permit us to tarry in Question 2, we should at least note that, contrary to what is often presumed, St Thomas does *not* bill Question 2 as an abstract inquiry into the mode of the union between God and man, or between the divine nature and the human, as if bracketing Christ's identity as the Son of the Father. Rather, Thomas says that he is investigating the union of *the Incarnate Word*, and references to "Son" and "Word" abound throughout. Further, Thomas's starting point is clearly the revelation that, in Christ, the Word became flesh; his principal objective is to plumb the intelligibility of that truth. His carefully refined use of the concepts of person, nature, union, and assumption in Question 2 is not an exercise in speculative philosophy for its own sake; rather, he is placing all of the resources of his

A. THE TERMINUS OF THE ASSUMPTION

Aquinas begins Question 3 with a key distinction for his Trinitarian appreciation of the mystery of Christ between the *principle* of the assumption of a human nature and its *terminus*. (In fact, this distinction is already present and operative in Question 2, though not yet placed at the center of St Thomas's analysis.)[4]

> Assumption implies two things, namely, the act of assuming and the terminus of the assumption. The act of assuming proceeds from the divine power, which is common to the three persons, but the terminus of the assumption is a person.... And therefore that which concerns the action in the assumption [of a human nature] is common to the three persons, but that which pertains to the *ratio* of a terminus belongs to one person and not the others. For the three persons act so that a human nature would be united to the one person of the Son.[5]

Thomas distinguishes *that by which* the incarnation is effected—the divine power possessed and exercised commonly by all three persons, by which they act[6] (he is speaking here in the register of efficient causality)—from the *terminus* of the assumption, which is the Son alone. This distinction is of capital importance both for Christology and for Trinitarian theology. It permits us to say, on the one hand, that Christ is the incarnate Son and that he is the Son *only*—i.e., Christ is neither the Father nor the Holy Spirit, and his actions are those of the Son—while, on the other hand, we can affirm the Trinitarian truth that the person of the Son is never separated from the Father and Holy Spirit, nor acts apart from them.

The first half of this distinction is a well-known feature of St Thomas's theology: the whole Trinity, by virtue of the one nature and one power of all three divine persons, is a *principle* of the Son's assumption of a human nature. On this point, Aquinas stands in a long tradition drawing on Scripture, conciliar decrees, and the Church

---

thought at the service of the understanding of this central Christian, and Trinitarian, mystery.

[4] See, e.g., *STh* III, q. 2, aa. 7 and 8.   [5] *STh* III, q. 3, a. 4.

[6] The sequence of Aquinas's account of God's action is nature–power–operation–effect. The mention of *virtus* (cf. the Greek term *dunamis*), that is, the perfection of power, echoes an important theme of Pro-Nicene Church Fathers. Cf. Michel René Barnes, *The Power of God: Δύναμις in Gregory of Nyssa's Trinitarian Theology* (Washington, D.C.: Catholic University of America Press, 2001), 220–307.

Fathers.[7] In fact, this is a concrete instance of the general principle we discussed in CHAPTER 2 that the divine persons act inseparably in all actions *ad extra*.

As for the other half of the distinction—that the assumption has a divine person as its *terminus*—this receives relatively little attention from contemporary commentators.[8] Yet, when we pay closer attention to it, it yields important insights for understanding Aquinas's Trinitarian Christology. What exactly does it mean, then, to say that the Son, and only the Son, is the terminus of this assumption of a human nature?

St Thomas offers his most complete explanation in his *Sentences* Commentary.[9] To summarize what we covered in CHAPTER 1, a divine mission implies an eternal procession from another and a temporal effect in which that eternal procession is disclosed and made present. And a mission's temporal effect has a relation to God both as a principle and as a terminus. This means that a mission's created effect is efficiently caused by all three divine persons, since the *principle* of the divine action that causes it is the divine nature that all three possess in common. But, in a divine mission, that effect is also related to one particular divine person in his personal property, *as a terminus*, so that the divine person who is sent in that effect is truly made present.[10]

Another way to put this is that, if a creature has a distinct relation to a divine person, it is a relation 'by which the creature is drawn into' that divine person 'as a terminus.'[11] In other words, the relation is a vector into the person, terminating in the divine person himself. To return to a text we analyzed in part in CHAPTER 1, Aquinas teaches that there are two possible kinds of such relations to a divine person relevant here:

> [One possible mode is] according to exemplar causality, as [for example]...in the infusion of charity where there is a termination in a likeness to the personal procession of the Holy Spirit.[12]

---

[7] See Ocáriz, Mateo Seco and Riestra, *The Mystery of Jesus Christ*, 77–8 (citing Heb. 10:5, Gal. 4:4, Phil 2:7, Luke 1:35, and Matt. 1:20, as well as St Augustine, the Eleventh Council of Toledo, and the Fourth Lateran Council).

[8] When contemporary commentators do mention it, it is typically to criticize Aquinas for saying (in article 5) that each of the three divine persons could serve as the terminus of such a union. We will discuss this in detail in SECTION D of this chapter.

[9] See, e.g., I *Sent.* d. 14. q. 2, a. 1, qla 1; d. 15, q. 1, a. 1 and a. 2; d. 30, q. 1, a. 2 and ad 3. The same distinction is operative in *STh* I, q. 43. See, e.g., *STh* I, q. 43, a. 2; q. 43, a. 6 ad 4; q. 43 a. 8. See also CHAPTER 1, pp. 21–2.

[10] For a detailed explanation of the foregoing, see CHAPTER 1, pp. 17–22.

[11] I *Sent.* d. 30, q. 1, a. 2.   [12] *Ibid.*

Thomas means that the gift of charity "joins" and "refers" the soul to the Holy Spirit, "assimilating" the soul to the personal procession of the Holy Spirit as its exemplar.[13] Charity thus generates a distinct relation to the Holy Spirit's personal procession, which "terminates" in the person the Holy Spirit himself. As CHAPTER 2 showed, this is how Aquinas speaks about the proper presence of both the Son and the Holy Spirit in the faithful in their respective invisible missions according to faith and charity.

There remains, however, another way—which we passed over in our earlier analysis—by which a creature can be drawn into a divine person as a terminus, the singular case of the Son's incarnation:

> Or there is a termination according to being [*esse*], and this mode belongs uniquely to the incarnation, through which the human nature is assumed into the being [*esse*] and unity of the divine person.[14]

Christ *is* the Son because his human nature is assumed, according to being, into a union that terminates in the person of the Son alone. The Trinity "assumes [a human nature] to a union to the person of the Son, and . . . the effect that follows . . . is that it is taken up into the personal unity of the Son."[15] St Thomas does not speak of the Son's presence in Christ's humanity in the first way (according to an assimilation of his soul to the Son's procession),[16] underlining instead the surpassingly greater union according to *subsistence* and *being*: Jesus *is* the Son in his very being. This is the greatest possible mode by which a creature (namely, Christ's human nature) can be related to a single divine person, as a terminus according to the Son's "personal *esse*."[17]

B. THE "PERSONAL *ESSE*" OF THE SON

This is an important advance in our grasp of how St Thomas understands Christ's human nature to belong uniquely to the Son: that

---

[13] I *Sent.* d. 14, q. 2, a. 1 qla 1.   [14] I *Sent.* d. 30, q. 1, a. 2.

[15] *In Epist. ad Hebr.* c. 1, lect. 3 (no. 52).

[16] Thomas certainly does speak of Christ's human soul receiving human knowledge of God's mystery by way of grace (discussed in CHAPTER 6). See, e.g., *STh* III, q. 7, a. 1 ad 2.

[17] *STh* III, q. 17, a. 2: "esse personale." See also I *Sent.* d. 16, q. 1, a. 3 ad 4; a. 4 ad 3; d. 17, q. 1., a. 1.

humanity has a relation to the Son "according to *esse.*" What is this "personal *esse*" in which Christ's human nature terminates? Aquinas explains that the Latin term "*esse,*" when used in this context, refers to an "act of being" or "act of existing." While it is often acceptable to translate this into English simply as "being," it is worth remembering that Thomas does not mean to designate a thing called "being," or something added to a nature, but rather an *act.*[18] "[W]hat has *esse* is made actually existing. Whence it is clear that what I call *esse* is the actuality of all acts and for this reason is the perfection of all perfections."[19]

Since our primary concern is to grasp how the incarnation's "terminus according to *esse*" is the divine person of the Word, and only the Word, we need not enter into the thorny question of whether and to what extent Aquinas conceives of Christ's humanity as having a "secondary" *esse* or act of being, and how precisely this is related to the divine *esse* (or simply is that *esse* as subsisting in a human nature). This is the subject of a long-standing and wide-ranging debate among students of Aquinas; it is indeed important for Christology, but, formulated in this way, is principally a question about the metaphysical status of Christ's human nature.

Instead, we would simply underline the point that is indisputably central to Aquinas's doctrine and that he everywhere emphasized: there is only one person and one supposit in Christ.[20]

> Although [Christ's] human nature is a certain individual in the genus of substance, nonetheless, because it does not exist separately through itself, but rather in something more perfect, namely, in the person of

---

[18] See, e.g., *De Pot.*, q. 7, a. 2 ad 9. On the meaning of *esse* in general according to Thomas Aquinas, see John F. Wippel, *The Metaphysical Thought of Thomas Aquinas: From Finite Being to Uncreated Being* (Washington, D.C.: Catholic University of America Press, 2000), 175.

[19] *De Pot.*, q. 7, a. 2 ad 9. See also *Quodlibet* IX, q. 2, a. 2.

[20] Aquinas's principal concern was to underline that Christ has only one substantial *esse*, just as Christ is one suppositum and one hypostasis, and to insist that Christ's humanity is not joined to his divinity as an accident, with an accidental being. Aquinas does not explain in any great detail precisely how he understands the existence of Christ's humanity—which has therefore given rise to a variety of interpretations by Thomas's followers. See Michael Gorman, "Questions Concerning the Existences of Christ," in *Philosophy and Theology in the Long Middle Ages: A Tribute to Stephen F. Brown*, eds Kent Emery, Jr., Russell L. Friedman, and Andreas Speer (Leiden: Brill, 2011), 709–35.

the Word of God, it follows that it would not have its own personhood. And thus the union was made in the person.[21]

Aquinas roots this core Chalcedonian truth in Christ's *being*:[22] there is only one person in Christ because, as he says here, Christ's human nature "does not exist separately through itself" but "in" the Word. Thus, however he might speak about some "secondary" human existence in Christ—in one text, the *De unione Verbi incarnati*, Aquinas does speak in this way, though exactly what he means remains disputed[23]—Aquinas is always clear (including in the *De unione*) that Christ's humanity exists neither "through itself," nor as an accident, but rather as united to something infinitely higher than a human person, the Word himself. Consequently, he affirms that Christ has only one "principal *esse* of his supposit,"[24] which is the "personal *esse*" of the Word.[25]

> Since the human nature is joined to the Son of God hypostatically or personally, and not accidentally, . . . it follows that no new personal *esse* comes to him according to his human nature, but only a new relation of the pre-existing personal *esse* to the human nature, such that that person would now be said to subsist not only according to [his] divine nature, but also according to [his] human nature.[26]

This, then, is what Aquinas means when he says that the assumption of a human nature "terminates" in the Word. From the first instant of Christ's human life, Christ's humanity has a "relation" to the divine

---

[21]   *STh* III, q. 2, a. 2 ad 3.

[22]   Ultimately, this is because "one" is founded upon "being." III *Sent.* d. 6, q. 2, a. 2.

[23]   Victor Salas contends that, with this expression, Aquinas is simply designating the personal *esse* of the Son as subsisting in a human nature, according to a "mixed relation" between that human nature and the terminus of the personal *esse* of the Son, and therefore that the *De unione* presents the same doctrine as that of *STh* III, q. 17, a. 2, as viewed from a different angle. Victor Salas, Jr, "Thomas Aquinas on Christ's *Esse*: A Metaphysics of the Incarnation," *The Thomist* 70 (2006): 595–600. See also Gorman, "Christ as Composite," 152. Others understand *esse secundarium* as an analogical term. See John Froula, "*Esse Secundarium*: An Analogical Term Meaning That by Which Christ Is Human," *The Thomist* 78 (2014): 557–80.

[24]   *De unione Verbi incarnati*, a. 4: "esse principale sui suppositi."

[25]   *STh* III, q. 17, a. 2: "esse personale." Cf. *Quodlibet* IX, q. 2, a. 2: "in Christo est unum esse substanciale, secundum quod esse proprie est suppositi." It is central to Aquinas's thought that the union is not accidental. See Thomas Joseph White, *The Incarnate Lord: A Thomistic Study in Christology* (Washington, D.C.: Catholic University of America Press, 2015), 78–91.

[26]   *STh* III, q. 17, a. 2.

Word himself, according to the Word's "pre-existing personal *esse*," a relation so profound and exalted that there is no merely human personhood in Christ, nor a human hypostasis or supposit, but only the personhood of the Word.[27]

Note that Aquinas speaks specifically of the Son's "personal *esse*." St Thomas refers to this elsewhere as the Word's "substantial *esse*," or the "proper *esse* of the supposit" who is the Son.[28] But what does this mean when we are speaking about a divine person? Is not the divine being identical to the divine essence, and absolutely one? Thomas himself affirms as much: "the divine persons have one *esse*."[29] In what sense, then, can Thomas also speak about there being also a "personal *esse*" of the Son—an expression that Aquinas uses again and again in the *Tertia pars*,[30] and which is the key to his claim that only the Son is incarnate? This is a question of capital importance not only for Christology, but also for Trinitarian theology.

Gilles Emery carefully outlines Aquinas's explanation. While "the being of the three persons is identical, their mode of being is distinct."[31] Thomas writes:

> Although the Father, Son, and Holy Spirit have the same nature, [that nature] does not have the same mode of existing [*modum existendi*] in the three, and I say "mode of existing" according to relation. For it is in the Father as not received from another, while in the Son it is as received from the Father.[32]

Emery notes that St Thomas is here making his own the Cappadocian Trinitarian doctrine formulated by Basil of Caesarea as it was passed on to the medieval West through John Damascene. "Each person exists in a distinct manner according to a relation. For Thomas, this means that the personal property designates the relational mode of being proper to each person."[33] This is founded on the order of the divine processions, so that, in speaking about a proper "mode of existing" for each person, Thomas is expressing the distinct

---

[27] Cf. *Quodlibet* IX, q. 2, a. 2.   [28] See citations in nn. 24–5.

[29] *STh* I, q. 30, a. 4 ad 3.

[30] St Thomas's account of the hypostatic union is peppered with this expression. See, e.g., *STh* III, q. 2, aa. 10–11; q. 4, a. 1 ad 2; q. 6, a. 6. and ad 1; q. 8, a. 5 ad 3; q. 9, a. 1 ad 3; q. 10, a. 1 ad 2; q. 17, a. 2.; q. 19, a. 1 ad 4; q. 21, a. 2 ad 3.

[31] Emery, "Personal Mode," 54.

[32] *De Pot.*, q. 3, a. 15, ad 17, as cited by Emery, "Personal Mode," 55.

[33] Emery, "Personal Mode," 55.

relational way in which the divinity exists according to those eternal processions.

> Although the complete and perfect Godhead is in each of the three persons according to a proper mode of existing, nonetheless it pertains to the perfection of the Godhead that there would be several modes of existing in God, namely, that there be one from whom another proceeds yet proceeds from no other, and one proceeding from another. For there would not be a complete perfection in the Godhead unless there were a procession of the Word and of Love.[34]

While there is only one divine nature or essence, the Father "is" that divine nature as the one from whom the Son and Holy Spirit proceed. The Son "is" that same divinity as received from the Father; so also the Holy Spirit, who is from the Father and Son.

At the beginning of his treatment of "what pertains to the Trinity of persons," in the *Summa Theologiae*, we find Aquinas clarifying precisely this critical point in slightly different terms:

> What is begotten in the divinity receives *esse* from the one begetting . . . insofar as he has the divine *esse* proceeding from another, not as if different from the existing divine *esse*. For in the very perfection of the divine *esse* is contained both the Word proceeding by intellect, and the principle of the Word.[35]

The Word receives the divine *esse* itself without limitation. His *esse* is simply the divine *esse* as received from the Father. For Aquinas, this is another way to speak about relations of origin:

> The Son has from eternity what he receives from the Father, and the Holy Spirit [has from eternity] what he receives from the Father and the Son. . . . Thus, "to receive" in God designates an order of origin.[36]

We are here at the heart of Thomas's speculative Trinitarian theology. The divine persons are distinguished because they are subsistent relations, relations that do not divide but that subsist in the one divine nature, relations that are founded on the order of processions in God: the Son is *from* the Father, and the Holy Spirit is *from* the Father and the Son. There is absolutely no distinction in the one God except with respect to these relations of origin, which imply this relational "mode of existing" of the divinity according to the order of

[34] *De Pot.*, q. 9, a. 5, ad 23.   [35] *STh* I, q. 27, a. 2 ad 3.
[36] *In Ioan.* c. 16, lect. 4 (no. 2107).

the processions. As Emery puts it, "the individualizing element resides in the relations of origin, such that the divine person is the
personal relation itself insofar as this relation takes on the mode of
existing of the individual substance."[37] In short, the persons are
"three subsistences,"[38] subsistent relations in the one divine nature.

Thus, when, in the *Tertia pars*, Aquinas uses the expression "personal *esse*" to refer to the terminus of the assumption of Christ's
human nature, Aquinas is signifying the divine being itself, but
according to the unique personal mode in which the Son subsists, a
mode that is purely relational: the Son *is* the infinite and perfect
divine *esse as received* from the Father, because the Son proceeds
from the Father as his Word, by way of intellect. The Son "has being
[*esse*] from the Father... from whom he also has his nature, because
he is God from God."[39] Only the Son subsists according to this
unique mode, but because it is relational, this mode cannot even be
conceived apart from the other divine persons, nor could it ever be
separated from them.

C. THE YIELD FOR A TRINITARIAN CHRISTOLOGY: CHRIST'S FILIAL MODE OF BEING AND ACTING

This speculative investigation of how the person of the Son is the
terminus of the incarnation offers a rich yield for a Trinitarian
Christology. It means that Christ's human nature is not only "related
to" the divinity or the divine *esse*, but specifically to the personal *esse*
of the Son, so that, in the deepest metaphysical sense, that human
nature is always marked by the filial mode of existing proper to
the divine Son who subsists in that human nature.[40] By speaking of

[37] Gilles Emery, "La Trinité, le Christ et l'homme: Théologie et métaphysique de la
personne," in *L'humain et la personne*, eds François-Xavier Putallaz and Bernard
N. Schumacher (Paris: Les Éditions du Cerf, 2008), 190.
[38] *STh* I, q. 29, a. 2 ad 2: "tres subsistentiae." "Subsistence" means the substance as
existing through itself (*per se existit*). Ibid., co.
[39] *In Ioan.* c. 5, lect. 3 (no. 749). Aquinas affirms this repeatedly: see, e.g., *In Ioan.*
c. 5, lect. 3 (no. 754); lect. 4 (no. 768); lect. 5 (no. 797); c. 14, lect. 8 (no. 1971).
[40] As Aquinas explains in the technical language of subsistence: "The Word of God
does not have subsistence from the human nature, but rather draws the human nature
to his own subsistence or personhood, for he does not subsist through it, but in
it.... He subsists through [*per*] the divine nature and not through [*per*] the human

this "filial mode," we mean that he—namely, the divine Son and consequently, Jesus Christ, the incarnate Son—is entirely relative to the Father, as receiving everything from the Father, including his personal being or personal *esse* itself. Two important Christological consequences for Christ's humanity flow immediately from this.

Christ's Humanity Bears the Son's Personal Property

First, because of this filial mode of existing that characterizes his person, Christ's humanity bears the Son's personal property. This is simply to restate Aquinas's central claim that the incarnation is the visible mission of the Son, such that Christ's humanity as united to the Son is the created effect in which the Son's visible mission is made. It thus "relates to" and "terminates in" the very eternal procession the Son according to being—the Son *has* and *is* the divine *esse* and the divine nature subsisting *as proceeding from the Father*—which is made present in a new way and is manifested in the world through that humanity. Though the whole Trinity is the efficient cause of this created effect (the whole Trinity unites a human nature to the Son, the whole Trinity causes the conception of Christ's human body),[41] Christ's human nature has, at its ultimate metaphysical foundation, an existence according to the filial mode of the Son.

This filial mode characterizes "every part of [Christ's] human nature," Aquinas reasons, because "a union in person is according to personal *esse*."[42] In other words, in virtue of the hypostatic union, Christ's humanity is the humanity of the divine Son to its deepest roots, according to its very being. Consequently, everything in that humanity takes on the filial mode of the Son. This is the case, for example, with Christ's human will. Aquinas explains that it is in perfect conformity with the divine will not because of anything coming from the human nature itself (not from anything "pertaining

---

nature; rather, he draws it to his subsistence so that he would subsist in it." *ScG* IV, c. 49. Levering underlines the importance of this subsistence language in Aquinas, concluding that, for Thomas, "Christ's status as a *subject* . . . is defined by the unique relation of the *Son* to the Father and to the Spirit. Even in his human nature, he embodies this relation, although he does so in a fully human way." Matthew Levering, *Christ's Fulfillment of Torah and Temple: Salvation according to Thomas Aquinas* (Notre Dame: University of Notre Dame Press, 2002), 36.

[41] *STh* III, q. 32, a. 1.   [42] *STh* III, q. 21, a. 2 ad 3.

to the nature ... considered absolutely"), but because his human nature, and thus his human will, is "in the divine hypostasis" of the Word, from which it acquires its "determined mode" of being moved in perfect harmony with what God wills.[43] It is even true of Christ's body, since the divine Son is sent visibly "through [his] flesh, ... namely, through a union not only in [his] soul, but also in [his] body."[44] "[T]he union not only includes his soul, but his body as well, and hence the body of Christ itself is the temple of God."[45]

To put this slightly differently, Aquinas says that as the eternal Son is eternally from the Father, so also the incarnate Son comes into the world in the mode of "being sent." "Through the incarnation, ... he came in the mode by which he was sent by the Father, from whom he was sent, insofar as he was made flesh."[46] The mode of "being sent," of course, is a reference to how the filial mode of the Son's eternal procession is made present in the world through the created effect of Christ's humanity. In other words, the same filial mode ("from the Father") characterizes the Son himself ("eternally begotten of the Father") *and the Son's visible mission* ("sent by the Father").

Consequently, Aquinas does not hesitate to say that whatever Christ has is from the Father:

> [H]is Father is the author [*auctorem*] from whom he both proceeds eternally in his divine nature, and from whom he has every good that he possesses in his human nature.[47]

Aquinas does not mean that the Father alone is the efficient cause of Christ's humanity, but that, like the Son in his divine nature, Christ in his human nature receives everything from the Father as from his personal principle. This is especially clear in St Thomas's Commentary on John's Gospel. For example, Aquinas paraphrases Christ's prayer (as man) to the Father—"everything that you have given me is from you"—thus:

> [W]hatever I have, I have from you; and these ones now know that "everything you have given me," namely, to your Son as man, "is from you;" "we saw his glory, the glory as of the only-begotten of the Father (John 1:14)," that is, we saw him as if having everything from the Father. And the Father is glorified by this, that they know this in their minds.[48]

---

[43] *STh* III, q. 18, a. 1 ad 4.   [44] I *Sent.* d. 16, q. 1, a. 1 ad 1.
[45] *In Ioan.* c. 2, lect. 3 (no. 399).   [46] *In Ioan.* c. 1, lect. 7 (no 165).
[47] *STh* III, q. 21, a. 3. See also a. 1 ad 1.   [48] *In Ioan.* c. 17, lect. 2 (no. 2199).

All that Christ has, *even as man*, is ultimately from the Father. "'The Father has put all things into his hands,' that is, in his power. God gave to Christ the man in time, what was in the Son's power from eternity."[49] This is precisely what Aquinas means when he describes the incarnation as the visible mission of the Son: the Son is sent into the world inasmuch as his personal property is made present ("as if having everything from the Father") and is disclosed ("these ones now know...") *in* and *through* Christ's human nature, which is drawn into the divine Son's filial relation to the Father.[50]

It is evident from this that Thomas's theology of the hypostatic union is about more than words. We do not only "say" that Christ is the Son, as if this were a kind of verbal rule. Rather, because Christ's humanity terminates in the Son's personal *esse*, the Son is really present and truly acts in the world in a new way—namely, in and through that humanity—with a personal presence that is proper to him and not to the other divine persons.

Christ Acts *from* the Father

There is a second important Christological consequence to Thomas's doctrine of Christ's personal *esse*: as Christ's very being itself is characterized by this filial mode, so also is his every word, gesture, and action—"*omnes passiones et actiones humanitatis Christi*."[51] When Jesus says, "I cannot do anything of myself," therefore, Thomas explains:

> his action, and his power, is his *esse*, but his *esse* is his from another, namely, from the Father; therefore, just as he does not exist from himself, so also he cannot do anything from himself: "From myself I can do nothing (John 8:28)."[52]

The mode of existing of the divine Word shapes his mode of acting—both are *from* the Father. "It is as if to say: 'I am equal to the Father, as I am from him...and whatever I have to do, is mine from the

[49] *In Ioan.* c. 13, lect. 1 (no. 1743). Aquinas makes the same point elsewhere, e.g., *In Ioan.* c. 17, lect. 1 (no. 2185).
[50] Cf. *In Ioan* c. 17, lect. 4 (no. 2246).
[51] *In Epist. ad Rom.* c. 4, lect. 3 (no. 380).
[52] *In Ioan.* c. 5, lect. 5 (no. 797). See also *In Ioan.* c. 5, lect. 3 (nos. 748–52).

Father.'"[53] "As the patterns of all things pass from the Father to the Son, who is the Father's Wisdom, so also the patterns of all things to be done. . . . by an eternal generation."[54]

Aquinas is explicit that this filial mode—that Christ receives all of his activity from the Father—applies as much to his human nature as to his divine nature:

> "It is necessary that I do the works of him who sent me." This can be referred to Christ as man, and then its sense is: "It is necessary that I do the works of him who sent me," that is, the works assigned to me by the Father, "the works which the Father has given me to do (John 6:36)." Later, he says: "Father, I have completed the work you gave me to do (John 17:4)." Or it can be referred to Christ as God, and then it would indicate his equality of power with the Father, so that the sense would be: "It is necessary that I do the works of him who sent me," that is, the works that I have from the Father. For everything that the Son does, even in his divine nature, he has from the Father: "The Son cannot do anything on his own, but only what he sees the Father doing (John 5:19)."[55]

Just as the Son receives everything that he does from the Father in the divine nature, so also the humanity of the Son receives everything—including all its actions—from the Father who sends him.

The Dominican master is always careful to maintain this strict correspondence between the Son's eternal procession and his visible mission. Indeed, this is central to the very definition of a divine mission that grounds his entire approach to Christology. When he speaks about Christ's human activity, therefore, Aquinas is simply following out its implications: Christ's humanity, including his activity, is intrinsically bound to his procession as Word ("from the Father"), insofar as his mission consists of what he is and what he does in this humanity. There is no merely nominal or "neutral" correspondence between Jesus's human words and the Son's eternal procession (as if the mystery of Christ's relation to the Father were "merely verbal").[56] Rather, that humanity's very personal being, and

---

[53] *In Ioan.* c. 5, lect. 3 (no. 747). This is a partial paraphrase of Augustine. Cf. *Catena Aurea in Ioan.* c. 5, lect. 3; Augustine, *Tract. In Ioh.* XX, 4 (CCL 36: 205). NB: The Marietti edition of the *Catena Aurea* misidentifies this quotation as coming from Tractate 18.

[54] *In Ioan.* c. 12, lect. 8 (no. 1723).

[55] *In Ioan.* c. 9, lect. 1 (no. 1304). Cf. *In Ioan.* c. 5, lect. 4 (no. 759).

[56] Rahner, *The Trinity*, 28.

consequently all its activity, belong to the Son precisely insofar as he is the Son—and so they are *from* the Father.

Christ's Human Actions Manifest and Lead to the Father

The corollary of this is that all of Christ's human actions (not only his words) *reveal* the Son as the Son, and therefore manifest the Father as his principle. St Thomas thus puts to work in his Christology the important Trinitarian truth discussed above in connection with the Word's eternal procession: "Everything that is from another manifests that from which it is—for the Son manifests the Father since he is from him."[57] Examples abound, especially in his Commentary on John, of Aquinas applying this not only to the Son as God, but also about Christ the Incarnate Word.

Consider, for example, Aquinas's explanation of how the Son glorifies the Father because the Father has given him "power over all flesh (John 17:1–2)."

> Every agent that acts from another, tends to lead from its effect to the manifestation of its cause: for by the action of a principle from a principle, the first principle is manifested. But whatever the Son has, he has from the Father, and hence it is necessary that, through what he does, he would manifest the Father, and hence he says "you have given him power".... According to Hilary, he says "you have given," by giving the divine nature through an eternal generation.... Or, "you have given to him," namely, to Christ the man, on account of the personal communion with your Son, so that he would thus have power over all flesh: "All power in heaven and on earth is given to me (Matt. 28: 18);" "He gave to him," namely, to the son of man, "power, honor, and kingship (Dan. 8:14)."[58]

Aquinas begins with the general principle that, in whatever he does, the Son manifests the Father because he is from the Father. This applies most obviously to the Son in his divine nature, as the citation to St Hilary indicates. But then Aquinas adds that this applies also to Christ as man, who acts according to the power he has received from the Father in virtue of the hypostatic union.

This is another way of speaking about Christ's theandric action, a subject to which we will return in CHAPTER 7. For now, it suffices to

---

[57] *In Ioan.* c. 16, lect. 4 (no. 2107).   [58] *In Ioan.* c. 17, lect. 1 (no. 2185).

note that Aquinas teaches that Christ's "human nature is, as it were, an instrument of the Word, not separated, but conjoined, . . . pertaining to his person" in virtue of the hypostatic union, so that it participates in the Word's own actions.[59] In other words, the Son's humanity is drawn into and participates in the Son's filial mode of action. The converse is also true: the Son acts *in* and *through* the properly human operations of his human nature (speaking, touching, suffering, and even dying), so that even these are from the Father and thus manifest the Father.

This has an extraordinary significance for Aquinas's Trinitarian Christology, and the hypostatic union is at its heart. That Christ's human nature is the instrument of the Word means, first, that every human action of Christ is an action of the divine Word in person—it belongs *properly* to him and *not* to the Father or the Holy Spirit.[60] It also means that everything that Christ does or suffers as man is not only salvific for us[61] in the sense that it has a kind of saving efficacy or causality, as important as this is, but also that Christ's every action is ordered to the end of the incarnation itself (which includes both sanctification and manifestation)—the restoration of man and of

---

[59] *ScG* IV, c. 41. Aquinas contrasts this union with that between a carpenter and his axe; though the axe participates in the carpenter's action, it remains distinct from the carpenter himself. Christ's humanity is more akin to a man's hand, which is the conjoined instrument of his soul. Yet even this analogy is insufficient, Aquinas explains, because Christ's human nature is united to the person of the Word "much more sublimely and intimately [*multo sublimius et intimius*]" than a soul to its own body. *ScG* IV, c. 41. Aquinas's deepest explanation of this most sublime and intimate union is that it is "according to personal *esse*." As such, Christ's humanity participates more closely in the Word's personal action than a body in the actions of its soul. *Ibid*; *STh* III, q. 13, a. 2; q. 19, a. 1. Cf. *In Ioan.* c. 11, lect. 5 (no. 1532).

[60] Students of St Thomas have not always understood Christ's human action in this way. For example, Kevin O'Shea argued that Christ's human activity belongs exclusively to the Word insofar as "we may appropriate *in a very special sense* to the Word the special divine efficient influence which moves the sacred humanity of Christ to act, and the immense divine charity which is its source." Kevin F. O'Shea, "The Human Activity of the Word," *The Thomist* 22 (1959): 230. O'Shea grounds this special appropriation in a unique formal influence of the Word on Christ's humanity by which that humanity is actuated, and through which the divine efficient causality passes. This argument suffers from a double difficulty: even if this is a "very special" appropriation, Christ's human actions remain appropriated to the Word; and it posits that Christ's humanity is formally modified by the hypostatic union itself. Both are theologically problematic, and neither can be accurately ascribed to St Thomas.

[61] See, e.g., *In Epist. ad Rom.* c. 4, lect. 3 (no. 380); *ScG* IV, c. 36; *STh* I–II, q. 112, a. 1 ad 1; III, q. 48, a. 6; *Compendium theologiae* I, c. 212.

118   *The Trinitarian Christology of St Thomas Aquinas*

the entire cosmos,[62] the revelation of the inner mystery of the Trinity,[63] and our being brought to the Father through him.[64] There is, therefore, always an element of revelation in Christ's actions, even when he is not preaching or speaking. Aquinas makes this point explicitly: "All the things that the Lord did or suffered in the flesh are saving teachings and examples."[65] In fact, he repeats with some frequency the axiom: "every action of Christ is our instruction."[66] Christ's actions are indeed examples for us to imitate, but, as Richard Schenk has shown in a careful study, Aquinas means more than this: Christ's actions teach us by revealing the truth about God.[67] (Indeed, Thomas himself described "those things that the incarnate Son of God did or suffered in [his] human nature"[68] as "the mysteries of the incarnate Word,"[69] a richly significant phrase.)[70] In short, everything that Christ does as man is a revelation, at least for those who have "eyes to see" and "ears to hear."

Christ's humanity reveals precisely because it is the created effect in which the Word is sent into the world, making the invisible visible. Take, for example, the concluding lines of a text we quoted in part in CHAPTER 3, where St Thomas says that the Word manifests the "secret things" of the Father:[71]

> Just as a man, wanting to reveal himself by the word of his heart that he proffers by his mouth, clothes that word, as it were, with letters or

---

[62] *STh* III, q. 13, a. 2; *Compendium theologiae* I, c. 213.

[63] *Compendium theologiae* I, c. 2; cf. I *Sent.*, prol.; *STh* II–II, q. 2, a. 8.

[64] *In Ioan.* c. 6, lect. 5 (no. 936); *ScG* IV, c. 8; *STh* III, q. 40, a. 1.

[65] *Puer Iesus.*   [66] *In Ioan.* c. 11, lect. 6 (no. 1555).

[67] Richard Schenk, O.P., "*Omnis Christi Actio Nostra est Instructio*: The Deeds and Sayings of Jesus as Revelation in the View of Thomas Aquinas," in *La doctrine de la révélation divine de saint Thomas d'Aquin*, Studi Tomistici, no. 37, ed. Leo Elders (Vatican City: Libreria Editrice Vaticana, 1990), 113–17. For a study of the significance of Christ's full humanity in Aquinas's thought, including its exemplarity, see Paul Gondreau, "The Humanity of Christ, the Incarnate Word," in *The Theology of Thomas Aquinas*, eds Rik Van Nieuwenhove and Joseph Wawrykow (Notre Dame: University of Notre Dame Press, 2005), 252–76.

[68] *STh* III, q. 27, prol.   [69] *STh* III, q. 60, prol.

[70] St Thomas intends this term to have a meaning that is quite broad: it includes "at the same time 'the divine plan of salvation' in the global sense it has in St Paul (e.g., Rom. 16:25; Eph. 3:3) and also the precise way in which this plan is accomplished in Jesus, by his whole life, by each of his actions, and by his preaching." Torrell, *Le Christ en ses mystères*, vol. 1, 22–3. Moreover, "[e]very event in the earthly life of Jesus is a 'mystery' in the sense that it signifies and realizes the entire 'mystery' of the love of God who reveals himself and acts in history." Torrell, *Le Christ en ses mystères*, vol. 1, 23.

[71] See CHAPTER 3, SECTION A, pp. 79–80.

sounds, so also God, wanting to manifest himself to men, clothes his Word, conceived from all eternity, with flesh in time. And thus no one can come to a knowledge of the Father except through the Son.[72]

A man, whom others know exteriorly (they see him, they observe his actions), reveals his "secret"—he discloses what is in his heart, giving a truly personal knowledge of himself—to his friends when he "clothes" his interior word in letters or sounds.[73] Likewise, the incarnate Word, clothed in the flesh of our nature and appearing in time, not only discloses things "about" God—human beings could already know something of God from God's "exterior" effects in creation—but manifests what is interior to the Trinity ("The Son of God came . . . publishing the name of the Trinity")[74] by manifesting himself and, consequently, the Father and the Holy Spirit as well. Moreover, Aquinas suggests that the humanity of Christ is related to the Word like a spoken word is related to the thought it expresses.[75] As vocal sounds bear within them the meaning of the interior word, which they reveal to others, so also the humanity of Christ is the manifestation in time of the Word himself, and thus of the Father who speaks him.[76]

Yet St Thomas goes further: Christ's humanity and his human actions not only reveal, but in revealing also lead us to the Father—which is another way of speaking about the incarnation as the visible mission of the Son. "[T]he effect of the mission of the Son was to lead [the faithful] to the Father."[77] "As man, Christ is the way; . . . he leads to the Father, as the way leads to its terminus or end."[78] Aquinas

---

[72] *In Ioan.* c. 14, lect. 2 (no. 1874). Cf. *ScG* IV, c. 46. Aquinas seems to have drawn this analogy from Augustine. See, e.g., *De Verit.* q. 4, a. 1 obj. 6; cf. Augustine, De Trinitate XV, c. 11 (CCL 50A:486–90); Sermo CXIX (PL 38:674–5).

[73] Cf. *In Ioan.* prol. (no. 11), where Aquinas explains that, because Christ had a special love for St John, he revealed his secrets to him in a special way, and above all, the truth of his divinity as the incarnate Word.

[74] I *Sent.*, prol.

[75] This is not a perfect analogy, says Aquinas: As a spoken word "manifests" an interior word, "so through flesh the eternal Word is manifested;" nonetheless, a spoken word is not perfectly identical to the word conceived in the heart, whereas "the incarnate Word is the same as the eternal Word, as also the word signified by a voice is the same as the word of the heart." *De Verit.* q. 4, a. 1 ad 6. See also ad 5, where Thomas distinguishes the way that the eternal Word "manifests" the Father to himself, from the way the incarnate Word manifests the Father "to all."

[76] See *In Symbolum Apost.* a. 3 (no. 897). See also *In Ioan* c. 5, lect. 4 (no. 773).

[77] *In Ioan.* c. 14, lect. 6 (no. 1958).

[78] *In Ioan.* c. 6, lect. 5 (no. 936). See also *In Ioan.* c. 6, lect. 5 (no. 648); c. 14, lect. 2 (nos. 1868–70).

underlines Jesus's words: "This is eternal life, that they would know you the only true God, and Jesus Christ, whom you have sent (John 17:3)," to which he adds, "that is, [he was sent] so that the Father would be glorified in the knowledge of men."[79] As the divine missions make present in a new way and reveal the Trinitarian processions, they are likewise the vectors of our return to the Triune God, with the Father as "the ultimate person to whom we return."[80] "Christ's humanity is the way for us to travel unto God."[81] Our access *to the Father* is built on the fact that Christ is *from the Father*, as both God and man: "When [St Paul] says [that we have access through him] 'to the Father,' he especially shows that whatever the Son has, he has from the Father."[82] As the incarnate Son, he "leads us to the vision of the Father."[83] This is our final end conceived in Trinitarian terms: "The vision of the Father is the end of all of our desires and all of our actions, such that nothing more is needed: 'You will fill me with the joy of your face (Ps. 15:11)," that is, in the vision of your face; 'He satisfies your desire with good things (Ps. 102:5).'"[84]

In light of this refined Trinitarian and Christological analysis, the Dominican *magister in sacra pagina* is ready to give full weight to Christ's affirmation that "he who sees me, sees the Father also (John 14:9)."

> It is as if he said . . . "I say truly that you have seen him". . . . For they saw Christ in his assumed flesh, in which was the Word, and in the Word, the Father—thus, in him, they saw the Father: "He who sent me, is with me (John 7:29)."[85]

The Word, and therefore the Father, is seen "in" Christ's very flesh. Aquinas also expresses this truth using St Paul's richly significant term, "mystery." "[T]he mystery [*mysterium*] of Christ's humanity . . . is the mystery [*sacramentum*] of godliness, as 1 Tim. 3 says.'"[86] "[T]he truth of this hidden mystery . . . [is] that God is the Father of Jesus Christ. Or that "the mystery of God the Father' is Christ."[87] Christ's

[79] *In Ioan.* c. 17, lect. 1 (no. 2186). See also *In Ioan.* c. 1, lect. 1 (no. 34).

[80] I *Sent.* d. 15, q. 4, a. 1. Cf. *In Ioan.* c. 16, lect. 7 (no. 2147) (Christ gives his disciples familiarity with and access to the Father, through knowledge and love).

[81] *In Ioan.* c. 7, lect. 4 (no. 1074). See also IV *Sent.* d. 15, q. 4, a. 5 qla 3 ad 1.

[82] *In Epist. ad Ephes.* c. 2, lect. 5 (no. 121).

[83] *In Ioan.* c. 15, lect. 3 (no. 2018).   [84] *In Ioan.* c. 14, lect. 3 (no. 1883).

[85] *In Ioan.* c. 14, lect. 2 (no. 1880).   [86] *STh* II–II, q. 1, a. 8.

[87] *In Epist. ad Col.* c. 2, lect. 2 (no. 80).

humanity, as hypostatically united to his divinity, is the "mystery" of the Son in the flesh and thus of the revelation of the Father. It is, as it were, a "sacrament,"[88] not only signifying or pointing to the Word, but making him present, causing our salvation, giving the Holy Spirit—all of which reveals the Father to us and gives us access to him through the Son and in the Spirit.

> [Through] the mystery of the humanity of Christ, . . . "we have access to the glory of the sons of God," as Romans 5 says. This is why John 17 reads: "This is eternal life, that they would know you, the true God, and Jesus Christ whom you have sent."[89]

The theological fulcrum for this is, of course, the fact that Christ's humanity terminates in the person of the Son himself, as Aquinas clarifies:

> But note that the Father was not in the flesh according to a unity of person, but was in the incarnate Word by a unity of nature—and it was in the incarnate Christ that the Father was seen: "We saw his glory, the glory as of the only-begotten of the Father (John 1:14)."[90]

The flesh of Christ is united only to the person of the Word; the Father did not become incarnate. But because of the unity of the divine nature and the mutual co-inherence of the divine persons (*perichoresis*), one who sees the humanity of Christ sees the person of the Son *in* his human nature, and thus the Father who is *in* the Son and consubstantial with him.[91]

Of course, while one who sees Christ's humanity truly sees the incarnate Son, it does not necessarily follow that he would *recognize* Christ as the Son and thus *know* the Father. St Thomas explains at length that, as long as the disciples only knew Christ as man, they did

---

[88] See, e.g., Edward Schillebeeckx, *Christ the Sacrament of the Encounter with God*, trans. Paul Barrett (London: Sheed & Ward, 1963), 13–17; Bernhard Blankenhorn, "The Instrumental Causality of the Sacraments: Thomas Aquinas and Louis-Marie Chauvet," *Nova et Vetera*, English ed. 4 (2006): 277–9.

[89] *STh* II–II, q. 1, a. 8.   [90] *In Ioan.* c. 14, lect. 2 (no. 1881).

[91] The doctrine of *perichoresis* also implies the mutual co-inherence of the Son and the Holy Spirit, so that one who sees the Son also "sees" the Holy Spirit. Christ does not reveal the Holy Spirit in the same way as he reveals the Father, however. The Father is Christ's principle, whom Christ reveals by virtue of his personal property, and to whom he leads us. As we will discuss later, the Holy Spirit is given to us by Christ who is a principle of the Holy Spirit, since the Spirit proceeds from the Father and the Son. Moreover, when Christ reveals the Father to us, Aquinas adds that he does this by giving us the Holy Spirit. *In Ioan.* c. 16, lect. 7 (no. 2152).

not know the Father; it is only when they recognized that he was truly the Word of God in the flesh that they not only "saw" but also "knew" him and the Father.

> "Philip, he who sees me, sees the Father also," as if to say: if you had known me, you would have known the Father; and thus you would not say "show us the Father," because having seen me, you would have then seen him: "If you knew me, you would know my Father also (John 8:19)."[92]

Thomas puts this in even stronger terms: God the Father is only known as Father when one grasps that he is:

> the Father of his only-begotten Son, Jesus Christ, and he was not at all known in this way [before the coming of Christ]; but he became known through the Son when the apostles believed [Christ] to be the Son of God.[93]

Here, we have pushed our analysis to its limit. Christ's actions are truly the actions of the Son; they are properly from the Father insofar as Christ's human nature participates in the filial mode of the Son's personal action. In themselves, when they are known for *what they truly are*, they reveal the Son and hence the Father.

> Christ willed to manifest the divinity through his humanity. And therefore, by living with men (which is proper to a human being), he manifested his divinity to everyone, by preaching, working miracles, and living innocently and justly among men.[94]

But though this was shown "to everyone" Christ met in the flesh, not everyone received it. That is, to know Christ's actions as they truly are is to know Christ as he truly is: as the Word made man, in person, according to being, sent by and entirely relative to the Father. This requires the gift of faith. Indeed, this is true even when Christ works the most striking of his miracles; without faith, the witnesses of such mighty works remain ignorant of who stands before them. But to account for this all-important gift requires us to speak in greater detail of the Holy Spirit and his relationship to Christ who is both God and man. This is the subject of PART III.

---

[92] *In Ioan.* c. 14, lect. 3 (no. 1886).   [93] *In Ioan.* c. 17, lect. 2 (no. 2195).
[94] *STh* III, q. 40, a. 1 ad 1.

D. COULD ANOTHER DIVINE PERSON
BECOME INCARNATE?

Let us conclude the present chapter by attempting to correct a widespread misunderstanding of St Thomas's approach to the incarnation. Many contemporary critics of Aquinas seize on his claim at *STh* III, q. 3, a. 5 that it would be possible not only for the Son to assume human flesh, but also for the Father or Holy Spirit to do so. They assume that this means that the shape of the salvation wrought by Christ is indifferent to his filial identity.[95] "Christ the God-man could just as easily have been the Father or the Holy Spirit," they think Aquinas is saying. "[T]here would be no difference in our experience if some other divine person constituted the subsistence of this human reality."[96] In other words, they suspect that Aquinas detaches Christ's concrete humanity from what is proper to the Word, rendering that humanity incapable of revealing his sonship and his relation to the Father, except insofar as Christ narrates this to us. The revelation of the Trinity would thus be "merely verbal," something that Christ says in words, but does not manifest through his very presence and action. According to one critic, it implies "that there is no necessary connection between what differentiates the Triune identities in God and the structure of God's work in time," which "bankrupts" the doctrine of the Trinity and detaches speculative theology from the biblical narrative.[97] This is all based on a misunderstanding of what Aquinas is saying and of why he proceeds as he does, and it causes a misperception of the whole tenor of his Christology.

---

[95] Karl Rahner is famous for having claimed that Aquinas's approach obscured the truth that the *Logos*, precisely as the *Logos* of the Father, "is *the one* who reveals to us (not merely *one* of those who might have revealed to us) the triune God, on account of the personal being which belongs exclusively to him." Rahner, *The Trinity*, 30. See also Karl Rahner, "Remarks on the Dogmatic Treatise 'De Trinitate,'" in *Theological Investigations*, vol. 4, trans. Kevin Smyth (Baltimore: Helicon Press, 1966), 77–102; Walter Kasper, *The God of Jesus Christ* (New York: Crossroad, 1984), 273–80; LaCugna, *God for Us*, 211; Jenson, *The Triune God*, 112–14. For a general account of this controversy (though unsatisfying, in our view—see n. 4), see Neri, *Cur verbum capax hominis*. More recently, Étienne Vetö sees this as part of the "paradoxical imbalance" and "unresolvable tensions" in St Thomas's Christology, with the result that, according to Vetö, Thomas's Trinitarian theology hardly marks his account of the *oikonomia*. Vetö, *Du Christ à la Trinité*, 120–2; 215–16.

[96] Rahner, *The Trinity*, 28.   [97] Jenson, *The Triune God*, 112.

Let us turn to the text of this much-maligned article itself. The opening stage of the body of St Thomas's response recalls the familiar distinction between the act of assuming and the terminus of the assumption:

> As was said, assumption implies two things, namely, the act itself of the one assuming and the terminus of the assumption. The principle of the act is the divine power, while the terminus is a person.[98]

To this point, Aquinas's analysis is uncontroversial. But in the second stage of his argument, Aquinas says that each divine person could serve as such a terminus; it is on this point that he is frequently misunderstood. If we examine the logic of his argument carefully, however, we can appreciate precisely what Aquinas is (and is not) saying. He continues:

> But the divine power commonly and indifferently regards [*se habet*] each of the persons. The same definition [*ratio*] of personhood is also common to the three persons, although their personal properties are different.[99]

This stage in the argument is purely Trinitarian, expressing a central truth about the Holy Trinity: the same notion of "personhood" belongs to each divine person. They are not persons in different ways, nor is there an analogical notion of personhood between the three; the notion of person is absolutely identical for the Father, the Son, and the Holy Spirit.[100] The only way to distinguish these persons is by their "personal properties," which themselves are based on the divine processions and are, in effect, simply another way of expressing the opposed relations of origin that constitute the persons.[101] Indeed, if the persons did not have the same *ratio* of personhood,

---

[98] *STh* III, q. 3, a. 5.   [99] *Ibid.*

[100] By contrast, the notion of personhood *is* analogical (rather than identical) between God and creatures (angels and men). *STh* I, q. 29, aa. 3–4.

[101] Two centuries after Aquinas, the Council of Florence expressed this truth thus: "These three persons are one God, not three Gods, because there is one substance of the three, one essence, one nature, one Godhead, one immensity, one eternity, and *everything is one where the opposition of a relation does not prevent this*." Council of Florence, in *Decrees of the Ecumenical Councils*, vol. 1, ed. Norman P. Tanner (Washington, D.C.: Georgetown University Press, 1990), 570–1, as modified and with emphasis added by Gilles Emery, *The Trinity: An Introduction to Catholic Doctrine on the Triune God*, trans. Matthew Levering (Washington, D.C.: Catholic University of America Press, 2011), 89.

there would be no basis for saying that there are three "persons" in God.

The third stage of Aquinas's argument then develops the way a power can regard different termini.

> Whenever a power regards [*se habet*] several indifferently, it can terminate its action in any of them, as is clear in rational powers that regard [*se habent*] opposites, both of which they are able to do.[102]

Throughout this article, Thomas uses the expression "*se habere*," a verb designating a relation, "to be situated,"[103] which we have translated as "to regard." Aquinas's example clarifies what he means by this. The human will, one of man's rational powers, "regards indifferently" opposing goods—e.g., the choice of reading the Bible or a detective novel—and can select either of them as the terminus of its action. It is related indifferently to—it is equally capable of selecting—either of its choices. That does not mean, of course, that the choice between them is arbitrary, that one action is as good as the other, or that the two would produce anything resembling the same result. Thomas only means that the power, considered in itself, is not determined to one or the other terminus.[104]

From here, Thomas arrives at his conclusion about the assumption of a human nature:

> Thus, therefore, the divine power could unite a human nature to the person of the Father or of the Holy Spirit, as it has united it to the person of the Son. And hence it must be said that the Father or the Holy Spirit could assume flesh, as also the Son.[105]

All the way through, Aquinas's argument is purely Trinitarian: it is about the relation of the divine power to the divine persons. If a human nature can be united to a divine person, then the divine power can unite it to any of the divine persons. Note that this argument *says nothing* about what would have to change on the created side in a world where the Father or the Holy Spirit became man; Aquinas leaves that question entirely out of account because this article is not exploring counter-factual hypotheticals (contrary to what is often

---

[102] *STh* III, q. 3, a. 5.

[103] Cf. Charlton T. Lewis and Charles Short, *A Latin Dictionary* (Oxford: Clarendon Press, 1955), s.v. "habeo."

[104] See, e.g., *STh* I, q. 82, a. 2 ad. 3.   [105] *STh* III, q. 3, a. 5.

supposed), but rather aims to clarify how the divine power, common to all three persons, is related to the one divine person who did in fact become incarnate.[106]

Perhaps even more important is the often-overlooked qualification that Aquinas adds in the second stage of his argument: "The same definition [*ratio*] of personhood is common to the three persons, *although their personal properties are different.*" Thomas's point is that the *ratio* of personhood (each divine person is a subsistent relation, a relation that *subsists* in the divine nature) is the decisive factor according to which a divine person serves as the terminus of the assumption of a human nature. As we have examined at length above, this terminus is "according to personal *esse*." Each of the divine persons *has* and *is* the divine *esse* in its complete perfection. But, as Thomas reminds us here, the personal mode according to which each person subsists is different for each divine person. This means that, while each divine person could equally be a terminus according to being, the personal mode that would characterize the resulting union would be different in each case. Consequently, according to the personal mode that characterizes its every aspect, *the incarnation of the Son would be vastly different from a hypothetical incarnation of the Father or the Holy Spirit.*

So Aquinas *is* saying that the incarnation of different persons would look—and be—very different indeed. Christ's humanity belongs uniquely to the Son because it terminates in the Son's personal *esse*. As we have shown above, this is also the foundation for the unique personal mode of Christ's action, in which Christ's humanity participates in the Son's own personal action. From the deepest roots of its metaphysical constitution to all its actions, gestures, words, and effects, Christ's humanity is marked by its relation to the Word according to his personal property.

Another way to put this is that, while there is nothing absolute on the side of God that requires an incarnation to terminate in the Son— it is within God's absolute power to do otherwise, since it would not involve a contradiction, and God remains sovereignly free with

---

[106] Joseph Wawrykow argues that, at *STh* III, q. 3, aa. 5–7, St Thomas explores hypotheticals about the incarnation only for the sake of shedding light "on the actual Christian dispensation." Article 8's inquiry into the fittingness of the Son's incarnation is therefore the true focus of the whole of *STh* III, q. 3. Wawrykow, "Wisdom in the Christology of Aquinas," 181–2. Matthew Levering argues in defense of Aquinas along very similar lines. Levering, *Christ's Fulfillment of Torah and Temple*, 34–5.

respect to creation and salvation—nonetheless, there *is* a "supreme fittingness," itself a kind of conditional necessity in view of the whole of the *dispensatio*, that the Son be the divine person who becomes incarnate. This is an important aspect of Aquinas's method. Contrary to what many suppose, his point is *not* to show that any person could have become incarnate (though, taken absolutely, any person could) but rather to demonstrate *how supremely fitting* it was that the Word alone be the one who took flesh, to unfold the wisdom of this divine plan. Aquinas's fundamental intention is to show why the Son—and *not* the Father or the Holy Spirit—became man, and how we can account for this truth.

When critics read Aquinas as if he held that God "surveyed the sets of possibilities open to him" and chose from among them as he pleased[107]—as if it "just so happened" that God chose the Son to become man, but it easily could have been otherwise—they are reading later modes of thought into that of the Dominican Master. In fact, such a position is much closer to the thought of John Duns Scotus, who inaugurated "a major shift" in thinking about necessity and contingency in opposition to the position of Aquinas.[108] Unlike Scotus (whose legacy lives on in much contemporary thought), St Thomas does not place an emphasis on God's will but rather on the wise ordering of creation that, while not absolutely necessary, nonetheless emerges from and reflects the eternal Wisdom of God and the processions of the divine persons according to a supreme fittingness. This is precisely what we examined in detail in CHAPTER 1. And, as we have shown in this chapter, the actual *dispensatio* is shaped all the way to its core by the fact that it was precisely the Son who became man.

* * *

As we have seen, St Thomas probes the rich intelligibility of the incarnation by considering it as the Son's visible mission by which man (and, in man, the whole universe), which proceeded from God as caused by and patterned upon the divine processions, is repaired after sin and is brought to his final perfection by returning to God

---

[107] Gelber, Hester Goodenough Gelber, *It Could Have Been Otherwise: Contingency and Necessity in Dominican Theology at Oxford, 1300–1350* (Leiden: Brill, 2004), 20.

[108] Gelber accounts for this shift in detail, citing an extensive body of literature on the novelty of Scotus's position. *Ibid.*, 111–50.

according to the same pattern of the personal processions. St Thomas's Christology is thus Trinitarian in a deep and thoroughgoing way. More than making occasional mention of some point of Trinitarian doctrine, St Thomas evidences a grasp of the whole mystery of Christ that emerges from a strikingly fecund understanding of the divine processions in the heart of the Trinity—an understanding of the way that those processions are the *ratio*, cause, and exemplar of creatures and also of the whole *dispensatio* of salvation (via the divine missions). Aquinas thus accounts for how the personal properties of the second person of the Trinity give him a unique and distinctive place at the center of that *dispensatio*—which is why *the Son* was the divine person who became incarnate.

Further, in his distinctive treatment of the hypostatic union, we can likewise discern the omnipresence of Aquinas's Trinitarian doctrine. That union is not merely the joining of a human nature to the divine nature; it terminates in the very person of the Son, according to his personal *esse*. That means that in the deepest metaphysical sense, even Christ's human nature is always marked by the filial mode of existing proper to the divine Son, namely, that he be from the Father. And as Christ's humanity bears the Son's personal property in itself, so also does Christ's every human action. In all that he says or does, Christ is from the Father and manifests the Father—a consequence of the strict correspondence that St Thomas always maintains between the Son's eternal procession and his visible mission in its every aspect. In the same way, as we shall see, this implies that all human action of Christ is related to the Holy Spirit, the Spirit whom he (together with the Father) sends to his own humanity and whom he pours out by the mysteries of his life in the flesh, especially his passion and exaltation. The hypostatic union thus becomes the foundation for Aquinas's doctrine that Christ's humanity is a conjoined instrument of the Word, so that Christ's human actions are elevated into the activity of the Word himself, participating in the Word's own divine power, and revealing the Father who sent him. And, in his coming in the flesh, the Son's humanity becomes the way by which we return to the Father.

Part III

Christ and the Holy Spirit

5

Like Splendor Flowing from the Sun

The Holy Spirit and Christ's Grace

Christ receives the Holy Spirit, is led by him, and gives the Spirit to his followers. Scripture and tradition testify abundantly to these truths, and no one would dispute that St Thomas also teaches them. And yet a nagging suspicion remains, even among Aquinas's contemporary disciples, that they do not have deep roots in his theology, and that the reach of their boughs is not wide; critics might even contend that St Thomas is repeating scriptural and Patristic formulas without grasping their profound implications. If we speak of Christ principally in terms of the hypostatic union, what scope is left for the movement of the Spirit in his life?[1] Does not Aquinas's account of our salvation suffer from a kind of "pneumatological amnesia," a "Christological domestication" of what Scripture ascribes to the Spirit?[2] This suspicion only grows when one pages through the *Tertia pars*, looking for the questions devoted to Christ and the Holy Spirit. "Outside of the treatise on the Trinity, . . . the Holy Spirit seems to have no place at all. Casual readers search in vain in the *Summa*'s Table of Contents for places where the question of the Holy Spirit is addressed in itself."[3] The Holy Spirit appears briefly at Christ's conception, again at his baptism, and at the transfiguration—but, at best, seems to have a supporting role, overshadowed by Aquinas's high *Logos*–Christology.

---

[1] See, e.g., Kasper, *Jesus the Christ*, 250–1.

[2] Marshall, "*Ex Occidente Lux?*," 25 and 40, articulating the criticisms of twentieth-century Orthodox theologians.

[3] Torrell, *Spiritual Master*, 153–4. See also Levering, *Christ's Fulfillment of Torah and Temple*, 35–41.

We will endeavor to show that this impression is mistaken. With Jean-Pierre Torrell, "we may say with certainty that, if we do not find the Holy Spirit here or there in Thomas Aquinas's work, it is because, in truth, he is everywhere."[4] This is especially true in Aquinas's Christology. Just as the incarnation of the Son always points us back to the Father (as we saw in CHAPTER 4), so it also always brings the presence and action of the Holy Spirit, both to the humanity that the Word assumes, and to the men Christ comes to save. Thomas's theology is profoundly Trinitarian: he thinks of the incarnation as the visible mission of the Word who breathes forth Love, and so Christ can never be without his Spirit. What is more, Christ as man relies on—indeed, cannot do without—the Holy Spirit in accomplishing the work given to him by the Father. As we shall see, the Holy Spirit is woven into the fabric of Thomas's speculative Christology itself.

A. THE HOLY SPIRIT'S MISSION AND CHRIST'S HABITUAL GRACE

The Holy Spirit is not only present in part or at certain moments in Christ's life; rather, Aquinas insists, "the whole Spirit (*totum spiritum*) is poured out upon Christ."[5] His soul is permeated with the Holy Spirit, by whom he is anointed and with whom he is filled, as man, from the first moment of his conception and ever afterwards. How does St Thomas understand this to be the case?

The *Tertia pars* mainly speaks of the Holy Spirit's presence in Christ in terms of Christ's habitual grace. Aquinas is quite clear that this grace corresponds to and, as it were, designates the invisible mission of the Holy Spirit to Christ.[6] As we discussed in detail in

---

[4] Torrell, *Spiritual Master*, 154. Thus, in writing the *Summa Theologiae*, Aquinas clearly assumed that the student of the *Tertia pars* would not read it as an autonomous treatment of a distinct domain, but, having already have studied the *Prima pars*, would bring forward its achievements into Christology. A principal motivation for composing the *Summa* was to avoid the "frequent repetition" of the same material which "has generated both loathing and confusion in the minds of students." *STh*, prol.

[5] *In Matt.* c. 12, lect. 1 (no. 1000).

[6] See, e.g., *STh* I, q. 43, a. 7 ad 6. This statement, which comes toward the end of the question on the divine missions, is built on what earlier articles of that question established: an invisible mission of the Holy Spirit designates the personal presence of

CHAPTER 2, the created effect of grace in the human soul is always secondary for Aquinas to the proper causality and personal presence of the Holy Spirit who is the cause and end of his created gifts.[7] "[I]n habitual grace," Aquinas explains, "the Holy Spirit is shown to be given to the soul of Christ, presupposing the union through which that man was the Son of God."[8] "Christ as man receives grace without measure, and therefore he receives the Holy Spirit without measure."[9] Moreover, this invisible mission is complete and perfect from the first instant, so that Christ always has the fullness of the Spirit dwelling in his humanity.[10] This presence of the Holy Spirit follows upon the hypostatic union "like splendor [flows from] the sun."[11]

The Grace of Union and Christ's Habitual Grace

Why is it important to underline this invisible mission of the Holy Spirit to Christ? Is it not enough to say that Christ is the Word of God in person, and therefore, as the God-man and in virtue of the hypostatic union, that he is both personally holy and capable of saving the world through what he does and suffers? Some have assumed that Aquinas thinks of Christ principally in such terms, and that the hypostatic union or the "grace of union" is the only explanation of Christ that is really needed.[12]

Aquinas does articulate this view, but only in objections—indeed, objections that he not only rejects, but that he regards as contrary to what Scripture has revealed and to what the great Christological councils have taught. The *Summa Theologiae* offers us a prime example in its treatment of Christ's habitual grace (*STh* III q. 7, a. 1). St Thomas sets out three related objections claiming that Christ did not need habitual grace: because he was God not by participation but "in truth," (objection 1); and because the hypostatic union itself

the Spirit in the soul of the recipient according to the created effect of habitual grace; this is the only mode in which an invisible mission is made.

[7] See, e.g., *In Epist. ad Rom.* c. 1, lect. 4 (no. 73), explaining that the person of the Holy Spirit is always understood when his gifts are mentioned, even if he is not explicitly mentioned.

[8] *De Verit.*, q. 29, a. 3.   [9] *In Ioan.* c. 3, lect. 6 (no. 543).

[10] *STh* III, q. 34, a. 1.   [11] *STh* III, q. 7, a. 13.

[12] The grace of union is defined by Aquinas as Christ's "personal *esse* itself [*ipsum esse personale*] which the divinity freely gives to the human nature in the person of the Word [and] which is the terminus of the assumption." *STh* III, q. 6, a. 6.

supplies all that Christ's humanity needed in order to be perfectly united to God through its operation (objection 2), and to act as an instrument of the divinity to save the world through his actions (objection 3). According to these objections, once we account for the hypostatic union, we have a complete account of Christ.

Aquinas's first response to this argument recalls (in the *sed contra*) Scripture's testimony that Christ possessed the Holy Spirit. In other words, to question Christ's possession of habitual grace is to question the presence of the Holy Spirit in Christ: "Isaiah 11 says 'The Spirit of the Lord will rest upon him.' But the Spirit is said to be in man through habitual grace, as was shown in the *Prima pars*. Therefore, in Christ there was habitual grace."[13] For Aquinas, it is inconceivable to have an economy of the Word without the presence of the Spirit.

Aquinas also brings the great Christological councils to bear on this question. The logic of Chalcedonian orthodoxy demands that Christ have habitual grace as man:

> Christ is true God according to his person and the divine nature. But because with the unity of person the distinction of natures remains, as was shown above [in an earlier discussion of the council of Chalcedon], the soul of Christ is not divine through its essence. Hence it must be made divine through participation, which is by grace.[14]

To hold that the hypostatic union elevates or divinizes Christ's humanity irrespective of habitual grace lets a kind of monophysitism enter through the back door.[15] If the union to the divine nature were itself to transform or divinize Christ's human nature as such, the result would be just the sort of confusion, mingling, and change of natures anathematized by Chalcedon.[16] Instead, the hypostatic union unites Christ's human nature to the Word in person, so that Christ's humanity is drawn into the personal mode of existing of the divine

---

[13] *STh* III, q. 7, a. 1 sc.

[14] *STh* III, q. 7, a. 1 ad 1. The authoritative account of St Thomas's interest in and research into the ecumenical councils is offered by Martin Morard, who explains that Aquinas was the first and the only one of the great scholastic theologians to have cited the councils with breadth and precision. Martin Morard, "Thomas d'Aquin lecteur des conciles," *Archivum Franciscanum Historicum* 98 (2005): 211.

[15] See Torrell, *Encyclopédie Jésus le Christ*, 996. In his *Sentences* Commentary, Thomas affirms unambiguously that Christ's divinity cannot formally sanctify his humanity; for that, the mediation of a created form is necessary, which is habitual grace. *Ibid.*, 1001, citing III *Sent.* d. 13, q. 1, a. 1.

[16] Thomas quotes Chalcedon on this point. *STh* III, q. 2, a. 1 sc.

Word while remaining fully and properly human. Saying this does not diminish the infinite dignity of Christ's person, nor the surpassing uniqueness of the hypostatic union, nor its central importance, but rather acknowledges that such a union calls for that nature to be elevated *as a human nature*, according to the way in which such a nature can participate in the divine life. In short, Christ's humanity is a true humanity, which implies a participated divinization proportioned to that humanity—namely, habitual grace.

Aquinas is therefore quite careful to distinguish between the divinization of that humanity as such through participation by habitual grace, and the union of that humanity to the person of the Son, which is not by participation.

> For the grace of union, which is not habitual grace, is rather a certain gratuitous gift given to Christ precisely so that he would be the true Son of God in his human nature, not through participation but through nature, insofar as the human nature of Christ is united to the Son of God in person. This union is called a grace because Christ has it by no preceding merits.[17]

Christ *is* the Son of God by nature, by virtue of the union. This does not change his human nature into the Son of God or into the divine nature; that human nature remains perfectly and truly created and human. And Christ also receives, as man, a really and formally distinct gift that is proportioned to his humanity, elevating it and divinizing it by participation.

The Relation between the Grace of Union and Habitual Grace

Given that Christ has habitual grace as well as the grace of union, what is the relation between these two gifts? The implications for a Trinitarian Christology are fundamental here, involving the relation in Christ between the personal presence of the Word (by the hypostatic union) and the gift of the Holy Spirit to his humanity (in habitual grace). If we are to dispel the suspicion that Aquinas leaves no room for the Holy Spirit's action in his Christology, we need to

---

[17] *In Ioan.* c. 3, lect. 6 (no. 544).

expose to view just how central this mission of the Spirit to Christ is for Aquinas.

The customary point of departure among Thomists on this issue is the very article we have been examining (*STh* III, q. 7, a. 1) where Thomas asks whether Christ's soul had habitual grace. In the main body of his response, Thomas writes:

> It is necessary to place habitual grace in Christ.... first, on account of the union of his soul to the Word of God. For the nearer a receiver is to the inflowing cause, the greater does it participate in that cause's influence. But the influx of grace is from God.... And hence it was supremely fitting that his soul would receive the influx of divine grace.[18]

This text, however, is ambiguous. Aquinas begins as if he will speak of the necessity that Christ have habitual grace, but the conclusion of his argument says that this grace is "supremely fitting." Which is it? What exactly is the relation between Christ's habitual grace and the hypostatic union? In fact, there are two opposing interpretations of Aquinas on this question. To prepare for our own assessment of the evidence on this key point, we will briefly review them.

The "Substantial Holiness" Position

For many later commentaries on the *Summa Theologiae*, article 1 of Question 7 is the *locus classicus* to launch into a discussion of Christ's "substantial holiness"—a claim that Christ is holy in his very being, in virtue of the hypostatic union itself. On this view, Christ's habitual grace is an effect of that union, but, more important, the true reason for and cause of Christ's holiness is the union itself. This position, often identified with the Thomist school, continues to color the reception of Aquinas's doctrine even today.[19]

To understand how this position came to be formulated in these terms—terms that St Thomas himself does not use—a brief review of its history is helpful. In the early fourteenth century, John Duns Scotus (and, after him, others like Durandus of Saint-Pourçain) not only distinguished but isolated Christ's habitual grace from the

---

[18] *STh* III, q. 7, a. 1.

[19] For a helpful account of the recent history of "the Thomist theology of the grace and holiness of Christ," covering the major twentieth-century figures of the Thomist school, see Philippe-Marie Margelidon, *Études thomistes sur la théologie de la rédemption, De la grâce à la résurrection du Christ* (Perpignan: Éditions Artège, 2010), 11–47.

grace of union. For example, Scotus argued that the only direct consequence of the union of Christ's human nature to the person of the Word is "its special dependence on the Word," since "no new absolute is posited in this nature through the union; therefore, as it remains the same nature with respect to every absolute, so it remains having the same capacity."[20] Richard Cross explains:

> The idea is that the relation of dependence on the Word appears to be logically independent of any other relational or non-relational property of the assumed nature. In particular, it does not affect the natural capacities of this nature. Thus, the relation of dependence [in the hypostatic union] does not entail that the human nature have grace.[21]

Scotus's move to render Christ's habitual grace separate from the hypostatic union is, according to Cross, a distinguishing mark of his Christology, with far-reaching consequences.[22] For Scotus, the hypostatic union entails neither any special knowledge in Christ, nor that he be impeccable.[23] Of course, Scotus affirms that Christ has these things, but only as distinct gifts of grace that do not follow from the hypostatic union; indeed, Scotus thinks that God could give the same gifts to another human being who was not united to the Son in person.[24] Scotus draws a related conclusion: Christ's acts in themselves do not have an infinite value; his passion satisfies for sin only because God "accepts" this offering (qualitatively the same sort of congruent satisfaction that other human beings with habitual grace can offer to God).[25]

In the sixteenth century, Dominican interpreters of St Thomas challenged Scotus's claims. The most famous Dominican theologian of the early sixteenth century, Thomas de Vio Cajetan (d. 1534) repeated St Thomas's teaching that habitual grace is an effect following the union, the "splendor" of the Son's presence in Christ's

[20] Scotus, *Ordinatio* III *Sent.* d. 13, q. 4 n. 10 [*Opera Omnia*, vol. 9 (Civitas Vaticana: Typis Vaticanis, 2006), 408].

[21] Richard Cross, *The Metaphysics of the Incarnation* (Oxford: Oxford University Press, 2002), 140–1.

[22] *Ibid.*, 318–24.

[23] Richard Cross, *Duns Scotus* (New York: Oxford University Press, 1999), 122.

[24] *Ibid.*, 124, quoting Scotus, *Ordinatio* III *Sent.* d. 13, q. 4, n. 8.

[25] Jan Rohof, *La sainteté substantielle du Christ dans la théologie scolastique: histoire du problème* (Fribourg: Suisse Éditions St-Paul, 1952), 46, citing John Duns Scotus, *Ordinatio* III *Sent.* d. 19, q. 1, n. 7. See also Scotus, *Ordinatio* IV *Sent.* d. 15, q. 1, n. 28 [*Opera Omnia*, vol. 13 (Civitas Vaticana: Typis Vaticanis, 2011), 64].

humanity.[26] Domingo de Soto (d. 1560) addressed Scotus more directly. While accepting Scotus's premise, he disputed his conclusion about satisfaction: even if Christ's human nature were to lack habitual grace, Soto reasoned, he would still be the Son in person by virtue of the hypostatic union, and hence his actions (actions *of* the Son *through* his human nature) would have an infinite value to God and would satisfy perfectly for sin, thus surpassing those of any mere human.[27] Domingo Bañez (d. 1604), Soto's most famous student, went further: he disagreed with Scotus's premise, arguing that it is impossible for Christ's human nature to be hypostatically united to the Son without receiving the further gift of habitual grace.[28] In all this, these sixteenth-century Dominicans largely used the same terms and categories of thought as St Thomas himself. Notably, none spoke of a "sanctification" of Christ's humanity by the hypostatic union. Each was careful to observe the distinction between person and nature in Christ. They argued that the *person* in Christ (the divine Son) has an infinite dignity and is perfectly pleasing to the Father, but they did not suggest that this itself sanctifies Christ's *human nature*; the supernatural perfection of Christ's human nature as such is only by habitual grace.

---

[26] *Commentaria Thomae de vio Caietani*, in Sancti Thomae Aquinatis *Opera Omnia*, vol. 11 (Rome: Ex Typographia Polyglotta S. C. de Propaganda Fide, 1903), at *STh* III, q. 6, a. 6, and q. 7, a. 13.

[27] For example: "For no matter how greatly we esteem Christ as man, it was nonetheless not the human nature that was acting in him, but the Son of God acting through that [nature]. But the Son of God was equal to the Father. For this reason, even if he would have received no created grace in his humanity, that man would have of himself been infinitely pleasing and a friend of God by reason of the union, and whatever he would have done would have been of itself a sufficient satisfaction to the equality of justice. Nay, any of his actions whatsoever would have been infinitely precious before God." Dominicus Soto, *De Natura et Gratia*, lib. 3, cap. 6 (Paris: Ioannem Foucher, 1549). One might wonder whether this is fully consistent with St Thomas's statements that any efficacious satisfaction must proceed from charity (*STh* III q. 14, a. 1 ad 1), and that it is necessary that Christ have perfect knowledge and grace in his soul in order to satisfy for sin (*STh* III q. 14, a. 4).

[28] "No grace is given to the man Christ out of the mercy and liberality of God, but rather he himself, insofar as he was the Son of God, both received and conferred this on his humanity. Just as, from the fact that one is a man, one is capable of laughter, so also from the fact that he was this man, it follows that such virtues were in the soul of Christ." Dominicus Bañez, *Tertia partis divi Thomae Aquinatis commentaria*, q. 1, a. 2, no. 27 [*Comentarios ineditos a la tercera parte de Santo Tomas*, vol. 1, *De Verbo Incarnato* (qq. 1–42), ed. Vicente Beltran de Heredia (Salamanca: Biblioteca de Teologos Españoles, 1951)]. Regarding whether the absolute power of God could do this, see *ibid.*, q. 7, a. 13, no. 3.

At the end of the sixteenth century, however, Jesuit theologians began to shift the categories in which this question was discussed, speaking of Christ's "holiness."[29] In the early seventeenth century, Francisco Suarez offered the definitive formulation of this new approach: "The humanity of Christ, or Christ as man, formally, by virtue of the grace of union itself, was absolutely and simply holy and pleasing to God."[30] Suarez held that, while habitual grace did in fact flow from the hypostatic union, this was neither necessary nor the true basis for Christ's human sanctity. "God could have assumed a human nature without habitual grace, although he could not assume it without making it pleasing to him."[31] "Christ would not need any created grace in order to be holy and pleasing to God, even as man . . . . Because of the sanctification [of Christ's soul and body by the grace of union], habitual grace was not necessary to Christ."[32] From this point forward, both non-Dominicans and Dominicans alike largely repeat Suarez's formulation.[33]

In its twentieth-century form, the "substantial holiness" position held that "the hypostatic union . . . sanctifies the humanity of Christ formally, that is, immediately, through itself, directly, and not only by a physically or morally necessary habitual grace."[34] While its advocates admitted that this position is not found in St Thomas, they argued that it was implied by his texts.[35] More recent historical and

---

[29] Francisco de Toledo (Toletus), writing in 1596, seems to have been the first. Rohof, *La sainteté substantielle du Christ*, 67–71.

[30] Francisco Suarez, *Commentaria ac Disputationes in Tertiam Partem D. Thomae*, q. 7, a. 1, disputatio 18, sec. 1, no. 5 [*Opera Omnia*, vol. 17 (Paris: Ludovicum Vivès), 1860).

[31] *Ibid.*, no. 15. This replicates Scotus's view about the independence of habitual grace from the grace of union, thought it disagrees with Scotus about what makes Christ's humanity pleasing to God.

[32] *Ibid.*, no. 3.

[33] Though John of St Thomas is often cited as holding this view, the text usually appealed to is not from his pen; in fact, the whole of the *Cursus Theologicus* dealing with the *Tertia pars* of Aquinas's *Summa Theologiae* was composed by one of his students and added after John of St Thomas's death. See Marco Forlivesi, "Le edizioni del *Cursus theologicus* di Joannes a Sancto Thoma," *Divus Thomas* (Bon.) 97 (1994): 15.

[34] A. Michel, "Jésus-Christ," in *Dictionnaire de Théologie Catholique* (Paris: Librairie Letouzey et Ané, 1947), vol. 8, col. 1276. Like Billuart, Michel cautions that this does not mean to say that there is "a form inhering in the soul of Jesus Christ (*principium quo*) by which it would be sanctified."

[35] *Ibid.*; see also Réginald Garrigou-Lagrange, *De Christo Salvatore* (Turin: R. Berruti, 1945), 182; Margelidon, *Études thomistes*, 27 (discussing the views of Charles-Vincent Héris).

textual research, however, raises serious questions as to whether such a position can be ascribed to Aquinas.[36]

In fact, Suarez's formulation involved a significant theological shift: thenceforth, the issue was no longer discussed according to the principal categories used by Aquinas and the pre-seventeenth-century Thomists, who had spoken of the "dignity" of the Son's person, the "infinite efficacy" of his actions, the "perfection" of Christ's soul, and the "participated divinization" of his human nature. Using those categories, there had been relatively little danger that what was true of Christ according to his person would be confused with what was true of his assumed human nature, or that the former would be predicated univocally or without qualification of his human nature. In Suarez's new formulation, however, this danger grew: the person–nature distinction no longer formed the central axis of the discussion. Instead, the holiness of the divine person was predicated directly of Christ's human nature—and not only by the communication of idioms, but according to substance.[37]

Additionally, by saying that Christ's humanity is "formally" holy by virtue of the grace of union itself, one might even be led to think that the hypostatic union modifies and elevates Christ's human nature as a

---

[36] As Rohof points out, the oft-cited text from the *Tertia pars* that seemed most clearly supportive of this position (*STh* III, q. 22, a. 2 ad 3) is inauthentic. The manuscript tradition contains no reply to the third objection of that article; editors in the latter part of the sixteenth century supplied one which later came to be taken, erroneously, as a text from St Thomas himself. Rohof, *La sainteté substantielle du Christ*, 42. The Leonine editors do not include this third reply in their edition.

The assertion that "St Thomas never calls Christ's habitual grace 'sanctifying grace,'" because Christ's sanctification comes from the grace of union," Ocáriz, Mateo Seco, and Riestra, *The Mystery of Jesus Christ*, 181, citing Garrigou-Lagrange, *De Christo Salvatore* at 182, is likewise incorrect. We have found at least two instances where Aquinas speaks of Christ as receiving sanctifying grace. See, e.g., *STh* III, q. 34, a.1; *In Ioan.* c. 3, lect. 6 (no. 543).

In any case, it is admitted by all that St Thomas does not speak in these terms—in fact, he does not often speak of Christ specifically in terms of "holiness." Where he does, he says things like "the abundance of the grace sanctifying Christ's soul is derived from the very union with the Word." *STh* III, q. 34, a. 1. To the extent that Aquinas speaks of the holiness of Christ as man, therefore, he is speaking of "a human sanctity" in contradistinction to that of the divine nature. See, e.g., *STh* III, q. 34, a. 1 ad 2: "*sanctitatem humanam.*"

[37] See, e.g., Suarez, *Commentaria ac Disputationes in Tertiam Partem*, q. 7, a. 1, disputatio 18, sec. 1, no. 18. This is not to say that Suarez confused the distinction between person and nature, but only that the categories in which he framed the issue are more susceptible to such confusion.

form.[38] There is a good reason why Aquinas is careful never to say any such thing: it endangers the central Christological truth affirmed by the Council of Chalcedon that the hypostatic union does not involve any confusion or mixing of natures. Indeed, St Thomas expressly denies that Christ's divinity might render his humanity perfect in its spiritual being formally (*formaliter*), that is, as a form or principle by which Christ's humanity is perfected.[39] He even argues that if the Word's divinity were added to the human nature as a form, Christ would no longer be human.[40] Rather, Christ is made "formally holy" by the same grace by which he justifies others, namely, his fullness of habitual grace.[41]

What is more, the substantial holiness position implicitly accepts Scotus's central claim, albeit on different grounds: for both Scotus and Suarez, the hypostatic union has no necessary connection to habitual grace, nor does habitual grace have a necessary connection to whether Christ is pleasing to God. The point of difference between them is principally whether, given the hypostatic union, Christ's humanity is necessarily pleasing to God (Scotus says no, Suarez says yes), but for

---

[38] Suarez comes close to saying this. For example: "[T]he Word is a quasi-form itself sanctifying the humanity and constituting this man as per se holy, because the Word is holiness itself through his essence, and is joined per se and intimately to that humanity. Further, the Word itself is that by which the man has this, that he would be the natural Son of God, and from this he has an infinite dignity, by reason of which he is endowed with infinite merit and sanctification." Suarez, *Commentaria ac Disputationes in Tertiam Partem*, q. 7, a. 1, disputatio 18, sec. 1, no. 10. Nonetheless, Suarez always maintains that the divinity cannot formally confer an accidental sanctification on Christ's humanity as an intrinsic formal effect.

[39] See Torrell, *Encyclopédie Jésus le Christ*, 1001, citing III *Sent.* d. 13, q. 1, a. 1 (quoted, p. 145).

[40] *ScG* IV, c. 35. The more nuanced advocates of the substantial holiness position thus took care to qualify the adjective "formally" in Suarez's phrase. See, e.g., Charles René Billuart, *Summa S. Thomae hodiernis academiarum moribus accomodata, sive cursus theologiae . . .* , vol. 3 (Würzburg: Ioannis Iacobi Stahel, 1758), Dissertatio 8, a. 1. When Garrigou-Lagrange advocates for the substantial holiness position, he admits that, if Christ's humanity were sanctified by the divine nature "as the informing form," then a confusion of natures would result. He argues, however, that the divine nature formally sanctifies Christ's human nature as "an act properly terminating" the nature. Garrigou-Lagrange, *De Christo Salvatore*, 185. (The background for this claim seems to be that Christ has only one *esse*, the divine *esse*, in which the human nature terminates.) However, this leads to the curious conclusion that Christ's human nature is "formally" sanctified without any "formal" change of the human nature, that is, without an intrinsic form as a *principium quo* of that sanctification. For a Thomist, it is also hard to reconcile with the explicit contrary statements of the Angelic Doctor himself.

[41] *STh* III, q. 8, a. 5 ad 2–3; see also *STh* III, q. 34, a. 3.

both of them, Christ's habitual grace is a separate matter. For both, Christ the God-man could be endowed with habitual grace or not, as God wills, without fundamentally changing the shape of the salvation wrought through the incarnation.

We can add a final difficulty: this approach focuses so much on the hypostatic union that the mission of the Holy Spirit to Christ's humanity is easily overlooked. For example, advocates of Christ's substantial holiness from Suarez through the twentieth century typically hold that the principal "anointing" of Christ's humanity is the hypostatic union itself, not his reception of the Holy Spirit as man.[42] While this usage is legitimate,[43] too strong an emphasis on the union risks marginalizing the principal emphasis of Sacred Scripture. Jesus says: "The Spirit of the Lord is upon me, because he has anointed me to preach good news to the poor," (Luke 4:18); in Acts, Peter confesses: "God anointed Jesus of Nazareth with the Holy Spirit and with power" (Acts 10:38). Aquinas, *magister in sacra pagina*, takes care to maintain this scriptural emphasis,[44] speaking principally of the Holy Spirit as anointing Jesus's humanity.[45] "[Christ] was anointed in a special way with an invisible oil, that is, [the oil] of the Holy Spirit.... [W]hence it says in Ps. 44:8: 'Your God has anointed you with the oil of gladness beyond your companions,' that is, beyond

---

[42] Ocáriz, Mateo Seco, and Riestra, *The Mystery of Jesus Christ*, 179; Michel, "Jésus-Christ," col. 1277. Even Matthias Scheeben, while acknowledging that the Holy Spirit anoints Christ's humanity, says that "the ointment ... is the Logos Himself." Matthias Joseph Scheeben, *The Mysteries of Christianity*, trans. Cyril Vollert (St Louis: Herder, 1946), 332–3. Yves Congar, while pleased with Scheeben's sensitivity to the place of the Holy Spirit in Christ, nonetheless regards this as an overemphasis on the hypostatic union. Yves Congar, *Je crois en l'Esprit Saint*, 2nd ed. (Paris: Les Éditions du Cerf, 1997), 46.

[43] Michel, echoing Suarez, cites several Fathers of the Church in defense of this usage. Michel, "Jésus-Christ," col. 1277.

[44] As Thomas cautions elsewhere, "man should not easily speak about God differently from how holy Scripture speaks." See, for instance (among many other passages), *Contra errores Graecorum* I, c.1; *STh* I, q. 32, a. 2, arg. 1.

[45] There are many such texts. Perhaps the clearest is *ScG* IV, c. 34, where Thomas explains that name "Christ" signifies an anointing of Jesus' humanity, which pertains to his reception as man of the Holy Spirit, and not the Word's incarnation itself. For other places where Aquinas speaks of the name "Christ" as signifying an anointing by the Holy Spirit, see *In Ioan.* c. 1, lect. 15 (no. 301); c. 1, lect. 16 (no. 332); c. 3, lect. 6 (no. 543); c. 6, lect. 8 (no. 1004), c. 11, lect. 14 (no. 1520); *ScG* IV, c. 60; *In I Epist. ad Cor.* c. 1, lect. 2 (no. 34); *In II Epist. ad Cor.* c. 1, lect. 5 (no. 44); *In Matt.* c. 1 (no. 96); c. 16 (no. 1374); *In Psalm.* 26 (no. 1); 44 (no. 5). We know of only one text where Aquinas uses "Christ" to designate the union of the divinity to Jesus's humanity: *In Epist. ad Tit.* c. 2, lect. 3 (no. 72).

all the saints, for all the saints are anointed with this oil, but he is singularly anointed, and is singularly holy."[46]

Jean-Pierre Torrell: Habitual Grace Is Supremely Fitting, Not Necessary

Among students of St Thomas, Jean-Pierre Torrell is a leading contemporary critic of the doctrine of Christ's substantial holiness; he represents the second principal response to the question of how the grace of union and habitual grace are related.[47] Unlike the advocates of Christ's substantial holiness, who argue that the humanity of Christ is holy in virtue of the hypostatic union "even independently of habitual grace,"[48] Torrell argues that Christ's human holiness depends on his habitual grace, but that this gift does not necessarily follow the union. Instead, Torrell underlines the fittingness that God would give the fullness of habitual grace to Christ's humanity. Torrell anchors his position on the conclusion of the argument in question 7, article 1: "it was supremely fitting that [Christ's] soul would receive the influx of divine grace."[49] For Torrell, this reference to fittingness in the opening article of the *Summa Theologiae*'s discussion of Christ's habitual grace qualifies all of Thomas's subsequent references to the necessity of that grace. While Aquinas repeatedly seems to speak of habitual grace as necessarily consequent to the union (for example, he compares it to the light that proceeds from the presence of the sun,[50] to the heat that is a natural property proceeding from the presence of fire,[51] and even says that it is "derived from the union of the Word itself"),[52] Torrell would

---

[46] *In Ioan.* c. 1, lect. 15 (no. 301). We must therefore register our disagreement with Congar's assessment of St Thomas on this point; Congar seems to assume that Aquinas holds the same position as the later advocates of the substantial holiness position. Yves Congar, *La Parole et le Souffle* (Paris: Desclée, 1984), 139–51.

[47] In contrast to Torrell, David Coffey uses Aquinas's categories in the service of his own personal account that inverts the traditional relationship between the grace of union and the hypostatic union, so that by the agency of the Holy Spirit, Christ's sanctification by habitual grace becomes the source of the hypostatic union. David Coffey, "The 'Incarnation' of the Holy Spirit in Christ," *Theological Studies* 45 (1984): 469. For a survey and evaluation of Coffey's position, see Ralph Del Colle, *Christ and the Spirit: Spirit Christology in Trinitarian Perspective* (Oxford: Oxford University Press, 1994), 91–140.

[48] Garrigou-Lagrange, *De Christo Salvatore*, 181.

[49] *STh* III, q. 7, a. 1, quoted at p. 136.   [50] *STh* III, q. 7, a. 13.

[51] *Ibid.*, ad 2.   [52] *STh* III, q. 34, a. 1.

not read those texts as expressing necessity in the strict sense, but as nested within the "supreme fittingness" of Question 7, article 1. Torrell explains:

> It is . . . very important not to transform this fittingness into necessity. The proximity of Jesus' humanity to the divinity not only does not transform it into the divine nature, but does not even entail a "natural" derivation or effusion from the divinity to Christ's humanity, and still less a necessary emanation. Even in the case of Christ, grace remains gratuitous and God is not constrained to give it.[53]

Torrell's concern is to safeguard the true humanity of Christ from any note of mingling or mixing with the divinity. To be sure, he moderates the impact of his warning when he speaks about Christ's human actions: Christ "needs" habitual grace in order to do what he does as man—in other words, we can be sure that God did in fact give Christ habitual grace because "if his soul were not elevated by grace, we would have something unheard-of: the Word as man would be a stranger to his own divine life."[54] Further, though he does not advert to it, Torrell would surely also agree with Aquinas that "Christ as man was predestined to be the Son of God,"[55] and that, according to Aquinas's logic, this must imply not only an eternal divine determination to bring about the incarnation through the grace of union, but also an eternal determination that Christ would receive the fullness of habitual grace (and every other gratuitous gift).[56] Still, for Torrell, it seems that Christ's habitual grace remains a causally distinct gift to

---

[53] Torrell, *Encyclopédie Jésus le Christ*, 1000.

[54] *Ibid.*, 1001.   [55] *STh* III, q. 24, a. 2.

[56] When Aquinas addresses Christ's predestination, he speaks principally and almost exclusively with respect to the grace of union, since what distinguishes Christ's predestination from ours is that, in Christ, "the rational creature is united [to God] . . . through a union in personal being, which is called the grace of union." *In Epist. ad Rom.* c. 1, lect. 3 (no. 46); III *Sent.* d. 11, a. 4 ad 4. See also *STh* III, q. 24, aa. 1–4; III *Sent.* d. 10, q. 3, a. 1, qla 1–3. Yet it must be the case, according to Aquinas's logic, that a determination to grant the fullness of habitual grace to Christ (as well as every other gratuitous gift) must have also been included in that one eternal decree that the Son would become incarnate. See, e.g., III *Sent.* d. 10, q. 3, a. 1, qla 1. Consequently, Torrell (and others who would agree with his reading of Aquinas on the relation of the grace of union and Christ's habitual grace) would indeed be able to say that Christ would certainly receive this grace according to an infallible and eternal divine decree; the question is simply whether this gift is a necessary consequence of the grace of union, or whether it is a causally distinct gift.

his humanity that does not *necessarily* follow from the union of Christ's humanity with the Word.

A Solution: Grace and Charity as Gifts of the Spirit's Mission

Torrell's critique of the doctrine of substantial holiness rightly points out that, in Aquinas's own words, the hypostatic union does not formally perfect Christ's humanity; a distinct gift of habitual grace must be given to Christ, something that cannot simply be reduced to the hypostatic union. Aquinas says:

> One must posit [habitual] grace in Christ's soul. For since it was most perfect in its spiritual being, there must be something perfecting it formally in that being. Yet the divinity does not formally, but rather effectively, perfect it. Thus one must posit a created form in [his soul], by which it is formally perfected; and this is grace.[57]

Insofar as some advocates of the substantial holiness position hold that Christ's humanity could be "perfect in its spiritual being" independent of habitual grace, they would seem to be departing from Aquinas's own teaching.[58] At the same time, Torrell's own reading of Thomas also has its difficulties, since Aquinas does link Christ's habitual grace quite closely to the union with the Word.

When we keep in view Thomas's theology of the divine missions, however, we can see that all of Aquinas's texts sound in consistent harmony with each other. Because of the order and connection between the divine missions, there *is* a certain necessary order between the hypostatic union and Christ's habitual grace, but it is not a necessity on the side of the creature, as if the principles of Christ's human nature caused him to receive grace, nor does it involve a mixing of Christ's two natures, as if Christ's human nature were formally sanctified in its human reality by the union itself. Rather, Aquinas appeals to the necessary relation between the divine processions themselves, and the distinct but inseparable presence of the divine persons in the created effects of the divine missions.

---

[57] III *Sent.* d. 13, q. 1, a. 1. Cf. *STh* III, q. 59, a. 3 ad 3.

[58] Such advocates often posit that habitual grace is necessary for Christ's connatural operation, but St Thomas claims in this text that it is necessary for the spiritual perfection of Christ's human soul, apart from any human operation.

The Key Text: *STh* III, q. 7, a. 13

Up till now, both sides of this controversy have dwelt on article 1 of Question 7, the *locus classicus* for discussing the substantial holiness of Christ. That article, however, does not purport to address the order between the grace of union and habitual grace; its purpose is simply to establish that Christ has created habitual grace, the root from which spring the virtues, gifts, and charisms covered in the remainder of Question 7. It is only after Thomas has shown that Christ has these virtues and gifts (including the gift of charity, by which a mission of the Holy Spirit is understood) that a complete account of the link between the hypostatic union and habitual grace can be given.

It is thus at the end of Question 7, in article 13, that Aquinas finally is ready to inquire into the order between the union and habitual grace, asking "whether habitual grace in Christ follows the union." His reply explicitly invokes his doctrine of the divine missions, revealing it as the key note to which his other texts are tuned.[59]

Aquinas begins by affirming that the grace of union and habitual grace are entirely simultaneous, but that there is nonetheless an ordering between them: "The union of the human nature to the divine person, which above we called the grace of union, precedes the habitual grace in Christ, not in time, but in the order of nature and of understanding."[60] From this starting point, Thomas gives three reasons or explanations for this priority of the grace of union.

---

[59] Although he does not explore it, Congar recognized the importance of Thomas's distinction between and coordination of the missions of the Son and the Spirit in Christ in *STh* III, q. 7, a. 13. "L'essentiel est d'honorer les deux missions du Verbe et de l'Esprit, selon leur succession qui découle des Processions intratrinitaires." Congar, *Je crois en l'Esprit Saint*, 50. Congar's own account of the place of the Spirit in the life of Jesus largely ceases to speak of this "essential point" of the simultaneous divine missions of the Son and Spirit in Christ, however; he prefers to leave to one side what he calls "*la théologie anhistorique*" of scholasticism and its emphasis on ontology (though he evidently regards its ontological account as largely true) in order to plunge into the "historical and concrete" manner of speaking used by the New Testament. Congar, *Je crois en l'Esprit Saint*, 733–42 (especially 734 and 739). See also François-Marie Humann, *La relation de l'Esprit-Saint au Christ: une relecture d'Yves Congar* (Paris: Les Éditions du Cerf, 2010), 46; cf. 115–21, 216–20.

[60] *STh* III, q. 7, a. 13. Albert Patfoort explains that "order of nature" here refers to the order of dependence between the two, while the "order of understanding" refers to the way in which we conceive of the relation between the two. Albert Patfoort, *La Somme de saint Thomas et la logique du dessein de Dieu* (Saint-Maur: Éditions Parole et Silence, 1998), 222 n. 8.

These reasons themselves are presented according to a definite hierarchical order: (1) the first concerns God in Himself with respect to the order among the immanent processions and the resulting order among the divine missions; (2) then Aquinas descends to the relation between God and creatures, specifically, the relation between created grace and its divine cause; (3) finally, Aquinas turns to the metaphysics of created being and the logical priority of a supposit over its *habitus* and actions.

THE FIRST REASON: THE ORDER OF THE PROCESSIONS The first reason why the grace of union precedes the habitual grace of Christ by order of nature and understanding, Aquinas continues, "is according to the order of the principles of each (*secundum ordinem principiorum utriusque*)." This starting point is crucial, a superb example of how Aquinas's Christology builds upon his doctrine of the missions, which in turn depends on his Trinitarian theology.

> For the principle of the union is the person of the Son assuming a human nature, and insofar as he assumes a human nature, he is said to be "sent" into the world. But the principle of habitual grace, which is given with charity, is the Holy Spirit, who consequently is said to be "sent" when he dwells in the mind by charity.[61]

Note how St Thomas places the accent on the action of the divine person who is sent. The Son is the principle of the incarnation, it is he who *assumes* a human nature, and hence he is the divine person "sent" in that mission. The Holy Spirit is no less active: in his invisible mission, he *dwells* in Christ's human mind, and he is the principle both of habitual grace and of charity. Note also that the created objects of these two missions in Christ's human nature are distinct: the visible mission of the Son is accomplished in the assumption of a human nature; its created effect is Christ's human nature itself insofar as it is united to the Word. The Holy Spirit is invisibly sent, however, in the *habitus* of charity that is always given with habitual grace. On the side of the created effects of the missions, therefore, we are already able to distinguish them.

Having reoriented the question along the lines of the divine missions, it then is easy for Aquinas to explain why Christ's habitual

---

[61] *STh* III, q. 7, a. 13.

grace follows the grace of union; this is simply the order between the mission of the Son and that of the Spirit:

> But the mission of the Son, according to the order of nature, is prior to the mission of the Holy Spirit, just as, by order of nature, the Holy Spirit proceeds from the Son and love proceeds from wisdom. Hence also, according to the order of nature, the personal union, in which we understand the mission of the Son, is prior to habitual grace, in which we understand the mission of the Holy Spirit.[62]

In this deceptively simple argument, St Thomas exposes to our sight the deepest foundations of his Trinitarian Christology. The grace of union (that is, the hypostatic union) is another way of signifying the visible mission of the Son, while the habitual grace of Christ is another way of referring to the invisible mission of the Holy Spirit to Christ's humanity. The most fundamental relation between these distinct graces is the ordering of their primordial principles, which are not only the missions but the eternal processions themselves, since the missions include the divine processions and "extend" them into time.[63] Reconceived in these terms, the invisible mission of the Spirit has an order to the visible mission of the Son insofar as the Holy Spirit proceeds from the Father *and the Son*. This does not mean, however, that the visible mission of the Son is earlier in time. As the divine processions are simultaneous, excluding every shadow of temporal succession (indeed, they exist in the very eternity of God), so also the Son's incarnation and the Spirit's invisible mission to Christ are simultaneous;[64] the eternal Word is eternally with the Holy Spirit that he breathes forth. Aquinas maintains only an order of nature between the missions, the same order as that between the divine processions and the divine persons themselves.[65]

---

[62] *STh* III, q. 7, a. 13. According to the recommendations of both Torrell and the editors of the two principal English editions of the *Summa Theologiae* (the English Dominican Fathers edition and the Gilby edition), we have followed here the Piana text ("*et a sapientia dilectio*") rather than the Leonine, which renders the final phrase of the penultimate sentence as "*et a Patre dilectio.*"

[63] *STh* I, q. 43, a. 2, ad 3; I *Sent.* d. 16, q. 1, a. 1.   [64] *STh* III, q. 2, a. 12.

[65] Aquinas stoutly avers that this "order" between the divine persons implies absolutely no priority whatsoever among them, "in no way, neither in time, nor nature, nor understanding, nor dignity," since the persons are distinct only by pure relation to each other. I *Sent.* d. 9, q. 2, a. 1. See also I *Sent.* d. 12, q. 1, a. 1. The only order between them is what he calls (with Augustine) an order of nature, "according to origin, without priority, . . . not as if one were before the other, but [only] as one is from the other." *STh* I, q. 42, a. 3.

But Thomas's response does not only show that the mission of the Son is "prior" according to the pure order of origin, but also points us to how the invisible mission of the Spirit into Christ's soul "follows" the Son's visible mission. The Son breathes forth the Spirit, not only eternally but also in his mission in the economy of grace. As the Son's eternal procession implies the procession of the Holy Spirit (the Father, in begetting his Son, gives the Son the power to spirate the Holy Spirit),[66] so also the Son's visible mission intrinsically implies the Word breathing forth the Spirit to that same humanity. In eternity *and* in time, the Word proceeds from the Father, breathing forth Love. As Thomas explains elsewhere (with a quotation he attributes to Athanasius), "Christ himself as God the Son sent the Spirit from above, and as man below he received the Spirit; from himself to himself, therefore, the Spirit dwells in his humanity from his divinity."[67]

This is exactly the sense of the two comparisons Aquinas offers in the passage from Question 7, article 13, quoted just above. The first is to the eternal procession of the Holy Spirit from the Son: "the mission of the Son [i.e., the hypostatic union], according to the order of nature, is prior to the mission of the Holy Spirit [i.e., the gift of charity given with Christ's habitual grace], just as, by order of nature, the Holy Spirit proceeds from the Son. . . . "[68] The order between the missions in Christ's humanity tracks the order of the Trinitarian processions, and it is according to this ordering that Aquinas would have us understand the relation between the grace of union and habitual grace. As the Word proceeds from the Father in eternity while also eternally breathing forth the Spirit with the Father (because the generation of the Word includes already, *virtualiter*, the procession of the Spirit),[69] so also the Word proceeds into the world in the incarnation, breathing forth the Spirit in a simultaneous temporal

---

[66] Emery, *Trinitarian Theology*, 290–4.

[67] *Contra errores Graecorum* II, c. 1. Aquinas takes from Athanasius and Cyril of Alexandria the important principle that the Spirit is the *proper* Spirit of the Son. Emery, "Missions invisibles," 80–1. For a brief discussion of Athanasius and Cyril on this point, see Dennis W. Jowers, "A Test of Karl Rahner's Axiom, 'The Economic Trinity is the Immanent Trinity and Vice Versa,'" *The Thomist* 70 (2006): 421–55.

[68] *STh* III, q. 7, a. 13.

[69] Because Aquinas understands the Word's spiration of the Spirit to be received from the Father, he is equally capable of saying that the Father sends the Spirit to Christ's humanity (cf. Acts 2:33), while also affirming that the Word breathes forth Love to his humanity. David Coffey's critique on this point is therefore wide of the mark, at least with respect to Aquinas. See Coffey, "A Proper Mission of the Holy Spirit," 237–8.

procession. For Aquinas, the divine persons come into the world as they are in themselves—which is to say, necessarily in relation to and interpenetrated by the other divine persons. The idea that a person could be sent into the world but might somehow fail to disclose and make present his eternal procession, or might somehow be severed from the other persons, would be self-contradictory for Aquinas.

This necessary and intrinsic coordination of the divine missions rests on a key insight of St Thomas's Trinitarian theology: the divine persons are constituted purely by their opposed relations, which means that to understand what it means to say "Son" also implies not only the Father but the Holy Spirit as well. "God the Father cannot be understood without the Word and without Love, nor is the converse possible; for this reason, in one of the three, all three are understood,"[70] Aquinas does not conceive of the Trinitarian processions as if first the Father is constituted as a person, who then generates the Son, and after these two have been constituted as persons, only in a third stage is the Holy Spirit breathed forth. Since the persons are constituted by relations—indeed, *are* subsisting relations—they exist coeternally, which means absolutely simultaneously, with neither succession nor priority. In short, the constitution of any one divine person always and eternally contains a reference to the other two divine persons.[71]

In the context of the divine missions, which include and disclose the eternal processions, Thomas's Trinitarian doctrine means, therefore, that the missions of the persons are necessarily simultaneous, inseparable, and coordinated. In fact, Thomas makes this point explicitly in Question 43 of the *Prima pars* in treating of the invisible missions: "one mission cannot be without the other because ... one person is not separated from the other."[72] This same Trinitarian reasoning now reappears in the *Tertia pars* precisely at the moment

---

[70] *ScG* IV, c. 23.

[71] By insisting that relation is what constitutes the divine persons, Aquinas takes a position unique among his contemporaries, famously diverging from St Bonaventure, for example, on how to define the personal property of the Father. See, e.g., *STh* I, q. 33, a. 4 and ad 1. For a detailed history and analysis of the medieval controversy over innascibility and relation with respect to the Father, see Durand, *Le Père, Alpha et Oméga*, 159–244; "Le Père en sa relation constitutive au Fils selon saint Thomas d'Aquin," *Revue Thomiste* 107 (2007): 47–72. See also see John Baptist Ku, *God the Father in the Theology of St Thomas Aquinas* (New York: Peter Lang Publishing, 2013), 85–98, 172–83.

[72] *STh* I, q. 43, a. 5 ad 3.

that Aquinas seeks to account for the coordination of the grace of union and the habitual grace in Christ's humanity: the ultimate foundation of that coordination is the necessary interrelation of the divine processions, and hence of the divine missions in Christ. The Son's visible mission does not only disclose his relation to the Father (the Son who is sent by the Father is manifested to be *from* the Father), but it also includes his relation to the Holy Spirit: to be the Father's Word means both to be from the Father, and to be the Word that breathes forth Love. The humanity in which there is a visible mission of the Son must therefore also receive an invisible mission of the Holy Spirit.

The second comparison Thomas makes in Question 7, article 13 for the order between the hypostatic union and habitual grace expresses this truth even more poignantly: the order between the mission of the Son and the Spirit's mission to Christ's humanity is like the way "love [*dilectio*] proceeds from wisdom," he says. While the first comparison referred to the *eternal processions* of the divine persons themselves, this second comparison refers to the interrelated *effects* (wisdom and love) of the divine missions, which reflect the order between the persons. These two comparisons are thus not essentially different; rather, they are like the two sides of the same coin, one uncreated, the other created.

Aquinas's brief reference to love and wisdom is rich with meaning for his Trinitarian theology; it rests on the same analogy Aquinas uses in the *Prima pars* to show that the missions of the Son and Spirit in sanctifying grace are reciprocal, and hence simultaneous and inseparable. To quote again a text we discussed in Chapter 2:

> [b]ecause the Holy Spirit is Love, through the gift of charity a soul is assimilated to the Holy Spirit; hence the mission of the Holy Spirit is observed according to the gift of charity. But the Son is the Word, not of whatever kind, but a Word breathing forth Love.... Therefore the Son is sent ... according to an intellectual illumination by which [the soul] breaks forth into the affection of love.... [which is] properly called wisdom.[73]

Wisdom is a perfection of the intellect that, by its nature, bursts forth into the will's act of love—such is the interpenetration of these two faculties of the soul.[74] For Aquinas, this is the best "similitude" for the

---

[73] *STh* I, q. 43, a. 5 ad 2.
[74] See Sherwin, *By Knowledge & By Love*, 84–94.

immanent processions within the Godhead of the Word and of the Holy Spirit; it is also his primary "similitude" for discussing the invisible missions of those persons in sanctifying grace.[75] By referring to this analogy again in the *Tertia pars*, Aquinas is once again underscoring the inseparability, simultaneity, and order between these missions to Christ's humanity—an order that originates in the necessary relations between the persons themselves, and that, on the created side, is reflected in the effects of the missions. When the Word is personally united to the human nature of Christ, that Word breathes forth or bursts into Love—that is, the Word bestows the Holy Spirit on that human nature in the gift of habitual grace, which blossoms in wisdom and love, so that Christ knows and loves God perfectly in that nature and according to a properly human mode.

This does not transgress the limits on necessity that Torrell has articulated: Thomas does not mean that the mission of the Spirit is a necessary emanation from God to the creature along Neoplatonic lines, nor is habitual grace something "owed" to the humanity of Christ as a created nature, as if the hypostatic union somehow changed the human nature itself. Rather, having graciously willed to send the Son in the incarnation, that implies also the gracious gift of the Spirit to Christ's humanity—these are paired just as the persons are inseparable. Just as the Word is eternally the Word who breathes forth Love, so the Word in Christ's humanity breathes forth Love to that humanity, namely, the Holy Spirit himself with habitual grace and the gift of charity. As Thomas explains elsewhere, "in the name 'Christ' is understood the Holy Spirit by reason of concomitance, because wherever Christ is, there also is the Spirit of Christ, just as wherever the Father is, there also is the Son."[76] Christ's human nature

---

[75] Of course, there is a fundamental difference between the invisible mission of the Son to a soul in grace and the personal union with the Son in Christ. (Aquinas sometimes compares this difference to the difference between a participated likeness of a thing and the thing itself. See, e.g., *STh* III, q. 2, a. 10 ad 2; q. 5, a. 4 ad 1. At other times, he compares it to the difference between a union depending on an operation or habit and a union based on "the personal being of the human nature itself." *STh* III, q. 6, a. 6 ad 1.) The Word is not only present in Christ by habitual grace, but is present by hypostatic union, a union excelling all others. *STh* III, q. 2, a. 9. But *mutatis mutandis*, Aquinas's analogy to the procession of love from wisdom stands: insofar as the Word is personally united to the human nature in Christ, that Word breathes forth or bursts into Love—that is, when the Word is united to his humanity by the hypostatic union, he breathes forth Love in person to that humanity.

[76] *Contra errores Graecorum* I, c. 13.

is hypostatically united to the Son alone, but it is simultaneously filled with the presence of the Holy Spirit because the Son and Spirit are never apart: the Holy Spirit is the Son's own Spirit. God acts in the economy of grace as he is in himself—as a Trinity of persons in which the Spirit proceeds from the Son.[77]

THE SECOND REASON: THE PRESENCE OF GOD IN CHRIST   Let us return to the text of Question 7, article 13. Having established the order of the processions as the most fundamental source of the order between the grace of union and habitual grace, Aquinas offers another reason. "The second reason for this order is taken from the relation of habitual grace to its cause." Thomas thus descends from the level of God in himself to the relation of a created effect to its divine cause:

> For grace is caused in man by the presence of the divinity, as light in air is caused by the presence of the sun.... But the presence of God in Christ is understood according to the union of the human nature to [his] divine person. Thus the habitual grace of Christ is understood as consequent to this union, as brightness is to the sun.[78]

One might think, at first glance, that this means that it is uniquely the personal presence of the Word that causes habitual grace in Christ, and that no more need be added. But the context belies such an interpretation, since these lines follow immediately upon Aquinas's account of the inseparability and order among the divine missions.

In fact, this passage does not limit the divine presence in Christ to the Word alone. Thomas says, quite precisely, that "the presence of

---

[77] In all this, St Thomas takes great care not only to preserve the order between the divine persons, but also to show how the incarnation manifests the truth about the Trinity. In this way, his understanding of the relation between *theologia* and *dispensatio*—between the order of the processions in themselves and how those processions are included in the divine missions and manifested to the world—is profoundly different than some contemporary theologians. Consider, for example, Hans Urs von Balthasar, who writes that, during Christ's earthly life, there is a "Trinitarian inversion" whereby the Holy Spirit mediates the Father's will to the Son and makes possible the Son's obedience to the Father. Hans Urs von Balthasar, *Theo-Drama: Theological Dramatic Theory*, vol. 3, *The Dramatis Personae: The Person in Christ*, trans. Graham Harrison (San Francisco: Ignatius Press, 1992), 183–91, 520–3. See also Hans Urs von Balthasar, *Mysterium Paschale: The Mystery of Easter*, trans. Aidan Nichols (San Francisco: Ignatius Press, 2000), 91; cf. 210–17. According to Balthasar, the Holy Spirit's unifying activity during this time actually obscures the Spirit's eternal procession from the Son: "For reasons of salvation history, however, this spiration has to go into hiding, as it were." Balthasar, *Theo-Drama* vol. 3, 188.
[78] *STh* III, q. 7, a. 13.

the divinity" causes grace. As we have seen, habitual grace is a created effect that always accompanies the divine presence in man, an effect that is efficiently caused by all three persons but in which the persons are made present to the human nature in distinct modes (the Son according to wisdom, the Holy Spirit according to charity, and the Father as the One to whom human beings are united by the gift of the Son and of the Holy Spirit). The minor premise ("the presence of God in Christ is understood according to the union . . . ") focuses on the preeminent presence of the Word in Christ's humanity. That satisfies the conditions of the major premise: if the Word is present in such a superexcelling mode—hypostatically or according to subsistence and not merely accidentally[79]—then certainly the divinity is present. Aquinas does not mean that *only* the Word is present, however; he showed the contrary a few lines earlier. The sense is rather "the divinity is present in Christ *above all* by the hypostatic union," such that the created effect of habitual grace must follow, and with it, the personal presence of the Holy Spirit in the gift of charity.[80]

In St Thomas's *Sentences* Commentary, he makes even more clear that the divine presence in Christ is of *both* the Son and the Spirit. Discussing how the "created gift" given to Christ (the "grace by which Christ's soul was formally perfected") is correlated with the "uncreated gift" of the divine presence in Christ, Aquinas affirms: "The uncreated [gift in Christ] was both the Holy Spirit himself, because, as Isaiah 11 says, the Spirit rested in Christ's soul; and the person of Word himself, because it is given to the human nature that it would be the human nature of the person of the Word."[81] The hypostatic union has a surpassing primacy in Christ (the Holy Spirit is not hypostatically united to Christ's humanity), but Thomas would not want us to play that note without also listening for the Holy Spirit's accompanying harmony.

Thomas reaches the same conclusion when he analyzes the divine presence in Christ according to the doctrine of *perichoresis* or circumincession:

---

[79] Aquinas remarks elsewhere that this union is unlike all other graces because it achieves "a full and perfect conjunction with God." *In Ioan.* c. 1, lect. 8 (no. 188).

[80] See also *ScG* IV, c. 34, where St Thomas argues that both the Word and the Holy Spirit dwell in Christ's humanity, although only the Word is present by way of hypostatic union.

[81] III *Sent.* d. 13, q. 1, a. 2, qla 2. Cf. *In Ioan.* c. 3, lect. 6 (no. 544); c. 4, lect. 2 (no. 577).

Since the Father is in the Son, and the Son in the Father, and both of them in the Holy Spirit, when the Son is sent, both the Father and the Holy Spirit simultaneously come, whether this is understood of the coming of the Son in the flesh, as he himself says at John 8:16: "I am not alone, but I and the Father who sent me;" or whether this is understood of his coming into the mind, as he says at John 14:23: "We will come to him and make our dwelling with him."[82]

Since the Son has the Father and the Holy Spirit in him, the visible mission of the Son brings with it, necessarily, the presence of the Father and Holy Spirit. The incarnation is the visible mission of the Son alone, but not the divine presence of the Son without the Father and the Holy Spirit.[83] This points us back to our analysis of the hypostatic union in CHAPTER 4: the incarnation terminates in a union of the human nature to the Son alone so that Christ is truly the Son in the flesh. But it does not follow that we cannot also speak of the presence of the Father and the Holy Spirit in Christ—indeed, Jesus himself says as much, as Thomas notes. Rather, it is the superexcelling way or mode of the Son's presence in the incarnation that is unique: it is a presence by hypostatic union. That is a surpassing mode of presence, but Thomas does not reduce the presence of the divinity in Christ, his holiness, or his power, to the hypostatic union alone and hence to the Son alone. He always insists that Christ's humanity is likewise filled with the presence of the Holy Spirit and the Father. (The Holy Spirit is sent, while the Father—who is not sent—dwells together with the Son and Spirit whom he sends.) These are not competing themes, but profoundly complementary ones, because the Son is always present and active with the Father and the Holy Spirit.

THE THIRD REASON: HUMAN NATURE REQUIRES A HABITUS TO ACT RIGHTLY
We can treat article 13's third reason for the priority of the grace of union over habitual grace briefly since we will return to this subject when we discuss the Spirit's role in Christ's action.

The third reason for this order can be taken from the end of grace, since it is ordered to right action. But actions are actions of supposits and

---

[82] I *Sent.* d. 15, q. 2, a. 1 ad 4.
[83] Aquinas even claims (albeit in a context likely more Eucharistic than strictly Christological) that "the flesh of Christ" is "conjoined to the Word and to the Spirit." *In Ioan.* c. 6, lect. 8 (no. 993).

individuals. Thus, action, and consequently grace ordaining to action, presupposes an acting hypostasis. But no hypostasis is presupposed in Christ's human nature before the union, as was shown above. And therefore the grace of union, according to understanding, precedes habitual grace.[84]

Christ became man in order to act. But in order to act as man, Christ must receive *habitus* disposing him to action (given in habitual grace), and those *habitus* can only exist in a subject (there is only one in Christ, the hypostasis of the eternal Son, to which the human nature is united through the grace of union).[85] It is thus that, in this third reason, St Thomas works his way back from the "end of grace" to the connection (now considered on the side of Christ's humanity) between the grace of union and habitual grace. Habitual grace can only be given to a person, and the only person in Christ is the eternal Son; the hypostatic union makes Christ's human nature the nature *of a person*, and hence capable of receiving the *habitus* of grace.[86] The Son's personal existence in a human nature, then, logically precedes the habitual grace given to Christ.

Further, the Son became incarnate to save us, and he accomplishes this through what he does and suffers in his human nature. As we will emphasize in CHAPTER 7, in order for Christ to undertake these human actions, his human nature stands in genuine need of the operative *habitus* given in habitual grace. "As an instrument animated by a rational soul that both is moved and moves itself, it is necessary for [Christ] to have habitual grace in order to act rightly."[87] Although this is only conditionally necessary in view of an end—namely, that Christ's humanity would be the perfect instrument of his divinity in the work of salvation—this is why the Son was sent in the flesh. Consequently, on the side of Christ's

---

[84] *STh* III, q. 7, a. 13.

[85] It is only through the grace of union that the human nature of Christ receives existence as the human nature of the Son and thus can receive a *habitus* ordaining it to action. From the first instant of its conception in the womb of the Virgin Mary, Christ's human nature was the humanity *of the person of the Son*. That human nature never existed apart from the divine hypostasis of the Son; apart from the union, there was no hypostasis capable of receiving a *habitus*.

[86] Thomas repeatedly adverts to this distinction between Christ's personal or hypostatic being and a *habitus* ordered to action. See, e.g., *STh* III, q. 6, a. 6 ad 1.

[87] *STh* III, q. 7, a. 1 ad 3.

human nature, there is also an authentic necessity that the visible mission of the Son be accompanied by the invisible mission of the Holy Spirit.

SUMMARY To summarize Aquinas's teaching in the *Summa Theologiae*, Christ's habitual grace is really and formally distinct from the grace of union and not merely reducible to it, but is also necessarily entailed by the grace of union according to a triple title: (1) on the side of God, the mission of the Holy Spirit always accompanies the mission of the Son just as, in God, the Spirit proceeds from the Son and love from wisdom; (2) from the perspective of the created effects of a divine mission (always efficiently caused by all three persons together), habitual grace is a created effect of the divine presence, which is understood in Christ par excellence by the union; (3) the end of the union is that Christ would act as man in the world, which requires, on the side of Christ's created nature, that he receive the *habitus* given in habitual grace that would dispose him to that action.

Personal Presence and Common Efficient Causality

These complementary reasons have their roots in Aquinas's Trinitarian theology, where the Dominican master is always careful to distinguish, without separating, what is proper to the divine persons and what is common to the divine essence. To avoid exalting one of the reasons why habitual grace follows the hypostatic union at the expense of the others—that is, in order to see how carefully Thomas elaborates their intricately interwoven nexus—it is important for us to see how, in this Christological context, Aquinas maintains a careful distinction between the modes of personal presence and causality of the divine persons in creatures on the one hand, and the common efficient causality of all three persons on the other.

When Aquinas analyzes in detail in his *Sentences* Commentary how the Son and Holy Spirit are present in Christ in different ways, he carefully differentiates two distinct modes of divine presence in Christ—the human nature hypostatically united to the Son, and the Holy Spirit dwelling in Christ by grace—both of which are simultaneously efficiently caused by all three divine persons. Christ's humanity is assumed "into the *esse* and unity of the divine person" of the Son as its terminus, and thus is united to the Son in an entirely unique and preeminent mode, so that it is the humanity of the Son himself.[88] The Holy Spirit is also in Christ's humanity, but in a very different mode: insofar as charity terminates in and conforms the soul to the Holy Spirit himself, who is the exemplar cause of charity.[89] Christ's humanity *is* the humanity of the Son incarnate, according to a "personal" or "hypostatic" union; he is not the Spirit, who is a distinct hypostasis present in him according to the accidental union of grace.[90] Both of these modes of divine presence in Christ are efficiently caused by all three persons of the Trinity, a fact that does not diminish in any way the reality of Christ's identity as the Son, or the reality of the Spirit's presence in his humanity. As Thomas suggests elsewhere, the important thing is not to distinguish different actions belonging to different divine persons, but to distinguish the divine persons within the one divine action.[91]

To summarize, the Dominican master has found a way to speak of Christ with respect to the causality of and presence of the Son (by the hypostatic union, so that Christ is the Son in person, in the flesh), of the Holy Spirit (indwelling Christ's soul by charity), and of the whole Trinity (as creative principle and efficient cause), each according to a different mode. Of course, the hypostatic union is always first and in a class by itself (since Christ *is* the divine Son), but despite its overwhelming importance, it is not the only register in which Aquinas speaks. More importantly for our purposes, each of these modes is intrinsically and inseparably interwoven with the others as a facet of the single reality of Christ. While there is an order among them, they cannot exist without each other. A complete account of Christ obliges us to accord each of them its proper place.

---

[88] I *Sent.* d. 30, q. 1, a. 2.

[89] I *Sent.* d. 17, q. 1, a. 1. Emery, *La Trinité créatrice*, 399–400.

[90] Aquinas is famous for insisting that, since Christ *is* the Son incarnate, the hypostatic union must be a substantial union, not an accidental one. See, e.g., *STh* III, q. 2, a. 6. A union by grace, however, is an accidental union on the ontological level. *STh* III, q. 2, a. 10. Consequently, Christ *is* the Son incarnate according to his person ("substance"), and the Holy Spirit, a distinct hypostasis, dwells in Christ according to the "accident" of grace.

[91] *In Ioan.* c. 17, lect. 5 (no. 2249), as cited by Bruce D. Marshall, "What Does the Spirit Have to Do?" in *Reading John with St Thomas*, eds Michael Dauphinais and Matthew Levering (Washington, D.C.: Catholic University of America Press, 2005), 69.

Conclusion

Aquinas's explanation of the relation between the hypostatic union and Christ's habitual grace in Question 7, article 13 is therefore the key to understanding the variety of other texts where he speaks of it. Sometimes, as Torrell notes, Thomas presents it as a question of fittingness; Christ's humanity, in its own right, is not "owed" grace but receives it as the supremely fitting complement to the hypostatic union. More often, however, St Thomas speaks of this as a necessity that goes beyond fittingness: in such cases, he is looking at the matter from the side of God; the Word is never present without his Holy Spirit. In both cases, Thomas is always vigilant to maintain the distinction between the proper presence of the divine persons in Christ's humanity and the causality of the divine essence common to all three persons.

Thus, "[h]abitual grace . . . is a certain effect of natural filiation in the soul of Christ,"[92] present from the first instant of his conception as man.[93] It is not reducible to the hypostatic union, which is formally distinct from it,[94] but it nonetheless "inseparably follows" that union "like a certain natural property,"[95] akin to the way light accompanies the sun and heat accompanies fire.[96] Consequently, there is a reciprocal relation between the presence of the divinity in that man and habitual grace, the created effect that is "derived" from that presence.[97] And in that gift of habitual grace (through the charity always present with habitual grace), "the Holy Spirit is shown to be given to the soul of Christ, presupposing the union through which that man was the Son of God."[98] The divine persons, in their inseparable yet distinct and complementary presence, are not competing causes of created grace, nor does the divine efficient causality of all created effects, which belongs to the whole Trinity, undermine the proper mode of causality and the distinct presence of each person.

---

[92] *STh* III, q. 23, a. 4 ad 2. Cf. *Compendium theologiae* I, c. 214, which speaks in nearly identical terms. Note that there is one filiation only in Christ, namely, his divine relation to the Father.

[93] *STh* III, q. 34, a. 4.

[94] III *Sent.* d. 13, q. 1, a. 1. See also *STh* III, q. 1, a 1 ad 1; *In Ioan.* c. 17, lect. 4 (no. 2231).

[95] *STh* III, q. 7, a. 13 ad 2. III *Sent.* d. 4, q. 3, a. 2, qla 1.

[96] *STh* III, q. 7, a. 13 and ad 2.

[97] *De Verit.* q. 29, a. 5 ad 1. *In Ioan.* c. 17, lect. 4 (no. 2231).

[98] *De Verit.* q. 29, a. 3.

B. CHRIST RECEIVES THE HOLY SPIRIT
"WITHOUT MEASURE"

It is by now pellucid that Christ's humanity receives an invisible mission of the Holy Spirit—something taught by Scripture, of which the Dominican *magister in sacra pagina* takes care to render full account.[99] But the Scriptures also testify that many others have received a mission of the Spirit: John the Baptist was "filled with the Holy Spirit, even from his mother's womb" (Luke 1:15), likewise his parents Zechariah and Elizabeth (Luke 1:41, 67), Simeon (Luke 2:25), the apostles and the Blessed Virgin Mary (Acts 2:4), Stephen (Acts 7:55), Paul (Acts 9:17), Barnabas (Acts 11:24), and the early Christian believers (Acts 2:38; 4:31; 8:17; 10:44; 11:15, 19:6). Indeed, St Paul says that all who believe receive the Holy Spirit (Rom. 5:7; 8:9–27), and Jesus himself promised that the Father will "give the Holy Spirit to those who ask him," (Luke 11:13), so that the Spirit himself will "dwell in" and "be in" those who believe in him (John 14:17; John 7:39).

This raises a theological question with important ramifications for both Trinitarian theology and Christology. Is there a difference between the way that Jesus receives the Spirit's mission, and the way that the Spirit is sent to the faithful? Since the Holy Spirit, as a divine person, is himself infinite, can there be differences in "how much" of the Spirit one receives?[100]

---

[99] Thomas's preferred scriptural *loci* for this subject include, *inter alia*, Isaiah 11:2 ("the Spirit of the Lord shall rest upon him"), Luke 4:1 (Jesus was "filled with the Holy Spirit"), and Matthew 12:18's reference to Isaiah 42:1 ("I will put my Spirit upon him"). See *STh* III, q. 72, a. 4 ad 4; *STh* III, q. 7, a. 13 sc; *In Matt.*, c. 12, lect. 1 (no. 1000). Many more Scripture citations could be added, the accounts of Christ's baptism not least among them.

[100] For a helpful approach to these and related questions in Luke-Acts, see James D. G. Dunn, *Jesus and the Spirit* (London: SCM Press, 1975), 157–96. Dunn concludes from his historical-critical analysis of the sacred text that, from the beginning, "religious experiences of the earliest community, including experiences like those enjoyed by Jesus himself, were seen as dependent on him and derivative from him." *Ibid.*, 196. He draws essentially the same conclusion when he considers the texts of the New Testament as a whole. James D. G. Dunn, *The Christ and The Spirit*, vol. 1, *Christology* (Edinburgh: T&T Clark, 1998), 152–3. However, Dunn seems to regard our reception of the Spirit as all-or-nothing; if there are no visible effects of the Spirit's coming to a believer (like "prophecy and witness"), Dunn suggests, based on Acts 8:14–24, that the Holy Spirit has not been received at all. Dunn, *The Christ and The Spirit*, vol. 2, *Pneumatology*, 226–8.

Christ Receives "the Whole Spirit"

In treating this, St Thomas most frequently turns to three texts from John's Gospel: "We saw his glory, the glory as of an only-begotten Son, full of grace and truth (John 1:14);" "from his fullness we have all received (John 1:16);" and "it is not by measure that God gives the Spirit" to Christ (John 3:34). According to Aquinas, these three verses are referring to different facets of the same reality: the mission of the Spirit to Christ's humanity according to the gifts of habitual grace, which Christ has in full, without measure. It is in this sense that Thomas quotes approvingly an evocative formula drawn from the *Glossa ordinaria*: Christ receives *totum spiritum:* "the whole Spirit," the Holy Spirit in his entirety.[101] "God gives the Spirit to men by measure, but to the Son without measure; . . . He gives his entire Spirit [*totum spiritum suum*] to the incarnate Son not in a particular fashion, nor by subdivision, but universally and generally."[102]

Aquinas is speaking of Christ's reception of "the whole Spirit" in his humanity (in his divinity, the Son is a principle of the Holy Spirit and so cannot be called the Spirit's beneficiary),[103] but this expression does not suggest that others receive only a part of the Spirit, as if a divine person could be partitioned and parceled out. On the contrary, every mission of the Holy Spirit entails the Spirit's presence according to his personal procession; on the side of the divine person, he is unchanging in his perfect divine simplicity. But the Spirit's presence in a creature is according to some created effect, which can be partial or "according to measure." "The Holy Spirit is given partially, not with respect to his essence and power (in this sense, he is infinite), but with respect to the gifts which are given by measure: 'But grace was given to each of us according to the measure of Christ's giving (Eph. 4:7).'"[104]

---

[101] Emery, "Missions invisibles," 82, quoting *In Matt.*, c. 12, lect. 1 (no. 1000).

[102] *De Verit.*, q. 29, a. 3, quoting the *Glossa ordinaria* with approval. As is clear in this article, Aquinas freely criticizes and sets aside other interpretations in the *Glossa ordinaria*; that he retained and repeated this quotation suggests that it accords with his own view.

[103] St Thomas agrees that God the Father gives the Spirit to the Son in his divinity "without measure" in the sense that he gives the Son the power of spirating the Spirit with the Father, but this should not be understood as if the Son, as God, is the beneficiary of the Spirit. Rather, the Son "as God has the Holy Spirit only as manifesting him, insofar as the Spirit proceeds from him." *In Ioan.* c. 3, lect. 6 (no. 543).

[104] *In Ioan.* c. 3, lect. 6 (no. 542).

It is not simply because the Holy Spirit is himself infinite, therefore, that Christ is said to have the perfect fullness of the Spirit. Were that the cause of Christ's fullness, Aquinas explains, "Christ would be no different" from "any other holy men," in whom "dwells the Holy Spirit" who, as "the third person of the Trinity, is infinite in himself."[105] Rather, Aquinas offers three marks of Christ's "fullness" of the Holy Spirit that distinguishes him from all others.

First, Christ has the perfect possession of the "whole Spirit" insofar as he receives the full *extent* of the Spirit's gifts, according to the categories of grace we have already discussed: Christ's humanity receives, in a unique and singular way, every possible created gift of grace ("whatsoever can pertain to the nature of grace,"[106] which includes habitual grace, the gifts of sanctifying grace, the virtues, the gifts of the Holy Spirit, and the charisms), and, above all, the Holy Spirit himself.[107]

Second, Aquinas underlines that, unlike other saints and prophets, Christ *always* has this fullness, which gives him a unique kind of possession of or dominion over the Spirit's gifts. This is especially important for understanding the New Testament portrayal of Christ's earthly life: at every moment, he has the fullness of the Spirit's power at his disposal.

> [A]s to [the charismatic gifts], it is proper to Christ that [the Holy Spirit] would remain with him always, because, in the fullness of his power he is always able to work miracles, to prophesy, and to do other things of this kind. But it is not so with others; because, as Gregory says, the spirits of the prophets are not subject to the prophets.[108]

Christ is not like a prophet who must wait for the Spirit to come to him. He receives, once and for all at the first instant of his conception,

---

[105] *De Verit.*, q. 29, a. 3.   [106] *STh* III, q. 7, a. 11; cf. a. 10.

[107] St Thomas's own teacher, Albert the Great, observes briefly that "anima Christi capax est gratiae totius Spiritus." Albertus Magnus, *Ennarationes in Joannem* 3.34 [*Opera Omnia*, ed. A. Borgnet, (1899) 24:149b]; cf. Giuseppe Ferraro, *Lo Spirito Santo nei commentari al quarto vangelo di Bruno di Segni, Ruperto di Deutz, Bonaventura e Alberto Magno* (Vatican: Libreria Editrice Vaticana, 1998), 148–9. Aquinas's analysis, and his emphasis that Christ receives the Holy Spirit himself and in full, is much more complete. We should note, however, that it is not certain that St Thomas knew this text of St Albert (it may have been composed after Thomas's death), though probably he was at least familiar with Albert's teaching on the fourth Gospel, having likely heard Albert lecture on it during his studies with him. See Sabathé, *La Trinité rédemptrice*, 586–7.

[108] *In Ioan.* c. 14, lect. 4 (no. 1915). See also *ibid.*, c. 1, lect. 14 (no. 273).

every possible gift of grace, so that, as man, he has a supreme freedom to act in the Spirit's power when and as he sees fit. Though Christ's humanity as such does not become the Holy Spirit's master (as a creature, it is infinitely less than the Holy Spirit who is God), St Thomas goes so far as to say that this gives Christ a kind of dominion over the "fullness" of the gifts that he receives from the Spirit.

> For others receive the use of grace for a time, since the spirit of the prophets is not always present to the prophets, but it is habitually in Christ, because in Christ there is always, at will, a dominion over this fullness. John 1:33: "He upon whom you see the Spirit descending and resting in him," etc.[109]

The gifts of grace that others receive only punctually are given to Christ habitually; he can use them as he wills. To be sure, they always remain *gifts* in Christ's humanity—they do not come from the principles of his human nature itself—but they are given to him in a singularly unique way, so that they are fully actual and available to Christ at every moment.

Finally, Christ has the infinite capacity to pour out the Spirit's gifts—and the Holy Spirit himself—on others with "a supreme fullness of communicative power."[110] This is a third mark that distinguishes the absolute fullness of Christ's possession of the Spirit from all others; even the fullness of the Blessed Virgin Mary's reception of the Spirit must be less than that of Christ, who has the Spirit "unto every effect of grace."[111] Thomas refers to this as Christ's capital grace (a subject we will discuss in CHAPTER 8); in fact, it is really the same as his habitual grace, differing from it only according to the aspect under which we view it.[112] In other words, Christ's own grace (his grace "as an individual man") is so full and perfect that Christ himself becomes the fount from which all others receive grace.

The ultimate source of these three facets of Christ's perfect fullness of the Spirit is the grace of union, the superexcelling unity of Christ's soul with the Word of God himself. The perfect visible mission of the Word is accompanied by the perfect invisible mission of the Spirit, who is present in Christ's humanity in the gifts of grace to the maximal possible degree. In short, the Word breathes forth the whole Spirit to the humanity he assumes. This is what Aquinas

---

[109] *In Epist. ad Col.* c. 1, lect. 5 (no. 50).   [110] Emery, "Missions invisibles," 82.
[111] *STh* III, q. 7, a. 10 ad 1.   [112] *STh* III, q. 8, a. 5.

means when he says, "only Christ has the Holy Spirit fully,"[113] and "Christ alone possesses the Spirit without measure."[114]

We can now infer why we do not find a question entitled "On Christ's Reception of the Holy Spirit" in the opening section of the *Summa Theologiae's Tertia pars*. Thomas's treatment of Christ's "fullness" and "infinity" of habitual grace in *STh* III, q. 7 has already treated the very mystery of the Spirit's mission to Christ, and has enunciated the key principles of a genuine Spirit-Christology. Question 8, on Christ's capital grace, discusses this same mystery insofar as, from that fullness, Christ is the source of grace for all others; indeed, this mystery is foundational for every Christological question that follows. But Aquinas's focus in this section of the *Summa* is on "the Savior himself," and, more specifically, on "the very mystery of the incarnation itself."[115] Because the incarnation is the formal object of his inquiry, the titles of the questions (q. 7: "the grace of Christ insofar as he is an individual man;" q. 8: "the grace of Christ insofar as he is head of the Church") refer in the first place to Christ, and the questions themselves examine the intrinsic features of the Son's visible mission as man. It is rather in the treatment of Christ's earthly life later in the *Tertia pars*, where he follows more closely the chronology of the Gospel rather than the order of speculative Christological doctrine, that we will find Aquinas bringing the Holy Spirit into the foreground.

Fullness of Grace: Finite and Infinite

As a creature, Christ's humanity is finite, and thus, in the most proper sense, considered a created accident inhering in that humanity, Christ's grace must be ontologically finite.[116] While Aquinas admits this to be true, strictly speaking, he nonetheless offers three arguments for how Christ's habitual grace—and thus his possession of the Spirit—can still be rightly considered "full," "without measure," or "infinite."[117] These arguments give us an important insight into the Trinitarian structure of Christ's grace.

---

[113] *In Epist. ad Hebr.* c. 6, lect. 1 (no. 289).

[114] IV *Sent.* d. 49, q 2, art 5, sc2; *In Epist. ad Rom.* c. 12, lect. 1 (no. 971).

[115] *STh* III, prologue: 'de ipso Salvatore;' 'de ipso incarnationis mysterio.'

[116] *STh* III, q. 7, a. 11.

[117] We will focus on the three arguments from *Compendium theologiae* I, c. 215. These arguments correspond word for word, with a few small (but sometimes

The first argument deals with the way in which God gives the gift of habitual grace: when God places no limitation on the grace he gives, then, considered from the side of the giver, grace is given "without measure."

> When someone is not given from the divine goodness as much as the natural capacity of its species, the gift to him seems to be according to some measure. But when his entire natural capacity is filled, the gift to him does not seem to be "by measure," because even if it would be "by measure" on the part of the recipient, it is not "by measure" on the part of the giver who is ready to give everything: as if someone bringing a pail to a river, finds water without measure prepared for him, although he can only take it by measure according to the limited size of his pail. In this way, the habitual grace of Christ, while finite in its essence, is said to be given infinitely and without measure, because as much is given as a created nature can receive.[118]

The Holy Spirit is like an infinite river, while the human nature of Christ is like a pail that receives as much from that river as it can possibly hold. If we focus on the pail (that is, considered from the recipient's side), the created grace it receives is ontologically finite, but this is not because God has chosen to withhold something from Christ. Rather, God pours out the surging abundance of the entire river on Christ; if we focus on the way God gives grace to Christ, we see it is given "without measure," with no limitation or reservation, so that Christ's grace is characterized by an infinite mode on God's side. God holds nothing back from Christ; the only limit to Christ's grace is due to the finitude of the human soul that receives it.

Aquinas's second argument concerns the essence of the gift of grace itself. While finite (as is every created essence), its intensity is infinite when it is perfectly realized in a subject.

> Thus the habitual grace of Christ is finite according to its essence, but is nonetheless called "without limit" and "without measure" because, whatever could pertain to the essence of grace, Christ receives it all [*totum*].

significant) variations, to the three arguments given at *In Ioan.* c. 3, lect. 6 (no. 544). We use the *Compendium theologiae* text because it exists in a critical Leonine edition. The same arguments are also present in abbreviated form in the *Summa Theologiae* (*STh* III, q. 7, aa. 10 and 11), and can be found in longer form at *De Verit.*, q. 29, a. 3, and formulated slightly differently (in terms of final, efficient, and formal causality) at III *Sent.* d. 13, q. 1, a. 2, qla 1.

[118] *Compendium theologiae* I, c. 215. Cf. *In Ioan.* c. 3, lect. 6 (no. 544).

Others, however, do not receive it all, but one, this much, and another, that much.[119]

This second argument centers not on the way God gives grace (as did the first), but on the various forms of grace and their intensity ("whatever pertains to grace," "all"): there is nothing of grace lacking to Christ.[120] St Thomas's wording echoes the dictum of the *Glossa ordinaria*: as Christ receives the whole Spirit (*totum spiritum*), so he receives the whole effect (*totum*) of the Spirit's presence.

His third argument connects Christ's grace to the hypostatic union—tracing the river back to its source, as it were—suggesting that the link between the mission of the Holy Spirit in grace and the mission of the Son in the hypostatic union is always presupposed by Aquinas.

> An effect is present in a certain way in its cause. Therefore, whoever has an infinite power to produce some infusion has what is infused without measure, and, in a way, infinitely. For example, if someone had a spring from which could flow out water to infinity, he would be said to have water without measure and infinitely. In this way, therefore, the soul of Christ has grace [that is] infinite and without measure because it has the Word united to it, who is the infinite and unfailing source of the entire emanation of all creatures.[121]

The Word, to whom Christ's human nature is united, is like a spring from which flows an infinite quantity of water—first to Christ's humanity itself, and through it, to all creatures.[122] Though Aquinas's text is somewhat ambiguous, he may be extending the metaphor of the river and pail from a few lines earlier. The infinite spring is clearly the Word and the water seems to be grace, which would suggest that the Holy Spirit is the infinite river flowing from the Word, a scriptural image for the Holy Spirit that Thomas uses elsewhere in his John Commentary (e.g., the Holy Spirit is called "a river because he proceeds from the Father and the Son").[123] If this is what Thomas

---

[119] *Ibid.* Cf. *De Verit.*, q. 29, a. 3.

[120] See, e.g., *STh* III, q. 7, a. 10. Cf. *De Verit.*, q. 29, a. 3.

[121] *Compendium theologiae* I, c. 215.

[122] In the lines that immediately follow this passage, Aquinas concludes that, if Christ himself received grace without measure, then he can pour out graces without measure on others as head of the Church ("*gratia ipsius secundum quod est Ecclesie caput est etiam infinita*").

[123] *In Ioan.* c. 7, lect. 5 (no. 1092). See also *In Ioan.* c. 15, lect. 5 (no. 2061).

means, then this passage nicely connects Christ's own reception of habitual grace (the water that fills the "pail" of his nature) to both the Holy Spirit and the Word from whom the Spirit proceeds. In any case, however, it is clear that Aquinas regards the Word himself, united to Christ's human nature, as a certain "source" of the fullness of Christ's grace.

A final caveat: St Thomas understands Christ's fullness of grace as thoroughly consistent with all that the Gospels say about the concrete historical life of Jesus—that he "increased in wisdom and in stature, and in favor with God and man (Luke 2:52)." In other words, Christ was always filled with the Spirit, but that does not mean that he was constantly working miracles or prophesying, or that he might not appear to others as anything but fully human. As Aquinas puts it, Christ's *habitus* of grace did not increase—it was perfect from the start—but his visible *acts* empowered by the Spirit's presence in him certainly did increase over time: "as he grew older, he did more perfect works, in order to show that he was truly a man." The *habitus* did not increase, but its visible effects did. "In this way, Christ increased in wisdom and in grace, as in age."[124]

The Holy Spirit, the Fullness of Christ

For Aquinas, Christ is not only full of created grace because his soul is united to the Word; there is another sense to this "fullness,"[125] namely, the Holy Spirit in person: "the fullness of Christ is the Holy Spirit, who proceeds from him, consubstantial with him in nature, in power, and in majesty."[126] Aquinas's theology of Christ's full reception of the Holy Spirit thus offers an authentic Spirit-Christology: it preserves the Trinitarian order of processions (the Spirit proceeds from the Son as God, and is given to Christ's humanity—the Word breathes forth Love to his assumed human nature), while accounting for the absolute uniqueness of Christ (by the hypostatic union, his humanity is made the humanity of the Word). It does so in such a way that the humanity of Christ is not mixed with the divine nature, but is supremely sanctified by the Holy Spirit's gift of grace in accordance with his human condition, so that the Holy Spirit is present in that

---

[124] *STh* III, q. 7, a 12 ad 3.   [125] *De Verit.*, q. 29, a. 5 ad 1.
[126] *In Ioan.* c. 1, lect. 10 (no. 202); see also c. 3, lect. 6 (no. 544).

humanity[127] according to the full capacity of a human nature for union with God.[128] The Spirit's presence in the man Christ is thus not in competition with Christ's divinity as the Word (from which it flows),[129] nor is it minimized as if it were only a footnote to the hypostatic union. The Holy Spirit's presence in Christ is, rather, of fundamental importance for understanding how that human nature is elevated *as a human nature* as a result of the hypostatic union.

The natural point to consider next would be Christ's capital grace, that is, how Christ, having received the Holy Spirit fully, then bestows that Spirit on all others. But in order to complete our investigation of the implications of the perfect presence of the Spirit in Christ himself, we will delay this consideration until CHAPTER 8.

Manifesting the Spirit: The Visible Missions of the Holy Spirit to Christ

Christ's grace, and therefore his possession of the Holy Spirit as man, was perfect from the first moment of his conception. Yet at two key moments of his earthly life—at his baptism by John in the Jordan, and at the transfiguration on Mount Tabor, the Holy Spirit's presence in him was manifested through a visible sign. These visible missions of the Holy Spirit to Christ did not produce anything new in Christ's humanity, but they do play an important role in the manifestation of the Trinitarian mystery of the incarnation. Further, they unveil for us how the way of salvation opened to us by Christ is a work of the whole Trinity.

Let us begin with what is most fundamental: Both at Christ's baptism and at his transfiguration, "the mystery of the Trinity is demonstrated"—the Son is present in his human nature, the Father's voice is heard, and the Holy Spirit is made known by the dove and the

---

[127] As we discussed in CHAPTER 2, for Aquinas, sanctifying grace *disposes* us to receive the Holy Spirit in person. The Holy Spirit is "possessed" when the soul is assimilated or conformed to him by charity, so that the soul is really united to the Holy Spirit himself as the object of fruition. See Emery, *Trinitarian Theology*, 379–87; *STh* I, q. 38, a. 1; q. 43, a. 3; q. 43, a. 5 ad 2.

[128] On the part of his human nature, then, Aquinas reasons that Christ's grace cannot increase because he is already as perfectly united to God as is possible for a human nature. *STh* III, q. 7, a. 12.

[129] *De Verit.*, q. 29, a. 5 ad 1.

luminous cloud.[130] Drawing on his speculative Trinitarian doctrine, St Thomas underlines that, in both theophanies, the Father reveals himself as one who speaks, and hence who is properly manifested through his Word.

> The Father is not demonstrated in the voice except as the voice's author, or as speaking through the voice. And because it is proper to the Father to produce the Word—which is "to say" or "to speak"—the Father is therefore most fittingly manifested through the voice, which signifies a word. Thus, the voice itself sent forth by the Father also bears witness to the filiation of the Word.[131]

The Father's speaking reveals what is proper to the Father, that he eternally speaks his Word. This simultaneously reveals the Word's filiation, since the voice identifies Christ as the "natural Son" of God, begotten by the Father in the same divine nature. "Both at the baptism and at the transfiguration, it was fitting that the testimony of the Father manifests Christ's natural filiation, because [the Father] alone, together with the Son and Holy Spirit, is perfectly conscious of that perfect generation."[132] The Father and his Word are thus manifested as intrinsically in relation to each other—the Father as the speaker of the Word, the Word as spoken by the Father.[133] Each side of this relation points to the other. Consequently, when Christ is manifested as the Father's Son, the Father is also revealed. As Aquinas explains in a text we saw in CHAPTER 3, "to manifest the name of the Father is the proper work of the Son of God, who is the Word," because it is proper to a Word "to manifest a speaker."[134] In fact, this also implies the Holy Spirit, who proceeds as the mutual love of the Father and Son. According to St Thomas, the Father's voice calls Christ his "beloved" Son for precisely this reason—that is, because "Love itself proceeds from the Father loving the Son, and from the Son loving the Father."[135]

Yet what makes these episodes *visible* missions is that they are accompanied by visible signs. "[The Father's] voice expressed, as it were, what the dove signified."[136] The Spirit was made visible "so that the Son of God made visible through the flesh would be manifested

---

[130] *STh* III, q. 39, a. 8, quoting St Jerome. See also *STh* III, q. 45, a. 4 ad 2; *In Ioan.* c. 1, lect. 14 (no. 268).

[131] *STh* III, q. 39, a. 8 ad 2.   [132] *STh* III, q. 45, a. 4.

[133] See *STh* I, q. 34, a. 3 ad 4.   [134] *In Ioan.* c. 17, lect. 2 (no. 2194).

[135] *In Matt.* c. 17, lect. 1 (no. 1436).   [136] *In Matt.* c. 3, lect. 2 (no. 302).

through the Holy Spirit by means of the visible species of a dove."[137] Considered as manifestations, therefore, the visible missions of the Son and Holy Spirit are alike, St Thomas explains, "because as the Son, existing from the Father, manifests the Father, thus also the Holy Spirit existing from the Son, manifests the Son." In both cases, the person visibly sent manifests that he exists from another.

As we noted in Chapter 2, however, an important difference between these visible missions remains. The dove at Christ's baptism was not assumed into a unity of person with the Holy Spirit, like the union between Christ's humanity and the divine Son. Rather:

> this appearance was formed anew to represent divine effects, as when the Lord appeared in the fire and the bush (Ex. 3:2), and in giving the law, in lightning and thunder (Ex. 19:16). Hence the dove was [made] to represent the influence of the Holy Spirit.[138]

The visible sign of a dove was made in order to demonstrate the otherwise invisible reality of the Spirit's presence in Christ's humanity.

> Note that a visible mission [of the Holy Spirit] is always a sign of an invisible mission.... But in Christ it does not signify a new effect, because from the instant of his conception he was full of grace and truth.[139]

The Holy Spirit "did not descend [upon Christ at his baptism] because of [Christ's] need, but for our sake, namely, so that his grace would be manifested to us."[140] The visible sign of the Holy Spirit manifests the Spirit, but that visible created effect remains on the level of a sign. The Holy Spirit's presence and action is signified by that sign, but the Spirit does not act through or by means of the sign.[141]

In fact, Aquinas explains that the visible signs of the Spirit's presence in Christ at the baptism and the transfiguration reveal more than that Christ himself has the fullness of grace. They also show "that [this] fullness is ordered to others, that this abundant grace would in some way overflow to them."[142] The Spirit's visible missions to Christ manifest that he is the founder and head of the Church,[143]

---

[137] *In Ioan.* c. 1, lect. 14 (no. 270).   [138] *In Matt.* c. 3, lect. 2 (no. 299).
[139] *Ibid.* (no. 301).   [140] *In Ioan.* c. 1, lect. 14 (no. 274).
[141] In contrast, the Son's humanity is more than a visible sign—through it, the Son acts as man to save us. *Ibid.* (no. 270).
[142] I *Sent.* d. 16, q. 1, a. 2.   [143] *STh* I, q. 43, a. 7 ad 6.

and that his humanity is the fount through which all graces flow.[144] In other words, the visible missions reveal publicly the very features of Christ's reception of the Holy Spirit that we have been discussing.

While this revelation is first of all about Christ himself—that as the Word Incarnate, he receives the Holy Spirit in full—there is a second dimension that is no less important: these visible missions reveal that the salvation Christ brings not only has a Trinitarian form (like the sacrament of baptism itself), but that this salvation has the whole Trinity as its end and its fruit.[145] Indeed, it is a work of the whole Trinity:

> As the baptism, where the mystery of our first regeneration was declared, was shown [to be] the work of the whole Trinity, through this that the incarnate Son was [present] there, the Holy Spirit appeared in the form of a dove, and the Father was there declared in the voice; thus also in the transfiguration, which is the sacrament of [our] second regeneration, the whole Trinity appeared, the Father in the voice, the Son as man, the Holy Spirit in the bright cloud, because as innocence is given in baptism, which is signified through the dove's simplicity, so in the resurrection he will give his elect the brightness of glory and rest from every evil, which is designated in the shining cloud.[146]

As Christ received the Holy Spirit in the form of a dove at his baptism, so our baptism, a work of the whole Trinity, gives us a share in the same Spirit, who renews our innocence and makes us as "simple as doves." And as Christ's humanity shone with the glory of the Holy Spirit at his transfiguration, so the Holy Spirit will conform us to Christ in his passion and death, so that we will also share in the glory of his resurrection.

---

[144] See, e.g., *Compendium theologiae* I, c. 215; *In Ioan.* c. 4, lect. 1 (no. 561).
[145] See, e.g., *In Matt.* c. 3, lect. 2 (no. 305). Cf. I *Sent.* d. 2, expos. text.
[146] *STh* III, q. 45, a. 4 ad 2.

6

The Holy Spirit and Christ's Human Knowledge

Although rarely appreciated, Aquinas recognizes an important role for the Holy Spirit in Christ's human knowledge. Because this is a point where Thomas's Christology is often criticized as giving short shrift to the Holy Spirit, it will be worth our effort to bring to light just how significant are the Spirit's presence and action in this domain.

In his *Summa Theologiae*, St Thomas identifies four types of knowledge in Christ: the divine knowledge of the Word himself, the beatific vision of Christ's human soul, his soul's infused supernatural knowledge, and finally Christ's experiential human knowledge.[1] Of these four types, we can set aside the first, a knowledge that belongs exclusively to Christ's divine nature—"this act could not be an act of Christ's human soul, since it is an act of a different nature."[2] We can also set aside the last, Christ's experiential human knowledge. Like us, Christ's experiential knowledge came to him through his senses. Such knowledge is important for Aquinas's Christology—St Thomas is the first medieval author who recognized in Christ a full "acquired knowledge" (*scientia acquisita*), and this only in his mature works[3]—but the Holy Spirit does not seem to have a special role in it, except perhaps insofar as he moves Christ in all his human acts. Our attention will therefore focus on the two remaining kinds of Christ's

---

[1] See *STh* III, q. 9.

[2] *STh* III, q. 9, a 1 ad 1. Just as they are one and the same essence, the three divine persons have, and are, one single divine knowledge.

[3] See Jean-Pierre Torrell, *Recherches thomasiennes* (Paris: Librairie Philosophique J. Vrin, 2000), 202. See also Torrell, *Encyclopédie Jésus le Christ*, 1018–24; and Jean-Pierre Torrell, "Le savoir acquis du Christ selon les théologiens médiévaux," *Revue Thomiste* 101 (2001): 355–408.

human knowledge, both of which are supernatural: first, Christ's beatific vision, and then his divinely infused knowledge.

A. THE BEATIFIC VISION AND THE HOLY SPIRIT

The beatific vision is the highest form of Christ's human knowledge. St Thomas holds that Christ's soul has an immediate vision of God that infinitely transcends all created images. "[F]rom the first instant of his conception, Christ fully beheld God in essence,"[4] and therefore his soul is perfectly blessed at every moment of his existence.[5] Aquinas speaks of this as a beholding of the Word himself: the soul of Christ "sees the Word more perfectly" than any other creature.[6] The hypostatic union is the reason that Christ's soul stands at the summit of all creation in this regard:

> The vision of the divine essence is accorded to all of the blessed insofar as they participate in the light that flows out [*derivantur*] to them from the fount of the Word of God, according to the text of Sir. 1: "The Word of God is the fount of wisdom on high." But the soul of Christ, which is united to the Word in person, is more closely joined to this Word of God than any other creature whatsoever. And hence it receives more fully than any other creature the inflowing of light from the Word itself in which God is seen.[7]

While this was a position unanimously held by Aquinas's contemporaries, it has come under fire from an array of critics.[8] Among them, some think it incompatible with the proper place of the Holy

---

[4] *STh* III, q. 7, a. 3. This is how Thomas generally speaks of what is commonly called the beatific vision: to see God "*per essentiam*," which renders the beholder blessed. See Jean-Pierre Torrell, "La vision de Dieu per essentiam selon saint Thomas d'Aquin," *Micrologus* 5 (1997): 43.

[5] *STh* III, q. 9, a. 2. For a detailed study of Aquinas on Christ's beatific vision and its Augustinian sources, see Pierre-Yves Maillard, *La vision de Dieu chez Thomas d'Aquin: Une lecture de l'*In Ioannem *à la lumière de ses sources augustiniennes* (Paris: Librairie Philosophique J. Vrin, 2001), 225–54.

[6] *STh* III, q. 10, a. 2; see also *STh* III, q. 9, a. 3; III *Sent.* d. 14, a. 2, qla 4.

[7] *STh* III, q. 10, a. 4.

[8] For a summary of the case against the traditional view that Christ had the beatific vision, see Gerald O'Collins and Daniel Kendall, "The Faith of Jesus," *Theological Studies* 53 (1992): 403–23. For other recent Catholic authors who question the Thomistic position on Christ's beatific vision, see, e.g., Balthasar, *Theo-Drama*

Spirit in Christ's life, arguing that Jesus's knowledge of God and his consciousness of his divine identity and mission come not from his identity as the divine Word made flesh, but from his anointing by the Holy Spirit.[9] Thomas Weinandy offers a good example of this sort of critique of Aquinas by a contemporary Catholic theologian. He sharply criticizes St Thomas's account, claiming that Christ did not have the beatific vision "in the Word," but rather progressively grew in awareness of his divine filial identity as he received, in greater and greater measure, the illumination of the Holy Spirit throughout his life, a process that only reached its full completion in the resurrection. For Weinandy, granting Jesus an objective vision of God throughout his life misunderstands and obscures the Spirit's proper role in the life of Christ and in the economy of salvation as a whole.[10]

For Aquinas, however, this poses a false dilemma, because he conceives of no rivalry in Christ between the Word and the Holy Spirit. Christ is the Word incarnate, a true man who is truly anointed, illumined, and led by the Holy Spirit. He possesses the beatific vision in the highest part of his soul as a gracious gift of the Word *and* of the Spirit who proceeds from the Word. Aquinas makes this explicit in his *Sentences* Commentary:

vol. 3, 172–6, 200; J. Galot, "Le Christ terrestre et la vision," *Gregorianum* 67 (1986): 429–50; Jean-Pierre Torrell, "S. Thomas d'Aquin et la science du Christ," in *Saint Thomas au XXe siècle*, ed. S. Bonino (Paris: Éditions St Paul, 1994), 394–409; Thomas G. Weinandy, "Jesus' Filial Vision of the Father," *Pro Ecclesia* 13 (2004): 189–201. On the other side of this issue, see Benedict Ashley, "The Extent of Jesus' Human Knowledge According to the Fourth Gospel," in *Reading John with St Thomas Aquinas*, eds Michael Dauphinais and Matthew Levering (Washington, D.C.: Catholic University of America Press, 2005), 241–53; Thomas Joseph White, "The Voluntary Action of the Earthly Christ and the Necessity of the Beatific Vision," *The Thomist* 69 (2005): 497–534; Thomas Joseph White, "Dyotheletism and the Instrumental Human Consciousness of Jesus," *Pro Ecclesia* 17 (2008): 396–422.

[9] See, e.g., Dunn, *The Christ and the Spirit*, vol. 2, 334–8; Dunn, *Jesus and the Spirit*, 41–67; G. W. H. Lampe, "The Holy Spirit and the Person of Christ," in *Christ, Faith and History*, eds S. W. Sykes and J. P. Clayton (Cambridge: Cambridge University Press, 1972), 124–6.

[10] Weinandy, "Jesus' Filial Vision," 196–8; see also Thomas G. Weinandy, *The Father's Spirit of Sonship: Reconceiving the Trinity* (Edinburgh: T&T Clark, 1995), 28–9, 45 (arguing that "the Spirit conformed Jesus to be the faithful Son on earth," that even for Jesus, "'Abba' can only be spoken in the Spirit," and that what Jesus knows of God is given him by the Spirit). For a critique of Weinandy's Spirit-Christology, see Gilles Emery, review of *The Father's Spirit of Sonship: Reconceiving the Trinity*, by Thomas G. Weinandy, *Revue Thomiste* 96 (1996) 152–4.

Only Christ has the Spirit "without measure," as John 3 says. But because Christ has the Spirit without measure, it belongs to him to know all things in the Word; for this reason, the Gospel goes on to say "the Father has given all things into his hand."[11]

Because he is the Word incarnate, Christ as man receives the whole Spirit (*totum spiritum*) and all of the Spirit's gifts, so that Christ as man has the most perfect beatific knowledge—a knowledge that is in the Word *and* from the Spirit.

It is therefore a mistake to read Thomas's texts on Christ's beatific vision as if he would connect that vision only to the hypostatic union, or as if the union were itself the sole explanation of the vision. Indeed, this is something Aquinas expressly denies: "on the part of the union itself, one cannot posit any knowledge in Christ. For that union is to personal being, while knowledge only belongs to a person by reason of some nature."[12] Even though assumed into a hypostatic union with the second person of the Trinity, Christ's human nature still needs to receive something *in that human nature* so that his soul can see the essence of God (something that also holds true for Christ's infused knowledge). The union itself does not itself change his human nature or endow it with this power.[13] Even though Christ *is* the divine Word, his human soul does not, by the mere fact of the union, behold the Word directly.[14]

Thus, in the first text quoted above (from *STh* III, q. 10, a. 4), Aquinas carefully distinguishes the Word itself from the light that flows out from the Word as from a fount, by which Christ's soul beholds the divine essence. This distinction draws on the account of

---

[11] IV *Sent.* d. 49, q. 2, a. 5, sc 2. Given the context, St Thomas is clearly speaking about the beatific vision here.

[12] *STh* III, q. 9, a. 1 ad. 3.   [13] *STh* III, q. 9, a. 2 ad 1.

[14] This is an interesting point of contrast with Karl Rahner, who does not mention a supernatural light, habitual grace, or the Holy Spirit, in connection with Christ's vision of the divine essence, but contends that the hypostatic union itself is its unique source. "The *visio immediata* is an intrinsic element of the Hypostatic Union itself." Karl Rahner, "Dogmatic Reflections on the Knowledge and Self-Consciousness of Christ," *Theological Investigations*, vol. 5, trans. Karl H. Kruger (Baltimore: Helicon Press, 1966), 206. "[T]his really existing direct vision of God is nothing other than the original unobjectified consciousness of divine sonship, which is present by the mere fact that there *is* a Hypostatic Union." *Ibid.*, 208. It is an "intrinsic and inalienable element of this Union." *Ibid.*, 215. Rahner explicitly rejects the argument that that vision is a distinct perfection granted to Christ "not ontologically bound up with the Hypostatic Union." *Ibid.*, 204.

the beatific vision Thomas elaborated in the *Prima pars*. That vision consists in a direct beholding of the divine essence involving no created likenesses in the mind of the beholder, but because this infinitely exceeds the capacity of any created intellect, the creature must receive a created gift, "the light of glory strengthening the intellect to see God."[15] Thomas explains this light thus:

> Everything that is elevated to something that exceeds its nature must be disposed to it by a disposition that is also above its nature.... And so it is necessary that some supernatural disposition be granted to an intellect [that would see the essence of God] in order to elevate it unto such sublime heights. Since a created intellect's natural power does not suffice to see the essence of God (as has been shown), its power of understanding must be increased further by divine grace. We call this increase of the intellective power an "illumination of the intellect".... It is about this light that Revelation 21 says that "the glory of God will illuminate them," namely, the society of the blessed who see God. By this light they are made "deiform," that is, like God, as 1 John 3 says: "when he appears, we will be like him, because we will see him as he is."[16]

The addition of a habitual disposition strengthening the intellect is a necessity for any human intellect that sees the divine essence, including Christ's. Even given the hypostatic union, Christ's intellect still must be supernaturally illuminated in order to do this.[17]

Thomas underlines this conclusion regarding Christ in a striking text from his *Sentences* Commentary. There, an objector had argued that no *habitus* was needed in Christ's soul for him to have the beatific vision because that soul was united directly to the Word in the hypostatic union. In replying, Aquinas makes clear that even given the grace of union, Christ still needs a supernatural light strengthening his intellect to see the divine essence directly.

> The union by which the Word is united to the soul of Christ in person is not the same as the union by which the Word is united to Christ's soul as what is seen [is united] to the seer; because the Word is united to the body in person, but it is not seen by the body. And hence, while there is no medium in that union by which the soul is united to the Word in person, it does not follow that there is no medium in the vision [of the

---

[15] *STh* I, q. 12, a. 2.   [16] *STh* I, q. 12, a. 5.
[17] *STh* III, q. 7, a. 1 ad 2; q. 9, a. 2 ad 2.

Word by Christ's soul] . . . [there is] a medium *under which* [*sub quo*] the Word is seen, like a light.[18]

This light of glory is not a medium in the sense that it is *what* Christ's intellect sees; the object of his vision is the divine nature itself, seen without the mediation of any created object "in which (*in quo*)" it is beheld. Rather, Aquinas explains, this light is a medium "under which (*sub quo*)" God is seen. As such, it is a grace, a supernatural *habitus* that Christ receives with the gift of habitual grace at his conception.[19] While Christ's human intellect sees God immediately (as its object), this immediate vision is achieved through the medium (the light *sub quo* or under which God is seen) of a gracious gift to his humanity. Aquinas certainly traces Christ's beatific vision back to the hypostatic union as its ultimate source, but he does so by way of the fullness of Christ's habitual grace and glory flowing from that union, in which Christ's human intellect is perfected with a surpassing gift of supernatural light so that it can behold the Word.[20]

Aquinas goes on to observe that there are different degrees of beatific knowledge among creatures. All see the same divine essence, but with a greater or lesser clarity depending on the limpidity of the supernatural light they receive. On this score, Christ's beatific knowledge surpasses that of all other creatures, even that of the highest angels, just as Christ's fullness of habitual grace surpasses the grace of any other creature.[21]

This brings us back to the Holy Spirit. Christ's beatific vision is supreme because his grace is supreme, because he is a man who

---

[18] III *Sent.* d. 14, a. 1, qla 3 ad 1. In the *Summa Theologiae*, Thomas reiterates that the light of glory can be called a medium "under which (*sub quo*) God is seen; this does not undermine the immediacy of the vision of God." *STh* I, q. 12, a. 5 ad 2. See also IV *Sent.* d. 49, q. 2, a. 1 ad 15.

[19] III *Sent.* d. 14, a. 1, qla 3 and ad 2; cf. IV *Sent.* d. 49, q. 2, a. 6.

[20] Thomas's analysis—the beatific vision as made possible by the *lumen gloriae* which is the medium *sub quo* the divine essence is seen—represents a solution to an important thirteenth-century question over the vision of God. As Torrell explains, though it was first formulated by Albert the Great (and, more distantly, Guerric of Saint Quentin), Thomas takes the intuitions of his predecessors to their logical conclusions and places them in a synthesis that is generally better organized. Torrell, "La vision de Dieu per essentiam," 55.

[21] III *Sent.* d. 14, a. 2, qla 3 ad 2. Aquinas also argues that the more one has charity, the more clear will be the beatific vision. *STh* I, q. 12, a. 6. Since Christ's charity is greater than that of all others because Christ receives the Spirit without measure, it would likewise seem to follow that Christ would have the beatific vision to the greatest degree. Thomas does not make this argument about Christ explicitly, however.

receives *totum spiritum*, the Holy Spirit "without measure." Because Christ is "full of grace and truth," his humanity is perfectly proportioned to the divinity to which it is united in person, formally perfected by every grace and gift that it can possess—including the supreme degree of supernatural light by which his soul sees the divine essence more clearly than the highest angel, in a vision that is fully actual and perfect at every moment.[22]

There is therefore no tension between St Thomas's claims that Christ's beatific vision comes "from the union,"[23] that the intellectual light by which Christ sees the divine essence flows out from the Word, and that "because Christ has the Spirit without measure, it belongs to him to know all things in the Word."[24] The visible mission of the Son in the incarnation brings with it, by way of an intrinsic relationship grounded in the eternal processions, the invisible mission of the Holy Spirit to Christ's humanity in the fullest possible measure, and consequently every grace, gift, and charism that a human nature can receive. The Holy Spirit is always a coprinciple of these gifts[25] (though never in competition with the hypostatic union, which remains foundational for Aquinas's Christology), insofar as the Spirit acts from the Father and the Son, according to the Trinitarian order. In technical terms, then, the Holy Spirit is rightly called a cause of the created light given to Christ as man, which is a *habitus*, an accident inhering in Christ's humanity distinct from the hypostatic union, "by which his soul is formally assimilated to the Word, so that it is capable of the vision of the Word."[26] Thomas perhaps would regard it as more appropriate to speak of this perfection of Christ's intellect as from the Word since it assimilates Christ's human soul to the Word,

---

[22] Christ's beatific knowledge is therefore not habitual but always perfectly actual, see *STh* III, q. 11, a. 5 ad 1; underlying it is the *habitus* of divine light strengthening his intellect.

[23] See, e.g., III *Sent.* d. 18, a. 4, qla 4 ad 2 and ad 3; III *Sent.* d. 18, a. 5.

[24] IV *Sent.* d. 49, q. 2, a. 5, sc 2.

[25] We could reprise here all that was said in CHAPTER 2 about the various modes of causality in grace, including the joint efficient causality of all three divine persons in every created effect, and how the Holy Spirit is the origin, *ratio* and exemplar (as Gift in person) of every grace. As a created effect, the light of glory is rightly appropriated to the Holy Spirit.

[26] III *Sent.* d. 14, a. 1, qla 3 ad 3. Aquinas also calls this supernatural light a gift of wisdom, insofar as "wisdom" is taken to mean all supernatural knowledge that makes God known. See, e.g., *STh* III, q. 10, a. 4.

but insofar as it is a created gift, it is also correct to acknowledge it as a gift from the Spirit.

Taking a wider perspective, St Thomas frames Christ's beatific knowledge in terms of Christ's supreme blessedness; here, the Holy Spirit is indisputably at work. Christ is blessed and a *comprehensor*—in technical terminology, Christ has a divine fruition or enjoyment of God—not only by knowledge, but also by love, with perfect charity.

> The fruition of God has a twofold aspect, according to the will and according to the intellect: according to the will which adheres perfectly to God by love, and according to the intellect which knows God perfectly. The perfect inhering of the will to God by love is through grace, through which man is justified. . . . for a man is made just because he adheres to God in love. The perfect knowledge of God is through the light of wisdom, which is the knowledge of divine truth. Therefore it was necessary that the incarnate Word of God would exist as perfect in grace and in wisdom of the truth; hence John 1:14 says: "the Word was made flesh, and dwelt among us, and we have seen his glory, the glory as of the only-begotten of the Father, full of grace and truth."[27]

For Aquinas, Christ's perfect charity must complement his perfect knowledge, since perfect intellectual knowledge leads to the will's act of love. As the Son is 'the Word breathing forth Love,' so perfect knowledge is wisdom that breaks forth into the affection of love. Christ as man cannot love God perfectly unless he knows him perfectly, and the perfect term of his perfect knowledge is a perfect love.[28] Indeed, St Thomas's phrasing echoes his earlier treatment of the divine missions in the gifts of wisdom and charity; he depicts Christ's humanity as perfectly conformed to the eternal processions by way of knowledge and by way of love. This confirms the conclusion we have already reached: Aquinas describes a profound coordination, cooperation, joint operation—indeed, a compenetration—of the Word and the Holy Spirit in their respective missions in Christ's humanity.

At this point, an objection arises. Does not this emphasis on the Holy Spirit's role in Christ's beatific knowledge cut against the grain of Aquinas's own Trinitarian theology, as well as his theology of divine indwelling? As we have seen, the gifts perfecting the intellect (faith, wisdom) assimilate the soul to the Word's procession by way of

---

[27] *Compendium theologiae* I, c. 213.   [28] See, e.g., *STh* II–II, q. 88, a. 4 ad 3.

knowledge, while charity perfects the will, assimilating the soul to the Holy Spirit's procession by way of love. It might seem to make little sense, according to Aquinas's own account, to attribute the perfection of Christ's human knowledge to the Holy Spirit.

To answer, we might observe, first, that the Dominican *magister in sacra pagina* is probing the mysteries expressed by sacred Scripture, which frequently attributes revelations, as well as man's supernatural knowledge, to the Holy Spirit. Aquinas follows Scripture's own way of speaking. "The Holy Spirit, as we are taught by Scripture, is the cause of every perfection of the human mind."[29] The Spirit inspires man, revealing to him God's wisdom and "the deep things of God (*profunda Dei*)."[30] True, the gracious illumination of one's mind grants a perfection that is representative of the Son, whose procession as Word is the exemplar cause to which the soul is assimilated, but the Holy Spirit, with the Father and Son, is equally an efficient cause of that illumination. When St Thomas explains the Holy Spirit's role in granting supernatural gifts perfecting the intellect, this is precisely the analysis he uses. The gift of wisdom, by which we know God, makes us like the Word; the Holy Spirit (with the Father and the Son) efficiently causes us to receive this gift. It is rightly appropriated to the Holy Spirit, for two reasons: the Spirit makes us intimate friends with God—"as if one heart" with him—and hence gives us to know the inner secrets of his heart; and it is a "gift" that comes from the Spirit who is "Gift" in person.[31]

St Thomas sees in Scripture's way of speaking about the Holy Spirit yet another profound truth about the Holy Spirit and the Triune mystery of God: the Holy Spirit "teaches" us, "insofar as he makes us participate the wisdom of the Son."[32] "The Holy Spirit leads to knowledge of the truth because he proceeds from the Truth.... [A]s proceeding from the Son, he leads us into knowledge of the Son."[33] This is exactly how Aquinas analyzes Jesus's promise to the disciples that the Holy Spirit "will teach you all things (John 14:26)." Why is this

---

[29] *ScG* IV, c. 18.

[30] *In I Epist. ad Cor.* c. 2, lect. 2 (no. 102). See also *In Ioan.* c. 14, lect. 6 (nos. 1958–60); *In Ioan.* c. 7, lect. 2 (no. 1039); *In I Epist. ad Cor.* c. 2, lect. 3 (nos. 109, 113, and 117); *ScG* IV, c. 21; *In I Epist. ad Cor.* c. 12, lect. 1 (no 718); *In Epist. ad Phil.* c. 1, lect. 2 (no. 17).

[31] *ScG* IV, c. 21.   [32] *In Ioan.* c. 14, lect. 6 (no. 1960).

[33] *In Ioan.* c. 14, lect. 4 (no. 1916).

teaching assigned to the Holy Spirit? Should not the Word teach the disciples?

> [S]ince the Son is the Word, it might seem that the gift of wisdom and of knowledge appropriately would pertain to him. . . . Nonetheless, because the Holy Spirit is [the Spirit] of the Son, what the Holy Spirit gives, he has from the Son; hence he attributes this gift of knowledge to the Holy Spirit (where he says "he will teach you all things," etc.), yet that is appropriated to the Son.[34]

St Thomas gives full weight to the Lord's words. The Holy Spirit proceeds from the Son, and thus all he does in the world and all he gives to us is also "from the Son."[35] The Holy Spirit, whom the Son sends, does not undermine the Son's prerogative as the Word and Wisdom of God, but rather the reverse: the Spirit's illumination of man's mind is itself from the Son and leads to a participation in the Son's wisdom.

To return to the thread of the argument with which we began, we now see why Aquinas's contemporary critics do not hit the mark. Christ's possession of the beatific vision does not mean that the Holy Spirit is superfluous to Christ's human knowledge. That vision is truly a vision "in the Word," which Christ's human mind possesses precisely as filled with the Holy Spirit.[36] For the Dominican master, it is thus quite true to say that Christ's beatific vision is a gift of the Spirit involving a genuine "illumination" of his human intellect by a light coming from the Holy Spirit. This is fully consistent with Aquinas's emphasis that Christ is the Word incarnate and sees

---

[34] *In Ioan.* c. 14, lect. 7 (no 1961). Thomas offers a similar explanation on several other occasions. See, e.g., *In Ioan.* c. 16, lect. 3 (nos. 2102–3); *In Ioan.* c. 14, lect. 4 (no. 1916); cf. *In I Epist. ad Cor.* c. 2, lect. 2 (no. 100). One might wonder why St Thomas says that the gift of knowledge to Christ's humanity is "appropriated" to the Son, rather than being proper to him as the Word. Aquinas may be using "appropriated" here in a general sense and not according to its strict meaning, or he may simply be speaking of efficient causality, since Christ's human knowledge is rightly appropriated to the Son as an efficient cause. Indeed, often enough, Aquinas appropriates the same reality to different persons under different aspects: the gift of knowledge can be appropriated to the Son insofar as it concerns the intellect, and to the Holy Spirit insofar as it proceeds from our friendship with God (the Holy Spirit is Love in person) and insofar as it is a gift (the Spirit is Gift in person). See, e.g., ScG IV, c. 21. In general, see Cabaret, *L'étonnante manifestation des personnes divines.*
[35] The same applies to the Son with regard to the Father: "*Filius quidquid operatur, habet a Patre.*" *In Ioan.* c. 15, lect. 5 (no. 2061). The Trinitarian order is key to Aquinas's explanations of the divine persons' agency.
[36] Cf. IV *Sent.* d. 49, q. 2, a. 5, sc 2, as quoted at p. 175.

God's essence "in the Word." Quite simply, Aquinas would never imagine any competition between the Word and the Holy Spirit in Christ: the Spirit whom the Son sends to his own humanity is the Son's own Spirit, who illuminates Christ's human mind with the divine light of the Word.

B. CHRIST'S INFUSED KNOWLEDGE AND THE HOLY SPIRIT

Also important for our inquiry is Christ's infused knowledge. Aquinas describes it as possessed by Christ's soul according to "intelligible species proportioned to the human mind."[37] Such infused knowledge must be carefully distinguished from the beatific vision (an unmediated vision of God without intelligible species in a mode exceeding the natural capacity of the human mind). Infused knowledge is not gained by sense experience; like the "evening knowledge" of angels, it is infused into Christ's intellect as a supernatural gift from God.[38] Such knowledge has two main components: infused "species" (e.g., intelligible forms), and an "infused divine light" by which the intellect understands what is revealed.[39] Speaking of both aspects, Aquinas notes that Christ's infused knowledge, considered "according to what it has from the inflowing cause," is "much more excellent than the knowledge of the angels, both in the number of things known, and in the certitude of his knowledge, because the spiritual light infused into the soul of Christ is much more excellent than the light that belongs to an angelic nature."[40]

This knowledge includes two subcategories. The first, of less interest for our study, is that Christ knows by a supernatural gift "whatever a man can know through the power of the light of the agent intellect—that is, whatever pertains to human sciences."[41] In other words, Christ received a divine infusion of intelligible species so that

---

[37] *STh* III, q. 9, a. 3.   [38] *Ibid.*   [39] *STh* III, q. 11, a. 6 ad 3.

[40] *STh* III, q. 11, a. 4. Aquinas also adds that, as received in a human nature, Christ's infused knowledge is lower than that of the angels, because the mode of human knowing is lower than the mode of angelic knowing.

[41] *STh* III, q. 11, a. 1.

he had habitual knowledge of all things that a human being could otherwise learn by his own natural light.[42]

The second subcategory plays a role of central importance for Christ's saving actions, however, and, here we encounter again the Holy Spirit.

> Second, through this [infused] knowledge Christ knew all those things that are made known to men through divine revelation, whether they belong to the gift of wisdom or to the gift of prophecy, or to any gift of the Holy Spirit whatsoever.[43]

While Aquinas's principal emphasis in accounting for this aspect of Christ's infused knowledge is on the role of the divine Word as united to Christ's possible intellect,[44] Aquinas also views it as akin to divine revelation, associating it with the Holy Spirit. As such, it is a dimension of Christ's plenitude of grace: having received every grace, Christ "knows most fully whatever can pertain to the mystery of grace."[45] As filled with the Holy Spirit, Christ as man knows everything that man is capable of knowing through the Holy Spirit.[46]

Christ presumably draws on this knowledge when he teaches his disciples and preaches to the crowds, because, unlike the beatific

---

[42] *Compendium theologiae* I, c. 216. Critics often regard this position as an excessive application of what is sometimes called the "principle of perfection"—the "presupposition that Christ's humanity must have the absolute best of everything." See, e.g., Gerald O'Collins, *Christology: A Biblical, Historical, and Systematic Study of Jesus*, 2nd ed. (Oxford: Oxford University Press, 2009), 208; Henk J. M. Shoot, *Christ the 'Name' of God: Thomas Aquinas on Naming Christ* (Leuven: Peeters, 1993) 179–83. Whatever its merits or demerits, however, we leave this issue to one side. For a discussion, see Torrell, *Encyclopédie Jésus le Christ*, 1024–9.

[43] *STh* III, q. 11, a. 1.

[44] See, e.g., *STh* III, q. 9, a. 3; q. 11, a. 1. Aquinas only occasionally argues from Christ's fullness of grace to the perfection of his infused knowledge; nonetheless, in both the *Summa Theologiae* and his Scripture commentaries, Aquinas clearly regards the Holy Spirit as a genuine principle of this knowledge. As we will argue below, this is yet another example of how Christ's habitual grace is concomitant with the hypostatic union.

[45] *Compendium theologiae* I, c. 216. This connection between the Holy Spirit, Christ's fullness of grace and consequent possession of all of the gifts, and his infused knowledge of all things, is implicit in Thomas's exegesis of the phrase from the prologue of John's Gospel that he often quotes, that Christ is "full of grace and truth." See *In Ioan.* c. 1, lect. 8 (no. 189).

[46] This is also connected to Christ's capital grace: because the Holy Spirit is given to us by Christ—and all the supernaturally infused knowledge that we can have from the Spirit—Christ himself must first possess that knowledge, because no one can give what he does not possess.

vision which cannot be directly translated into human words and images, Christ's infused knowledge functions in a way analogous to prophetic knowledge, according to images proportioned to his human mind.[47] Following the usage of Scripture, Aquinas suggests that this knowledge is infused in Christ's mind *"per Spiritum Sanctum."*[48] In this sense, St Thomas says that Christ's teaching is not his own (insofar as he is considered as man), since he speaks it "from the Holy Spirit."

> He says "my teaching," which I have according to my created soul, and which I proclaim by my body's mouth, "is not mine," that is, it is not mine as from myself, but from God: because every truth, by whomever it is spoken, is from the Holy Spirit.[49]

Aquinas also puts it this way: Christ's words "have a spiritual sense, because they are from the Holy Spirit. 'It is the Spirit who speaks mysteries (1 Cor. 14:2).'"[50]

In other words, Christ as man is truly a prophet who reveals to men the mysteries of God,[51] and whose prophetic knowledge comes to him as a gracious gift from the Holy Spirit. Yet Christ is greater than every other prophet; possessing the fullness of the Holy Spirit, Christ's prophetic knowledge surpasses that of all others in four ways. First, the supernatural knowledge given by the Spirit informs everything that Christ says, whereas other prophets only sometimes spoke from the Spirit. Christ's prophetic knowledge is continuous, not intermittent. "Christ, who received the Spirit without measure and in every respect (*quantum ad omnia*), therefore speaks the words of God in all that he says (*quantum ad omnia*)."[52] Second, as we noted when we discussed the "fullness" of Christ's grace, other prophets did not have the power to prophesy at will; in contrast, Christ has such a plenitude of the Spirit's

---

[47] *STh* III, q. 7, a. 8 ad 1; White, "The Voluntary Action of the Earthly Christ," 516–18; Torrell, "S. Thomas d'Aquin et la science du Christ," 394–409; Torrell, *Encyclopédie Jésus le Christ*, 1026–7.

[48] *STh* III, q. 11, a. 1 sc.

[49] *In Ioan.* c. 7, lect. 2 (no. 1037). On the last phrase of this quotation, see Serge-Thomas Bonino, "'Toute vérité, quel que soit celui qui la dit, vient de l'Esprit-Saint.' Autour d'une citation de l'*Ambrosiaster* dans le corpus thomasien," *Revue Thomiste* 106 (2006): 101–47.

[50] *In Ioan.* c. 6, lect. 8 (no. 992).

[51] *STh* III, q. 7, a. 8; q. 31, a. 2; *In Matt.* c. 13, (no. 1212).

[52] *In Ioan.* c. 3, lect. 6 (no. 541).

gifts that he can prophesy "at will."[53] Third, his prophetic knowledge extends vastly beyond that of other prophets. For example, "none of the prophets knew all future things from himself, but only Christ, who did not have the Holy Spirit by measure. Thus, Isaac, a great prophet, was deceived by Jacob."[54] Finally, as we quoted Aquinas saying just above, Christ's infused knowledge is supremely certain: on this measure, it is "much more excellent than the knowledge of the angels."[55]

Aquinas also includes in Christ's infused knowledge whatever is known through the gifts of the Holy Spirit:

> Isaiah 11 says that "he will be filled with the Spirit of wisdom and understanding, of knowledge and of counsel;" under which fall all things knowable: knowledge of all divine things pertains to the gift of wisdom; knowledge of all immaterial things belongs to the gift of understanding; knowledge of all conclusions belongs to the gift of knowledge; and knowledge of all things that can be done belongs to the gift of counsel. Therefore it seems that Christ, insofar as he has knowledge infused by the Holy Spirit, knows all.[56]

Aquinas does not identify Christ's infused knowledge with the gifts; his point is rather to underline the *extent* of Christ's infused knowledge (it includes *all* that can be supernaturally known, according to whatever gracious gift), and in so doing, he also reiterates its connection to the Holy Spirit.[57]

Here, one might rightly point out that, since Christ's infused knowledge is a perfection of his human intellect (specifically, of his possible intellect), Aquinas often attributes it to the Word. In

---

[53] See p. 162, quoting *In Epist. ad Col.* c. 1, lect. 5 (no. 50). See also *In Ioan.* c. 14, lect. 4 (no. 1915). At *STh* III, q. 11, a. 5, Aquinas further explains that Christ's infused knowledge is habitual. Presumably, therefore, he adverts "at will" to what he always knows habitually.

[54] *In Epist. ad Philemon.* lect. 2 (no. 29).   [55] *STh* III, q. 11, a. 4.

[56] *STh* III, q. 11, a. 1 sc. See also the body of St Thomas's response following this *sed contra*, as well as *Compendium theologiae* I, c. 216; *STh* III, q. 11, a. 1.

[57] An investigation into the cognitive dimension of the gifts of the Holy Spirit, though interesting, is beyond the scope of this study. As St Thomas's work on the gift of wisdom shows, it generates a knowledge that is in the intellect as its subject, but, because it arises from charity (and hence is from the Holy Spirit), it involves a connaturality with divine realities. The person endowed with the gift of wisdom is like someone with the *habitus* of chastity, who judges rightly of what pertains to chastity, not as a result of learning moral theology, but by a certain connaturality. "This *compassio* or connaturality with divine realities is generated by charity.... and therefore the gift of wisdom has a certain cause in the will, namely, charity, but its essence is in the intellect, whose act is to judge rightly." *STh* II–II, q. 45, a. 2.

STh III, q. 9, a. 3, St Thomas argues that "one must affirm an infused knowledge in Christ, insofar as intelligible species are impressed in Christ's soul by the Word of God personally united to it."[58] One question later, Thomas says that infused knowledge "is caused in Christ's soul by the union to the Word (*ex unione ad Verbum*)."[59] And two articles after that, Aquinas explains that Christ's infused knowledge did not come through angels, but that his soul "was filled with knowledge and grace immediately by the Word of God himself."[60] When these texts are considered all together, however, one can see that Aquinas is making the same argument he made about the connection between habitual grace and the hypostatic union: infused knowledge flows into Christ's intellect *because of* the union, according to the created gifts given to that humanity through habitual grace. While some texts rightly emphasize the immediacy of the Word's influence, Thomas also affirms that this knowledge comes to Christ's soul "insofar as his human nature was perfected by grace,"[61] which is to say, by grace as the proper effect of the invisible mission of the Holy Spirit. It is a case of both–and, not either–or. The ultimate explanation for this is that the Holy Spirit eternally proceeds from the Son. As the Son receives everything he is and everything he does from the Father, so also the Holy Spirit receives everything he is and everything he does from the Father *and the Son*: "what the Holy Spirit gives, he has from the Son."[62]

* * *

Regarding Christ's supernatural human knowledge, Aquinas offers a balanced synthesis of all the data of revelation, whether they accent the Spirit's agency or the Word's. At work are two fundamental principles of Trinitarian theology. The first is the inseparability of the action of the three divine persons: the Son always acts inseparably with the Spirit. The second is the Trinitarian order: just as all that the Son *is* and *does* is *from* the Father, so also all that Spirit *is* and *does* is *from* the Father and the Son, such that the gifts that the Spirit gives to Christ's humanity have their principle in the Son. This is why it is true to say *both* that Christ knows all things in the Word, and that this knowledge is given in the fullness of the Holy Spirit's grace.

---

[58] *STh* III, q. 9, a. 3.   [59] *STh* III, q. 12, a. 2 ad 3.
[60] *STh* III, q. 12, a. 4.   [61] III *Sent.* d. 14, a. 3 qla 2 ad 1.
[62] *In Ioan.* c. 14, lect. 7 (no. 1961).

7

Christ's Action and the Holy Spirit

The Holy Spirit stands at the center of Aquinas's account of Christ's human action. "[I]t is obvious that the soul of Christ was most perfectly moved by the Holy Spirit, as Luke 4 says: 'Jesus, full of the Holy Spirit, returned from the Jordan and was led by the Spirit into the desert.'"[1] To Aquinas's mind, this was a truth so evident, and so abundantly attested to in Scripture, that it almost need not be mentioned. While the Dominican master of sacred Scripture does not frequently elaborate on it, it appears at key points in his discussion of the mystery of Christ's work of salvation. Thus, in the prologue to his *Sentences* Commentary, the young Thomas speaks of Christ as impelled by the Spirit to save the world: "As if by a kind of impetus of love for our restoration, Christ fulfilled the mystery; whence Isaiah 59:19 says: 'When he shall come as a rushing stream, driven by the Spirit of the Lord.'"[2] Later, echoing Jesus's own words, St Thomas explains that the Holy Spirit sends the Son "according to his assumed nature" to preach good news to the poor.[3] Likewise, the mature Aquinas holds that Jesus was moved by a special impulsion of the Holy Spirit to offer himself on the cross for the salvation of the world.[4] In short, Christ is truly a man of the Spirit, the Word-made-flesh whose every gesture is anointed by the Spirit's invisible unction. As the Word cannot be without the Spirit whom he breathes forth, neither can the Word incarnate act without the empowering presence of the Holy Spirit.

---

[1] *STh* III, q. 7, a. 5. Aquinas repeats this in near-identical terms at *ScG* IV, c. 34. Note how St Thomas is careful always to maintain the Trinitarian *ordo*: the Holy Spirit moves Christ's soul (i.e. his humanity), but does not move the Son in his divinity. See, e.g., *ScG* IV, c. 24.
[2] I *Sent.* prol. [3] *ScG* IV, c. 24.
[4] See, e.g., *In Epist. ad Hebr.* c. 9, lect. 14 (no. 444); *STh* III, q. 47, a. 3.

A. HABITUAL GRACE, CHARITY, AND THE PERFECTION OF CHRIST'S HUMAN CAPACITY FOR ACTION

This presence of the Holy Spirit is fundamental to St Thomas's Christology, first of all, because the Dominican *magister in sacra pagina* builds his theological account of Christ's action as man on the scriptural truth that the Holy Spirit's anointing *empowered* Christ to undertake his saving actions. Since Christ "does all things well," not only as true God but also as true man, Aquinas explains, "it is necessary that he have habitual grace through which his human action is perfected."[5] And the principle of this gift of habitual grace is, of course, the Holy Spirit, through whom Christ is perfected as man,[6] and who dwells in Christ's humanity according to the perfect charity he infuses. Indeed, Aquinas here is drawing conclusions from what Scripture reveals: Christ is the perfectly virtuous man,[7] the first teacher of the faith,[8] the greatest prophet,[9] a man perfectly moved by the Holy Spirit.[10] All things that are possible to him, Aquinas argues, because he receives as man the fullness of habitual grace that elevates his human nature (entitative *habitus*),[11] and in which he receives the perfection of his powers (operative *habitus*) that make his human nature capable of such actions. These operative *habitus* (all the virtues, the gifts of the Holy Spirit, and the charisms) are themselves given in the fullness of habitual grace.[12] And, as we have seen, the Holy Spirit is the uncreated Gift received by Christ as man, through whom he receives all gracious gifts.

This point is more important for Aquinas's theology than might at first appear. Human nature has certain natural powers, and is also open to a supernatural elevation so as to act beyond its natural

---

[5] *STh* III, q. 7, a. 1 ad 2. See also *ibid.* ad 3; a. 13; III *Sent.* d. 13, q. 1, a. 1; *De Verit.*, q. 29, a. 5 ad 2. St Thomas does not mean that there is a strict or absolute necessity on the side of Christ's humanity that he have habitual grace. He is speaking instead of a kind of conditional necessity, which is also a sort of fittingness: given that God has willed to become man to save us through his *acta et passa* (something not at all necessary in itself), it was necessary for God to grant through a supernatural infusion the operative *habitus* to Christ's humanity in order that he could accomplish his mission.

[6] *In I Epist. ad Cor.* c. 15, lect. 7 (no. 993).

[7] *STh* III, q. 7, a. 2.   [8] *STh* III, q. 7, a. 7.

[9] *STh* III, q. 7, a. 8.   [10] *STh* III, q. 7, a. 5.

[11] For a note on the use of this term, see CHAPTER 2, p. 27.

[12] Cf. *STh* III, q. 7, a. 2.

capacity (its "obediential potency"), but in both cases, a perfecting disposition (*habitus*) of those powers is needed so that one can employ them promptly and easily in virtuous action.[13] A man lacking the *habitus* for virtuous action would at best find it difficult to do such things—and when it is a question of supernaturally elevated human action, would be completely incapable of them. Had Christ as man lacked the anointing of the Holy Spirit in habitual grace (*per impossibile*), he would thus have been incapable of acting as the Gospels show he did, because he would have lacked the operative *habitus* rooted in habitual grace that empower a human nature to do such things.

In fact, Aquinas envisions precisely the sort of role for the Holy Spirit in Christ's life that one finds in the work of some contemporary exegetes:[14] the Holy Spirit "anoints" Christ such that, as man, he becomes empowered in a unique and supernatural way: "Christ is called anointed by reason of the power of the Holy Spirit."[15] As Jesus says, "it is by the Spirit of God that I cast out demons (Matt. 12:28)," and "the Spirit of the Lord is upon me, because he has anointed me to preach good news to the poor (Luke 4:18)." This is just what St Thomas is getting at: the Holy Spirit's anointing in habitual grace empowers Christ as man by giving him the *habitus* that rightly prepare, dispose, and enable his human nature for the actions, both natural and supernatural, that he will undertake.[16]

B. CHRIST'S HUMAN ACTION AND THE GIFTS OF THE HOLY SPIRIT

This brings us to Christ's unique mode of acting as the God-man, "a key idea" of St Thomas's Christology,[17] and also one where the gifts

---

[13] See, e.g., *STh* I–II, q. 49, where St Thomas discusses habits in general as an intrinsic principle (along with the powers of human nature) of human acts.

[14] See, e.g., James D. G. Dunn, *Christology in the Making: A New Testament Inquiry into the Origins of the Doctrine of the Incarnation*, 2nd ed. (Grand Rapids: Wm. B. Eerdmans Publishing Co., 1996), 137–8.

[15] *ScG* IV, c. 60.

[16] Thomas likewise explains (speaking about operative *habitus*) that it is the "anointing" of the Holy Spirit that makes us capable of the "perfect operations" by which we attain to God. *ScG* IV, c. 21.

[17] Torrell, *Encyclopédie Jésus le Christ*, 362.

of the Holy Spirit play a crucial role. Indeed, in the larger picture, Aquinas's account of Christ's actions is important for two reasons. First, it occupies a critical place in the whole of the economy of salvation; it is central to the *Tertia pars*—and indeed to Aquinas's whole theology—that all Christ did and suffered in the flesh, all of his *acta et passa* (and not only his death on the cross), are salvific for us. It is through his humanity that Christ gives grace to us, sending us the Spirit.[18] Accounting for how the Word works in and through his assumed human nature is thus a critical task. Second, Aquinas's mature teaching on Christ's theandric action represents an important contribution to Western theology; Aquinas recovered for the West a robust understanding of Christ's human nature as an instrument of the divinity (a doctrine developed in the Patristic period, especially by Athanasius and Cyril of Alexandria), in a way that surpassed his medieval predecessors, giving that doctrine its definitive form for centuries to come.[19] Consequently, the fact that we also find here the Holy Spirit and his gifts shows just how important the Spirit's role is for his Christology.

This is not the place for a detailed exposition of Aquinas's doctrine on Christ's action; we will sketch only its main lines. The first principle of Aquinas's treatment is that, as the Third Council of Constantinople teaches,[20] Christ has not only two natures, but two wills and two operations, one human and the other divine. Each operation thus produces effects proper to the nature that is acting. By distinguishing Christ's human operation from his divine operation, Aquinas makes clear that he has a complete human nature, and

---

[18] See Gilles Emery, "Réflexions sur l'apport d'une christologie trinitaire et pneumatique en théologie chrétienne des religions," in *Le dialogue interreligieux*, eds Mariano Delgado and Benedict T. Viviano (Fribourg: Academic Press Fribourg, 2007), 57.

[19] The classic study of the history and significance of this doctrine is Theophil Tschipke, *L'humanité du Christ comme instrument de salut de la divinité*, trans. Philibert Secrétan (Fribourg: Academic Press Fribourg, 2003) (originally published in German in 1940). Tschipke avers that "Thomas was the first Latin scholastic to take up again the expression '*organon tēs theotētos*,' and the only one among the masters of high scholasticism to discuss the doctrine of the instrumental efficacy of Christ's humanity." *Ibid.*, 136. For a more recent study, see Paul G. Crowley, "Instrumentum Divinitatis in Thomas Aquinas: Recovering the Divinity of Christ," *Theological Studies* 52 (1991): 451–75. See also Blankenhorn, "The Instrumental Causality of the Sacraments," 255–94.

[20] For a careful study of Thomas's access to and use of Constantinople III, see Morard, "Thomas d'Aquin," 305–16.

that his human operation has an intelligibility and integrity of its own—a fundamental Christological truth. "As it says in the letter of Pope Leo, each nature does what is proper to itself in communion with the other nature."[21] Thus, "the human nature in Christ is not an instrument that is only moved, but it also is a principle of action insofar as it has dominion over its acts."[22] Considered in themselves, Christ's human actions genuinely produce effects proper to a human nature (he touches a leper, he writes in the dust, he overturns tables in the temple). This does not render a complete picture of Christ's action, of course, but it is important to Aquinas that we recognize the relative integrity of Christ's human action as human, so as to better grasp how it is drawn into the divine operation without being overwhelmed or obliterated by that infinitely higher nature.

Following closely upon this first principle, Aquinas articulates a second. The two operations of Christ's two natures are not merely parallel; rather, Christ's human nature serves as a living, proper, and conjoined instrument of the divine nature, so that the divine Word acts *through* the human nature:

> In Christ, the human nature has its own proper form and power through which it operates, and likewise the divine nature. And thus his human nature has a proper operation distinct from the divine, and vice versa. Nonetheless, the divine nature uses the operation of the human nature as the operation of its own instrument, and similarly the human nature participates in the operation of the divine nature, as an instrument participates in the operation of the principal agent.[23]

Following the Greek Fathers, Aquinas uses a special name for this action; it is:

> "theandric," that is, "God-manly" or "divino-human," not through some confusion of the operations or of the powers of the two natures, but because Christ's divine operation uses his human operation, and his human operation participates in the power of the divine operation.[24]

As Emery summarizes, "the human action of Christ can be considered in two ways: (1) according to its proper form, and thus it differs essentially from his divine action; and (2) as an instrument of the divinity, and under this second aspect the human operation of Christ

---

[21] *De unione Verbi incarnati*, a. 5 ad 2.   [22] *Ibid.*, ad 4.
[23] *STh* III, q. 19, a. 1.   [24] *STh* III, q. 19, a. 1 ad 1.

participates in the power (*virtus*) of the divine operation itself, as its instrument."[25] "*Ut res*," as a human reality, Christ's human action produces human effects. But "*ut instrumentum*," Christ's human action produces divine effects, effects proper to his divinity that uses his humanity as an instrument. Aquinas concludes his analysis with a third point: this dual activity of Christ's divine and human natures produces a single "work" of Christ the God-man: "Healing the leper is a proper work of the divine operation, while touching him is the proper work of the human nature. Both operations concur in one work insofar as one nature acts in communion with the other."[26] In fact, Aquinas offers two reasons for this: it is because an instrument participates in the act of its principal agent; and because the act is performed by a single supposit in virtue of two forms or natures, like a red-hot knife both cuts (in virtue of the form of sharpened steel) and burns (in virtue of the form of heated steel) at the same time.[27]

Here, a question arises: how broad is this category of action? It is important for understanding certain of Christ's miracles (like healing a leper by the touch of his hand), but does Christ's humanity *always* act as an instrument of his divinity—for example, when he is walking along the seashore, preaching to the crowds, or reclining at table? In those cases, the divine nature does not seem to be working any visible miracles through Christ's humanity, and so one might be tempted to say that Christ's humanity is not the Word's instrument in those actions. Aquinas, however, does not restrict theandric action in this way: he speaks boldly and broadly of *all* of Christ's actions as theandric, because he sees *all* of Christ's actions as salvific.

> The operation of the human nature in Christ had a certain power from the divinity, beyond human power: for that he would touch a leper was an action of his humanity, but that that touch would cure him of leprosy proceeded from divine power. In this way, *all of his human actions and sufferings were salvific* by virtue of his divinity, and so Dionysius calls

---

[25] Gilles Emery, "Le Christ médiateur: l'unicité et l'universalité de la médiation salvifique du Christ Jésus suivant Thomas d'Aquin," in *Christus—Gottes schöpferisches Wort: Festschrift für Christoph Kardinal Schönborn zum 65. Geburtstag*, eds George Augustin, Maria Brun, Erwin Keller, and Markus Schulze (Freiburg: Herder, 2010), 350–1.

[26] *STh* III, q. 19, a. 1 ad 5. While Thomas takes care to distinguish the two operations proper to Christ's two natures, he also shows how they are one *secundum quid*, in a certain respect.

[27] III *Sent.* d. 18, a. 1 ad 5.

the human operation of Christ theandric, that is, God-manly, namely, because it proceeded from his humanity in such a way that the power of the divinity was at work in it.[28]

Aquinas repeats this point in several places,[29] and it is of central importance. *All* that Christ does, every part of the Son's visible mission, is salvific, including even what seem to be the most quotidian of Christ's actions.

Why does Aquinas say this about *every* action of Christ's humanity? Although he offers a variety of reasons (for example, that Christ's human will was always ordered under the divine will, so that he acted as man according to the disposition of the divine will,[30] or that the divine power was always at work in his humanity),[31] these resolve into a primary and overarching one: Christ's humanity is joined to the Word as its instrument, so that all of Christ's human actions are instrumental actions of the Word—and consequently are theandric and salvific.[32] Ultimately, therefore, this category of action englobes *every* act of Christ as man because every such act is done by the person of the Word, operating through Christ's humanity as his instrument.

The root of this is Aquinas's grasp of the hypostatic union as central to the mystery of Christ, allowing him to articulate not only the distinction between Christ's divine and human operations, but also how they are "in communion" with each other. That is, a focus on the hypostatic union directs our attention to the person who acts through that human nature: the Word himself. As St Thomas explains, Christ's human nature is much more than an inanimate instrument like an axe, which is separate from the carpenter. It is a proper and *conjoined* instrument, the human nature of the Word himself.[33] The actions of the human nature are not simply the actions of a separated instrument, but are properly attributed to the Word himself as the subject who is acting *in* and *through* that human nature. "[T]he soul

---

[28] *Compendium theologiae* I, c. 212. Emphasis added.
[29] See, e.g., *STh* III, q. 48, a. 6; *ScG* IV, c. 36; *In Epist. ad Rom.* c. 4, lect. 3 (no. 380); cf. *STh* I–II, q. 112, a. 1 ad 1.
[30] *ScG* IV, c. 36.   [31] *Compendium theologiae* I, c. 212.
[32] As is clear from the context of the passages where he discusses it, Thomas's account of Christ's instrumental action concerns all that Christ willingly or intentionally did or suffered. Non-voluntary acts (e.g., Christ's digestion) are not properly "human acts" according to Aquinas (see, e.g., *STh* I–II, q. 1, a. 1 ad 3).
[33] *ScG* IV, c. 41.

sees by virtue of the [body's] eye; and in this way, the eternal supposit [of the Word] was acting by virtue of [Christ's] human nature."[34] In fact, Aquinas's account of Christ's action follows the same logic as the communication of idioms:

> In Christ, there is a communication of idioms, not that there would be some confusion of natural properties, but because the properties of each nature are said of the same supposit. And the communication of operations works in the same way, because each operation (divine and human) is attributed to the same supposit.[35]

The hypostatic union is therefore an indispensable foundation for a complete account of Christ's human action.

But the hypostatic union alone is not enough to account for how Christ's humanity acts as an instrument of his divinity. There are two more elements in Aquinas's explanation. First, Christ's human nature, a rational nature that both is moved by God and simultaneously moves itself, must be properly disposed within itself to act as that instrument. Second, that nature must be actually moved by the divinity, with a motion that originates above it and yet that is interior to it.

The Gifts Dispose Christ's Humanity to Be Moved as an Instrument

As we have just seen in SECTION A, Aquinas is clear that Christ must receive the Holy Spirit and thus the supernatural operative *habitus* given in habitual grace that make possible the acts he does. There, we focused on the *habitus* needed for Christ's human acts in general. Here, our concern is more specific: because Christ's humanity acts as an instrument, Aquinas explains, it needs a *habitus* to dispose it to be moved by the divinity "*ut instrumentum*": "[A]s an instrument animated by a rational soul that both is moved and moves itself, ... it is necessary for [Christ] to have habitual grace in order to act rightly."[36] "Thus, as a slave needs a *habitus* in order to carry out in

---

[34] *De unione Verbi incarnati*, a. 5 ad 5.   [35] *Ibid.*, ad 9.

[36] *STh* III, q. 7, a. 1 ad 3. As Emery explains, "[t]he humanity of Jesus is *constituted* as an 'instrument of the divinity' by the hypostatic union, and it is *perfected* by the Holy Spirit to accomplish its instrumental action of salvation." Emery, "Le Christ médiateur," 350. For a general discussion of the relationship between Christ and the gifts, see Joseph Wawrykow, "Christ and the Gifts of the Holy Spirit According to Thomas Aquinas," in *Kirchenbild und Spiritualität: Dominikanische Beiträge zur*

a fitting way the command of his master, so also the soul of Christ [needs *habitus*] in order that he be moved perfectly [as an instrument] by the divinity."[37] St Thomas offers another analogy: just as our bodily appetites need a special *habitus* that disposes them to obey the commands of reason (the virtue of temperance, for example), so also, when man is moved by God as an instrument, his soul needs a special *habitus* that disposes it to be moved while at the same time moving itself freely.[38] This *habitus* is distinct from those virtues by which man rules himself, and it brings him to a special perfection: he becomes capable of receiving God's supernatural "inspiration" from within, according to a divine impulse or "instinct" that does no violence to his reason or his freedom, but rather empowers and elevates them.

This is precisely what the gifts of the Holy Spirit do—in us (in a limited way) and above all in Christ (in the most full and perfect way). They provide Christ's humanity with the *habitus* necessary to prepare it to be perfectly moved *"ut instrumentum,"* as an instrument. As Thomas teaches in the *prima secundae* of the *Summa Theologiae* (where he begins to lay out his influential and original mature form of the theology of the gifts),[39] the gifts involve a movement that originates not from within man, but from God: "the human virtues perfect man insofar as man is made apt to be moved by reason . . . [but the gifts] are higher perfections of man according to which he is disposed to be moved divinely."[40] The gifts of the Holy Spirit are thus distinct from not only the acquired and infused moral virtues, but also from the theological virtues, which do not involve the same

Ekklesiologie und zum kirchlichen Leben im Mittelalter, Festschrift für Ulrich Horst OP zum 75. Geburtstag, eds Thomas Prügl and Marianne Schlosser (Paderborn: Ferdinand Schöningh, 2007), 43–62.

[37] III *Sent.* d. 13, q. 1, a. 1 ad 4. See also *De Verit.*, q. 29, a. 1 ad 9; a. 5 ad 2.

[38] *STh* I–II, q. 68, a. 3 and ad 2.

[39] Edward D. O'Connor, "Appendix 4: The Evolution of St Thomas's Thought on the Gifts," in *Summa Theologiae*, vol. 24, *The Gifts of the Spirit (1a2æ.68–70)* (London: Blackfriars, 1974) , 119. O'Connor also surveys the positions of Aquinas's predecessors and contemporaries, showing the originality of Aquinas's synthesis. *Ibid.*, "Appendix 3: Scholastic Thought Before St Thomas," 99–109. We should add, however, that even within the *Summa Theologiae*, Aquinas's treatment of the gifts evolves, leaving one to wonder whether Aquinas himself was fully satisfied with it.

[40] *STh* I–II, q. 68, a. 1. Aquinas says that Scripture calls the gifts "spirits," suggesting that the type of divine motion involved is that man be moved "by divine inspiration." *Ibid.*

sort of direct movement of the soul by God.[41] "The gifts exceed the common perfection of the virtues, not with respect of the genus of the acts, . . . but according to the mode of action, according to which man is moved by a higher principle."[42] As *habitus*, therefore, the gifts prepare man to be moved directly by God; they "proportion" and "dispose" man's powers and even his supernaturally infused virtues and charisms, so that the divine movement of them is not extrinsic (like a movement by violence), but rather profoundly interior. Neither do man's powers and virtues merely "cooperate with" the divine movement, as if acting alongside and parallel to the divine movement; rather, they are disposed to be "inspired" or actuated by God according to what Thomas calls a "divine instinct."[43] We will have more to say on the unique interiority implied by the word "instinct" very shortly; the key point here is that, in order to be moved in this way, Christ's human nature needs the preparatory dispositions given by the Holy Spirit.

We can grasp the particular character of the perfection brought to Christ's humanity by the gifts if we reflect for a moment on Aquinas's use of the term "divine instinct."[44] A beast who acts by instinct acts purposefully, directed by God towards an end, but according to a plan that is above its capacity to know. The gifts of the Holy Spirit are analogous: while the spiritual man certainly understands more of

---

[41] How to distinguish the gifts from the virtues perplexed more than a few of Aquinas's predecessors and contemporaries; the Dominican master's solution was quite original. See M. Michel Labourdette, "Dons du Saint-Esprit: saint Thomas et la théologie thomiste," in *Dictionnaire de spiritualité*, vol. 3 (Paris: Dabert-Duvergier Beauchesne, 1957), cols. 1616–17. Despite this distinction, we should add that the gifts are given *with* the theological virtues in habitual grace.

[42] *STh* I–II, q. 68, a. 2 ad 1.

[43] On the gifts as perfecting the virtues, as more than a passive capacity, and as "the guidance and assistance of the Paraclete" himself, see O'Connor, "Introduction," in *Summa Theologiae*, vol. 24, xviii–xix.

[44] See, e.g., *In Epist. ad Rom.* c. 8, lect. 3 (no. 635). For a classic study of Aquinas's use of the term "*instinctus*," see Max Seckler, *Instinkt und Glaubenswille nach Thomas von Aquin* (Mainz: Mattias Grünewald Verlag, 1961). Seckler shows that Aquinas's use of this term marks a development in his thought after his discovery of the Council of Orange's condemnation of Semi-Pelagianism. *Ibid.*, 90–8. See also Servais Pinckaers, "Morality and the Movement of the Holy Spirit: Aquinas's Doctrine of *Instinctus*," in *The Pinckaers Reader: Renewing Thomistic Moral Theology*, eds John Berkman and Craig Steven Titus (Washington, D.C.: Catholic University of America Press, 2005), 385–95; Sherwin, *By Knowledge & By Love*, 139–44. Cf. Henri Bouillard, *Conversion et grâce chez s. Thomas d'Aquin: Étude historique* (Paris: Aubier, 1944), 138–40.

what he does and why, he still does not have a perfect comprehension of the divine plan—a plan as infinite as Divine Providence itself—and so he is given an *instinctus* from God that inclines him to act according to God's plan, by a movement that is free and operates through his powers, virtues, and gifts, but that has a mode and direction surpassing his nature. This *instinctus* does not originate in his intellect's apprehension of a desirable good, but in a divinely given impulse. Indeed, left to himself, even if his actions in their material aspect would be identical with what God wills, he would not grasp in full (as the divine intellect does) the goodness of these acts, and his rational appetite would necessarily fall short of willing them according to the perfect mode in which God himself wills them, insofar as a man's will can only desire and act in accord with his finite understanding.[45] The gifts thus dispose man to a mode of action transcending the human, a mode of action in perfect accord with the divine plan.[46]

In the case of Christ's humanity, the operative principles found in his soul are finite and thus less than those of his divine nature. Were his human actions to come only from the finite perfection of his humanity, they could fall short of the perfect mode by which God wills them. To put it another way, such a movement would originate principally in Christ's human nature, as his will responds to what his intellect grasps. This is why Aquinas underscores the role of the gifts of the Holy Spirit here: as a full possessor of the gifts, Christ has a perfect divine instinct. His heart is moved perfectly to desire and act precisely in accord with the divine will, in a mode higher than that of which a human nature—even a human nature perfected by the theological virtues—is capable. St Thomas says this explicitly when explaining why Christ, though perfect in every other respect (in his human nature, in his infused virtues, and in all other gifts of grace), still needs the gifts of the Holy Spirit in order for his action to be perfect:

> What is perfect in the order of its nature needs to be helped by what is of a higher nature; just as man, however perfect he be, needs to be helped by God. And in this way the virtues [in Christ] need to be helped by the

---

[45] See also *STh* I–II, q. 68, a. 2, where Aquinas argues that, even informed and elevated by faith, man's "movement of reason is insufficient to his supernatural final end," and hence man needs the "instinct and motion of the Holy Spirit" which is given in the gifts. Cf. III *Sent.* d. 20, a. 5, qla 1, ad 3.

[46] Cf. *STh* I–II, q. 68, a. 2 ad 1.

gifts, which perfect the powers of the soul insofar as they are moved by the Holy Spirit.[47]

Through the gifts, Christ acts in a higher mode, the mode of God's own action. This is a critical ingredient for Christ's action; to act as the Word's instrument in the fullest sense, Christ's humanity must not only be moved by the divinity, but it must also be put, *as human* (according to its "proper form" as human) in perfect harmony with God, perfectly prepared to be the proper and conjoined instrument of the Word, which instrument acts *as man* according to the divine mode of the Word's own action. This is precisely what the gifts of the Holy Spirit bring about.

Finally, with respect to efficient causality, we should note that the created effects produced in Christ's humanity by the gifts of the Holy Spirit are rightly appropriated to the Spirit but are not efficiently caused by the Spirit alone. Even so, the gifts themselves are rooted in and given with charity, by which the Holy Spirit indwells the soul in person; in discussing the gifts, Thomas consistently underlines this connection to the Holy Spirit's personal presence.[48] Likewise, the perfection of Christ's human action as such has a special affinity to the Spirit's personal procession, since it involves the presence of the beloved by way of a kind of impulsion and movement.[49]

Christ's Humanity Is Moved as the Word's Instrument

This brings us to the second element (in addition to the hypostatic union) in Aquinas's explanation of Christ's action: because Christ's

---

[47] *STh* III, q. 7, a. 5 ad 1. Cf. *SThIII*, q. 13, a. 1 ad 2.

[48] *STh* I–II, q. 68, a. 5. In the *Summa Theologiae*, Aquinas does not use the language of appropriation when speaking about the gifts of the Holy Spirit. It is true that, as a created effect, the gifts are caused efficiently by all three divine persons—Thomas made that point explicitly in his youthful *Expositio super Isaiam*, where he had not yet fully worked out how the gifts are best understood as involving the motion of the Holy Spirit. See *Expositio super Isaiam* c. 11. But the later Aquinas shifts his focus elsewhere when he treats of the gifts. Having grasped that they are habitual dispositions to be moved by the Holy Spirit, Aquinas explains the gifts in the *Summa Theologiae* as habitual dispositions rooted in charity, through which the creature is moved by the divine inspiration that comes from the Holy Spirit. See also *In II Epist. ad Cor.* c. 5, lect. 3 (no. 181) and *In II Epist. ad Tim.* c. 1, lect. 3 (no. 14), where Thomas suggests that being led by the Spirit is an effect of charity, which stimulates us to action.

[49] See *STh* I, q. 27, a. 4; *In Ioan.* c. 14, lect. 4 (no. 1916); c. 15, lect. 5 (no. 2062); see also Emery, *Trinitarian Theology*, 66, 223–4.

human nature always acts as an instrument of the Word, it follows that, in its action, that humanity is *actually moved* by the principal agent, that is, by the Word. As Thomas explains, "an instrument receives its instrumental power in two ways: when it receives the form of an instrument, and when it is moved by the principal agent."[50] Christ as man receives the form of an instrument of the Word—indeed, is ontologically constituted as such an instrument—by the hypostatic union, and is perfected as an instrument by the operative *habitus* he receives as gifts from the Spirit. But this instrument must also be moved; Thomas insists on this point. "It is proper to an instrument that it is moved by the principal agent."[51] An instrument acts "according to the power of the one who moves it."[52] If Christ's humanity were to act in perfect conformity with the divine will but without being *moved* by the divinity, his actions would not be truly instrumental or theandric. But in truth, Christ's own proper human operation is drawn into the very divine action itself, as its instrument. This is because:

> the operation that belongs to a thing that is moved by another is nothing other than the action of the mover himself, just as making a bench is not an action of an axe apart from the carpenter. And hence . . . the instrument participates in the operation of its mover, and the mover uses the instrument; in this way, each acts in communion with the other.[53]

This leads St Thomas to the conclusion that, in Christ, "the human nature participates in the operation of the divine nature, as an instrument participates in the operation of the principal agent."[54] As Tschipke puts it, "[i]n its instrumental activity, the human action is implicated in the divine act. That is why the instrumental activity of Christ's humanity belongs more to God than to itself. God is its principal agent."[55]

Yet, when the divine nature moves Christ's human nature, it does so according to the singular nobility of that humanity, which is "a living instrument." Thomas explains:

> It is proper to an instrument that it be moved by the principal agent, but in different ways according to the properties of its nature. For an

---

[50] *STh* III, q. 72, a. 3 ad 2. IV *Sent.* d. 1, q. 1, a. 4.
[51] *STh* III, q. 18, a. 1 ad 2. See also *STh* III, q. 19, a. 1.
[52] *STh* III, q. 64, a. 5. Tschipke devotes an entire section of a chapter to this point. Tschipke, *L'humanité du Christ*, 156–62.
[53] *STh* III, q. 19, a. 1.   [54] *Ibid.*
[55] Tschipke, *L'humanité du Christ*, 169.

inanimate instrument, like an axe or a saw, is moved by an artisan through a purely bodily motion. A living instrument with a sensitive soul is moved through its sense appetite, like a horse by its rider. But a living instrument with a rational soul is moved through its will, as a servant is moved to do something through the command of his master: the servant, indeed, is like "a living instrument," as the Philosopher says in *Politics* I. In this way, therefore, the human nature of Christ was an instrument of the divinity, as moved through its own will.[56]

A saw is moved "bodily" by physical force, but a horse, a nobler "instrument," is not. The rider does not push or drag it by brute physical strength; he "moves" the horse to move itself according to the rider's will by stimulating the horse's own sense appetites. More noble still is a human being with a rational soul. That instrument's full nobility is realized when, for example, a servant puts at the service of his master the full power of his rational nature, acting freely through his own will, with intelligence and creativity, to fulfill the master's command. Christ's humanity was moved *through* Christ's own human will.

Even this does not capture the unique interiority of this movement of Christ's human will. A servant receives an order from outside and then chooses to obey it. But the Word is not "outside" Christ's humanity. The movement of Christ's human will produces an action that *is* the human action of the Word, according to a union far more intimate than that between a master and his servant, or even between a soul and its body. This motion comes from above yet is *interior* to Christ's human nature, producing human actions that are at the same time moved by God *and* are voluntary.

In the *Summa Theologiae*, when an objector argues that, because "everything in Christ was moved according to the divine will," Christ could not have had his own proper human will,[57] we find Thomas agreeing with the objector's premise: every movement in Christ's humanity originates in God.[58] The objector's conclusion, however, does not follow, because the divine will moves Christ's human will from within:

Whatever was in the human nature of Christ was moved at the bidding of the divine will, but it does not follow that in Christ there was no movement of will proper to his human nature, for even the pious wills of other saints are moved according to the divine will, "which works in

[56] *STh* III, q. 18, a. 1 ad 2.   [57] *STh* III, q. 18, a. 1 obj. 1.
[58] *Ibid.* ad 4.

them to will and to accomplish," as Philippians 2 says. For although the will cannot be moved from within [*interius*] by any creature, yet it can be moved from within [*interius*] by God, as was said in the *Prima pars*. And thus Christ followed the divine will according to his human will, as the psalm says: "I have desired to do your will, my God."[59]

Christ's human will is real and truly moves itself. It is a properly human will. No other creature can force it. Yet it is moved from within, freely, by God who created it.

While something similar happens when God moves other saints to act, Christ's humanity is the noblest possible instrument with the closest possible link to its principal agent, and hence we are dealing with an instrumentality that vastly surpasses that of any other saint. The perfection of Christ's grace ensures that the human side of his movement is most perfectly conformed to and penetrated by the divine impulse. What is more, the instrument of Christ's humanity is itself *conjoined to* and *proper to* the Word because of the hypostatic union, so that the action of that humanity is truly an act of the Word itself in his assumed human nature.

C. CHRIST AS MAN IS ALSO MOVED BY THE HOLY SPIRIT

As we have seen, it is a fundamental principle of Christology that, in every human action of Christ, the divine Word is the principal agent, the person who acts. The Holy Spirit is also implicated in this, because Christ's humanity must be properly disposed to receive such a divine movement, as "anointed" by the Holy Spirit with grace, especially with the gifts of the Holy Spirit given with habitual grace. Yet there is still more to say: The New Testament also clearly speaks of the Holy Spirit as "leading" Christ, and St Thomas does not hesitate to give the full

[59] *STh* III, q. 18, a. 1 ad 1. See also *De unione Verbi incarnati*, a. 5. Corey Barnes shows how Aquinas's account evolved to emphasize more and more that Christ's human will both is moved by God, and acts freely—and that this is important for Aquinas's account of Christ's human nature as an instrumental efficient cause of salvation. Corey L. Barnes, *Christ's Two Wills in Scholastic Thought: The Christology of Aquinas and Its Historical Contexts* (Toronto: Pontifical Institute of Mediaeval Studies, 2012), 172–4.

sense to this scriptural witness. In addition to the Holy Spirit's action in conferring habitual gifts of grace, Thomas attributes movement to the Holy Spirit: Christ's "heart is moved by the Holy Spirit," "inclined" to act "from the instinct of the Holy Spirit."[60] In doing this, however, Aquinas does not confuse the Spirit's movement with Christ's instrumental or theandric action, as we shall see.

Thomas consistently distinguishes the motion of the Holy Spirit from the Spirit's habitual gifts. This is clear from, for example, Aquinas's insistence that "the operation of the Holy Spirit, by which he moves and protects us, is not circumscribed by the effect of the habitual gift he causes in us; beyond this effect, he moves and protects us simultaneously with the Father and the Son."[61] Speaking specifically of Christ's humanity, for example, Aquinas explains that Christ is "sent" by the Holy Spirit to preach to the poor.[62] As a created effect, this motion is efficiently caused by all three divine persons and is appropriated to the Holy Spirit with respect to efficient causality. It is especially fitting to appropriate it to the Holy Spirit, Thomas thinks, since the name "*Spiritus*" implies a certain impulsion, as does the name "*Amor*."[63] At the same time, however, the Holy Spirit is personally and properly present in the soul in charity insofar as, through charity, the soul is assimilated to the Spirit's eternal procession by way of love (exemplar causality).[64]

Charity and the Gifts of the Holy Spirit

There are two principal (and overlapping) ways in which St Thomas speaks about Christ being moved by the Holy Spirit.[65] The first is with

---

[60] *In Epist. ad Rom.* c. 8, lect. 3 (no. 635).

[61] *STh* I–II, q. 109, a. 9 ad 2. For a general discussion of Thomas's distinction between habitual grace and the actual movement of the soul by the Holy Spirit (principally referring to texts from the *Summa Theologiae*), see John Rziha, *Perfecting Human Actions: St Thomas Aquinas on Human Participation in Eternal Law* (Washington, D.C.: Catholic University of America Press, 2009), 149–54. On this distinction with reference to the gifts of the Holy Spirit, see O'Connor, "Introduction," in *Summa Theologiae*, vol. 24, xvi. Finally, note that someone without charity can nonetheless be moved to say or do something by the Holy Spirit. *In Epist. ad I Cor.* c. 12, lect. 1 (no. 718).

[62] *De Pot.* q. 10, a. 4 ad 14.   [63] *ScG* IV, cc. 19 and 20.

[64] See, e.g., I *Sent.* d. 17, q. 1, a. 1. For a more detailed treatment of these matters, see CHAPTER 2, pp. 36–42.

[65] We set aside here a third way, common to the movement of will of every rational creature, by which a created will must be reduced from potency to act by God. See, e.g., *STh* I–II, q. 9, a. 6 ad 3.

reference to charity, the "medium" through which "the [Holy Spirit's] operation mov[es] the will to the act of love."[66] "The will is moved to love by the Holy Spirit in such a way that it would itself also be making this act."[67] As Thomas explains in more technical terms, charity as a *habitus* is the form in the soul caused by the Holy Spirit through which the Holy Spirit actually moves the soul.[68]

[T]he Holy Spirit, who is uncreated charity, is in the man who has created charity, moving his soul to the act of love, as God moves all things to their acts, to which they are nonetheless inclined from their own forms. And it is thus that he disposes all things sweetly, because he gives forms and virtues to all things inclining them to that to which he himself moves them, that they would tend to it not by constraint, but as if spontaneously.[69]

Thus, the Holy Spirit *moves* man to a supernatural act of love *through* an inclination truly belonging to him (in virtue of his *habitus* of charity, itself given by the Spirit), so that the act of love that results is *both* from the motion of the Holy Spirit[70] *and* from man's own will acting according to that inclination. While St Thomas does not go into this sort of technical detail when he speaks of Christ's charity, he surely has it in mind when he says, for example, that Christ was "led by the Spirit" insofar as he was moved by the "impetus of charity,"[71] or that "the cause why Christ shed his blood . . . was the Holy Spirit, by whose motion and instinct—namely, by charity for God and for neighbor—he did this."[72]

---

[66] I *Sent.* d. 17, q. 1, a. 1 ad 1. Even in this early text, Aquinas holds that, through charity, the Holy Spirit actually moves the soul. See also Édouard-Henri Wéber, *Le Christ selon saint Thomas d'Aquin* (Paris: Desclée, 1988), 183–7.

[67] *STh* II–II, q. 23, a. 2. While Thomas famously dissents from Peter Lombard's claim that charity is a movement in us from the Holy Spirit without a mediating *habitus*, he nonetheless holds that charity is a movement from the Holy Spirit according to the *habitus* of charity. Ibid.; *De Caritate*, aa. 1 and 12; I *Sent.* d. 17, q. 1, a. 1 and ad 1. In many other texts, Aquinas simply says that the Holy Spirit moves man by charity. See, e.g., *STh* II–II, q. 8, a. 4; q. 24, a. 3 ad 1; q. 24, a. 11. Cf. *STh* I–II, q. 109, a. 2.

[68] *De Caritate*, a. 1 ad 1 and ad 2.

[69] *Ibid.*, a. 1. See also *De Caritate*, a. 12.

[70] By appropriation—see CHAPTER 7, SECTION C.

[71] *In Matt.* c. 4, (no. 310) (speaking about Christ as man being led into the desert).

[72] *In Epist. ad Hebr.* c. 9, lect. 14 (no. 444). Cf. *In Epist. ad Rom.* c. 8, lect. 5 (no. 694), where Aquinas suggests, albeit indirectly, that the Holy Spirit is at work when Christ conforms his human will to the Father's will in the Garden of Gethsemane. See also *STh* I–II, q. 114, a. 6: "anima Christi mota est a Deo per gratiam."

The second way that Thomas speaks of Christ's soul as moved by the Holy Spirit is through the gifts of the Holy Spirit. This is related to the first way (and in a sense derived from it) because man is moved by the Holy Spirit only insofar as he is united to the Spirit by charity, through and in which the gifts are given.[73] Yet the gifts involve a special motion of the Holy Spirit, because (as we have seen) through them man is moved by a higher instinct, according to a higher mode than charity's impulse.[74]

We find an excellent example of this in St Thomas's Commentary on Romans 8:14 ("Those who are led by the Spirit of God are sons of God"). He first explains how the Spirit can move man from within using the terminology of his theology of the gifts of the Holy Spirit, and then applies this to Christ who is "led by the Spirit."

> The first thing to be considered is how one is led by the Spirit of God. This could be understood thus: . . . that one is guided as by a leader and director, which is something that the Spirit does in us, insofar as he interiorly illuminates us about what we should do: "Let your good Spirit guide me," etc. (Ps. 142:10).[75]

This is not a sufficient exegesis of St Paul's text, Aquinas thinks, because it does not account for how one is truly *led* by the Spirit. When one acts based on an intellectual illumination, one's movement

---

[73] *STh* I–II, q. 68, a. 4 ad 3; a. 5.

[74] *STh* I–II, q. 68, a. 2 ad 1; see O'Connor, "Introduction," in *Summa Theologiae*, vol. 24, xvi–xvii; Labourdette, "Dons du Saint Esprit," 1626–7; Yves Congar, "Le Saint-Esprit dans la théologie thomiste de l'agir moral," in *Tommaso d'Aquino nel suo settimo centenario: Atti del Congresso internazionale*, vol. 5, *L'agire morale* (Napoli: Edizioni Domenicane Italiane, 1977), 10–13. Many interpreters of Aquinas have traditionally considered the motion imparted by the gifts of the Holy Spirit to be distinct from the more general category of the *auxilium* of grace. See, e.g., John of St Thomas, *The Gifts of the Holy Ghost*, trans. Dominic Hughes (New York: Sheed & Ward, 1950), 35, 57–8; Ambrose Gardeil, *The Holy Spirit in Christian Life* (St Louis: B. Herder Book Co., 1953), 5–7. Joseph Wawrykow explains that the gifts "are infused as additional habits in the person who possesses habitual grace and the infused virtues, to make that person more prone to the promptings of the Spirit in *auxilium*," seemingly implying that the same divine *auxilium* is more effective because of the habitual dispositions conferred by the gifts. Wawrykow, "Christ and the Gifts of the Holy Spirit," 50. John Meinert's extended study of this question leads him to read Aquinas as if actual grace (or the *auxilium* of grace) were identical with the *instinctus* of the Holy Spirit involved in the gifts. John Meinert, *Donum Habituale: Grace and the Gifts of the Holy Spirit in St Thomas Aquinas* (Ph.D. dissertation, Catholic University of America, 2015), 302–13.

[75] *In Epist. ad Rom.* c. 8, lect. 3 (no. 635).

arises from one's own will (as the intellect grasps its object, the will naturally desires it insofar as it is good). Such an action might be counseled by the Spirit, but it would not properly be an action *led* by the Spirit. Aquinas thus probes more carefully the meaning of St Paul's words:

> But it is necessary to understand better this phrase "those who are led by the Spirit," since one who is led does not act from himself: the spiritual man is not only instructed by the Holy Spirit about what he should do, but his heart is also moved by the Holy Spirit. For those who are led are moved by a certain higher instinct. Thus, we say that animals do not act but are led, because they are moved to their acts from nature and not from their own impulse. Similarly, the spiritual man is inclined to do something not as if principally moved by his own will, but from the instinct of the Holy Spirit, ... as Luke 4:1 says, Christ was led by the Spirit into the desert.[76]

The Holy Spirit does grant an intellectual illumination (as in Christ's infused knowledge), but the Spirit is not only a "leader and director (*ductor et director*)." Thomas's key insight here is that "being led" is not just a motion, but a motion of a particular type—a motion that comes from above. "Those who are led are moved by a certain higher instinct," he says. When a spiritual man is led by the Spirit, his action does not originate principally in his will, but rather comes from the Spirit who moves him to action, something that Aquinas variously describes as a movement of the heart, an instinct, and an impulse. Though he does not here expressly name the gifts of the Holy Spirit (the habitual dispositions to follow well such "instincts" of the Spirit), the context and Thomas's terminology suggest that he has them in mind.[77] This is how Christ's human nature was moved by the Holy Spirit, Aquinas concludes, when Christ was led by the Spirit into the desert.

As we have seen, that Aquinas uses the word *instinctus* to speak about the gifts of the Holy Spirit is distinctive and quite important: the gifts dispose one to "follow well a divine instinct," the "instinct

---

[76] *Ibid.*

[77] For example, at *STh* I–II, q. 68, a. 2, and *STh* III, q. 7, a. 5, Thomas makes similar arguments; in both cases, he is explicitly speaking about the gifts of the Holy Spirit. The latter text suggests that Christ was led into the desert by the Spirit through the gifts.

and motion of the Holy Spirit," that surpasses the "instinct of reason."[78] The Dominican master is trying to express how this movement is *from* the Spirit (i.e., above and outside man) and yet does not
move man from outside. Man is moved *within*, by a movement fully
consistent with his freedom but that surpasses his reason without
contradicting or opposing it. Through the gifts, the Holy Spirit
activates man's own powers and virtues, including even the theological virtues, in a higher mode, according to the infinite and perfect
wisdom of God himself,[79] so that he is "led by the Spirit" in a way
distinct from the way the Spirit moves him in charity. Charity's
inclination seems to "belong" to the soul in a way that the "instinct
of the Holy Spirit" does not.[80]

The Spirit's Impulse and Theandric Action: Distinction in Unity

At this point, one might wonder if the Spirit's movement of Christ
is distinct from Christ's instrumental action, where the Word is the
principal agent of Christ's human acts. In fact, if one examines
the created effects in Christ's human nature—for example, that his
human will is moved interiorly by a divine impulse (whether from the

---

[78] *STh* I–II, q. 68, a. 2. In general, see Servais Pinckaers, "Morality and the
Movement of the Holy Spirit," 385–95.

[79] Labourdette, "Dons du Saint Esprit," 1626–7.

[80] Though a thorough examination of this point is beyond the scope of this study, it
seems to us that, in *De Caritate*, a. 1, Aquinas accounts for the Holy Spirit's movement
of the soul in charity by pointing to the inclination really given to the soul in that
habitual gift, an inclination to love God above all things. As such, that inclination
"belongs" to the soul according to a human mode as elevated by grace. In contrast, at *In
Epist. ad Rom.* c. 8, lect. 3 (no. 635), Aquinas speaks of the gifts of the Holy Spirit as
giving the "instinct of the Holy Spirit" to the soul, which involves an inclination that,
although fully consistent with the will's freedom, is more properly viewed as originat-
ing *above* the soul, and which does not "belong" to the soul according to the same
human mode because it involves a higher mode of action. Thomas says this explicitly at
STh I–II, q. 68, a. 2 ad 1 and ad 2: the gifts involve "a certain superior instinct of the
Holy Spirit," (ad. 2) by which "man is moved by a higher principle" than the virtues,
thus giving his action a higher mode (ad. 1). This seems to be consistent with what
Labourdette has in mind when he writes about the perfection brought to the theological virtues by the gifts. Labourdette, "Dons du Saint Esprit," 1626–7. For a study of
Thomas's usage of the terms "inspiratio" and "instinctus" suggestive of (though
certainly not proving) the above distinction, see O'Connor, "*Instinctus* and *Inspiratio*,"
in *Summa Theologiae*, vol. 24, *The Gifts of the Spirit*, 131–41.

Word, or from the Holy Spirit)—it is hard to offer any clear distinction. Both the movement of Christ's human nature as the Word's instrument and the movement of Christ's humanity by the Holy Spirit are *interior* in their "way of working within" Christ. Both impart a motion that enhances rather than diminishes human freedom in a way possible to God alone. (As Thomas explains the Spirit's motion through the gifts: "[T]his does not mean that spiritual men would not act through their will and free choice, because the Holy Spirit causes in them the very movement of the will and of free choice, as Phil. 2:13 says: 'God is at work in you both to will and to work.)"[81] Both require the gifts of the Holy Spirit disposing Christ's humanity to be perfectly moved by God. Thus, when Scripture says that Christ is "led" by the Holy Spirit, Thomas does not suggest that this "being led" involves an *effect* in Christ's humanity somehow different from the human dimension of Christ's action as the Word's conjoined instrument.

Rather, the distinction resides in the utterly unique union of Christ's humanity to the Word: it is assumed into the very person of the Word, so that when Jesus walks or heals, there is only one act belonging to one person (the Word), exercised in two natures.[82] Even if, simultaneously, his "heart is moved by the Holy Spirit,"[83] so that Christ as man can also be said to be led by the Spirit in that action, what results is a theandric act belonging *properly* to the Word (who concurrently moves Christ's humanity as conjoined to it).

In contrast, the Holy Spirit's influence on Christ is always on the human nature *of the Word*. To put it another way, the Holy Spirit may work *within* Christ's human will, but the Holy Spirit himself remains a distinct actor, a distinct subject. (Elsewhere, Thomas speaks of this sort of interior divine motion of the will as being "as if from an exterior principle (*sicut ab exteriori principio*);"[84] here, despite his interior way of working, the Holy Spirit is a principle that is, in a sense, exterior to Christ insofar as the Spirit is a distinct *supposit*.) When we say that Christ is moved to do something by the Holy Spirit, therefore, we are speaking about the action of one person by reference to another. The Spirit's influence may be quite important or even decisive, but the action can be attributed only in an improper

---

[81] *In Epist. ad Rom.* c. 8, lect. 3 (no. 635). See also *ibid.*, c. 9, lect. 3 (no. 777).
[82] *STh* III, q. 19, a. 1 ad. 3.
[83] *In Epist. ad Rom.* c. 8, lect. 3 (no. 635).   [84] *STh* I–II, q. 9, a. 6.

and attenuated sense to him.[85] When Peter is moved to act by the Holy Spirit, the resulting action is Peter's. It is the same with Christ. There is only one supposit and hypostasis in him. Every one of Christ's actions is an action of that hypostasis, which is the Word.[86]

St Thomas makes exactly this distinction in his *Sentences* Commentary when he distinguishes how the Holy Spirit moves a man's soul in charity from the unique case of the hypostatic union:

> The union of the human nature in Christ terminates in the one *esse* of the divine person, and hence the act of the divine person and of the assumed human nature is numerically the same. But the will of a saint is not assumed into the unity of the supposit of the Holy Spirit. Thus, since an action has unity and diversity from the supposit, [such an action of a saint] cannot be understood to be one action of [his] will and of the Holy Spirit, except in the way by which God works in any given thing.[87]

Note the principle that governs Aquinas's analysis: "an action has unity and diversity from the supposit." Where there is one acting supposit, the resulting act is numerically one. Since there is only one supposit in Christ, there is therefore one single act ("*opus operatum*") of the Word and his assumed human nature, resulting from the two distinct operations of his two natures.[88] The unity of Christ's theandric action is rooted in this unity between the Word and his human nature. This is not the case with the Holy Spirit, who moves Christ's humanity from within through charity and the gifts (and is therefore a genuine principle of Christ's acts), but who always remains a distinct hypostasis. In the strict sense, therefore, the Holy Spirit's action is distinct from that of Christ. Christ's resulting human action is not the proper action of the Holy Spirit himself, but only that of the Word.[89]

---

[85] Even then, this attribution is by appropriation, since the Holy Spirit moves Christ's heart as an efficient cause together with the Father and the Son. *STh* I–II, q. 109, a. 9 ad 2. In contrast, the attribution of Christ's action to the Word is proper and not by appropriation.

[86] See, e.g., *STh* III, q. 19, a. 1 ad 3.   [87] I *Sent.* d. 17, q. 1, a. 1.

[88] Thomas adds that the theandric act of Christ is only one in a certain respect, *secundum quid*, and not absolutely, since it is the action of one supposit in virtue of two distinct natures. See III *Sent.* d. 18, a. 1 ad 1–5.

[89] To approach this from a slightly different perspective, we could say that each of Christ's actions is a unified and single action, even though, as the God-man, there are distinct operations of the divine and human natures in that single action. Christ's every action is therefore an action of the Word himself. Christ is likewise always moved by the Holy Spirit to his actions, so in every action of Christ, we can also discern a concurrent action of the Holy Spirit.

Thus, when Christ is "led by the Spirit" into the desert, Christ's action can in one sense be attributed to the Holy Spirit's interior movement of Christ's will through the gifts of the Holy Spirit (and also, in a more general sense, through charity). Yet, strictly speaking, this act is not the Holy Spirit's. Rather, it is per se an action of the Word in his human nature. The Word acts in and through Christ's human nature *as hypostatically united to it*; the Holy Spirit concurrently moves Christ's human will from within, but as a distinct divine person dwelling in Christ's humanity by grace. Consequently, Christ's action is always properly attributed to the Word but never to the Spirit, though both are implicated in it (in different and complementary ways). The Holy Spirit's movement of Christ's humanity is not a fiction—the Spirit really moves Christ's humanity and is a principle of Christ's every action (indeed, the Word and the Spirit always act in perfect harmony and simultaneity)—but the Spirit's action remains distinct from that of Christ, whereas Christ's human action is the very action of the Word in his proper and conjoined human nature.[90]

Finally, according to the Trinitarian order, every action of the Spirit *comes from the Word himself*, both in the inmost life of the Trinity as well as in the economy—and so the Holy Spirit's "impulse" moving Christ's heart also comes from the Word. The Word is always breathing forth love, and the Holy Spirit is always being breathed forth by the Word, so that the Holy Spirit who moves Christ's humanity is the Spirit who proceeds from the Father and Son and has received all from them.

* * *

In sum, then, Aquinas holds that Christ, having received the Holy Spirit in full in his human nature, receives all of the gifts of the Holy Spirit in the greatest possible degree, and is impelled by the Spirit to act in perfect love and in perfect harmony with the divine will. There are four principle elements to the teaching that Christ is moved by the

---

[90] These important distinctions are often overlooked. For example, when Étienne Vetö discusses Aquinas's account of Christ as moved by the Holy Spirit, he posits that this is entirely by appropriation, and that in fact, when St Thomas says that Christ is moved by the Holy Spirit, he really means that the divinity in general moves Christ—and that, to the extent he would attribute this to one divine person, it would be the Word, not the Holy Spirit. Vetö, *Du Christ à la Trinité*, 108–10. Unfortunately, this overlooks a great many of Aquinas's texts that suggest otherwise, as we have attempted to show in this chapter.

Holy Spirit. (1) Christ's humanity is constituted as the instrument of the Word by the hypostatic union since this humanity is the Word's proper humanity, hypostatically conjoined to him. (2) Christ's humanity is perfected by the grace of the Holy Spirit, and in particular by the gifts of the Holy Spirit, which dispose that humanity to act by a movement coming from God in unerring harmony with the divine will, and which thus make it perfectly suited to be "used" by the divine Word as his human instrument. (3) Christ's humanity is actually moved as the Word's conjoined instrument to acts that are properly theandric, the human acts of the Word himself. (4) Complementing this theandric action, it is also true to say that Christ's humanity is moved by the Holy Spirit, who acts "from" the Word; though a distinct divine person and not himself the principal agent of Christ's actions, the Holy Spirit nonetheless is rightly said to impart an impulse or motion to Christ's humanity, both by charity and through the gifts of the Holy Spirit.

8

Christ Gives the Holy Spirit

Christ is not only the beneficiary of the Holy Spirit, but is the source of the Spirit for the world. Attentive to what Scripture clearly attests, that "Christ gives the Holy Spirit,"[1] St Thomas explains that "because he received the gifts of the Spirit without measure, he has the power of pouring them out without measure."[2] This makes Christ "a spiritual fount.... 'With you is the fount of life (Ps. 35),' namely, the Holy Spirit, who is the Spirit of life."[3]

A. THE SON SENDS THE HOLY SPIRIT

As we begin examining this teaching, we should recall a fundamental point both for Aquinas's Trinitarian theology and his theology of the divine missions: the Holy Spirit eternally proceeds from the Father and the Son, and is sent in time by the Father and the Son. That Christ sends the Spirit to the world as the divine Son, therefore, manifests in the world the order of the eternal processions within the Triune God.[4] According to St Thomas, this is why Christ always mentions both the Father and the Son whenever he speaks of the sending of the Holy Spirit:

> The mission of the Holy Spirit is jointly from the Father and the Son, as signaled in Revelation: "He showed me a river of living water," that is, the Holy Spirit, "proceeding from the throne of God and of the Lamb,"

---

[1] *In Epist. ad Tit.* c. 3, lect. 1 (no. 93).   [2] *Compendium theologiae* I, c. 215.
[3] *In Ioan.* c. 4, lect. 1 (no. 561).
[4] We should add, with Bruce Marshall, that "[t]hat Christ gives—or more precisely, sends—the Holy Spirit does not mean, Thomas also observes, that the Spirit's coming is anything less than his own free action." Marshall, "What Does the Spirit Have to Do?" 64.

that is, of Christ (Rev. 22:1). For this reason, concerning the mission of the Holy Spirit, Christ mentions both the Father and the Son, from whom the Spirit is sent by their equal and identical power. Whenever Christ speaks of the Father sending, he does not leave out the Son, as at John 14:26: "the Paraclete, the Holy Spirit, whom the Father will send in my name." But whenever he mentions himself sending, he does not do so without the Father, as here where he says: "[the Paraclete] whom I will send you from the Father," because, in fact, whatever the Son does, he does from the Father: "the Son cannot do anything from himself (John 5:19)."[5]

We should not pass too quickly over the connection between the Spirit's procession and his mission lest we neglect its profound import for St Thomas's thought. As we have seen, it is impossible, according to Aquinas, to separate the divine missions of the Son and the Holy Spirit from their eternal processions, since a divine mission includes and discloses the eternal procession upon which it is founded. Indeed, the missions extend those processions into time, as it were. There is therefore an internal logic to the divine "pedagogy" by which God reveals himself to us. The Son is the *Auctor sanctificationis*: he who, in the eternity of the Triune Godhead is a principle (with the Father) of the Holy Spirit, is likewise the one in history who, through his saving actions (above all, his suffering, death, and exaltation), gives the Holy Spirit to the world. Similarly, the Holy Spirit, who is Love and Gift in person, is the uncreated *Donum sanctificationis*; it is by giving the Holy Spirit to the world that the saving mission of Christ is accomplished. To Aquinas's mind, it would be as nonsensical to separate these two aspects as to separate the divine persons from each other: The Son does not act in the world without the Spirit, and so the whole of the mystery of Christ aims at and is accomplished in the outpouring of the Holy Spirit on the world. These are aspects of one single reality, our salvation by the Triune God according to a Trinitarian pattern.

This is exactly how Thomas interprets the opening lines of St Paul's Letter to the Romans, where the Apostle summarizes the whole of the Gospel:

It is proper to the divine power to sanctify men by the gift of the Holy Spirit: "It is I the Lord who sanctify you (Lev. 20:8)." It is he alone who can give the Holy Spirit.... and thus it is clear that Christ has divine power, because he himself gives the Holy Spirit.... We are sanctified by

---

[5] *In Ioan.* c. 15, lect. 5 (no. 2061).

his power, as 1 Cor. 6:11 says: "But you are sanctified and justified in the name of our Lord Jesus Christ and by the Spirit of our God." St. Paul says, therefore, that the fact that Christ is *"the Son of God in power"* appears *"according to the Spirit of sanctification,"* that is, insofar as Christ gives the Spirit who sanctifies.[6]

The incarnation itself is for the sake of our salvation, which is accomplished when the Holy Spirit, the *Donum sanctificationis*, is given to us through the incarnate Son, *manifesting* the Son and also *configuring* us to the Son so that we become adopted sons and daughters of the Father.[7] "One who receives the Holy Spirit from the Father and the Son, that one knows the Father and the Son and comes to them."[8] Or, to return to the perspective of CHAPTER 1, that of the divine processions themselves, "the procession of the persons . . . is the *ratio* of the return [of creatures] to their end, so that as we were created through the Son and the Holy Spirit, likewise we also are joined through them to our ultimate end."[9] For this reason, Thomas says, "the Holy Spirit is called the nearest to us, insofar as through him all gifts are given to us."[10]

B. CHRIST GIVES THE HOLY SPIRIT AS MAN

What role does Christ's humanity play in the giving of the Spirit? In the Western theological tradition, this question has largely been treated in the context of Christ's capital grace, and in this domain, at least for the Latin theologians of the thirteenth century and for the early Thomas, the principal authority was St Augustine.

The Heritage of St Augustine

To Augustine's mind, Christ's capacity to give the Holy Spirit is a proof of his divinity, since the gift of the Holy Spirit can only come from Christ's divine nature:

> How is the one who gives the Holy Spirit not God? Rather, how truly is he God who gives God! For none of his disciples gave the Holy Spirit;

---

[6] *In Epist. ad Rom.* c. 1, lect. 3 (no. 58).   [7] *In Ioan.* c. 14, lect. 6 (no. 1957).
[8] *In Ioan.* c. 14, lect. 6 (no. 1959).   [9] I *Sent.* d. 14, q. 2, a. 2.
[10] III *Sent.* d. 2, q. 2, a. 2, qla 2, ad 3. Cf. III *Sent.* d. 1, q. 2, a. 2 ad 5.

instead, they prayed that the Spirit would come upon those on whom they laid their hands, but they did not give him. The Church has preserved this custom even now in regard to its leaders.[11]

Human beings can merely pray that God will give the Holy Spirit, because only God can give God. Augustine concludes, therefore, that Christ "received [the Holy Spirit] as man, and poured him forth as God."[12]

According to Yves Congar, Augustine's view is bound up with his theory of intellectual illumination. "Only God illumines souls, being alone superior to them. . . . Christ gives life to souls as Son of God, and to bodies merely as son of man."[13] Gérard Philips likewise summarizes Augustine thus: "if the body can touch the corporeal, only the spirit can influence the spiritual."[14] The Spirit acts in our souls "after having acted on the humanity of Jesus, but his action, strictly speaking, does not pass through this humanity."[15] Influenced

---

[11] Augustine, *De Trin.* lib. 15, c. 26 (CCL 50A: 526).   [12] *Ibid.*

[13] Yves Congar, "Saint Augustin et le traité scolastique 'De gratia Capitis,'" *Augustinianum* 20 (1980): 92. See also Augustine, *Tract. In Ioh.* XXIII, 13 and 15 (CCL 36: 242–4), where Augustine holds that Christ gives life to souls as consubstantial with the Father, while it is accorded to his humanity to be the source of the resurrection of bodies.

[14] Gérard Philips, "L'influence du Christ-chef sur son corps mystique suivant saint Augustin," in *Augustinus Magister: Congrès International Augustinien*, vol. 2 (Paris: Études Augustiniennes, 1954), 810.

[15] *Ibid.*, 813. Gérard Remy takes issue with Philips's conclusion that, unlike the Greek fathers, "Augustine in no way presents the humanity of Christ as an instrument of salvation." Remy shows that, for Augustine, Christ is mediator as man, and that his later thought dropped the sharp distinction between what Christ does as Son of God and what he does as Son of Man. Augustine had a nuanced and realistic understanding of the role of Christ's humanity in our salvation, says Remy, who suggests that the logic of Augustine's later thought implies that Christ's humanity must somehow mediate the gift of the Spirit to his members. Remy's case for a nuanced reading of Augustine is well taken, but his positive argument about the humanity of Christ and the giving of the Spirit in Augustine remains somewhat hypothetical, since he does not marshal texts that show the bishop of Hippo explicitly adopting such a view. See Gérard Remy, "La théologie de la médiation selon saint Augustin: son actualité," *Revue Thomiste* 91 (1991): 603 and 618–20. See also Stanislaus J. Grabowski, "St Augustine and the Doctrine of the Mystical Body of Christ," *Theological Studies* 7 (1946): 75–7, who attempts to harmonize Augustine with the Greek Fathers and the later Aquinas on the instrumentality of Christ's humanity. Congar does a careful analysis of twelve different texts of Augustine that might be susceptible to such a reading, concluding that, while for Augustine, there is an "exemplary anticipation and assurance for our hope" in Christ our glorified head insofar as there is a communion and "unity of destiny between the Head and his body," he never affirms a causal

by Neoplatonism and lacking a robust category of instrumental causality, Augustine thus does not speak of Christ as giving the Holy Spirit as man. This is something that only God does.

The young Aquinas follows Augustine when discussing Christ's capital grace in his *Sentences* Commentary, quoting the passage excerpted above in his first objection: "The Holy Spirit is not diffused in the Church by Christ as man, but only as God, because, as Augustine says, . . . [Christ] received the Holy Spirit as man and poured him out as God."[16] In his reply to this argument, the Dominican bachelor elaborates the meaning of Augustine's text, distinguishing the two ways of giving the Spirit implicit in it: authoritatively (*auctoritate,* by origin or authority), and ministerially (*ministerio,* by an office or ministry). Only God gives the Holy Spirit authoritatively, Aquinas says, while "men are also said to give the Holy Spirit ministerially, insofar as the Spirit is given by God through their ministry." And so, Thomas concludes, "in this way, Christ as man could give the Holy Spirit ministerially."[17] The early Aquinas thus places Christ's human nature in the same category as the apostles, who also give the Holy Spirit ministerially—a position hardly distinguishable from Augustine's.

A few years later, however, when Thomas raises the subject of Christ's capital grace in Question 29 of the *De Veritate,* he takes up the notion, recently recovered from the Greek Fathers, that Christ's humanity is an instrument of his divinity, which he uses to deepen his reflections and to distinguish Augustine's dictum. "As Damascene says, the humanity of Christ was, as it were, an instrument of the divinity, and hence his actions could be salutary for us."[18] Christ as man, in all that he says and does, accomplishes our salvation instrumentally. This potent understanding of instrumental causality leads to a bold claim for the role of Christ's human nature, well beyond what Augustine says: "Because Christ in a certain way infuses the effect of grace in all rational creatures, he is therefore in a certain

influence of Christ as man in giving grace or the Holy Spirit. Congar, "Saint Augustin," 89–90.

[16] III *Sent.* d. 13, q. 2, a. 1, obj. 1.   [17] *Ibid.,* ad 1.

[18] *De Verit.,* q. 29, a. 5. See also a. 4, ad. 1, explaining that, while only Christ's divinity vivifies souls as a principal agent, his humanity does so as an instrument of his divinity. Aquinas thus reads Augustine's statement that souls are vivified by Christ's divinity and bodies by Christ's humanity as a type of "appropriation" in order to highlight the causality of Christ's resurrection for our future bodily resurrection.

manner the principle of all graces according to his humanity, as God is the principle of all being."[19] Christ's humanity is thus far more than a merely ministerial cause (comparable to the apostles) of the gift of the Holy Spirit. "Christ works our salvation as if from his own power, and so it was necessary that the fullness of grace would be in him."[20] Aquinas here links the instrumentality of Christ's humanity to his capital grace. "[A]s the whole perfection of being is concentrated in God, so also the complete fullness and power of grace is found in Christ, through which he not only can perform gracious works, but he can also bring others to grace."[21] To illustrate this, Aquinas takes from John Damascene the image of iron heated to the point of catching fire, transposing it from a generic example of theandric action to a specific illustration of how Christ's humanity gives grace instrumentally: Christ's humanity is like iron so aflame with the Holy Spirit that he can set others ablaze with that same fire.[22]

From this point onward in his career, Aquinas does not hesitate to say that Christ gives the Holy Spirit as both God and man: "We find two natures in Christ, and it pertains to both that Christ gives the Holy Spirit."[23] Thus, when St Thomas addresses Christ's capital grace in the *Summa Theologiae*, he distances himself from St Augustine, whom he quotes in an objection: "As Augustine says, ... Christ does not give the Holy Spirit as man, but only as God. Therefore, it does not belong to him as man to be the head of the Church."[24] Aquinas's reply is direct. While not openly contradicting Augustine, he distinguishes the bishop of Hippo's *dictum* by emphasizing the instrumentality of Christ's humanity.

> To give grace or the Holy Spirit belongs to Christ as God authoritatively, but as man it belongs to him instrumentally, since his humanity was the instrument of his divinity. In this way, his actions were

---

[19] *Ibid.*, a. 5.   [20] *Ibid.*, ad. 3.   [21] *Ibid.*, a. 5.

[22] *De Verit.*, q. 29, a. 4. Cf. John Damascene *De Fide Orthodoxa: Versions of Burgundio and Cerbanus*, ch. 63, ed. Eligius M. Buytaert (St Bonaventure, New York: The Franciscan Institute, 1955), 259.

[23] *In Epist. ad Tit.* c. 3, lect. 1 (no. 93). See also *In Epist. ad Hebr.* c. 8, lect. 1 (no. 382), which explains that, insofar as his humanity is an instrument of his divinity, "the man Christ is a minister" of the heavenly sanctuary "because all goods of glory are dispensed through him;" *In Epist. ad Rom.* c. 8, lect. 7 (no. 718). Cf. *Compendium theologiae* I, c. 239.

[24] *STh* III, q. 8, a. 1 obj. 1.

salvific for us from the power of his divinity, as causing grace in us both through merit and through a certain efficiency. Augustine, however, negates that Christ as man gives the Holy Spirit authoritatively. Yet instrumentally, or ministerially, even other saints are said to give the Holy Spirit, as Gal. 3 says: "He who gives the Holy Spirit to you," etc.[25]

This reply is both technically dense and theologically important. First, as we have seen before, "to give grace" and "to give the Holy Spirit" are interchangeable expressions for Aquinas; habitual or sanctifying grace is the created effect of the indwelling of the Holy Spirit in person. Christ does not give the one without the other. In fact, the gift of the Holy Spirit in person is absolutely primary.[26] When St Thomas says that Christ gives or causes grace, this implies that Christ gives the Holy Spirit in person.[27]

Second, Thomas places the instrumentality of Christ's humanity at the center of his explanation.[28] Implicit is Thomas's integration of the patristic doctrine of Christ's theandric action into his own account of the hypostatic union and of Christ's grace. The main body of this article stressed the interconnection of those two realities in a passage that is, in effect, a concise theological commentary on the prologue of St John's Gospel: as the Word made flesh, Christ's humanity, more closely united to the divinity than any other creature, receives the Holy Spirit in full and hence "the perfect fullness of all graces: 'We saw him full of grace and truth (John 1:14).'" Consequently, as man, he is an instrument with "the power of giving grace to all the members of the Church: 'From his fullness we have all received (John 1:16).'" To call Christ "head of the Church" is to underscore this dimension of his reception of the Holy Spirit.[29]

Finally, Christ's actions "caus[e] grace in us both through merit and through a certain efficiency." Christ's saving death on the cross *merited* for us the gift of the Holy Spirit, but that is not all: his actions "have a certain efficiency" in giving grace or the Holy Spirit. Augustine does not speak in this register about Christ's humanity; it is a

<hr/>

[25] *STh* III, q. 8, a. 1, ad 1. Aquinas reads Gal. 3:5 as referring to St Paul giving the Holy Spirit to the Galatians through his ministry.
[26] See I *Sent.* d. 14, q. 2, a. 1, qla 2, as discussed in Chapter 2, pp. 41–2.
[27] Cf. *In Ioan.* c. 3, lect. 6 (no. 543).
[28] See Emery, "Le Christ médiateur," 349–52. [29] *STh* III, q. 8, a. 1.

genuine contribution of the Master from Aquino,[30] and a point on which Aquinas was unique among thirteenth-century theologians.[31] Christ's human life and human acts are not only important because, by his passion, he satisfied for our sins;[32] Thomas's reappropriation of instrumental causality permits him to give a supreme importance and salvific significance to everything that the man Christ did and suffered[33]—"*omnes actiones et passiones Christi.*"[34] Aquinas gives Christ's humanity and its concrete history a weight and scope vastly greater than his contemporaries.[35]

---

[30] Torrell, *Encyclopédie Jésus le Christ*, 220. Congar, "Saint Augustin," 89–90. Congar goes on to recount how the idea that Christ is the cause of the influx of grace first appears towards the end of the twelfth century: Robert of Melun speaks of the gifts of the Holy Spirit "descending from Christ to the Church," while Gilbert de la Porrée affirms that Christ's fullness of grace means that "we received from his fullness," so that every grace we have is in Christ "*per causam.*" *Ibid.*, 91 nn. 39 and 40. Aquinas certainly stands in this line of development, but the Dominican master gives it a far more detailed and sophisticated treatment.

[31] For example, the *Summa Fratris Alexandri* held that "*Christus homo influit gratiam . . . membris eius*" by merit, as an exemplar, and as head. Regarding headship, however, it does not hold that Christ as man is the source of grace, but rather that Christ loves his members, and that the Holy Spirit completes this desire of Christ "on account of his love for us." *Summa Fratris Alexandri*, Tract. III, q. 1, tit. 2, mem. 2, c. 3, a. 2, prob. 1 [Quaracchi ed. (1948), 4:157–8]. St Albert expressly denies that Christ's humanity exercises any efficient or instrumental causality in the giving of grace: "Christ's capital grace flows to his members efficiently, but not insofar as Christ is man." Albertus Magnus, III *Sent.* d. 13A, a. 3 [*Opera Omnia*, ed. A. Borgnet (1894) 28:239]. St Bonaventure hews closely to St Augustine, writing that Christ prepares us for grace as man (by satisfying for our sins and disposing us to receive grace), concluding that "Christ only gives grace as God," for which he cites Augustine: "It is God alone who illuminates pious minds." Bonaventure, III *Sent.* d. 13, a. 2, q. 1; see also qq. 2 and 3 [*Opera Omnia*, vol. 3, Quaracchi ed. (1887)].

[32] Bonaventure puts his emphasis here: Christ's humanity removes the obstacles to grace by satisfying for our sins. Bonaventure, III *Sent.* d. 13, a. 2, q. 1.

[33] Emery, "Le Christ médiateur," 351.   [34] *STh* III, q. 48, a. 6.

[35] In Aquinas's Commentary on John (which dates from 1270 to 1271 or perhaps even 1272), there are two passages that seem to return to his earlier Augustinian position about Christ giving the Holy Spirit as God. See *In Ioan.* c. 14, lect. 4 (no. 1910), and c. 16, lect. 2 (no. 2088). When read carefully, however, these texts do not negate Aquinas's claim in the *Summa Theologiae* and other mature works that Christ as man gives the Holy Spirit instrumentally. Aquinas simply omits the fact that Christ's humanity does function as an instrument in giving the Spirit, perhaps because he is focused on a different point. Moreover, earlier in the John Commentary, Aquinas affirms that Christ as man causes grace to be given to us—which means that he gives the Holy Spirit: "'From his fullness we have all received [John 1:16].' . . . There is a fullness of efficient causality and outflowing, which belongs exclusively to the man Christ, as the author of grace." *In Ioan.* c. 1, lect. 10 (no. 201).

Christ Pours Forth the Spirit He Received in Full

How does Christ's human nature have this *"efficientiam quandam"* of giving the Holy Spirit? Here, Aquinas offers an answer with two facets: the first concerns Christ's full possession of the Holy Spirit, and the second has to do with the instrumentality of Christ's humanity in giving the Spirit. These two elements are formally and really distinct (just as Christ's grace is distinct from the hypostatic union), but Aquinas unites them quite closely in his theological account of Christ's work of salvation.

On the one hand, Aquinas frequently identifies Christ's own perfect possession of the Holy Spirit as the source of Christ's giving the Spirit. It is because he receives the Spirit without measure that Christ gives the Spirit to the world.

> For from the fact that he has it, [Christ] pours it forth. Thus, because Christ received the gifts of the Spirit without measure, he has the power of pouring out these gifts without measure . . . so that his grace not only would be sufficient for the salvation of some men, but of all the men of the whole world, as 1 John 2:2 says: "He himself is the propitiation for our sins, and not only for ours, but for those of the whole world." One could even add "and for many worlds," if they existed.[36]

Such is the plenitude of Christ's grace, "a superabundance of grace enough for an infinite number of worlds, if they existed!"[37]

On the other hand, Aquinas sometimes points to the hypostatic union: insofar as his humanity is joined to his divinity as its instrument, Christ *as man* acts in the power of the divinity.[38] "The humanity of Christ has the power of infusing grace insofar as it is conjoined to the Word of God,"[39] Aquinas says. This is the better-known element of Aquinas's theology of Christ's capital grace.

---

[36] *Compendium theologiae* I, c. 215. Aquinas repeats this argument, nearly word for word, at *In Ioan.* c. 3, lect. 6 (no. 544). Cf. Emery, "Réflexions," 56. In both cases, this explanation follows immediately after Thomas identifies the hypostatic union as the root of Christ's power to give grace.

[37] *In Ioan.* c. 1, lect. 8 (no. 190).

[38] Cf. *STh* III, q. 48, a. 6, which distinguishes a principal efficient causality from an instrumental efficient causality. For Aquinas, Christ's humanity can only ever exercise an instrumental efficient causality in giving grace or the Holy Spirit; the principal cause is God.

[39] *STh* III, q. 8, a. 2. Thomas elaborates on this argument in two nearly identical texts, where he compares Christ's humanity, hypostatically united to the Word, to a

For Aquinas, these two elements are embedded in the meaning of John 1:16, "from his fullness we have all received," a Scripture verse to which he often adverts. Aquinas comments:

> To show this singular fullness of Christ's outpouring and efficient causality [with respect to grace], the Evangelist says "from his fullness we have all received," namely all apostles, patriarchs, and prophets; all the just who ever have been, who are, and who will be; and even all angels.[40]

Christ's giving of the Spirit, flowing out from his perfectly sanctified humanity, is for Aquinas the origin of the whole dispensation of salvation, the foundation of the Church, and of all sacraments, and the source of every other grace in the history of the world.

Aquinas then underlines that this "fullness" also designates the Holy Spirit himself. That "from his fullness we have all received," means that the very same Spirit fills Christ's humanity and, through him, fills, sanctifies, and unites the Church.

> [T]he fullness of Christ is the Holy Spirit, who proceeds from him, consubstantial with him in nature, in power, and in majesty. For although the habitual gifts of grace in the soul of Christ are different from those in us, the very same Holy Spirit who is in him, fills all the sanctified.[41]

Christ's humanity is thus the instrumental efficient cause and the source of grace, so that Christ is the author of the outpouring of the Spirit, the author of the gift of graces; this is the ultimate layer of meaning in this rich verse of the Johannine prologue:

> Sometimes the preposition "from" [i.e., "from his fullness"] denotes efficient causality or original causality . . . and according to this reading, "from" designates the efficiency or authorship of grace that is in Christ, because the fullness of grace in Christ is the cause of all graces that are given to all intellectual creatures, as Sir. 24:26 says: "Come to me, all you who desire me, and with my fruits," which proceed from me, "be filled" by participating in my all-sufficing plenitude.[42]

---

spring that has an infinite capacity to pour out water. See *In Ioan.* c. 3, lect. 6 (no. 544); *Compendium theologiae* I, c. 215.

[40] *In Ioan.* c. 1, lect. 10 (no. 201).
[41] *In Ioan.* c. 1, lect. 10 (no. 202).   [42] *Ibid.*

Our reception of grace is a participation in the plenitude of Christ, a sharing in the Spirit which is given to him without measure.[43] Christ our head is anointed with the Holy Spirit, and the oil of the Spirit's gladness flows down "the beard of Aaron, running down on the collar of his robes (Ps. 132:2)."[44] Christ has this anointing "principally and first, while we and others [have it as] flowing out from him . . . . Thus, others are called holy, but he is truly the Holy of Holies, for he is the root of all holiness."[45] This is why Ephesians 1:23 calls the Church "the fullness of Christ," according to St Thomas: "all spiritual under-standing, all gifts—in short, whatever can exist in the Church—all of this is superabundantly in Christ, and flows from him into the Church's members."[46] The Holy Spirit does not come to us inde-pendently of Christ's humanity, but precisely as flowing *from* it (personal and capital fullness) and *through* it (instrumentality).

This permits us to articulate the ordered and complementary relation between the two principal elements of Aquinas's account of Christ's capital grace: Christ's possession of the Holy Spirit "without measure" (and thus his fullness of grace) is deployed *through* the instrumental actions of his humanity. The former refers to Christ's humanity as a source of grace (as filled with the Spirit), and the latter as the instrument by which grace is poured out. As a source, Christ's humanity has most perfectly and fully what it gives: the Holy Spirit in person. As an instrument, Christ's humanity produces a divine effect as an efficient cause of salvation (all of Christ's *acta et passa* are salvific), because it is joined to the Word in the hypostatic union. Consequently, acting as both God and man, Christ sends the Holy Spirit visibly to the apostles on the evening of the resurrection and at Pentecost, so that they would in turn give a share of the Holy Spirit to all the faithful. In this way, Christ's humanity serves as a fount of living water, pouring forth salvation for the whole world.

---

[43] Cf. *STh* III, q. 8, a. 5, which holds that Christ gives to others from the very grace he receives "*secundum maximam eminentiam.*"

[44] *In Epist. ad. Hebr.* c. 1, lect. 4 (nos. 63–5); *In Psalm.* 44 (no. 5); *In Epist. ad. II Cor.* c. 1, lect. 5 (no. 44).

[45] *In Epist. ad Hebr.* c. 1, lect. 4 (no. 65).

[46] *In Epist. ad Ephes.* c. 1, lect. 8 (no. 71). Likewise, the Church is the mystical body of Christ because it receives its spiritual unity from the Holy Spirit, "the Spirit of unity," who "is derived to us from Christ." *In Epist. ad Rom.* c. 12, lect. 2 (no. 974).

Aquinas concludes his exegesis of this passage by contrasting Christ's fullness of the Holy Spirit with our partial reception of the Spirit:

> The Evangelist notes that the part [received] in those who receive is derived from a fullness. For [Christ] received every gift of the Holy Spirit without measure, according to a perfect fullness, but we have through him a certain partial participation in his fullness, as God alone apportions us by measure, "to each of us grace is given according to the measure of the giving of Christ (Eph. 4:7)."[47]

Christ's gift of the Spirit to us is not only a matter of instrumentality and efficient causality, but also of participation—our reception of the Holy Spirit is a participation in Christ's fullness of the Spirit.

The field of vision that this opens up is vast. Our reception of the Spirit implies our participation in Christ's grace, our conformity to him in his human nature, in his *acta et passa*, even in his march to Calvary and, ultimately, in his resurrection from the dead. All of this is accomplished in us by the Holy Spirit, who, coming to us through the historical acts of his humanity, conforms us to Christ and gives us a share in his sonship, making us adopted sons and daughters of the Father.

The Trinity, Christ's Humanity, and Salvation in the Holy Spirit

We could hardly do better than by concluding this section with a text that "contains in miniature" Aquinas's whole Trinitarian and Christological understanding of the giving of the Holy Spirit.[48] Commenting on St Paul's Letter to Titus—"he saved us by the washing of regeneration and renewal of the Holy Spirit, whom he poured out upon us abundantly through Jesus Christ our Savior (Tit. 3:5–6)"—St Thomas asks after the cause of this washing of regeneration and renewal. His answer: "This power is from the holy and undivided Trinity." He then briefly summarizes the Trinitarian shape of our salvation: we are

---

[47] *In Ioan.* c. 1, lect. 10 (no. 202). Cf. *In Epist. ad Ephes.* c. 4, lect. 3 (no. 204), underlining that it is Christ who apportions graces to us from the fullness that he received.
[48] Emery, "Le Christ médiateur," 352; Cf. Emery, "Réflexions," 60.

washed and regenerated by the Holy Spirit (who is from the Father and the Son) through the humanity of Christ:

> [T]he Holy Spirit does this. Ps. 103:30: "You send forth your Spirit [and they are created, and you renew the face of the earth]." Likewise, our regeneration is through the Spirit. Gal. 4:6: "God has sent the Spirit of his Son into our hearts, crying: Abba, Father." . . . But God the Father gives this Spirit, "whom he pours out upon us abundantly." "The Paraclete whom I will send to you . . . (John 16:7)." This also is given by Christ Jesus . . . . For we find two natures in Christ, and it pertains to both of them that Christ gives the Holy Spirit. As to the divine nature, because he is the Word; from both the Word and the Father the Spirit proceeds as Love . . . . As to his human nature, Christ receives the highest fullness of the Holy Spirit, so that through him it derives to all others. John 1:14,16: "We saw him full of grace and truth . . . and from his fullness we have all received, grace upon grace." John 3:34: "God gives his Spirit without measure."[49]

The Father is the ultimate source of our salvation; the Son, who is the Word of the Father, receives from the Father the power to breathe forth the Spirit. He does this as God, but also as man who receives the Spirit in full and thus pours him out on all others. In short, our salvation comes from the Trinity, always through Christ and mediated by his sacred humanity.

C. THE HOLY SPIRIT MAKES CHRIST'S SALVATION EFFECTIVE IN US

Up to this point, we have mainly discussed the elements of St Thomas's Trinitarian Spirit-Christology under the rubric of the divine missions: God comes to save us in the incarnation of the Son who, with the Father and through his assumed human nature, sends the Holy Spirit to us. Yet, as CHAPTER 1 notes, Aquinas does not conceive of this as a linear movement, and even less a one-way journey; it is part of a perfect circular movement, "a certain circulation [*circulatio*] or circling-back [*regiratio*], such that everything returns to that from which it proceeded as a principle, as if returning to its end."[50] The

---

[49] *In Epist. ad Tit.* c. 3, lect. 1 (no. 93).   [50] I *Sent.* d. 14, q. 2, a. 2.

divine missions involve not only the divine persons coming to us, but also us being drawn into God.[51]

There are two fundamental aspects to the Holy Spirit's role in our return to God through Christ. First, the Holy Spirit *leads us to know his Principle*: he makes Christ known by faith, and, in Christ, the Father himself. Second, the Holy Spirit *conforms us to his Principle*, giving us a share in Christ's sonship and holiness. Both of these are indispensable to the very saving work of Christ himself. It is not like a second movement of a symphony that begins only after the first is concluded; rather, the Son and Holy Spirit always work simultaneously and inseparably, coming to us and drawing us into them, just as the parts of an orchestra play in simultaneous harmony to produce a single piece of music.

Thus, Aquinas insists quite clearly that what Christ teaches, even about himself, would be ineffective without the Holy Spirit also working *in us*—Jesus Christ would be, quite literally, a Word falling on deaf ears. Consider St Thomas's Commentary on John 14:26 ("[The Holy Spirit] will teach you all things"):

> Anyone who teaches [divine truths] from the outside, labors in vain unless the Holy Spirit interiorly gives understanding, because unless the Spirit is present to the hearts of the listeners, the speech of a teacher is useless ... so that even the Son himself speaking through the instrument of his humanity would be of no avail, unless he works interiorly through the Holy Spirit.[52]

Absent the Spirit's action, the teaching that Christ gives through his words and deeds would remain exterior to, and unknown by, the very men and woman he came to save. This is why St Thomas underlines the intrinsic connection between Christ's action, both as God and man, and that of the Holy Spirit; neither acts without the other. We see here the care with which the Dominican master anchors all that he says about the dispensation of our salvation—through Christ and in the Holy Spirit—to his Trinitarian reflections: in their temporal processions, the divine persons are never separated, never act alone, and always act according to the mode and order of their eternal

---

[51] *Ibid.*

[52] *In Ioan.* c. 14, lect. 6 (no. 1958). St Thomas makes the same point in his sermon *Emitte spiritum*. See Peter A. Kwasniewski and Jeremy Holmes, "Aquinas's Sermon for the Feast of Pentecost: A Rare Glimpse of Thomas the Preaching Friar," *Faith & Reason* 30 (2005): 118.

processions. Divine revelation, which is accomplished above all through the Son's incarnation, is a work of the Trinity who draws us into the Triune life by giving us to know (and hence love) the Trinity. In this work, each divine person has a proper role. "For, as the effect of the mission of the Son is to lead to the Father, so the effect of the mission of the Holy Spirit is to lead the faithful to the Son."[53]

As we discussed in CHAPTER 4, this is rooted in the Trinitarian order between the persons in their eternal processions. The Son manifests the Father because he is from the Father, and the same principle is at work regarding the Holy Spirit: he manifests and brings the faithful to Christ.

> "He [the Holy Spirit] will glorify me," that is, he will make known my glory, . . . illuminating the disciples . . . who are enabled to know the majesty of Christ's divinity by the Holy Spirit. . . . The reason for this is that the Son is a principle of the Holy Spirit. For each thing that is from another, manifests that from which it is: the Son manifests the Father, because he is from the Father. Therefore, because the Holy Spirit is from the Son, it is proper to him to glorify the Son.[54]

It is *proper* to the Spirit to glorify, to manifest, and to lead us to the Son (and, of course, the Father) because the Spirit is from the Son; this relation to the Son is not only included in the Spirit's mission, but it is its first feature.[55] And thus to receive the Holy Spirit is also to be brought to know the Son precisely as the divine Word of the Father; this is the incarnate Son's glory. This means, once again, that the Holy Spirit's mission in the world is not independent of Christ or of his humanity, but flows from the Incarnation and always refers us back to Christ, God and man.

> The Son, since he is begotten Wisdom itself, is the Truth itself ("I am the way, the truth, and the life," John 14:6). And hence the effect of the Holy Spirit's mission is to make men sharers in divine wisdom and knowers of the truth. The Son, as the Word, gives us his teaching, but the Holy Spirit makes us capable of receiving that teaching.[56]

---

[53] *In Ioan.* c. 14, lect. 6 (no. 1958).

[54] *In Ioan.* c. 16, lect. 4 (nos. 2106–7). On this point, Aquinas and Bonaventure are in agreement. See Ferraro, *Lo Spirito Santo*, 109.

[55] Cf. *STh* I, q. 34, a. 2 ad 5; q. 43, a. 7 ad 6. See also Marshall, "What Does the Spirit Have to Do?" 66–8. St Thomas even suggests that the Father sends the Holy Spirit to the faithful to reveal Christ's true identity, "demonstrating him to be his Son . . . through an internal revelation." *In Ioan.* c. 6, lect. 5 (no. 935).

[56] *In Ioan.* c. 14, lect. 6 (no. 1958).

"Receiving that teaching" means more than grasping an intellectual concept: made "sharers in divine wisdom," we come to *know* the Truth in person, bringing us into the very life of the Trinity itself. "To know" here means to be somehow *transformed* into the thing known—in a word, divinization.

This brings us to the second aspect of the Spirit's role: he conforms us to Christ. For example, when St Thomas explains how Christ's passion frees us from the penalty of sin, he appeals to the Holy Spirit's work:

> As Christ first had grace in his soul with a passible body, and [then] came to the glory of immortality through his passion, so also we, who are his members, . . . first receive the "Spirit of adoption of sons" in our souls, . . . and then, "having been configured to the passion and death of Christ," we are led into immortal glory, as the Apostle says: "if sons, heirs also; heirs indeed of God, and coheir with Christ: yet so, if we suffer with him, that we may be also glorified with him."[57]

The Holy Spirit's grace in Christ's soul is a pattern for our sanctification and glorification, and then, when the Holy Spirit comes to us, he configures us to Christ our exemplar.

Aquinas also speaks of the Holy Spirit transforming us into the likeness of Christ with respect to our knowledge. Commenting on 2 Corinthians 3:18 ("We all beholding the glory of the Lord with unveiled faces, are transformed into his likeness, from glory to glory, as by the Spirit of the Lord"), Thomas writes:

> we behold [God] when man rises from a consideration of himself to some knowledge of God, and he is transformed. For since all knowledge involves the knower's being assimilated to the thing known, it is necessary that those who see be in some way transformed into God. . . . "When [Christ] appears [we shall be like him] (1 John 3.2)." . . . But where does this come from? Not from the letter of the law, but rather from the Spirit of the Lord. "Whosoever is led by the Spirit of God [are the sons of God] (Rom. 8:14)." "Your good Spirit will guide [me] (Ps. 142:10)."[58]

---

[57] *STh* III, q. 49, a. 3 ad 3.

[58] *In II Epist. ad Cor.* c. 3, lect. 3 (nos. 114–15). Emery, *Trinitarian Theology*, 401. On knowledge as an assimilation to the thing known, see Gilles Emery, *Trinity, Church, and the Human Person: Thomistic Essays* (Naples, Florida: Sapientia Press, 2007), 73–114.

Thus, "the one who receives the Holy Spirit from the Father and the Son, that one knows the Father and the Son and comes to them."[59] The knowledge of the Son given by the Holy Spirit is a sanctifying knowledge that brings us to the Son, conforming us to Christ's humanity (including his suffering, death, and resurrection), thus "transforming" and "assimilating" us to his filial divinity. In short, it belongs to the Holy Spirit "to make us like his principle."[60]

Even here, Thomas emphasizes, the Holy Spirit's power does not stand alone or work independently;[61] this power is from the Father and the Son, just as the Spirit's mission in the world always includes and discloses his eternal procession.

> [The Holy Spirit] will teach them by the power of the Father and the Son, "because he does not speak from himself," but from me, because he will be from me. For as the Son does not act from himself but from the Father, so the Holy Spirit, who is from another, namely, from the Father and the Son, "will not speak from himself, but whatever he hears"—by receiving the divine knowledge as he receives the divine essence, from eternity—"this he will speak," not corporeally, but by interiorly illuminating the mind.[62]

The Holy Spirit teaches the same truths as the Son because everything that the Spirit has, comes from the Father and the Son, who give everything they have (except their paternity and sonship) to him.[63] The Holy Spirit does not speak "corporeally," as does the incarnate Son, but "by interiorly illuminating the mind"—a way of influencing man's intellect that is especially fitting to the Holy Spirit.

The deepest account Aquinas offers of how and why the Holy Spirit manifests Christ, however, draws on the Spirit's proper name, Love, and his procession by way of love.

> The Holy Spirit leads to knowledge of the truth because he proceeds from the Truth: "I am the way, the truth, and the life." For, in us, our love of the truth follows upon our grasping and considering it, so also in God, Love proceeds from the truth conceived, who is the Son. And as

---

[59] *In Ioan.* c. 14, lect. 6 (no. 1959). See also *In Ioan.* c. 16, lect. 7 (no. 2152) (Christ reveals the Father to us by giving us the Holy Spirit).

[60] *In Ioan.* c. 16, lect. 3 (no. 2102). *In Ioan.* c. 15, lect. 5 (no. 2062). See also Sabathé, *La Trinité rédemptrice*, 494–6.

[61] Thomas attributes the illumination of hearts to both the Word and the Holy Spirit. Sabathé, *La Trinité rédemptrice*, 183, citing *In Ioan.* c. 3, lect. 2 (no. 452).

[62] *In Ioan.* c. 16, lect. 3 (no. 2103).   [63] See the discussion at pp. 180–1.

proceeding from the Son, he leads us into knowledge of the Son.... "No one can say 'Jesus is Lord' except by the Holy Spirit (1 Cor. 12:3)."... To manifest the truth belongs to the personal property of the Holy Spirit [namely, love]. For it is love that makes one reveal one's secrets: "I have called you friends, because everything that I have heard from my Father, I have made known to you (John 15:15)."[64]

This exposes to view how profoundly the roots of our salvation in Christ penetrate into the heart of the Triune mystery. The whole structure of the economy of grace emerges—not of necessity, but freely—from the eternal processions of the Son and Holy Spirit by way of knowledge and of love. Indeed, this passage is a fine illustration of the principle that the processions of the persons are the *ratio*, cause, origin, and exemplar of both creation and salvation: we return to God according to the same pattern as the world was created, namely, the pattern of the eternal processions themselves.

There is, however, a difference in how Christ and the Holy Spirit teach the truth, based on their respective personal properties. As God, Christ teaches by giving a participation in his personal property as the Word and Wisdom of the Father. (The gift of the Son's invisible mission is precisely wisdom, a participation in his personal property as Word.) Similarly, as man, Christ teaches by his human words and deeds, and by sending the Holy Spirit who conforms us to the Word.

As for the Holy Spirit, his mode of teaching is that of Love. He *disposes* the disciples to receive Christ's teaching through love, giving them a pure heart and hence a "sense" of divine things; and the Holy Spirit, as Love, *moves* the disciples to know Christ, since love implies impulsion, motion.[65] This has a great spiritual significance. The Holy Spirit does not merely give us facts about Christ. As Love in person, he infuses into us a love of Christ that permits us to seize upon the deepest mysteries of Christ's identity as God made man who has come to save us. Truly to know Jesus is to be made his friend, to be drawn into the closest intimacy with him, to be caught up in love.[66] All this is indispensable if one is really to know him as he is—as the Word made flesh, from the Father, who breathes forth Love. And thus the Holy Spirit's illuminating action is essential to Christ's mission: it

[64] *In Ioan.* c. 14, lect. 4 (no. 1916).
[65] Emery, *Trinity, Church, and the Human Person*, 105–10.
[66] Thomas speaks of this as a kind of affective knowledge. See Sabathé, *La Trinité rédemptrice*, 184–5.

is the Holy Spirit who brings us to know and love Christ as our savior, true God, and true man.[67]

According to Aquinas, this knowledge and love of Christ that the Holy Spirit gives is equally a knowledge and love of each of the divine persons, granting us a participation in the very inner life of the Trinity. This is the import of Christ's prayer to the Father on the eve of his passion, among the most privileged revelations of the Triune mystery and of our participation in it: "I have made your name known, and I will make it known, that the love, by which you have loved me, would be in them, and I in them (John 17:26)." St Thomas's exegesis of this passage integrates his Trinitarian theology, his Christology, and his theology of the Holy Spirit. He begins with the eternal procession of the Word and his incarnation:

> The root and fount of the knowledge of God is the Word of God, namely Christ.... This knowledge is derived to men from the Word, because insofar as they participate the Word of God, they know God.[68]

The mission of the Son in the incarnation was to bring this knowledge to the faithful, "by instructing them exteriorly with words," and "by giving them the Holy Spirit" who grants them "an interior knowledge," initially "of faith" and ultimately of "the vision of glory in our heavenly homeland, where we will see 'face to face.'"[69] Aquinas thus links the work of the Son and the Spirit in giving knowledge, and then expands on their intertwined roles in accomplishing our Trinity-shaped salvation through it: "The fruit of this knowledge is 'that the love by which you have loved me would be in them, and I in them.'"[70] This can be explained in two ways, says Aquinas.

> First and better: it says that the Father loves the Son.... The consequence is that the Father loves all those in whom the Son is, and the Son is in them insofar as they have knowledge of the truth. This is the sense of the passage: "I will make your name known." By the fact that they know you, I, your Word, will be in them; and by the fact that I am in them, "the love by which you have loved me will be in them," that is, will be derived to them, and you will love them as you have loved me.[71]

---

[67] Cf. *In Ioan.* c. 16, lect. 4 (no. 2106); lect. 3 (no. 2101).
[68] *In Ioan.* c. 17, lect. 6 (no. 2267).   [69] *Ibid.* (no. 2269).
[70] *Ibid.* (no. 2270).   [71] *Ibid.*

This first exegesis of Christ's words places the personal indwelling of the Son as Word at center stage. The Father loves the Son, and consequently the Father loves all those in whom the Son indwells. Two aspects are closely interconnected in this doctrinal exegesis: (1) the Father loves the disciples insofar as the Son is present in them; (2) the Son is present in them insofar as they know the truth, since the Son is the Word and Truth. Because of this, the love by which the Father loves the Son—the Holy Spirit in person—is derived to those who share in the Son by knowing the truth. Here, sanctifying knowledge of the truth accounts for the indwelling of the Son and, consequently, for the gift and indwelling of the Holy Spirit.[72] It is by one and the same Spirit that the Father loves the Son and loves the faithful.[73]

Thomas immediately changes registers to speak of the created effects in the faithful caused by the Spirit's indwelling:

> Or, second: "as the love by which you have loved me," that is, they will love by participating in the Holy Spirit, which is the very same way that you have loved me. And because of this, I will be in them as God dwells in his temple, and they will be in me as members are in their head. "He who remains in love, remains in God, and God in him (1 John 4:16)."[74]

This second exegesis of Christ's words places the spotlight on the Holy Spirit. While the first presented the gift of the Holy Spirit as a consequence of the indwelling of the Son, the second exegesis presents the indwelling of the Son as a consequence of the gift of the Holy Spirit. These two complementary interpretations bring to light the interlaced network of causes, relations, and effects that are implicated by the inseparable missions of the Son and Holy Spirit, and the necessary nexus in St Thomas's thought between Trinitarian doctrine, Christology, and the work of the Holy Spirit.

* * *

St Luke tells us that Christ was "filled with the Holy Spirit," a point emphasized by contemporary exegetes. In the history of Western theology, we must number St Thomas among the theologians with a great sensitivity to this pneumatological dimension of the mystery

---

[72] Emery, *Trinity, Church, and the Human Person*, 103–5.
[73] Cf. *STh* I, q. 37, a. 2 and ad 1.   [74] *In Ioan.* c. 17, lect. 6 (no. 2270).

of the incarnation.[75] Indeed, on an important point—that Christ gives the Holy Spirit as man—Aquinas broke with the Augustinian consensus of his day in order to emphasize precisely this. His synthesis is admirably balanced and eminently scriptural: Christ is at the same time the Word made flesh and a man anointed by the Spirit, from whose fullness we have all received. Once attuned to the way Thomas Aquinas speaks of the Holy Spirit in his Christology— according to the invisible mission of the Holy Spirit to Christ's humanity, a mission that necessarily accompanies the visible mission of the Son in the incarnation according to the hypostatic union—one grasps both the extent and the importance of the Spirit not only for understanding the technicalities of Christology, but for the entirety of the economy of grace and the whole dispensation of salvation. There is no domain of theology where the Spirit is missing; there is no gift of grace where the Spirit is absent; Christ himself does not work our salvation without the perfectly complementary action of the Holy Spirit.

---

[75] Notwithstanding the originality of his synthesis, St Thomas's conclusions about Christ's grace and the Holy Spirit sound in profound harmony with the common patristic heritage of both East and West. See, e.g., Boris Bobrinskoy, "The Indwelling of the Spirit in Christ: 'Pneumatic Christology' in the Cappadocian Fathers," *St Vladimir's Theological Quarterly* 28 (1984): 49–65; Anthony Briggman, "The Holy Spirit as the Unction of Christ in Irenaeus," *Journal of Theological Studies* NS 61 (2010): 171–93.

Conclusion

How is St Thomas's Christology Trinitarian? The explanations are manifold, but can be best summarized under four main headings. The first offers the broadest perspective: the incarnation is, above all, *the visible mission of the divine Son*. By definition, then, the incarnation makes present in the world and extends into time the Son's eternal procession from the Father. This teaching has profound and far-reaching implications. It means that Christ's humanity bears within itself and discloses the Son's procession, and hence what is proper to the divine Son. Aquinas's Christology is therefore fundamentally Trinitarian. The Son is constituted as a distinct divine person by his relation to the Father, which includes his relation to the Holy Spirit (he is from the Father, and breathes forth the Holy Spirit with the Father), and so the unique presence of the Son in his visible mission (in every aspect of his humanity, in all he does and suffers) and that mission's disclosure of the Son's personal identity, also *necessarily* implicates both the Father and the Holy Spirit. Consequently, as the incarnation—i.e., the visible presence and life of the eternal Son as man—makes Jesus Christ known as the divine Word, it also *necessarily* reveals the Father and the Holy Spirit as well. This is precisely what Aquinas has in mind when he says, for example, that it is proper to Christ to reveal the Father or to give the Holy Spirit. For Aquinas, then, Christ's coming as man is *from the Trinity* (its origin, cause, and *ratio* is the eternal processions), and is necessarily ordered to *making present and revealing the Trinity* in time.

A corollary to this is that St Thomas's Christology always includes within it his speculative Trinitarian doctrine. We could even say that, as Jesus Christ is the Father's eternal Word who takes on flesh in a historical place and time, so also Aquinas's study of Christ incorporates and clothes with flesh, as it were, his Trinitarian theology. There are, therefore, two major Trinitarian axes to Aquinas's Christology, corresponding to the two "personal relations" of the divine person of the Son: Christ's relation to the Father, from whom he proceeds as Word, Son, and Image; and Christ's relation to the Holy Spirit who proceeds from him (and the Father). These formed the subject matter of PARTS II and III of our study.

In addition to this, at the core of St Thomas's whole theology is the principle that the Trinitarian processions are not only the origin, cause, *ratio*, and exemplar of the coming-forth of creatures, but also of their return. The entire dispensation of salvation emerges from the Trinity and returns to it, according to the pattern of the divine processions. In the incarnation, the Son's visible mission both opens the way, and *becomes* the way, of man's return to the Father. And Christ does this precisely in the Trinitarian mode proper to him: as from the Father, and as the giver of the Holy Spirit.

Placing St Thomas's Christology in this cosmic setting gives a new and richer Trinitarian resonance to the explanations Thomas offers for why it was the second person of the Trinity who became incarnate. For example, when he considers God in himself (*theologia*), Aquinas teaches that, in proceeding as Word, the second person is "perfectly expressive" of the Father, containing all that is in the Father. Aquinas then sees this aspect of the Son's eternal procession extending to the *exitus* of creatures: the Father creates all things through his Word, who is their perfect exemplar (the ideas of all things are in the Word who is "spoken" by the Father), like an architect who builds a house according to the design he conceives in his mind. Finally, in the *dispensatio* of salvation, the Word's eternal procession extends even more fully into time: the Father sends the Word as man in order to restore his fallen creation through the same divine exemplar through which he created it, like the restorer of a damaged house who uses the architect's original blueprints (the idea and exemplar of the house) to repair it. For Aquinas, then, the deepest reasons for Christ's coming to save the world can only be fully understood—and hence Christology itself can only be fully understood (to the extent possible to a finite mind)—if one grasps these truths about the Son's procession as the Father's Word, the Word's proper role in creation and recreation, and the Holy Spirit's procession from the Father and the Son. In all of this, the Word's eternal procession is an unfathomable wellspring (as origin, cause, *ratio*, and exemplar) of the whole dispensation of creation and salvation.

This brings us to our second principal heading: Aquinas's Christology is Trinitarian not only in its origins (the Trinitarian processions in themselves) and its end (our return to the Trinity), but also in *its very shape and internal structure*, somewhat like a large crystal whose smallest molecule has the same shape and structure as the whole. We saw this, first of all, in Christ's very constitution as the God-man in the hypostatic union, which has, fundamentally, a Trinitarian shape. It is a union between the divine and human natures in the person of the Son: Christ's human nature "terminates" in the Son's "personal being [*esse*]," which is the divine being as received from the Father. The hypostatic union entails that Christ, both as God and as man, is "from the Father" to his very core. He not only tells us about the Father, but is relative to the Father and reveals the Father in everything that he is, that he has, that he says, and that he does. "He who has seen me has seen the Father (John 14:9)."

Similarly, the personal presence of the Holy Spirit in Christ as man (according to the Spirit's invisible mission) flows from the hypostatic union as its necessary consequence. Just as the divine persons cannot be separated from each other, neither can the divine missions be separated. The Word is sent by the Father to assume a human nature into the unity of his person, and in doing so, he does what is proper to him as Word: he breathes forth Love. The Holy Spirit thus dwells in Christ's human nature according to the gifts of grace. What is more, Christ as man needs those gracious gifts to elevate and perfect his human nature supernaturally, so that it would be apt to act as the perfect instrument of the divine Son. The hypostatic union cannot, by itself, account for this supernatural perfection of Christ's humanity; the Holy Spirit's empowering presence is indispensable for Christ to carry out his saving work. Aquinas avows, therefore, that the Holy Spirit is a veritable cause of all that Christ does and suffers as man. The Spirit's gifts dispose Christ's humanity to act freely and in perfect harmony with the Father's divine plan; they irradiate Christ's human mind with the divine light by which it sees and knows that divine plan (and, indeed, the divine essence itself) as perfectly as is possible for a created intellect. The Spirit moves Christ as man to his saving actions: Christ is a man anointed by and led by the Spirit. Indeed, Aquinas offers a robust Spirit Christology that flows from, rather than competing with or displacing, the hypostatic union. The Spirit's presence and action in Christ's humanity—i.e., the Spirit's visible and invisible missions to Christ—are the necessary and perfect complements to the Son's visible mission.

We find the third main way in which Aquinas's Christology is Trinitarian when we look at it *in detail and "in action"* in the events of Christ's life. Because our study has been structured around the theological principles of St Thomas's Trinitarian Christology and not the sequence of events in the Gospels, we have not had this aspect principally in view, but we have been able to catch a few glimpses along the way of what such an approach would offer.

We saw that, in his teaching activity, Christ unveils his true identity, and the identities of the Father and Holy Spirit. In doing so, he imparts to his disciples a knowledge that breaks forth into love—he does not only teach about the Trinity, but puts those who receive his teaching in living contact with the Triune persons who come to dwell in them according to wisdom and love. In his public miracles, Aquinas explains, Christ both shows his dependence on the Father and glorifies the Father; likewise, as man, he performs his public miracles through the Holy Spirit, as moved by and empowered by the Spirit. They confirm his teaching and lead to belief in him as the Son. In his prayer, Christ shows that he is from the Father and that, even as man, he is oriented entirely to the Father. In his passion, Christ manifests the Trinity, and, in saving us, draws us into the Trinity. He is moved by the Father and the Holy Spirit to offer himself freely to the Father for the world's salvation. In doing so, Christ manifests the Father's love and glorifies the Father, while at the same time displaying both the truth of his passible human nature and the infinite charity with which his humanity was filled by the Spirit's presence. This perfect sacrifice is therefore a Trinitarian event: sent by the Father, the Son is impelled by the Spirit to offer himself in total freedom to the Father for our sake, that we might be saved. Although we did not examine it in detail, the resurrection is similarly Trinitarian for Aquinas: raised by the whole Trinity, Christ's human nature shines with the Father's glory, manifesting most fully that he is the Father's divine Son made man. And the trajectory of Christ's passion and resurrection reaches its apex in Christ's breathing forth the Holy Spirit upon the Apostles and the Church. The Holy Spirit's mission to Christ as man is the Christological foundation for this: having received "the whole Spirit" in his fullness of grace, Christ pours out the Spirit upon the Church through his human nature.

This brings us to the fourth principal heading: the Trinitarian shape of our salvation is derived from the Trinitarian shape of the mystery of the incarnation. For Aquinas, our return to the Father through the Son and in the Holy Spirit is not a postscript to Christology but its Trinitarian crowning and completion: it is by receiving the Holy Spirit that one receives, interiorly and effectively, the revelation of the Triune God that Christ brings through his teaching, his deeds and miracles, his passion, and his exaltation. And the Holy Spirit is the Gift of sanctification and salvation whom Christ gives, making effective in the individual believer the salvation Christ accomplished on the cross. When the Spirit comes, he conforms his recipients to Christ, according to what Christ did and suffered in the flesh (since sanctifying grace has Christ as its source, it is always Christ-shaped). In doing so, the Holy Spirit makes them into adopted sons and daughters of the Father, in the Son; all three persons of the Holy Trinity thus dwell in them. What is more, having received faith and charity in sanctifying grace, the faithful are vivified and energized by the Holy Spirit, who impels them on the trajectory of their return to God as they imitate and follow Christ crucified and glorified, so that they return to the Father according to the pattern of the processions of the Son (faith assimilating them to the Son's procession by way of knowledge) and of the Holy Spirit (charity assimilating them to the Holy Spirit's procession by way of love). In brief, the Father sends his Word into the world as man, so that, having fulfilled his dispensation, he would breathe forth the Holy Spirit upon the world and thus bring to completion all that he did and suffered in the flesh.

* * *

We hope it is now clear that St Thomas's Christology has a Trinitarian shape. Why is this important to affirm? Why study this dimension of the mystery of Christ in Aquinas? What is its significance and what are its implications?

To begin, it dispels a concatenation of misconceptions about St Thomas's theology that have been repeated in varying combinations for more than a century. For example, it has often been said that Aquinas's philosophical account of the one divine essence (his treatise *de Deo uno*) is in the driver's seat in his theology, and that he puts in the back seat what pertains to the Trinity—the distinction and plurality of the divine persons and their personal properties. Others have already shown this to be false with respect to Aquinas's Trinitarian theology in itself,[1] and

---

[1] See, e.g., Emery, *Trinitarian Theology*, 36–50.

our study bolsters this conclusion by showing the fundamental role in Aquinas's Christology (and the whole of the dispensation of salvation) played by the divine persons in what is proper to each of them. Related to this, some have thought that Aquinas's Christology (and his whole theology of the dispensation of salvation) has little to do with the Triune mystery or is even detached from it; Aquinas may say that Christ is the Son who reveals the Father (so they claim), but this remains superficial, a merely verbal affirmation, often only a matter of appropriations. As we have seen, however, quite the opposite is true. Aquinas's theology of Christ delves deeply into Christ's identity as the Word who proceeds from the Father and who breathes forth the Holy Spirit; little in St Thomas's Christology is untouched by this truth. Indeed, it is one of the first principles that structures his whole treatment of Christ, and it explains a great deal of his thought. Far from separating Christology from the Trinity, or treating Christ principally as the God-man (instead of the Word-made-flesh), Thomas depicts Christology as the Son's Trinitarian procession as extended into time. Christology is Trinitarian theology clothed in flesh, as it were.

As such, St Thomas's Trinitarian account of the incarnation provides a potent alternative to Karl Rahner's "economic Trinity/immanent Trinity" schema that one encounters frequently in contemporary theology.[2] For St Thomas, the dispensation of salvation, and above all the Son's coming in the flesh, makes present and discloses the eternal processions of the persons. There is no possible gap or divergence between the Trinity in itself and the Trinity revealed by Christ. Rather, Christ bears within himself the mystery of his eternal procession from the Father, and of the Holy Spirit's procession from the Father and the Son. This Triune mystery is present in time, unveiled as it is in itself, through the Son's visible mission and the accompanying visible and invisible missions of the Holy Spirit. The presence and activity of the divine persons in the dispensation necessarily manifest who they are in themselves.

The converse is also true: we know the Triune God as he is in himself because he is revealed to us by Christ, the Father's incarnate Word. The refrain that one hears from some contemporary theologians

---

[2] For a more complete argument on this point focused on the divine missions in general, see Emery, "*Theologia* and *Dispensatio*," 557–61. See also Sabathé, *La Trinité rédemptrice*, 17–28.

writing on the Trinity—that because Thomas begins the *Summa Theologiae* with God as he exists in himself, treated in the abstract with all its refined distinctions, he effectively divorces the Triune God in himself from the divine mystery revealed in history through Christ—is therefore deeply mistaken. The *Summa* follows the *ordo disciplinae*, the order of subjects best suited to presenting the material according to its own intelligibility, but this simply rearticulates the revelation brought to us by Christ in the *dispensatio*. Other than the mode of presentation, there is no difference between the two. "In Christian doctrine, the starting point and principle of our wisdom is Christ as the wisdom and Word of God, that is, according to his divinity. But with respect to us, the principle is Christ himself, as the Word made flesh, that is, according to his incarnation."[3]

This produces a Christology that is thoroughly scriptural. We have seen this in St Thomas's biblical commentaries, which generally present the same teaching as his systematic works but articulate it in the resonant tones of sacred Scripture itself. In them, it is some-times easier to perceive that Aquinas's speculative doctrine is rooted in and emerges from sacred Scripture, which it aims to understand and to unfold. In fact, Thomas's Christology is a kind of refined theological exegesis of Scripture, although in the *Summa Theologiae* and other systematic works, the Dominican master reorganizes the material in an order suited for teaching. The more we appreciate St Thomas's close attention to the sacred text (even in his systematic works) and the fundamental role it plays in his thought, the easier it is to dismiss the suspicion that his theology is hostage to foreign philosophical presuppositions, or to scholastic abstractions and hypo-theticals. To the contrary, St Thomas's doctrine is firmly grounded in what the Triune God has actually done in the historical dispensation of salvation.

Next, studying the Trinitarian shape of Aquinas's theology of the incarnation brings into view the key role of the Holy Spirit in Christology and in the whole dispensation of salvation. Aquinas accounts for this without compromising the central place of Christ's identity as the Word, or of the hypostatic union; the presence of the Holy Spirit in Christ is their necessary counterpart. What is more, Thomas's theology explains why there is no economy of the Holy

---

[3] *In Ioan.* c. 1, lect. 1 (no. 34).

Spirit apart from Christology: given the order of the divine processions in God (a pure order of origin), there is also a corresponding order between the missions of the Son and Holy Spirit in the dispensation. The Son's visible mission precedes and entails the visible missions of the Holy Spirit; the Holy Spirit is only bestowed in full on the world by the incarnate Son acting in and through his human nature.

Aquinas's Trinitarian Christology likewise illuminates all of Christ's deeds, in all that he does and suffers. There is thus a Trinitarian dimension to every element of Christ's life, given the very structure of Christ's constitution as the Father's Word made flesh, always from the Father and oriented to him, and endowed as man with the Holy Spirit in full. This disperses whatever clouds of doubt might remain about whether the Trinity is a saving mystery for Aquinas, or whether he divorces Christology from Trinitarian theology. In fact, it helps us to contemplate Christ in all of his actions as showing us and leading us to the Father, through the Holy Spirit whom he gives to us, and who conforms us to him.

The incarnation's Trinitarian dimension has a special importance for Aquinas's theology of Christ's passion. When some contemporary theologians formulate a Trinitarian theology of the cross, they posit that the passion is an intra-Trinitarian event: that the Son on the cross assumes in obedience the full weight of human sin and is thereby alienated from the Father, which manifests and enacts an infinite distance between the Father and the Son in the Trinity itself. Although we did not study it in detail, we can nonetheless note that Aquinas's approach is quite different: the passion is indeed a Trinitarian event that manifests the Trinity and draws us into the Trinity, but it is not an intra-Trinitarian event whereby the Son is separated from the Father. Rather, in the passion (as in all of Christ's actions), the incarnate Son shows himself to be perfectly from the Father, "obedient" to the divine will which he "hears" or receives from the Father, and oriented entirely to the Father, whom he loves with a charity received from the Father. As man, the incarnate Son is moved by the Holy Spirit to accept freely the suffering of the cross; on the cross, he is the perfect icon and revelation of the Father and of the Father's love for his fallen creatures, which knows no limits. Thus, in the passion, the Father, Son, and Holy Spirit act together to reveal themselves to the world and to restore fallen man to the most intimate communion with them. Moreover, Aquinas's Trinitarian theology of our redemption through the cross does not stop here:

Aquinas extends his analysis from the passion to Christ's resurrection, ascension, and his sending of the Holy Spirit, each of which has its proper place in the Trinitarian dispensation of salvation.

Finally, understanding Aquinas's Trinitarian perspective on Christology also leads us to appreciate how it is an integral part of his larger theological vision, since theology for Aquinas is a unified whole and a single discipline. More specifically, the divine missions link Trinitarian theology to the whole dispensation of salvation, and Christology stands at the center of the movement of the divine missions. As the visible mission of the Son in the incarnation clothes the Son's eternal procession in flesh, as it were, so also it founds our return to God—which is to say, the whole of the theology of grace and of moral theology, the sacraments, ecclesiology, and so forth.

From here, a wide field for further research opens before us. Our study has focused on the principal Trinitarian shape and structure of the mystery of the incarnation in Aquinas—the roots, trunk, and main branches of the tree—but we have been obliged to forgo exploring its offshoots and have only sampled its fruits. For example, Aquinas's treatment of the mysteries of Christ's life remains to be studied in detail. (Among other things, we have left *STh* III, qq. 27–59, largely unexamined.) To this could be added additional material from Aquinas's two Gospel commentaries (on John and Matthew), and from his commentaries on the letters of St Paul. We have also left aside the details of St Thomas's teaching that, by the invisible mission of the Holy Spirit, the faithful are configured to Christ according to the mysteries of his life.

Other rich subjects for further study could include how Aquinas's Trinitarian Christology unfolds in the sacraments, is at work in the prayer of each Christian, and founds and animates the whole life of the Church. Further research in St Thomas's theology of grace as both Trinitarian and Christoform (flowing through Christ's humanity and conforming its recipients to Christ) could also provide valuable insights, especially with respect to the theological virtues and the gifts of the Holy Spirit, but also with respect to the other virtues and, indeed, the whole of the Christian life.

* * *

We began this study with St Thomas's commendation to Brother Reginald, his *socius* and secretary. St Thomas exhorted him to keep always before his eyes the divinity of the Trinity and the humanity of

Christ, since Christ is the way by which we return to the Triune God. We have now seen that, in his theology of the incarnation, Aquinas follows his own advice: he never loses sight of the deep Trinitarian mystery that the incarnation reveals and draws us into. It is our hope that, insofar as this study helps us better to appreciate how, in Aquinas's thought, the mystery of Christ is Trinitarian, we may better take St Thomas's advice to heart, so that we may follow the way opened to us by Christ: to the Father, through the Son, in the Holy Spirit.

Bibliography

For works of St. Thomas Aquinas, see the table on page xiii.
Patristic and medieval authors in the Patrologia Latina or Graeca (PL, PG)
and in the Corpus Christianorum, Series Latina (CCL) are not included in
this bibliography.

Albert the Great. *Opera Omnia*. Edited by A. Borgnet. 38 vols. Paris: Apud
Ludovicum Vivès, 1890–99.

Ashley, Benedict. "The Extent of Jesus' Human Knowledge According to the
Fourth Gospel." In *Reading John with St. Thomas Aquinas: Theological
Exegesis and Speculative Theology*, edited by Michael Dauphinais and
Matthew Levering, 241–53. Washington, D.C.: Catholic University of
America Press, 2005.

Bailleux, Emile. "Le cycle des missions trinitaires, d'après saint Thomas."
Revue Thomiste 63 (1963): 165–92.

Bailleux, Emile. "A l'image du Fils premier-né." *Revue Thomiste* 76 (1976):
181–207.

Balthasar, Hans Urs von. *Theo-Drama: Theological Dramatic Theory*. 5 vols.
Translated by Graham Harrison. San Francisco: Ignatius Press, 1988–98.

Balthasar, Hans Urs von. *The Theology of Karl Barth: Exposition and Interpretation*. Translated by Edward T. Oakes. San Francisco: Ignatius Press,
1992.

Balthasar, Hans Urs von. *Mysterium Paschale: The Mystery of Easter*. Translated by Aidan Nichols. San Francisco: Ignatius Press, 2000.

Bañez, Dominicus. *Comentarios ineditos a la tercera parte de Santo Tomas*.
Vol. 1, *De Verbo Incarnato (qq. 1–42)*, edited by Vicente Beltran de
Heredia. Salamanca: Biblioteca de Teologos Españoles, 1951.

Barnes, Corey L. "Necessary, Fitting, or Possible: The Shape of Scholastic
Christology." *Nova et Vetera*, English edition 10 (2012): 657–88.

Barnes, Corey L. *Christ's Two Wills in Scholastic Thought: The Christology of
Aquinas and Its Historical Contexts*. Toronto: Pontifical Institute of Mediaeval Studies, 2012.

Barnes, Michel René. *The Power of God: Δύναμις in Gregory of Nyssa's
Trinitarian Theology*. Washington, D.C.: Catholic University of America
Press, 2001.

Belloy (de), Camille. *La visite de Dieu: Essai sur les missions des personnes
divines selon saint Thomas d'Aquin*. Geneva: Éditions Ad Solem, 2006.

Billuart, Charles René. *Summa S. Thomae hodiernis academiarum moribus accomodata, sive cursus theologiae* . . . Vol. 3. Würzburg: Ioannis Iacobi Stahel, 1758.

Blankenhorn, Bernhard. "The Instrumental Causality of the Sacraments: Thomas Aquinas and Louis-Marie Chauvet." *Nova et Vetera*, English edition 4 (2006): 255–94.

Blankenhorn, Bernhard. *The Mystery of Union with God: Dionysian Mysticism in Albert the Great and Thomas Aquinas.* Washington, D.C.: Catholic University of America Press, 2015.

Bobrinskoy, Boris. "The Indwelling of the Spirit in Christ: 'Pneumatic Christology' in the Cappadocian Fathers." *St. Vladimir's Theological Quarterly* 28 (1984): 49–65.

Boland, Vivian. *Ideas in God according to Saint Thomas Aquinas: Sources and Synthesis.* Leiden: E. J. Brill, 1996.

Bonaventure. *Opera Omnia*, edita PP. Collegii a S. Bonaventura. 10 vols. Ad Claras Aquas (Quaracchi): 1883–902.

Bonino, Serge-Thomas. " 'Toute vérité, quel que soit celui qui la dit, vient de l'Esprit-Saint.' Autour d'une citation de l'*Ambrosiaster* dans le corpus thomasien." *Revue Thomiste* 106 (2006): 101–47.

Bouillard, Henri. *Conversion et grâce chez s. Thomas d'Aquin: Étude historique.* Paris: Aubier, 1944.

Briggman, Anthony. "The Holy Spirit as the Unction of Christ in Irenaeus." *Journal of Theological Studies* NS 61 (2010): 171–93.

Cabaret, Dominique-Marie. *L'étonnante manifestation des personnes divines: Les appropriations trinitaires chez saint Thomas.* Les Plans-sur-Bex, Switzerland: Éditions Parole et Silence, 2015.

Cajetan, Thomas de Vio. *Commentaria Thomae de vio Caietani.* In Sancti Thomae Aquinatis *Opera Omnia*, vol. 11. Rome: Ex Typographia Polyglotta S. C. de Propaganda Fide, 1903.

Coffey, David. "The 'Incarnation' of the Holy Spirit in Christ." *Theological Studies* 45 (1984): 466–80.

Coffey, David. "A Proper Mission of the Holy Spirit." *Theological Studies* 47 (1986): 227–50.

Congar, Yves. *Chrétiens désunis: Principes d'un 'oecuménisme' catholique.* Paris: Éditions du Cerf, 1937.

Congar, Yves. "Le Saint-Esprit dans la théologie thomiste de l'agir moral." In *Tommaso d'Aquino nel suo settimo centenario: Atti del Congresso internazionale*, vol. 5, *L'agire morale*, 9–19. Napoli: Edizioni Domenicane Italiane, 1977.

Congar, Yves. "Saint Augustin et le traité scolastique 'De gratia Capitis.'" *Augustinianum* 20 (1980): 79–93.

Congar, Yves. *La Parole et le Souffle.* Paris: Desclée, 1984.

Congar, Yves. *Je crois en l'Esprit Saint.* 2nd ed. Paris: Éditions du Cerf, 1997.

Cross, Richard. *Duns Scotus.* New York: Oxford University Press, 1999.

Cross, Richard. *The Metaphysics of the Incarnation.* Oxford: Oxford University Press, 2002.

Crowley, Paul G. "*Instrumentum Divinitatis* in Thomas Aquinas: Recovering the Divinity of Christ." *Theological Studies* 52 (1991): 451–75.

Cunningham, Francis L. B. *The Indwelling of the Trinity: A Historico-Doctrinal Study of the Theory of St. Thomas Aquinas.* Dubuque, Iowa: Priory Press, 1955.

Dauphinais, Michael A. "Loving the Lord Your God: The *Imago Dei* in Saint Thomas Aquinas." *The Thomist* 63 (1999): 241–67.

Del Colle, Ralph. *Christ and the Spirit: Spirit-Christology in Trinitarian Perspective.* Oxford: Oxford University Press: 1994.

Doolan, Gregory T. *Aquinas on the Divine Ideas as Exemplar Causes.* Washington, D.C.: Catholic University of America Press, 2008.

Drilhon, Bruno. *Dieu missionnaire: Les missions visibles des personnes divines selon saint Thomas d'Aquin.* Paris: Éditions Téqui, 2009.

Dunn, James D. G. *Jesus and the Spirit.* London: SCM Press, 1975.

Dunn, James D. G. *The Christ and the Spirit.* vol. 1, *Christology.* vol. 2, *Pneumatology.* Edinburgh: T&T Clark, 1998.

Durand, Emmanuel. "Le Père en sa relation constitutive au Fils selon saint Thomas d'Aquin." *Revue Thomiste* 107 (2007): 47–72.

Durand, Emmanuel. *Le Père, Alpha et Oméga de la vie trinitaire.* Paris: Éditions du Cerf, 2008.

Elders, Leo J. *Sur les traces de saint Thomas d'Aquin, théologien: Étude de ses commentaires bibliques, Thèmes théologiques.* Translated by Véronique Pommeret. Paris: Presses universitaires de l'IPC, 2009.

Emery, Gilles. *La Trinité créatrice: Trinité et création dans les commentaires aux* Sentences *de Thomas d'Aquin et de ses précurseurs Albert le Grand et Bonaventure.* Paris: Librairie Philosophique J. Vrin, 1995.

Emery, Gilles. "Review of *The Father's Spirit of Sonship: Reconceiving the Trinity*, by Thomas G. Weinandy." *Revue Thomiste* 96 (1996): 152–4.

Emery, Gilles. "The Personal Mode of Trinitarian Action in Saint Thomas Aquinas." *The Thomist* 69 (2005): 31–77.

Emery, Gilles. "Missions invisibles et missions visibles: le Christ et son Esprit." *Revue Thomiste* 106 (2006): 51–99.

Emery, Gilles. "Réflexions sur l'apport d'une christologie trinitaire et pneumatique en théologie chrétienne des religions." In *Le dialogue interreligieux: Situation et perspectives*, edited by Mariano Delgado and Benedict T. Viviano, 51–64. Fribourg: Academic Press Fribourg, 2007.

Emery, Gilles. *Trinity, Church, and the Human Person: Thomistic Essays.* Naples, Florida: Sapientia Press, 2007.

Emery, Gilles. "La Trinité, le Christ et l'homme: Théologie et métaphysique de la personne." In *L'humain et la personne*, edited by François-Xavier

Putallaz and Bernard N. Schumacher, 175–93. Paris: Éditions du Cerf, 2008.

Emery, Gilles. "Le Christ médiateur: l'unicité et l'universalité de la médiation salvifique du Christ Jésus suivant Thomas d'Aquin." In *Christus—Gottes schöpferisches Wort: Festschrift für Christoph Kardinal Schönborn zum 65. Geburtstag*, edited by George Augustin, Maria Brun, Erwin Keller, and Markus Schulze, 337–55. Freiburg: Herder, 2010.

Emery, Gilles. "*Theologia* and *Dispensatio*: The Centrality of the Divine Missions in St. Thomas's Trinitarian Theology." *The Thomist* 74 (2010): 515–61.

Emery, Gilles. *The Trinitarian Theology of Saint Thomas Aquinas*. Translated by Francesca Aran Murphy. Pbk ed. Oxford: Oxford University Press, 2010.

Emery, Gilles. *The Trinity: An Introduction to Catholic Doctrine on the Triune God*. Washington, D.C.: Catholic University of America Press, 2011.

Emery, Gilles. "L'inhabitation de Dieu Trinité dans les justes." *Nova et Vetera* 88 (2013): 155–84.

Faricy, Robert L. "The Trinitarian Indwelling." *The Thomist* (1971): 369–404.

Fejérdy, Áron. *L'Eglise de l'Esprit du Christ: La relation ordonnée du Christ et de l'Esprit au mystère ecclésial: une lecture de Vatican II*. S.T.D. thesis, Université de Fribourg, 2012.

Ferraro, Giuseppe. *Lo Spirito Santo nei commentari al quarto vangelo di Bruno di Segni, Ruperto di Deutz, Bonaventura e Alberto Magno*. Città del Vaticano: Libreria Editrice Vaticana, 1998.

Forlivesi, Marco. "Le edizioni del *Cursus theologicus* di Joannes a Sancto Thoma." *Divus Thomas* (Bon.) 97 (1994): 9–56.

Froula, John. "*Esse Secundarium*: An Analogical Term Meaning That by Which Christ Is Human." *The Thomist* 78 (2014): 557–80.

Galot, Jean. "Le Christ terrestre et la vision." *Gregorian um* 67 (1986): 429–50.

Gardeil, Ambrose. *The Holy Spirit in Christian Life*. St. Louis: B. Herder Book Co., 1953.

Garrigou-Lagrange, Réginald. *De Christo Salvatore*. Turin: R. Berruti & Co., 1945.

Garrigou-Lagrange, Réginald. *De Gratia*. Turin: R. Berruti & Co., 1947.

Geiger, L. B. "Les rédactions successives de *Contra Gentiles* I, 53 d'après l'autographe." In *Saint Thomas d'Aquin aujourd'hui*, Recherches de philosophie 6, edited by R. Jolivet et al., 221–40. Paris: Desclée de Brouwer, 1963.

Geiger, L. B. "Les idées divines dans l'oeuvre de S. Thomas." In *St. Thomas Aquinas 1274–1974: Commemorative Studies*, edited by Armand A. Maurer et al., 175–209. Toronto: Pontifical Institute of Mediaeval Studies, 1974.

Gelber, Hester Goodenough. *It Could Have Been Otherwise: Contingency and Necessity in Dominican Theology at Oxford, 1300–1350.* Leiden: Brill, 2004.

Gondreau, Paul. "The Humanity of Christ, the Incarnate Word." In *The Theology of Thomas Aquinas,* edited by Rik Van Nieuwenhove and Joseph Wawrykow, 252–76. Notre Dame: University of Notre Dame Press, 2005.

Goris, Harm. "Theology and Theory of the Word in Aquinas: Understanding Augustine by Innovating Aristotle." In *Aquinas the Augustinian,* edited by Michael Dauphinais, Barry David, and Matthew Levering, 62–78. Washington, D.C.: Catholic University of America Press, 2007.

Gorman, Michael. "Christ as Composite according to Aquinas." *Traditio* 55 (2000): 143–57.

Gorman, Michael. "Questions Concerning the Existences of Christ." In *Philosophy and Theology in the Long Middle Ages: A Tribute to Stephen F. Brown,* edited by Kent Emery, Jr, Russell L. Friedman, and Andreas Speer, 709–35. Leiden: Brill, 2011.

Grabowski, Stanislaus J. "St. Augustine and the Doctrine of the Mystical Body of Christ." *Theological Studies* 7 (1946): 72–125.

Greenstock, David L. "Exemplar Causality and the Supernatural Order." *The Thomist* 16 (1953): 1–31.

Haight, Roger. "Sin and Grace." In *Systematic Theology: Roman Catholic Perspectives,* edited by Francis Schüssler Fiorenza and John P. Galvin, 375–430. 2nd ed. Minneapolis: Fortress Press, 2011.

Hamman, A. G. *L'homme image de Dieu.* Paris: Desclée, 1987.

Healy, Nicholas M. *Thomas Aquinas: Theologian of the Christian Life.* Burlington, VT: Ashgate, 2003.

Hofer, Andrew. "Dionysian Elements in Thomas Aquinas's Christology: A Case of the Authority and Ambiguity of Pseudo-Dionysius." *The Thomist* 72 (2008): 409–42.

Holmes, Jeremy. "Aquinas's Sermon for the Feast of Pentecost: A Rare Glimpse of Thomas the Preaching Friar." *Faith & Reason* 30 (2005): 99–139.

Humann, François-Marie. *La relation de l'Esprit-Saint au Christ: Une relecture d'Yves Congar.* Paris: Éditions du Cerf, 2010.

Hunt, Anne. *The Trinity and the Paschal Mystery: A Development in Recent Catholic Theology.* Collegeville, MN: Liturgical Press, 1997.

Jenson, Robert. *Systematic Theology.* vol. 1, *The Triune God.* Oxford: Oxford University Press, 1999.

John Damascene. *De Fide Orthodoxa: Versions of Burgundio and Cerbanus.* Edited by Eligius M. Buytaert. St. Bonaventure, New York: Franciscan Institute, 1955.

John of St. Thomas. *The Gifts of the Holy Ghost.* Translated by Dominic Hughes. New York: Sheed & Ward, 1950.

Jowers, Dennis W. "A Test of Karl Rahner's Axiom, 'The Economic Trinity is the Immanent Trinity and Vice Versa.'" *The Thomist* 70 (2006): 421–55.

Juárez, Guillermo A. *Dios Trinidad en todas las creaturas y en los santos: Estudio histórico-sistemático de la doctrina del* Comentario a las Sentencias *de Santo Tomás de Aquino sobre la omnipresencia y la inhabitación*. Córdoba, Argentina: Ediciones del Copista, 2008.

Kasper, Walter. *Jesus the Christ*. Translated by V. Green. Pbk ed. London: Burns & Oates, 1977.

Kasper, Walter. *The God of Jesus Christ*. New York: Crossroad, 1984.

Klimczak, Paweł. *Christus Magister: Le Christ Maître dans les commentaires évangéliques de saint Thomas d'Aquin*. Fribourg: Academic Press Fribourg, 2013.

Ku, John Baptist. *God the Father in the Theology of St. Thomas Aquinas*. New York: Peter Lang Publishing, 2013.

Kwasniewski, Peter A. and Jeremy Holmes. "Aquinas's Sermon for the Feast of Pentecost: A Rare Glimpse of Thomas the Preaching Friar." *Faith & Reason* 30 (2005): 99–139.

La Soujeole (de), Benoît-Dominique. "De l'actualité des missions *visibles* du Fils et de l'Esprit." *Revue Thomiste* 113 (2013): 399–410.

Labourdette, M. Michel. "Dons du Saint-Esprit: saint Thomas et la théologie thomiste." In *Dictionnaire de spiritualité*, vol. 3, col. 1610–35. Paris: Dabert-Duvergier Beauchesne, 1957.

LaCugna, Catherine Mowry. *God for Us: the Trinity and Christian Life*. San Francisco: HarperCollins, 1991.

Lampe, G. W. H. "The Holy Spirit and the Person of Christ." In *Christ, Faith and History*, edited by S. W. Sykes and J. P. Clayton, 111–30. Cambridge: Cambridge University Press, 1972.

Legge, Dominic. "Fittingness and Necessity in the Manifestation of the Trinity According to St. Thomas Aquinas." Licentiate thesis, Pontifical Faculty of the Immaculate Conception, Washington, D.C., 2008.

Levering, Matthew. *Christ's Fulfillment of Torah and Temple: Salvation according to Thomas Aquinas*. Notre Dame: University of Notre Dame Press, 2002.

Levering, Matthew. *Scripture and Metaphysics: Aquinas and the Renewal of Trinitarian Theology*. Oxford: Blackwell Publishing, 2004.

Maillard, Pierre-Yves. *La vision de Dieu chez Thomas d'Aquin: Une lecture de l'*In Ioannem *à la lumière de ses sources augustiniennes*. Paris: Librairie Philosophique J. Vrin, 2001.

Manzanedo, M. F. "El hombre come 'Microcosmos' según santo Tomás." *Angelicum* 56 (1979): 62–92.

Margelidon, Philippe-Marie. *Études thomistes sur la théologie de la rédemption: De la grâce à la résurrection du Christ*. Perpignan: Éditions Artège, 2010.

Marshall, Bruce D. "*Ex Occidente Lux*? Aquinas and Eastern Orthodox Theology." *Modern Theology* 20 (2004): 23–50.

Marshall, Bruce D. "What Does the Spirit Have to Do?" In *Reading John with St. Thomas*, edited by Michael Dauphinais and Matthew Levering, 62–77. Washington, D.C.: Catholic University of America Press, 2005.

Meinert, John. *Donum Habituale: Grace and the Gifts of the Holy Spirit in St. Thomas Aquinas*. Ph.D. dissertation, Catholic University of America, 2015.

Merriell, D. Juvenal. *To the Image of the Trinity: A Study in the Development of Aquinas' Teaching*. Toronto: Pontifical Institute of Mediaeval Studies, 1990.

Michel, A. "Jésus-Christ." In *Dictionnaire de Théologie Catholique*. vol. 8. Paris: Librairie Letouzey et Ané, 1947.

Moltmann, Jürgen. *Der gekreuzigte Gott: Das Kreuz Christi als Grund und Kritik christlicher Theologie*. Munich: Chr. Kaiser Verlag, 1972.

Morard, Martin. "Thomas d'Aquin lecteur des conciles." *Archivum Franciscanum Historicum* 98 (2005): 211–365.

Mühlen, Heribert. *Der Heilige Geist als Person*. Münster: Aschendorff, 1963.

Narcisse, Gilbert. *Les raisons de Dieu: Argument de convenance et esthétique théologique selon saint Thomas d'Aquin et Hans Urs von Balthasar*. Fribourg: Éditions Universitaires, 1997.

Neri, Francesco. *Cur verbum capax hominis: Le ragioni dell'incarnazione della seconda Persona della Trinità fra teologia scolastica e teologia contemporanea*. Rome: Editrice Pontificia Università Gregoriana, 1999.

Ocariz, F., L. F. Mateo Seco, and J. A. Riestra. *The Mystery of Jesus Christ*. Dublin: Four Courts Press, 1994.

O'Collins, Gerald. *Christology: A Biblical, Historical, and Systematic Study of Jesus*. 2nd ed. Oxford: Oxford University Press, 2009.

O'Collins, Gerald and Daniel Kendall. "The Faith of Jesus." *Theological Studies* 53 (1992): 403–23.

O'Connor, Edward D. "Appendix 4: The Evolution of St. Thomas's Thought on the Gifts." In *Summa Theologiae*, vol. 24, *The Gifts of the Spirit (1a2æ.68–70)*, edited by Edward D. O'Connor, 110–30. London: Blackfriars, 1974.

O'Shea, Kevin F. "The Human Activity of the Word." *The Thomist* 22 (1959): 143–232.

Patfoort, Albert. *La Somme de saint Thomas et la logique du dessein de Dieu*. Saint-Maur: Éditions Parole et Silence, 1998.

Philips, Gérard. "L'influence du Christ-chef sur son corps mystique suivant saint Augustin." In *Augustinus Magister: Congrès International Augustinien*, vol. 2, 805–15. Paris: Études Augustiniennes, 1954.

Pinckaers, Servais. "Morality and the Movement of the Holy Spirit: Aquinas's Doctrine of *Instinctus*." In *The Pinckaers Reader: Renewing Thomistic*

Moral Theology, edited by John Berkman and Craig Steven Titus, 385–95. Washington, D.C.: Catholic University of America Press, 2005.

Rahner, Karl. "Some Implications of the Scholastic Concept of Uncreated Grace." In *Theological Investigations*, vol. 1, translated by Cornelius Ernst, 319–46. Baltimore: Helicon Press, 1961.

Rahner, Karl. "Remarks on the Dogmatic Treatise 'De Trinitate.'" In *Theological Investigations*, vol. 4, translated by Kevin Smyth, 77–102. Baltimore: Helicon Press, 1966.

Rahner, Karl. "Dogmatic Reflections on the Knowledge and Self-Consciousness of Christ." In *Theological Investigations*, vol. 5, translated by Karl H. Kruger, 193–215. Baltimore: Helicon Press, 1966.

Rahner, Karl. *The Trinity*. Translated by Joseph Donceel. New York: Herder and Herder, 1970.

Remy, Gérard. "La théologie de la médiation selon saint Augustin: son actualité." *Revue Thomiste* 91 (1991): 580–623.

Rohof, Jan. *La sainteté substantielle du Christ dans la théologie scolastique: histoire du problème*. Fribourg: Suisse Éditions St-Paul, 1952.

Rosato, Philip J. "Spirit Christology: Ambiguity and Promise." *Theological Studies* 38 (1977): 423–49.

Rziha, John. *Perfecting Human Actions: St. Thomas Aquinas on Human Participation in Eternal Law*. Washington, D.C.: Catholic University of America Press, 2009.

Sabathé, Martin. *La Trinité rédemptrice dans le Commentaire de l'évangile de saint Jean par Thomas d'Aquin*. Paris: Librairie Philosophique J. Vrin, 2011.

Salas, Victor, Jr. "Thomas Aquinas on Christ's *Esse*: A Metaphysics of the Incarnation." *The Thomist* 70 (2006): 577–603.

Scheeben, Matthias Joseph. *The Mysteries of Christianity*. Translated by Cyril Vollert. St. Louis: Herder, 1946.

Schenk, Richard. "*Omnis Christi Actio Nostra est Instructio*: The Deeds and Sayings of Jesus as Revelation in the View of Thomas Aquinas." In *La doctrine de la révélation divine de saint Thomas d'Aquin*, Studi Tomistici, no. 37, edited by Leo Elders, 104–31. Vatican City: Libreria Editrice Vaticana, 1990.

Schillebeeckx, Edward. *Christ the Sacrament of the Encounter with God*. Translated by Paul Barrett. London: Sheed & Ward, 1963.

Schindler, David. "Christology and the Imago Dei: Interpreting Gaudium et Spes." Communio 23 (1996): 156–84.

Scotus, John Duns. *Opera Omnia*. 21 vols. Civitas Vaticana: Typis Vaticanis, 1950–.

Seckler, Max. *Instinkt und Glaubenswille nach Thomas von Aquin*. Mainz: Matthias Grünewald Verlag, 1961.

Sherwin, Michael S. *By Knowledge & By Love: Charity and Knowledge in the Moral Theology of St. Thomas Aquinas*. Washington, D.C.: Catholic University of America Press, 2005.

Shoot, Henk J. M. *Christ the 'Name' of God: Thomas Aquinas on Naming Christ*. Leuven: Peeters, 1993.

Somme, Luc-Thomas. *Fils adoptifs de Dieu par Jésus Christ: La filiation divine par adoption dans la théologie de saint Thomas d'Aquin*. Paris: Librairie Philosophique J. Vrin, 1997.

Soto, Dominicus. *De Natura et Gratia*. Paris: Ioannem Foucher, 1549.

Suarez, Francisco. *Commentaria ac Disputationes in Tertiam Partem D. Thomae* . . . vol. 17 of *Opera Omnia*, edited by Carolo Berton. Paris: Ludovicum Vivès, 1860.

Summa Theologica seu sic ab origine dicta Summa Fratris Alexandri. Studio et cura PP. Collegii S. Bonaventurae. 4 vols. Ad Claras Aquas (Quaracchi): 1924–48.

Torrell, Jean-Pierre. "Saint Thomas d'Aquin et la science du Christ: une relecture des questions 9–12 de la 'Tertia Pars' de la Somme de Théologie." In *Saint Thomas au XXe siècle: Actes du colloque du Centenaire de la 'Revue thomiste'*, 394–409. Paris: Éditions Saint-Paul, 1994.

Torrell, Jean-Pierre. *Saint Thomas Aquinas*. Translated by Robert Royal. vol. 1, *The Person and His Work*. vol. 2, *Spiritual Master*. Washington, D.C.: Catholic University of America Press, 1996–2003.

Torrell, Jean-Pierre. "La vision de Dieu per essentiam selon saint Thomas d'Aquin." *Micrologus* 5 (1997): 43–68.

Torrell, Jean-Pierre. *Le Christ en ses mystères: La vie et l'oeuvre de Jésus selon saint Thomas d'Aquin*. 2 vols. Paris: Desclée, 1999.

Torrell, Jean-Pierre. *Recherches thomasiennes*. Paris: Librairie Philosophique J. Vrin, 2000.

Torrell, Jean-Pierre. "Le savoir acquis du Christ selon les théologiens médiévaux." *Revue Thomiste* 101 (2001): 355–408.

Torrell, Jean-Pierre. *Encyclopédie Jésus le Christ chez saint Thomas d'Aquin*. Paris: Éditions du Cerf, 2008.

Torrell, Jean-Pierre. *Christ and Spirituality in St. Thomas Aquinas*. Translated by Bernhard Blankenhorn. Washington, D.C.: Catholic University of America Press, 2011.

Tschipke, Theophil. *L'humanité du Christ comme instrument de salut de la divinité*. Translated by Philibert Secrétan. Fribourg: Academic Press Fribourg, 2003.

Vall, Gregory. "*Ad Bona Gratiae et Gloriae*: Filial Adoption in Romans 8." *The Thomist* 74 (2010): 593–626.

Vetö, Étienne. *Du Christ à la Trinité: Penser les mystères du Christ après Thomas d'Aquin et Balthasar*. Paris: Éditions du Cerf, 2012.

Villar, José Ramón. "Christo, imagen de Dios invisible (Col 1, 15a). Tradición exegética y comentario de santo Tomás de Aquino." *Scripta Theologica* 42 (2010): 665–90.

Wawrykow, Joseph P. *God's Grace and Human Action: 'Merit' in the Theology of Thomas Aquinas*. Notre Dame: University of Notre Dame Press, 1995.

Wawrykow, Joseph P. "Wisdom in the Christology of Thomas Aquinas." In *Christ among the Medieval Dominicans: Representations of Christ in the Texts and Images of the Order of Preachers*, edited by Kent Emery, Jr, and Joseph P. Wawrykow, 175–96. Notre Dame, University of Notre Dame Press, 1998.

Wawrykow, Joseph P. "Hypostatic Union." In *The Theology of Thomas Aquinas*, edited by Rik Van Nieuwenhove and Joseph Wawrykow, 222–51. Notre Dame: University of Notre Dame Press, 2005.

Wawrykow, Joseph P. "Christ and the Gifts of the Holy Spirit According to Thomas Aquinas." In *Kirchenbild und Spiritualität: Dominikanische Beiträge zur Ekklesiologie und zum kirchlichen Leben im Mittelalter, Festschrift für Ulrich Horst OP zum 75. Geburtstag*, edited by Thomas Prügl and Marianne Schlosser, 43–62. Paderborn: Ferdinand Schöningh, 2007.

Webb, Eugene. *In Search of the Triune God: The Christian Paths of East and West*. Columbia, MO: University of Missouri Press, 2014.

Wéber, Édouard-Henri. *Le Christ selon saint Thomas d'Aquin*. Paris: Desclée, 1988.

Wéber, Édouard-Henri. *La personne humaine au XIIIe siècle: l'avènement chez les maîtres parisiens de l'acception moderne de l'homme*. Paris: Librairie Philosophique J. Vrin, 1991.

Weinandy, Thomas G. *The Father's Spirit of Sonship*. Edinburgh: T&T Clark, 1995.

Weinandy, Thomas G. "Jesus' Filial Vision of the Father." *Pro Ecclesia* 13 (2004): 189–201.

Weinandy, Thomas G. "Trinitarian Christology: The Eternal Son." In *The Oxford Handbook of the Trinity*, edited by Gilles Emery and Matthew Levering, 387–99. Oxford: Oxford University Press, 2011.

White, Thomas Joseph. "The Voluntary Action of the Earthly Christ and the Necessity of the Beatific Vision." *The Thomist* 69 (2005): 497–534.

White, Thomas Joseph. "Dyotheletism and the Instrumental Human Consciousness of Jesus." *Pro Ecclesia* 17 (2008): 396–422.

White, Thomas Joseph. *The Incarnate Lord: A Thomistic Study in Christology*. Washington, D.C.: Catholic University of America Press, 2015.

Williams, A. N. "Deification in the *Summa theologiae*: A Structural Interpretation of the Prima Pars." *The Thomist* 61 (1997): 219–55.

Williams, A. N. *The Ground of Union: Deification in Aquinas and Palamas*. Oxford: Oxford University Press, 1999.

Wippel, John F. *The Metaphysical Thought of Thomas Aquinas: From Finite Being to Uncreated Being*. Washington, D.C.: Catholic University of America Press, 2000.

Index

accidents 107n20, 108, 154, 158, 164, 178

action *ad extra* of God common to three persons 21, 22–3, 36–7, 38, 43, 47, 70n44, 105

adoption 39, 45, 58, 82–9, 99, 213, 222, 226, 236

Albert the Great, Saint 13, 162 n107, 177n20, 218n31

Alexander of Hales 74, 218n31

Ambrose, Saint 82n105

angels 25, 51, 78n82, 124, 177, 182, 220

apostles 11, 48, 56–8, 71, 122, 160, 215, 216, 220–1, 235

appropriations 37, 48, 117n60, 198n48, 208n85, 215n18, 237

ascension of Christ 240

assimilation to a divine person 30–1, 33–6, 39–40, 77, 84–7, 95–6, 168n127, 178

assumption of human nature. *See* Christ, assumption of human nature

Athanasius, Saint 149, 190

Augustine, Saint 12, 33, 45, 50, 70, 76, 82n105, 148n65, 213–18,

auxilium of grace. *See* grace

Balthasar, Hans Urs von 3, 153n77, 173n8, 239–40

Bañez, Domingo 138

baptism, sacrament of 58, 171

Barnes, Corey L. 201n59

Basil of Caesarea, Saint 109

beatific vision 14, 77, 78, 173–82

beatitude 2, 45, 55

being. See *esse* (being)

Billuart, Charles René 139n34, 141n40

Boethius 70

Bonaventure, Saint 13, 74, 150n71, 218nn31–2, 225n54

Cabaret, Dominique-Marie 37

Cajetan, Thomas de Vio 137–8

causality
efficient 21–2, 36–7, 38, 40–1, 43, 65, 68–9, 104–5, 157–8, 219–22
exemplar 20, 33, 38–9, 40, 43, 67–9, 95, 105
final 2, 13, 39, 48, 68n34, 78, 82, 120
formal 27, 30, 41–2, 68n34, 134n15, 135, 140–1, 145
quasi-formal 38n57, 141n38

Chalcedon, Council of 108, 134, 141

charisms 146, 162, 178, 188, 196

charity vii, 25, 31, 36, 39, 40–2, 43–8, 98–9, 105–6, 188–9, 202–6, 236

Christ
acta et passa
in general 55, 96, 102, 114, 222, 239
as salvific 55, 96, 190, 192–3, 217–18, 221
actions of 116–22, 126
anointed by the Holy Spirit 132, 142–3, 174, 187, 188–9, 201, 221, 231, 234
ascension of 240
assumption of human nature 20, 49–51, 62, 103–6, 108, 111, 123–7, 147
as Author of Salvation 50, 52–3, 58, 63, 96–102, 220
baptism of 17, 48, 51, 53, 57, 95n158, 99, 131, 168–71
beatific vision of 6, 173–82
capital grace of 56, 163, 164, 170, 215, 235
as *comprehensor* 179
conformity to 56, 58, 83, 87, 92–6, 171, 222, 224, 226–7, 236
death of 95n158, 171, 190, 212, 217, 226
dignity of 135, 138, 140, 141n38
divine nature of 108–10, 111–13, 115, 121, 128, 134–5, 167, 169, 172, 191–5, 199, 213
esse of. *See* Christ, personal *esse* (being) of
esse secundarium of 107–8

256   *Index*

form 35n47, 38n57, 69, 71–2, 134n15,
    139n34, 139–41, 145, 191–2, 198,
    199, 203
formal causality. *See* causality, formal
friendship with God 45, 119, 138n27,
    180, 228

Garrigou-Lagrange, Réginald 27n13,
    140n36, 141n40
Gaudium et Spes 92n150
gift of wisdom (gift of the Holy
    Spirit) 180–1, 183, 185
gifts of the Holy Spirit. *See* Holy Spirit,
    gifts of
Gilbert de la Porrée 218n30
glory 14, 27, 32, 55, 113, 121, 171,
    216n23
grace
    actual. *See* grace, *auxilium* of
    auxilium of 26–7, 33n40, 204n74
    as formal cause 27, 30, 41, 134n15,
        135, 140–1, 145, 154, 178
    as God's love 27, 42, 46
    habitual 14, 25, 26–9, 30, 36–48,
        86–7, 98–9, 133–56, 164, 188–9,
        220. *See also* Christ, habitual
        grace of
    sanctifying. *See* grace, habitual
    uncreated 26, 29–36, 42
    of union. *See* Christ, grace of union
Greenstock, David L. 38n55, 69n39
grundaxiom (Rahnerian) 3, 123–8, 237
Guerric of Saint Quentin 74, 177n20

habitus 24, 26–9, 155–7
    entitative 27–9, 48
    operative 27–9, 33n40, 48, 156
Hilary of Poitiers, Saint 12, 16,
    82n105, 116
Holy Spirit
    acts from the Father and the Son 178,
        186, 209, 227
    as cause of incarnation 16
    as cause of passion 187, 189, 203,
        234, 235
    and charity 20, 25, 31, 35n47, 38, 40,
        42, 45–7, 98–9, 105–6, 158,
        188–9, 202–10
    and Christ's action 187–210
    and the Church 13, 56–8,
        170–1, 216–17, 220–1,
        235, 240

as conforming believers to Christ 56,
    58, 88, 96, 171, 222, 224, 226–8,
    239–40
and creation 13, 16, 62, 228
form of a dove 24, 50–1, 53, 57,
    168–71
as from the Father and the Son 148–9,
    166, 169, 170, 178, 186,
    211–12, 225
as Gift 15–17, 38, 98–9
    as Gift of sanctification 50, 52, 97,
        99, 102, 212–13, 236
gifts of 28, 37n51, 183, 185, 189–201,
    202–6, 207, 209–10
and grace 12, 40, 42, 43–8, 97, 102,
    160–8, 170, 183, 188, 215–22
indwelling of 25, 31–4, 43–8, 50–1,
    98–9, 147–9, 154–5, 160, 198,
    217, 230, 236
inspiration of 180, 195–8, 206n80
instinct of 195–8, 202–6
invisible mission to Christ's humanity.
    See Christ, invisible mission of
    Holy Spirit to
invisible mission to saints 160
as Love 15–17, 38, 46, 97–8, 169
makes us participate in wisdom of
    Son 180–1
as manifesting Christ 53–4, 170, 213,
    225–30
mission of Holy Spirit as essential to
    Christ's mission 211–12,
    219–23, 223–31
order of missions 147–53
Pentecost v, 13, 17, 24, 48, 53, 57, 99,
    219–22
procession of 11, 15, 20, 30, 97–9, 169
    as understood in Father and
        Son 150, 152
visible mission to apostles 51, 56–8
visible mission to Christ's
    humanity 49–51, 56–7, 168–71
hope 214n15
human nature in general 27–9
hypostatic union. *See* Christ, hypostatic
    union

Image
    as proper name 15, 83n107, 89–93
    as likeness of Father 15, 70, 83n107,
        91n145
    incarnation of 89–96

Index of Scripture Citations

Printed and bound by CPI Group (UK) Ltd, Croydon, CR0 4YY